Aging and Biography

James E. Birren, PhD, DSc, is Associate Director of the UCLA Center on Aging at the Multicampus Program of Geriatric Medicine and Gerontology, and Adjunct Professor of Medicine/Gerontology, University of California, Los Angeles. He also is Professor Emeritus of Gerontology and Psychology at the University of Southern California. He received his M.A. and Ph.D. from Northwestern University, and was invited to be a Visiting Scientist at the University of Cambridge, England. Dr. Birren's career includes: founding Executive Director and Dean of the Ethel Percy Andrus Gerontology Center at the University of Southern California, founding Director of the Anna & Harry Borun Center for Gerontological Research, and past President of the Gerontological Society of America, the Western Gerontological Society, and the Division on Adult Development and Aging of the American Psychological Association. In addition, he has served as Chief of the Section on Aging of the National Institute of Mental Health. He is Series Editor of the internationally renowned *Handbooks on Aging* and has over 250 publications in academic journals and books.

Gary M. Kenyon, PhD, occupies the Chair in Gerontology at St. Thomas University, Fredericton, New Brunswick, Canada, where he directs a certificate and a degree program. He is also Adjunct Professor, Centre on Aging, Faculty of Medicine, McGill University, Montreal, Quebec. Dr. Kenyon is a Fellow of the Andrew Norman Institute for Advanced Studies in Gerontology and Geriatrics, University of Southern California, has been a post-doctoral scholar at the University of Linkoping, Sweden, and is a frequent visiting scholar in Sweden, Finland, and Germany. His recent publications include *Metaphors of Aging in Science and the Humanities* and a special issue of the *Canadian Journal on Aging* (Guest Editor).

Jan-Erik Ruth, PhD, is Director of research at the Kuntokallio Center for Gerontological Training and Research, Östersundom, Finland, Senior Research Fellow at the Academy of Finland, and Associate Professor of Psychology at Helsinki University as well as Associate Professor of Social Gerontology at Abo Akademi. Dr. Ruth has been a Fulbright grantee at the E.P. Andrus Gerontology Center, USC and visiting scholar at the Borun Center for Gerontological Research, UCLA. He is founding member of the Finnish Society for Growth and Aging Research and the Finnish Psychogeriatrics Society. Dr. Ruth is the editor and author of several books in his field and listed in biographical source books such as *Who is Who in the World.*

Johannes J. F. Schroots, PhD, is founding Executive Director of ERGO (Europees Researchinstituut voor Gezondheid en Ouder Worden/European Research Institute on Health and Aging), Coordinator of EuGeron (EC Concerted Action on Gerontology), and Adjunct Professor of Gerontology at the Department of Psychology, University of Amsterdam. Dr. Schroots is also an Associate Professor of Life-Span Psychology at the Department of Developmental Psychology, University of Leiden. From 1985–1986 he was an invited Fellow of the Andrew Norman Institute for Advanced Study in Gerontology and Geriatrics at the E.P. Andrus Gerontology Center, USC. He is co-editor of a number of publications.

Torbjorn Svensson, PhD, is Principal Researcher at the Gerontology Research Center, Lund, Sweden. He is Director of the Lund 80+ Study, a longitudinal sequential study being conducted in Lund, Sweden. Dr. Svensson is also coordinator of a similar study in Iceland. His recent publications include a contribution to the volume *The Concept and Measurement of Quality of Life in the Frail Elderly*. Dr. Svensson is a frequent visiting scholar in North America.

Aging and Biography

Explorations in Adult Development

James E. Birren, PhD
Gary M. Kenyon, PhD
Jan-Erik Ruth, PhD
Johannes J.F. Schroots, PhD
Torbjorn Svensson, PhD
Editors

Gary M. Kenyon
Jan-Erik Ruth
Editorial Coordinators

SPRINGER PUBLISHING COMPANY

Springer Publishing Company, Inc.
536 Broadway
New York, N.Y. 10012-3955

Cover design by Tom Yabut
Production Editor: Joyce Noulas

Library of Congress Cataloging-in-Publication Data

Aging and biography : explorations in adult development / James E. Birren . . . [et al.], editors.
p. cm.
Includes bibliographical references and index.
ISBN 0-8261-8981-4
1. Adulthood. 2. Aging. 3. Gerontology–Biographical methods. 4. Social sciences–Biographical methods. I. Birren, James E.
HQ799.95.B54 1995
305.24–dc20 95-2876
CIP

Contents

Contributors

Betty A. Birren
Director
California Council of Gerontology and Geriatrics
Los Angeles, CA

Irene Burnside, Ph.D.
Adjunct Professor
San Diego State University
San Diego, CA

Bertram J. Cohler, Ph.D.
William Rainey Harper Professor
Department of Behavioral Sciences
University of Chicago
Chicago, IL 60637

Thomas R. Cole, Ph.D.
Professor and Graduate Program Director
Institute for Medical Humanities
University of Texas Medical Branch
Galveston, TX

Peter Coleman
Professor
Departments of Geriatric Medicine and Social Work Studies
University of Southampton
UK

Brian de Vries, Ph.D.
Assistant Professor
Department of Family Studies
University of British Columbia
Vancouver, BC
V6T 1Z4

Brian Gearing, Ph.D.
Senior Lecturer in Health and Social Welfare
The Open University
Walton Hall, Milton Keynes,
MK7 6AA, UK

Kenneth J. Gergen, Ph.D.
Professor
Department of Psychology
Swarthmore College
Swarthmore, PA 19081

Riita-Liisa Heikkinen, Ph.D.
Professor
Gerontology Research Centre
Department of Health Sciences
University of Jyväskylä
Jyväskylä, Finland SF-40100

Allen J. Lehman
Graduate Student
Department of Family Studies
University of British Columbia
Vancouver, BC

Wilhelm Mader, Ph.D.
Professor, Adult Education and Practicing Psychoanalyst
University of Bremen
Bremen, Germany

Dan P. McAdams, Ph.D.
Professor
Department of Education and Social Policy
Northwestern University
Evanston, IL 60208

Peter Öberg
Research Associate
University of Uppsala
Sweden

Donald E. Polkinghorne, Ph.D.
Professor of Counselling Psychology
University of Southern California
Los Angeles, CA 90007

William L. Randall, Ph.D.
Instructor, Department of English
Seneca College of Applied Arts and Technology
North York, ON

Foreword

Why is there such a surge of interest in autobiographies, diaries, and other personal narratives? I think it is due to a belief by researchers, scholars and the informed public that something important has been left out of our scientific knowledge-generating system in its studies of adult change and aging. It is becoming clear that what has been omitted are the experiences of growing old and of being old. Impersonal measurements, rating scales, and observations have contributed immensely to our knowledge about aging. However, such approaches do not lend themselves easily to examining aging from the inside. How people experience and feel about their physical appearance, symptoms, and long-term friendships, and their attachment to objects and symbols from their earlier lives merits attention. There is something absorbing about reading a personal narrative about a long life and the way in which a person views the experiences of growing up and growing old and puts them into perspective. The ripening process that evolves into wisdom, or the increasing sour look of a bitter life, emerges from the firsthand stories of life by the individuals who lived them.

What this book provides is a fresh look at the inside experiences of life, of aging, of getting beyond the slings and arrows and the laboratory measurements and what our cells and tissues tell us about time. The book is an invitation to share the current enthusiasm for using personal narratives as an additional and important access to the interpretations of life. Stories of life offer not only new knowledge but also provide pathways to helping all persons—including the helpless and hopeless—heal the bruises of life. It is quite natural that the "caring" professions are interested in lifestories. How can you help care for a person unless you know where they came from and "where they are coming from?"

Who are the authors of these chapters? Many professional fields are represented, including sociology, psychology, nursing, social work, education, and the humanities. The scope is clearly multidisciplinary, since the content of lives is not a particular profession's exclusive territory, whether it involves the scientific analysis of narrative content or healing people in practice.

What is the challenge? Many aspects of the subject matter need further work to realize the promise that lies in studying personal accounts of life. There is a scientific challenge to develop new methods of analysis of autobiographical content. Determining reliable ways to isolate the goals and life strategies of individuals and to characterize their perceptions of the events of their lives is not simple. Nor is it simple to find patterns in lives that appear to yield diverse outcomes. New combinations of qualitative and quantitative methods will no doubt follow the present high level of interest in content. It is also a challenge to find the most effective ways of gathering lifestories including open ended monologues or guided methods that encourage the narrator to speak about general themes of significance.

There is also a challenge to refine our use of autobiographies to uncover pathways of living with fewer pitfalls, and to make available to others the experience of wisdom of mature persons. Narratives invite us to walk through lives–to some extent to reexperience lives–and to think about ways to help others walk through life safely and contentedly. The use of this new knowledge in practice will involve a wide range of professional activities, from pastoral counselling to nursing.

The reading of autobiographies and other personal narratives does not have to end with the reader's pronouncement, "Well, I never knew that." The material can be digested and comparative research can be undertaken with many different goals in mind. Not the least of these is gaining insight into how lives in different cultures, living conditions, historical periods, and circumstances are interpreted. Personal narratives provide research with a rich source of new insights into human aging.

There are chapters in this volume that offer the reader clues about how individuals derive meaning in life, and how they transcend the consequences of catastrophies of health, loves, and the whims of nature. The blending of emotion and thinking in our interpretations of life is observed in the chapters. This is unlike the content from laboratory research methods, which avoid the individual's feelings, thinking, and doing. The material here shows us convincingly that all these dimensions come together in the experiencing person's being.

This book is itself a product of a ripening process that extended over many years and several continents. The editors, as primary contributors to the growth of the ideas, met at different times: in the Black Forest and Bremen, in Germany, in Los Angeles, and in Budapest. As we continued to meet to discuss how methods and theories of development and aging can be advanced, it seemed that there was something here to share. The idea of the book was born and others interested in the "new look at the inside of aging" were invited to contribute their thoughts about the personal interpretation of life.

JAMES E. BIRREN, PHD
UCLA Center on Aging
Los Angeles, California

Acknowledgments

We would like to thank the Department of Human Resources Development Canada for providing an opportunity to engage Kim Doucet as editorial assistant for the book. We would also like to thank Kim Doucet for her efficiency, dependability and flexibility throughout the duration of this project.

We would further like to thank the Academy of Finland for a research grant to Jan-Erik for Ruth the completion of the editorial process.

Kerry Smith also deserves a note of gratitude for his considerable problem-solving and clerical contributions.

Finally, the editors would like to thank the chapter contributors who were very responsive to deadlines and editorial suggestions.

1

Biography in Adult Development and Aging

Jan-Erik Ruth, Ph.D., and Gary Kenyon, Ph.D.

According to Sartre (1957), the ego is the spontaneous, transcendent unification of our psychological states and overt actions, and the phenomenological life world that the ego creates can be studied through the subjectivity of the individual. This comment notwithstanding, many studies in gerontology view aging from the "outside," analyzing, for example, changes in health in aging organisms, or appropriate roles for the retired in society. The "inside" of aging has largely been forgotten. The limitations of our longstanding traditions of knowledge and truth within psychogerontology have also become evident. Many models of the aging individual can be characterized as mechanical, atomistic, and abstract in the extreme. It is difficult to gain a comprehensive understanding of an aging *person* on the basis of many of these views. It seems that the more distinctly human dimensions, such as sociocultural and experiential aspects of the aging individual, have been neglected. One reason for this could be that, in classic philosophy of science terms, the urge to explain and predict has been stronger than the motive to describe and understand (Cole, Achenbaum, Jakobi, & Kastenbaum, 1993; Kenyon, 1988; Moody, 1988; Polkinghorne, 1988, this volume). This emphasis has resulted in a paucity of studies employing biographical approaches due to a focus on hypothesis testing, abstract theory and, some authors would agree, scientism at large (Gadamer, 1981; Runyan, 1982).

As Carr (1986) notes,

> We often explain someone's action by citing its "reasons," and the question is whether and how such an explanation differs from one which assigns causes. A long tradition affirms that there are fundamental differences between the two. To understand an action is to know not what caused it but rather what justified it, either in general or in the eyes of the agent. (p. 31)

There is growing awareness in both academic and professional communities of the importance of understanding the individual aging process. The way people perceive their lives is of vital importance, not only as a means of exploring the aging process, but also as a guideline for social policy and the delivery of care in an aging society. The basic argument of this chapter is that an understanding of the phenomenon of growing older can only be fully shaped through an investigation of personal meanings of aging, which are expressed in metaphors, images, and lifestories (Kenyon, Birren, & Schroots, 1991).

The transitions we undergo as we age, how we develop throughout the life span, and how individuals experience and value their own lives can effectively be explored by analyzing a person's own inner images. Moreover, since people often act on the basis of their interpretations of life events rather than on the life events themselves, it is essential to study such things as self- perceptions and meaning in order to understand the aging process in depth. Every aging person is unique in important ways and, by emphasizing this uniqueness, we gain access to a rich perspective for the study of aging and adult development in general.

Biographical approaches, such as narratives, lifestories, and autobiographical material, provide an excellent medium for investigating both the idiosyncratic and shared aspects of human aging over the life span. For example, we can analyze personal recollections of developmental tasks, turning points, stresses, and individual coping strategies. These sources of information facilitate insight into how a life has been lived, how it is lived, and how it can be lived. By employing biographical approaches we are also able to describe how cultures, subcultures, or family patterns are reflected in individual lives, and how particular people adapt to or expand the possibilities and limits set by the historical time period in which they live (Ruth, 1993; Ruth & Öberg, 1992).

In sum, biographical materials and approaches are useful, on the one hand, at a general level in generating theories and interpretations of adult development and aging. On the other hand, they are also indispensable in facilitating our understanding of social and personal aspects of aging as lives progress. Finally, biography is also important in determining ways to enhance quality of life.

The present chapter will provide a discussion focusing on three general areas of aging and biography. First, there will be a discussion of theoretical issues and the philosophical foundations of biography in adult development and aging. This will be followed by a consideration of historical precedents in research. The final section of the chapter will explicate a number of ethical issues pertaining to the employment of biographical materials in research and practice.

AGING AND BIOGRAPHY: THEORY

The importance of biography in the field of aging is highlighted by statements such as "Older people do not perceive meaning in aging itself; rather, they perceive meaning in being themselves in old age" (Kaufman, 1986, p. 6). It is the focus on the ageless self that gives one an understanding of personal meanings of aging, and not a focus on aging or being old, per se (Kaufman, 1986). It follows that one gains important knowledge about meaning in aging not by concentrating exclusively on what it is to be old, but by studying, observing and listening to older lives, selves, or in other words, *persons* (Kenyon, this volume).

The activity of ascribing meaning is a given in human nature; it is an ontological and not only a psychological characteristic. From this point of view, the mind itself is a system of meaning structures (Lundh, 1983). This implies that a fundamental aspect of human development and aging is that people idiosyncratically ascribe meaning through creating, interpreting and choosing.

Biography is important because, as has been noted, meaning is manifested or expressed through metaphors, which are raw materials out of which one constructs one's narratives, life stories, and autobiography. In other words, "the story of my life" is made up of images and perceptions that are figurative and creative, not literal imprints of factual events. Consequently, the relationship between personal meanings of aging and biography is fundamental in that not only do people express or communicate meaning through stories of various kinds, but also storytelling is basic to the organization of experience (Kenyon, this volume; Prado, 1986). From this point of view, human beings are always constructing narratives or stories which reflect an intersection of genetic dispositions, past experience (intra- and interpersonal and sociocultural), and choice or interpretation.

In what follows, the terms "narrative" and "story" will be employed interchangeably, except in cases where the technical differences in meaning are under discussion. In agreement with Randall (1995), a broad discussion enables one to make maximum use of the term "story". For example, we do not say, "the narrative of my life," or "the same old narrative." Further, "narrative" or "story" refers to both the process of making a story and to the results, which are also called tales, histories, and autobiographies. The minimum elements required for something to be called a story are: (1) a storyteller or point of view, (2) a character or set of characters, and (3) a plot or action.

Biographical accounts such as autobiographies and lifestories include highly subjective matter that provide an echo of personal development. There are accounts of the hand that was dealt, that is, the resources that derive from family background, life experiences, education, social networks, and health and economic status. The term "resources" in this context refers to the hereditary and environmental influences on who we are that constrain or facilitate developmental change. Autobiographies also reveal how the narrator or storyteller has met various demands of life concerning such things as gender, intimacy, social role, ideological commitments, and survival.

Lifestories provide a picture of the self, including a person's main goals in life, their self-concept, the factors that give meaning to their life, and whether they have attained wisdom (Ruth, 1993). The individual not only tells us who they are, but also who they are *not*. Biographies are filled with personal interpretations of ethical issues, and personal ways of pursuing careers, family life, and lifestyles. Here the narrator tells us not only how "most people" function or think, but also how he or she differs from the crowd in many respects (Bruner, 1990).

However, life stories do not only provide data on an individual level, but are also firmly grounded on a societal level. Lifestories give glimpses of the historical periods of the society that the narrator has lived through. Individual narratives add up to what can be called a *collective subjectivity* (Alasuutari, 1990), that is, shared experiences in a society such as wars and hard economic times, as well as great leaps forward in the development of a culture, for example, welfare states. Lifestories thus can also be seen as individual interpretations of cultural conditions of earlier times (Roos, 1985).

Lifestories reveal the canonical rules of the society at a certain time, its mores, behavioral expectations, and taboos; they give a picture of earlier *categorical imperatives* (Bruner, 1990). Life stories further reflect standard mythical scenarios in a culture drawn from literature, drama, and sacred heroes of the past, as well as present media heroes from TV and film (Coleman, 1990; McAdams, 1993). For example, through lifestories the postmodern transient self emerges saturated with impulses for modification and change (Gergen, 1990). The self is described by Gergen as changing from time to time according to the demands put on the individual: "Under postmodern conditions, persons exist in a state of continuous construction and deconstruction (in a) world where anything goes and can be negotiated" (Gergen, 1990, p. 7). These personality processes have been described as "person-situation interaction" by Ruth and Schultz-Jorgensen (1984). The self in postmodern life been described as many-fold and de-centered, as "a set of separate situational role players," where the self can be seen as a bundle of loosely connected sub- or quasiselves (Featherstone, 1992). Through narrative research it may be possible to capture the way in which these subselves are manifested in varying real life situations, and how they change during different periods of life.

It follows from the foregoing that human beings are only partly the authors of their own stories, and only partly in control of the content of their stories (Sampson, 1985). This is because we are being created by our world and other persons, as we simultaneously and paradoxically create the world and ourselves. To some extent, then, we are always beyond ourselves, we are larger than our individual selves, and our stories or autobiographies reflect this phenomenological situation (Kenyon, this volume). The basic assumption here is that lifestories are *influenced* by societal and environmental factors, as they are also influenced by genetic predispositions. However, who we are is not *determined* exclusively by one or both of these factors. We are co-authors of "the stories we are" by virtue of our capacity for creating and discovering meaning.

One result is that our stories are accessible to one another, that is, they are, in principle, capable of being *communicated* and shared by other persons. In other words, it may be important for us to tell our stories and it is possible for us and others to "story-listen," as well. The central challenge here is for the listeners or readers, for example, researchers and interveners, to gain insight into the limits of their experience vis-à-vis that of the narrator. The more understanding concerning the relevant phenomenon or theme possessed by the researcher, the more open, flexible, and genuinely interested they can be and as a result, the better the possibilities are to bridge the potential gap of *intersubjectivity*. But intuition and empathy are only part of what defines a good reader or listener. Cognitive factors are also important; that is, the more methodologically advanced the researcher is, and the more fruitful questions or working hypotheses they can formulate about the material, the better are their chances of entering the life world of the narrator (Gergen, 1990; Ruth, 1991).

As indicated earlier, the link between personal meaning and biography occurs at an existential-phenomenological level of discourse. That is, in lifestories, one is dealing with individual perceptions, attributions of meaning, and interpretations. Paraphrasing Wicker, one's story does not contain the answer to something, *it is the answer* (Prado, 1986). In other words, biography is the way the world is for someone (Coleman, 1986; Kaufman, 1986; Prado, 1986; Reker & Wong, 1988). In a biography one finds the structure of a life in the form of the structure of the narrating self. Biographies and autobiographies thus can be seen as structured individual selves, or as the personal plot or the myth one creates concerning oneself in life (Kohli, 1981; McAdams, 1993, this volume; Polkinghorne, 1991).

Moreover, these perceptions, meanings, interpretations, or stories are also the basis for action. This means that it can be shown that understanding and predicting human behavior may effectively take place on this basis and not only on the basis of a more traditional objective assessment of a situation (Kenyon, 1988; Olbrich, 1985; Prado, 1986; Thomae, 1980). It is for this reason that lifestories are theorized to involve the whole person, including cognitive, affective, and motivational dimensions (Birren, 1988; Lundh, 1983; Reker & Wong, 1988).

One example is provided by Thomae's (1980, 1992) cognitive theory of adjustment to aging. According to this theory, it is essential to strike a balance between cognitive and motivational structures of the aging individual. The *perception* of life events and change in areas such as health and socioeconomic levels, rather than objective change, is essential for understanding adaptation. The cognitive representations of life situations are perceived and stored in memory out of the dominant concerns of the individual, and the basis for action depends on the perception of present, past, and future (Thomae, 1992). These aspects of human functioning can be studied in the narratives of the aging individual (Ruth & Oberg, this volume).

Since the entire being of a person is involved in ascribing meaning in an individual life course, there are interesting issues raised in this context regarding the relationship between such things as the human mind, reality, and behavior that deserve further attention. For example, for one person such experiences as a serious illness, divorce, or death will lead to spiritual insight or even possibly a self-cure of an illness, whereas another person will suffer from long-term dysfunctions.

What one observes in biographies are individual and unique patterns (Kaufman, 1986), situations idiosyncratically interpreted, new strategies and solutions to life events (Thomae, 1980, 1992), adaptation to never-before-seen circumstances (Birren & Hedlund, 1987; Ruth, 1993) and expressions of the human spirit. However unique, lifestories may share common qualities. It is through these commonalities that more generalized *patterns* may evolve. Through the characteristics that define the patterns, we can make statements about a group of persons concerning the adaptation styles they use in encountering demanding life events, or the "ways of life" they employ as strategies utilizing inner and outer resources (Ruth & Oberg, this volume).

A potentially optimistic feature of viewing human aging biographically is that there is an *openness* or flexibility to the human journey (Kenyon, 1991; this volume). While there is continuity, there is also change and the possibility for change. In other words, there may be no necessary connection between the events of our lives, our number of years, and the meaning ascribed to those events; stories can be rewritten, plots altered, and metaphors traded in and traded up (Birren, 1987), according to the needs of the self.

Development is *time-bound* and future-bound. As we grow, mature, and age in time we gradually form and reform ourselves and the stories we tell about ourselves. Human identity can be seen as constructions by individuals in a certain cultural environment and at one point in time (Sarbin, 1986). Nevertheless, time passes, persons change, and the story of the self is modified accordingly. As mentioned earlier, in one way of speaking the story *is* the Self and both are developmentally bound. The story about the self is always told from the vantage point of the present and reflects back on the past in order to make a coherent and credible account (McAdams, 1993; Polkinghorne, 1991). Our understanding of time is an important aspect of the discussion of aging and biography (Kenyon, this volume).

There are important aspects of biography in gerontology that require further theoretical discussion as well as empirical research. For example, there is the question as *to whom* the stories are told and why. The narrative may be produced out of very special concerns, such as to provide an authorized career biography, to write an intimate family biography, to enhance change in therapy, or to lend consolation in spiritual counselling. The narrator will present him- or herself in a specific way according to the audience. The reasons for telling the story as well as the medium partly form the message. Perhaps it is not a question of the story of my life, but rather the *stories* that constitute my life (Kenyon, this volume; Randall, 1995).

Currently, studies exploring the reality within stories are receiving increased attention in research. Questions concerning the presumed reader of the text, the relation between storyteller and their society, and questions concerning culturally rooted expressions in lifestories are, at present, considered fruitful topics of investigation (Tigerstedt, Roos & Vilkko 1992). It is important to investigate the process of narration and the communication of stories (Cohler & Cole, this volume; Gergen, this volume) and to identify factors that co-construct life stories, for example, the social and cultural dimensions of stories. Nevertheless, the researchers must admit that they will never be able to fully enter into the life-world of the narrator. The most important issue remains that of concentrating upon the subjective meaning that is communicated concerning central issues or in decisive situations in life, within the restrictions of those outer factors that are co-constructing the discourse and the stories (Coupland & Nussbaum, 1993). Borrowing from Gubrium's (1993) comments on the notion of a critical gerontology, the goal of efforts in aging and biography should

> . . . be a critical empiricism; its aim on the one hand, is to make visible the variety, contingency, and inventiveness in any and all efforts to present life, and on the other hand, to resist the temptation to put it all together into an analytically consistent and comprehensive framework privileging certain voices and silencing others. (p. 62)

Another central aspect of biography is the function of memory in storytelling. More knowledge and models are needed concerning reminiscence (Burnside, this volume), particularly of distant events in later life, as well as phenomena such as childhood amnesia (Coleman, 1990). The reinterpretation of narratives of the life lived is also tied to memory, and we therefore need studies of *autobiographical memory* based on a life span, as well as an "everyday" psychological approach (Rubin, 1986). Issues such as the creative and integrative process involved in self-defining memory and the importance of emotions for the development of personality have recently been described by Jefferson and Salovey (1993).

The issues of a consciously selective presentation of the self according to audience and a more unconscious interpretation (or even distortion) do not necessarily mean that the lifestory would be completely altered every time it is told. The life events behind the story have many elements that are anchored not only in a subjective but also in an objective reality. However, the perception of the importance of the material, the cognitive evaluation of it, and the meaning ascribed to it will be altered from time to time. Therefore, the *social context of narration* and the factors affecting how the story will be constructed is a challenge for researchers and practitioners within the field.

According to our view the experiential, phenomenological perspective is the central one and needs much more attention than it traditionally has received within the fields of gerontology and adult development, especially at a time when such notions as individuality, autonomy, and integrity are being stressed with respect to older persons. It might be sufficient here to acknowledge that, it is highly unlikely we will ever establish a total picture of "the truth" about an individual and of his or her aging. Rather, we will understand only fragments of the inner world of aging individuals, as they are manifested in social arenas or in social communication. These fragments, tied together, might give us patterns of the experience and the symbolic relevance of different aspects of aging shared by some individuals (Heikkinen, this volume; de Vries & Lehman, this volume). To look for "the truth" about aging persons or "the inner self" or even "the aging self" would appear futile, keeping in mind the multidimensionality of social constituents, developmental change, the possiblity to choose what to tell in a story of life, and our ontological situation as human beings (Kenyon, this volume). This multitude of aspects attests to the phenomenological richness of aging (Raz, 1993). These issues and others are taken up in more detail in the next section of the chapter which considers the historical development of research in aging and biography.

EARLIER USE OF BIOGRAPHY IN SCIENCE AND THE HUMANITIES

Biographical materials have been used in a variety of disciplines: psychology, sociology, political science, anthropology, literature, and history, to mention just a few (Polkinghorne, 1988). Biographical accounts such as lifestories thus cut through many disciplines and have great potential as a multidisciplinary research approach, where questions central to many areas can be addressed.

Nevertheless, there is no single biographical method or approach. The chosen approach is a function of the research problem. This way of proceeding is crucial in order to minimize the tendency to reduce a life to an inappropriate theoretical construct. As Haldemann (1993) points out, "Toutefois, plus le phénomene a étudier est delimité et construit sur le plan theorique, plus il détermine le choix des methodes" (p. 120). (The more the phenomenon to be studied is constructed and limited by the theoretical framework, the more *that* determines the choice of methods.) For this reason, self-reports, subjective or guided autobiographies, thematic interviews, and personal documents including diaries and letters as well as archival data have been used (Bertaux & Kohli, 1984; Birren & Hedlund, 1987; Gubrium & Sankar, 1994; Runyan, 1982). According to the question posed, not only the content but even the level of inquiry varies. Nevertheless, there is a continuum of research questions addressing, at one extreme, individual subject matter and, at the other extreme, sociocultural issues.

There are also different levels of generality in the answers obtained from the study of lives by narrative or biographical approaches. Some of the findings are claimed to hold true only for individual lives, some for groups of persons or lives and some constitute universals; they are claimed to be applicable to all persons (Runyan, 1982). In some research projects combinations of different data sources have been employed and a biographical approach was created in which both asking the questions and generating the answers is validated by the concomitant use of different methods (Elder, 1984; Ruth & Oberg, this volume; Schutze, 1980).

Although the narrative method has its roots in North America in the symbolic interactionist perspective of the Chicago School (Blumer, 1969) and in Europe with the work of Dilthey (Rosenmayr, 1982), it has been used in so many different disciplines and with such varied theoretical frameworks that it seems to have passed the test of credibility. Phenomenology, personology, ethnopsychiatry and ethnosociology, cultural psychology and sociology, structuralism, literature studies based on a psychoanalytical perspective, psychobiography, and even cultural variants of Marxism have used the narrative method (Bertaux & Kohli, 1984; Devereux, 1980; Runyan, 1982).

The idea of using methods other than those of natural science to study the individual or "character" goes back to John Stuart Mill in the 1850s. Further, Wilhelm Wundt advocated that "characterology," the way of studying individual character and its forms, should be based on a more practical form of analysis than the traditional experimental one (de Waele, 1983). Sigmund Freud also used case histories with narratively reconstructed plots to add real-life understanding of problems that emanated from his patients' discourse. At first, Freud held the view that his patients' accounts represented historical truth, but later had to admit that some of it could have been based on fantasies and could have been given meaning out of the present concern of the individual (Spence, 1982).

The classic distinction between nomothetic and idiographic methods, which later was used by Allport (1968) and now represents a standard distinction in psychological methodology, was first used by Stern in 1911 (see Polkinghorne, 1988). According to Stern, we need both nomothetic research methods, where distributions and correlations of characteristics across populations are calculated, and idiographic methods, where research is concentrated on one or some individuals, whose various characteristics are studied (Polkinghorne, 1988).

In the 1920s Stanley Hall used autobiographies as a source for developing theories on adolescence, and Murray (1938) in his classic work *Explorations in Personality*, although employing various psychological methods, stated that autobiographies gave him the most indispensible data (Annis, 1967). For Murray, the trends and themes around which behavior was organized were revealed in the autobiographies. Since Murray (1938), held the view that "the history of the organism is the organism" (p. 9), methods that addressed individual developmental issues along the lifespan were essential for his purposes. In agreement with Birren and Deutchman (1991), "perhaps we should add to Murray's statement the thought that the individual's interpretation of history, as well as history itself, is the individual" (p. 128).

One of the early books on methodology using narratives and other personal documents to study the individual was produced by Gordon Allport (1942). His basic idea was that the human disciplines should adopt multiple approaches. Allport held that the uniqueness of the person would be revealed by concentrating on the individual case and choosing the most suitable methods on that basis. Biographies and other narratives were but one of many possibilities, but by using proper control they would provide an inner view of the person that no other method provided.

Another early effort to formulate scientific rules for the biographical approach called the *life history method* was made by John Dollard (1935). In "*Criteria for the Life History*," the interdependency of the individual and society is clearly spelled out. Dollard claimed that it is necessary to blend a structure of principles from cultural studies and clinical psychology. According to Dollard, the subject telling the story must be viewed as a specimen in a cultural setting, and the motives for action ascribed must be socially relevant. The question of how personal material is tied to social action must be raised, as well as the social situation in which the story is told. Dollard also stressed that the continuous experience from childhood through adulthood should be put in focus. A life span perspective can be observed in Dollard's thinking, even if the lifespan does not extend from adulthood to old age.

The Polish Peasant in Europe and America by Thomas and Znaniecki (1927) was a sociological study based on life histories where the object of inquiry was a group of persons. According to Thomas and Znaniecki, the subjective life histories were suited for making generalizations or laws concerning the social group. While pondering the relationship between the subjective and the objective, they coined the now classic expression that when people define something as real it becomes real in its consequences. The biographies for this and many other studies at that time were collected by public competitions announced in newspapers on different topics, such as "life as a young peasant" or "life as an industrial worker." These competitions became very popular and are still going on (Bertaux & Kohli, 1984). Further, the foregoing approach has recently been adopted by Roos (1985), in an effort to describe different generations or cohorts of Finns from a more subjective perspective, as well as in a comparative study on European lives (Roos, 1993). In Norway (Gullestad, 1989) and in Russia (Roos, 1993) written autobiographies have been collected, organized, and published and in Germany (Heinriz, 1991) several collections of written autobiographies exist. In Italy, written life stories are even published at public festivals (Roos, 1994). Finally, the American autobiographic archive of James Birren at USC started in 1974.

The Chicago School of Sociology in America drew inspiration from "*The Polish Peasant*," and many studies within the symbolic interactionist tradition used biographies to study the unique or deviant through intensive case studies (Bertaux & Kohli, 1984). In this tradition, the symbols and language in a culture are seen as constitutive of human behavior. Studies by Shaw (1930, 1931, 1936) provide a good example of this approach and include *Jack The Roller: A Delinquent Boy's Own Story*, *The Natural History of a Delinquent Career*, and *Brothers in Crime*. Later, this tradition can be seen in works such as a study of transsexuals by Garfinkel (1967), a study of heroin addicts (Rettig, Torres, & Garrett, 1977), and a study of a woman dying of cancer (Strauss & Glaser, 1977). Only recently have studies on more normal life trajectories emerged within symbolic interactionism, such as the works of Denzin (cited in Bertaux & Kohli, 1984), but even Denzin shows an interest in marginal groups, such as alcoholics (Denzin, 1993).

Biographical approaches and especially life histories have also been found fruitful as a supplementary method within anthropology. The first studies mapped the life world of the American Indian, such as Radin's *Crashing Thunder: The Autobiography of an American Indian* (1926) and Simmons' *Sun Chief: The Autobiography of a Hopi Indian.* (1942) In Simmons' view, the autobiographies of natives have a holistic or synthetic power in that everything is there (Simmons, 1942). A later example is the widely known book by Oscar Lewis (1961), *Children of Sanchez: Autobiography of a Mexican Family*. In this work, Lewis shows human dignity existing within a culture of poverty. He wanted to raise the voice of the poor themselves, and tone down the voice of "the middle-class researcher," in order to avoid either a brutalization or romanticization of the life of the poor that an interpreter supposedly would add to the stories.

However, Frank (1979) has refuted these kinds of claims and pointed out that a biography in many cases is a result of a joint effort of the subject and the researcher, and that it is almost impossible to point to their respective parts in the story as a whole (see also Danielsen, 1992). Clifford and Marcus (1986) state that the impact of the researcher is crucial in ethnographic research; the researcher rewrites the statements of his or her informants, and writes his/her own analysis into the accounts, that is, writes the *research story*. Bertaux and Kohli (1984) state that in a work like Lewis' *Children of Sanchez*, where the researcher is both a scientist and a *literateur*, the formal aspect of science perhaps plays a minor part, while the personal skill of the investigator plays the dominant part. For Bertaux and Kohli (1984), this is true for many qualitative studies within various areas of research, and therein lies the big challenge (see also Gubrium & Sankar, 1994). According to Bertaux (1977), aesthetic features of a scientific presentation are not a sign of prescientific activity, but a positive and developmental aspect of science.

Very few studies based on narrative methods are evident in any fields between the mid 1940s and late 1960s, with exceptions such as Oscar Lewis, mentioned above, Erik H. Erikson (1958) and his study *Young Man Luther*, and Robert White (1952, 1966, 1972), with his studies on lives and personality. Further, Charlotte Buhler (1933) developed a stage theory of development across the lifespan during this period using biographical material (Buhler & Massarik, 1968). In the sixties, studies on personality were carried out by a group of investigators at the University of Chicago, in which 40-to-80-year-old-persons were involved in a sequence of interrelated studies with measures ranging from questionnaires and projective tests to structured and unstructured interviews (Neugarten, Havinghurst, & Tobin, 1968). These studies, partly relying on narrative data, revealed a now commonly discussed aging pattern, namely, a change from active to passive mastery of the environment and a change from outer-world to inner-world orientation (Neugarten, 1977).

Another exception to the scientism of the period from the 1940s to the 1960s is the German psychogerontologist Hans Thomae. From the early fifties on, Thomae has strived to bridge the gap between idiographic and nomothetic methods in the study of responses to stress, beginning with data concerning the development of delinquent boys (Thomae, 1953). These studies are included in the Bonn longitudinal study of aging (Thomae, 1976). Semistructured interviews and lifestories were used in these studies, in which the subjects freely recounted their perceptions of stressful situations and their responses to them, and in which the interviewer did not intervene by suggesting responses. The classification system of responses to stress developed by Thomae preserved the semantics of the information given by the subjects, and the responses were classified according to the domain of stressors encountered (Thomae, 1987). This procedure is in accordance with ontological demands on authenticity in using personal documents as data sources (Allport, 1942; Vaillant, 1977), and consistent with recent demands to consider the context in which accounts of life are given (Gergen, 1990, 1993).

The fruitfulness of narrative methods is also acknowledged in some recent studies on stress and coping in later life, as revealed in the following quotation: "The checklist (of coping strategies) might limit the participants' responses by discouraging them from considering their unique coping effects" (Meeks, Carsten, Tamsky, Wright, & Pellegrini, 1989, p. 134). Further, "comparisons of the stresses reported by study participants with conventional checklist measures suggest that at least a third of the stresses described by our respondents would have been missed if a checklist had been used. This finding illustrates the importance of permitting older persons to define stress in terms meaningful to them" (George & Siegler, 1982, p. 157).

Glaser and Strauss' (1965, 1968; Strauss & Glaser, 1977) intensive studies of the relationship between nurses' experiences of the social value of patients in terminal care constitute a major contribution both to empirical research and research methodology in biography. The focus of the research was the interplay between staff and the dying patient, and the strategies the staff employed to cope with the situation. The care of the patients (the substantive theory) was elevated to a theory of professional service-giving to clients at large (the formal theory,) all of which is based on the social value of the client. Glaser and Strauss's (1967) textbook *The Discovery of Grounded Theory* constituted a breakthrough in methodology at the time. Elaborated and user-friendly versions of these thoughts have been published by Strauss (1987) and Strauss and Corbin (1990).

Glaser and Strauss' research on the care of the dying has also inspired additional research focussing on geriatric wards (Kappeli, 1984; Perakyla, 1988). Together with Giorgi's (1970, 1975) works on phenomenological psychology, they have inspired both experiential nursing research theory (Lynch-Sauer, 1985;

Munhall, 1988; Parse, 1981, 1992) and research methodology within the caring sciences (Parse, 1981, 1987, 1990, 1992).

Beginning in the 1970s, a renewed strong interest in the study of lives and biographical approaches in general is evident. For example, Lowenthal, Thurnher, and Chiriboga (1975), in *Four Stages of Life, a Comparative Study of Women and Men Facing Transitions*, used a multimethod approach in which the lifestory was crucial. Another study encompassing several periods of the life span is *The Seasons of a Man's Life* by Levinson, Darrow, Klein, Levinson and McKee (1978). In this study, the focus is on "a man's engagement with his environment–his relationships, roles, involvements in the world, as well as his fantasies, conflicts and abilities" (p. xii). These researchers report that they drew upon a multidisciplinary approach, using thinking within sociology, anthropology, history, and political science, along with psychology and psychiatry, in the study. Biographical approaches were the main instruments for obtaining data.

In the late 1970s Roger Gould's (1978) study, *Transformations, Growth and Change in Adult Life*, appeared, in which both direct observation and interviews were used as data sources. The sometimes turbulent adult periods of development were described in detail and a handful of false assumptions about life were seen as obstacles for mature development. An earlier attempt to describe predictable crises of adulthood was Gail Sheehy's book *Passages* (1974) that became a longtime best seller. Sheehy's conclusions were based on extensive lifestories analyzed in a journalistic manner.

The revival of biographical methods within sociology is most evident in the work of Bertaux and Bertaux-Wiame (1981a,b). In studying the professional life of the French baker, topical life histories were collected in a single milieu focusing on activities or practices rather than on perceptions or feelings. From these practices, patterns of sociocultural relationships affecting the baker's career and life trajectories were inferred by the researchers. This ethnomethodological study is focused on revealing the ordinary, mundane world of their subjects, and the researcher's aim is to be faithful to the procedures and practices that the subjects use in constructing and making sense of their social world (Benson & Hughes, 1983; Rosenmayr, 1982).

A deepened interest in biographical research calls for a refinement of research procedures, however, and since the 1980s, the methodological debate has intensified. McKinley Runyan's (1982) book *Life History and Psychobiography* is still a rewarding source of methodological reflection within psychology and psychiatry, along with Bertaux's *Biography and Society: The Life-Story Approach in the Social Sciences* (1981) within sociology. Later major contributions include Sarbin's *Narrative Psychology* (1986) and Polkinghorne's *Narrative Knowing and the Human Sciences* (1988), in which the potentials for narrative material are discussed.

In the first *Handbook of the Psychology of Aging* (1977), David Gutmann published the first "Notes toward a comparative psychology of aging." Gutmann describes the changes that occur by age in the masculine and feminine psyche and the changes that follow in the social status of the old in different cultures. David Unruh's *Invisible lives: The Social World of the Aged* (1983) was the first attempt to study the lives of ordinary older Americans where taped recollections were used to map the profiles and the integration of the social world of the aged. Within the English culture Peter Coleman's (1986) *Ageing and Reminiscence Processes: Social and Clinical Implications* was a breakthrough in gerontological narrative research. When it appeared, it was considered one of the most promising and talked about gerontological scientific books of the year, mainly because of its hermeneutical approach, the scientific credibility of which was debated at the time. As can be seen in the different chapters of this work, it continues to have an impact on biographical research and is often cited, especially where gerontological intervention based on reminiscence processes is concerned.

The same year as Coleman's presentation was published in England, Sharon Kaufman's *The Ageless Self* (1986) appeared. Through conversations and participant observation of daily routines, Kaufman created rather intimate pictures of aging individuals, including how they coped with aging and their interpretations of participation in the social world. The feeling of personal constancy of self in spite of chronological aging is one finding often cited from this piece of gerontological life history research. A third gerontological presentation based on life history research that appeared the same year is Erik Erikson's *Vital Involvement in Old Age*, where his well known theory of individual development through life, and the need for integration of personality in old age, is further elaborated (Erikson, 1982, 1984; Erikson, Erikson & Kivnick, 1986).

In England Paul Thompson (1978) and Thompson, Itzin & Abdnstern (1990) have been early advocates of life history research with their works entitled respectively *The Voice of the Past: Oral History*, and *I Don't Feel Old: Subjective Ageing and the Search for Meaning in Later Life.* Thompson et al. conclude in the latter volume that later life is seen as a time for constant reconstruction, and it is only through lifestories that we can hope to understand an individual's own construction of identity over a lifetime. Thompson (1992) states that "I don't feel old is a cry of protest against a myth which causes both pain and fear: a call for the recognition of human individuality and resourcefulness at any age" (p. 43). Malcolm Johnson is another British gerontologist who has shown interest in biographical research (Johnson, 1976, 1988), along with the British sociologist Peter Townsend (1957), who used diaries and conversational interviews as complementary data to preconstructed questions when studying the family life of older people. One of the most recent presentations within the gerontological field is Barbara Meyerhoff's (1992) *Remembered Lives: The Work of Ritual, Storytelling and Growing Older*. This work is based on several research projects carried out at the Andrus Gerontology Center in Los Angeles in the 1970s, projects that resulted in scientific presentations well as a play and a film. *Remembered Lives* is an edited collection of Meyerhoff's writing and includes an empirical study of "ethnicity and aging," specifically, a group of elderly Jews at a retirement center in Venice. The collection also includes an essay entitled "Reflexive perspectives in Anthropology" and an insightful introduction to anthropological aging research by Marc Kaminsky.

It is interesting to note that one of the first collections of ethnographic accounts on aging in different cultures was published out of the need for material for course work at Stanford University. In Amoss and Harrell's *Other Ways of Growing Old: Anthropological Perspectives, (1981)* the roles and social status of the aged in such different societies as India, New Guinea, Taiwan, and Micronesia, as well as North America and Northern Canada, were compared. In this work it is evident how respect for the aged is tied to traditional values and mythological beliefs in a society, and that values and respect are altered through the process of modernization.

At the Andrus Gerontology Center, University of Southern California, guided autobiography classes aimed at elderly students were started by the Center's founder, James Birren, in 1976. The aim of this activity was to "promote well-being, develop friendships and increase feelings of self-efficacy in older adults" (Birren & Deutchman, 1991, p. ix, see also Birren & Birren, this volume). The collected autobiographies have been used as data for research on the meaning of life in adulthood (Hedlund, 1987), attitudes toward death and dying (De Vries, this volume; De Vries, Bluck & Birren, 1993), and adaptation styles and the life lived (Ruth, 1993). Theoretical papers concerning contributions of autobiography to developmental psychology (Birren & Hedlund, 1987; Reedy & Birren, 1980), and a practice guide on conducting autobiography groups, have also appeared (Birren & Deutchman, 1991).

Lately, efforts to bridge the gap between quantitative and qualitative methods have been made, and some theoreticians such as Silverman (1989), have made a plea for using "a cautious positivism" in case studies toward enhancing the possibilities of generalizing from biographical or narrative data. An effort to combine the life review approach with standard statistical procedures has recently been attempted in Germany at the Max-Planck-Institute in a study on intellectual development throughout the life span (Staudinger, 1989). These authors argue that social scientists must begin to seek cumulative generalizations that are theoretically derived and that also are *refutable*. More emphasis should be put on systematic analysis and methodology, in order to tell convincing scientific stories (Silverman, 1989).

At present there appears to be a boom in the production of literature on the use of conversation and narrative from an interactionist and constructivist standpoint in social psychological research. In 1993 a book series on the narrative study of lives was launched (Josselson & Lieblich, 1993) and an *International Yearbook of Oral History and Life Stories* was published in 1992. Several textbooks have appeared, including Gubrium's *Speaking of Life: Horizons of Meaning for Nursing Home Residents*, (1993), Sarbin's *Constructing the Social*, (1993), Gergen's *Toward Transformation of Social Knowledge*, (1993), Silverman's *Interpreting Qualitative Data: Methods of Analyzing Talk, Text and Interaction*, (1993), and Harris and Gillett's *The Discursive Mind* to mention but a few. Further, the first *Handbook of Qualitative Research* has just appeared (Denzin, 1994).

The next section of the chapter will consider several important ethical issues related to the use of biographical materials in the context of research and intervention.

ETHICAL ISSUES IN AGING AND BIOGRAPHY

Biographical forms of intervention, dealing as they do with fundamental aspects of individual lives, require considerable maturity and integrity on the part of both researchers and interventionists. The following five points address this issue, which may be termed "the ethical imperative of aging and biography."

First, an absolute requirement when biographical accounts are used is an informed consent from the narrator. This is essential whether the accounts are published as citations in research journals or in books for the general public, and when they are stored in medical or psychological data banks. As Fischer (1994) notes, "Social research holds out the promise of anonymity for respondents, but detailed individual stories may violate this promise" (p. 4). This is a serious issue, since people are often relating pieces of their lifestories, for example, about intimate relationships that concern "feelings or actions that they have not told one another" (Fischer, 1994, p. 4). A ground rule would be to obtain written consent at the time when the account is given and to have the main future use of accounts spelled out. All possible uses might not be known when the consent is given, however. A recommended approach is to always contact the persons involved, if they are still living, before extensive documents of their lives are published. This suggestion applies equally to semi-official or public use of psychiatric or medical data perhaps only remotely connected to the original reasons for collection.

Second, it follows from the foregoing discussion of the nature and use of biography that the activity of creating meaning applies to all older persons, whether frail or well. The point here is that if someone is alive, they are engaged in attributing meaning; they are still creating their story and have a story to tell. Under the present interpretation, storytelling can be considered as a basic characteristic of human nature, constituting an existential or spiritual dimension that is as important as the body or intellect. Thus, a dementing or otherwise frail person is, in principle, a legitimate candidate for biographical intervention, both in the context of assessment and diagnosis, in such areas as competence (Checkland & Silberfeld, 1993; Harrison, 1993) and community care (Coleman & Gearing, this volume), and in the context of therapy modalities such as life review and reminiscence (Burnside, this volume) in a geriatric unit or nursing home. Another area of concern in the context of frail older persons is the increasing use of living wills and advance directives. Boetzkes (1993) suggests that while these documents are important and appropriate, a biographical approach may be necessary to protect the autonomy of frail older persons in the process of making life-and-death decisions.

However, the third point is that even though the activity of self-reflection upon self and life is a basic human capacity, this does not mean that everyone should be forced to engage in the process to attain mental health or some other desirable end-state (Kenyon, this volume). It is interesting to note in this regard that Coleman (1986), for example, encountered people who did not have a need for reminiscence. These older persons were accepting of their lives and had not, at least formally, engaged in the process of reminiscence. Other current research suggests that in cases of such things as depression, recent trauma, and even certain basic personality traits, biographical forms of intervention may be experienced "as invasive, coercive, or otherwise threatening to clients who feel they have been inappropriately and/or prematurely engaged in such programs" (Webster, 1994, p. 68). There is a good practical lesson to be learned from this, namely, that biographical reflections are not necessarily for everyone, nor should storytelling be viewed as the sole key to successful aging.

A fourth point has to do with the purpose of biographical interventions. The ground rules of various approaches need to be clarified and respected in training and implementation. For example, life-review in Butler (1963) and reminiscence in Coleman (1986) are most often intended as forms of therapy and can assist older people to resolve neuroses, psychoses, and other conflicts. Properly trained interventionists are required in this context. In contrast to these approaches, guided autobiography (Birren & Birren, this volume) constitutes an educational, existential form of biographical intervention. Here, there is an emphasis on creating personal meanings of aging specifically, as well as in other important aspects of life. The process of guided autobiography employs a written component, an oral component, and an intersubjective component as people read their autobiographies to each other in a group. While guided autobiography may have therapeutic outcomes, it is not a form of therapy, and it is important to maintain the important distinction between learning and therapy (Alheit, 1992) in the design and implementation of such programs. The ethical implication here is that quality of life can be damaged as well as enhanced through intervention, and that certain criteria concerning skill and suitability must be applied by the person implementing various programs.

The fifth ethical issue for interventionists in this area to consider is the need to reflect carefully on their own conceptions and attitudes, their "meanings" of aging. This is particularly important in a situation where a younger interventionist is engaged with older persons. The issue of transference and counter-transference is another central one. Biographical material gives a younger person access to information about aging and history; however, this is a history that has been *lived* by the older person (Prado, 1986). This is why it is so important to understand this information from the point of view of the individual narrator. A suggested guideline here is that the more knowledge of aging that a person has, the more he or she has reflected on their own meanings, and the less the researcher or interviewer infers or assumes, the better.

The intervener plays a singularly essential role in keeping the journey of life going forward, by sharing another's journey and communicating metaphors of hope and dignity to a person who is often vulnerable. In this regard, techniques and training are necessary.That training must include a reflected understanding of one's own journey and one's own attitudes and metaphors of aging, life and death; and a willingness to risk involvement in another's journey, coupled with a noninterference directive (Kenyon, 1989; Schroots, Birren, & Kenyon, 1991).

CONCLUSION

Narrative methods have been found to be useful in numerous studies representing the various disciplines within social science and the humanities. The level of inquiry in these studies, as well as the levels of generality, span the unique to the universal, the individual to society. Within psychology, however, relatively few studies can be found using biography to describe the process of adult development and aging. Therefore, following Jerome Bruner (1986, 1990), we would suggest that a new research paradigm within psychology—cultural psychology or "everyday" psychology—is called for, where narration is seen as a basic form of cognitive action. In this view, individuals and their culture co-constitute each other, they are a part of each other (Stigler, Shweder & Herdt, 1990). Narratives originate in our culture, and through the language and symbols lifestories provide, we can understand each other, ourselves, and our social environment. Therefore, the narratives of individuals in different life situations, in different cultures, and even in different time periods will constitute the most important data sources in this new psychology (Bruner, 1990; Stigler et al., 1990).

At present there is a credo within the social sciences to acknowledge the quality of human reflexivity that can be found in the narratives of human beings and which constitutes a sign of creative science (Bourdieu, 1992). "Narrative" seems to have become the construct around which much of the postmodern social research is centered at present, as can be seen from the foregoing discussion. The following quotation expresses these sentiments succinctly: "All human actions are enacted narratives" (MacIntyre 1981, p. 197), and Hardy's "narrative of narratives" has been widely cited; "We dream in narrative, daydream in narrative, remember, anticipate, hope, despair, believe, doubt, plan, revise, criticize, construct, gossip, learn, hate and love in narrative" (cited in Featherstone, 1992, p. 167). Therefore, it seems fruitful to explore what can be learned about human development through narratives, and to develop methodological approaches that lend increased credibility and effectiveness to this scientific and humanistic endeavor.

2

The Meaning/Value of Personal Storytelling

Gary M. Kenyon, Ph.D.

> Each individual's experience of life is always potentially fresh, growing—up and old—resembles a continuous journey down a river flowing inexorably toward the sea. (Cole, 1992)
>
> Our private inward experience does not tell us the number of our years; no fresh perception comes into being to show us the decline of age. (de Beauvoir, 1973)

INTRODUCTION

The discussion of personal storytelling or *biographical aging*, the storied aspects of aging, involves one in the issue of basic assumptions or ontological images of human nature. An important question here is that of what a human being has to be in order for the notion of biography or storytelling to have any epistemological or cognitive content. Without the elaboration of this ontology, the story of a life is at risk of being reduced to an epiphenomenon characterized by such statements as "spinning your wheels."

For example, personal storytelling can be seen to be exclusively the result of sociocultural conditioning, on the one hand, or, on the other hand, lifestories simply reflect various biopsychobehavioral reactions over a life span. In both of these cases, "The story of my life" is not really mine. Yet, at the other extreme, it does not seem plausible to argue that our stories are created in a void, or in an hermetically sealed individual space, for example, a la Wittgenstein's private language argument (Wittgenstein, 1976).

It is possible to identify four interrelated dimensions of personal storytelling or biographical aging. First, there are the structural aspects or constraints to the creation of our own stories, which include such things as social policy and power relations in a society. Second, there is social aging, or the social meanings associated with storytelling, including such relationships as professional and client, or employer and older worker. This dimension also includes the ethnic and cultural aspects of storytelling. Third, there is an interpersonal aspect of one's story, which refers to relationships of intimacy, confidants, families, and love. Finally, there is the dimension of personal meaning or personal storytelling, per se. This is the dimension consisting of the creation and discovery of one's life history or herstory; the way in which the pieces make or do not make sense to a person.

The purpose of this chapter is to explore the issue of personal storytelling by placing it within an existential philosophical context, in order to contribute to clarifying this complex phenomenon and to consider the practical value and limitations of personal storytelling in both research and practice in gerontology. The rendering of personal storytelling that follows provides a framework for accomodating the four dimensions just discussed, while focussing on the personal dimension itself.

HUMAN NATURE AS PERSONAL EXISTENCE

The term "personal existence" (Kenyon, 1988) refers to the basic elements of our being-in-the-world (Heidegger, 1962). Two of these elements are particularly important to the present inquiry. First, human beings are embodied. As biological organisms, and therefore part of nature, human beings are born, they develop and age, and they die. However, so far as we know, the distinctive feature of "human" life is that we alone are aware that we have bodies.

The second element of personal existence is that not only are human beings aware of their bodies, but the body is the basis for our perspective on the world. This is what is meant by "situatedness" (Heidegger, 1962). By virtue of my body I am *here* and not *there*. Moreover, from my perspective, as an "opening through perception" (Merleau-Ponty, 1962), I am aware of a physical and human environment (Heikkinen, this volume). It is important to the discussion of storytelling to emphasize the point that the human condition is one of finding oneself in a particular context, a particular situation. That is, the process of perception establishes us in a world which becomes a field of practice, the basis of more explicitly reflective activity (Carr, 1986). This active, creative perceptual activity refers to the fact that human beings are intentional; they have a will to meaning (Frankl, 1962).

This dimension has been variously referred to in different traditions as the meaning-giving, self-determining, self-creating, self-constructing aspect of human nature (Birren, 1988; Heidegger, 1962; Kenyon, 1988; Reker & Wong, 1988). To add one other term for present purposes, Sartre (1956) calls this the dimension of being-for-itself (*être-pour-soi*). It follows from the foregoing that human beings are not only situated, they are also characterized by relatedness. This relatedness is existential in the sense that my body itself is both a physical and a social object that, as Gadow (1986) notes, "belongs to the world as well as to the self" (p. 249).

From this perspective, a human being, or more precisely, a *person* , is not separate from the physical world (Lundh, 1983; Prado, 1986), nor is one individual separate from other persons. The term "person," which has a rich history in philosophy, is intended to call attention to aspects of being that are ostensibly specific to "human" nature, and which are often underemphasized in those traditions that focus on such things as instinctual drives and behavioral reactions to a physical or social environment. Personalists– and, in the present context, this would include humanistic psychologists– are interested, among other things, in features of human nature such as love, meaning, appreciation of beauty, altruism, and autonomy. These phenomena are considered to be ways in which people not only cope with life, but express life, and by which they are able to achieve some degree of harmony with themselves and other persons (Maslow, 1976).

The statement that people are not, in the end, separate from one another sometimes assumes either a mystical association or becomes a cliché. However, in the present context it means that we are presented with a fundamental paradox of human nature: we create our world personally, idiosyncratically and dynamically; yet, to a significant extent, we are also influenced and created by a world that is larger than ourselves, individually speaking. On the one hand, this means that part of what "I am" is established, completed, or constituted by another person, as well as a culture and a social structure. Nevertheless, on the other hand, as a self-aware being, I am both aware of the other person's activity in this regard, and also engaged in the activity of constituting the other person. This approach is significantly different from some versions of, for example, symbolic interactionism (Ruth & Kenyon, this volume) insofar as the latter view sometimes reduces reality to social reality; that is, a person is viewed as exclusively socially constructed (Kenyon, 1985).

From the point of view of personal existence, human beings are not conceptualized as totally socially constructed, but neither are they seen as egoistic or solipsistic entities. In other words, we are not self-enclosed individuals, but rather we have a fundamental interpersonal dimension. The *cogito*, or "I think, therefore, I am" of Descartes, is really the reverse, namely "I am, therefore, I think." Furthermore, this *tacit cogito* (Merleau-Ponty, 1962) refers to a deeper connectedness. Borrowing from Luborsky (1993), in storytelling terms the biographical unit is not to be equated with the biological body. J.P. Sartre's (1956) way of expressing this insight is to argue that there is an aspect of who we are that is derived from our being-for-the-other (*être-pour-autrui*). As Plank (1989) explains,

> It is important to understand that the contribution of the other to our being is not merely on the order of the psychological, but that it has the impact of the ontological, that is, in a very straightforward way it constitutes an aspect of our self, and creates an integral part of that self. (p. 21)

This relatedness can take many forms, from the early Sartre's (1955) notion, "Hell is other people" to Marcel's rendering of "Presence" and participation (Kenyon, 1980, 1991; Marcel, 1962). That is, there is a broad range of possible human interrelatedness; from trust, love and acceptance, to betrayal, hate and rejection, as well as disillusionment, resentment, and indifference. The argument here is that we are primarily connected to each other, part of a larger reality, and then there are different qualities of that relationship. As Ricoeur (1992) notes, "Otherness is not added on to selfhood from the outside as though to prevent its solypsistic drift, it belongs instead to the tenor of meaning and to the ontological constitution of selfhood" (p. 317).

If we take this interpretation seriously, then the primary form of our being-in-the-world is one of participation (Marcel, 1962), and, conversely, such notions as "hell is other people" (Sartre, 1955) are secondary. This is not to suggest that ways of life based on separation and closure are not common; however, it is to suggest that they may not always be necessary, or at least that other forms are possible. The elements of contingency, risk, and opacity (Kenyon, 1991) are also basic to human nature, and negative and unexpected experiences create separation and despair, sometimes temporary and sometimes apparently permanent. However, human life also offers the possibility of hope, communion, compassion, openness, and change (see also McAdams, this volume). In what follows it will be argued that lifestories offer an effective vehicle for exploring these possibilities.

To sum up the discussion to this point, human beings possess bodies, and live in specific historical and sociocultural contexts. However, all of this, our situation, is subject to interpretation; it all has meaning for us; it is not simply present in a totally predetermined, a priori, manner. The challenge for research and practice in adult development and aging is to "hold" these distinct and yet interrelated dimensions in mind at the same time, and resist the temptation to prematurely reduce aging phenomena to one dimension or another.

THE STORIES WE ARE

> In the complex actions and experiences of everyday life we are subjects or agents, narrators, and even spectators to the events we live through and the actions we undertake. (Carr, 1986)

The connection between meaning and biography is fundamental (Ruth & Kenyon, this volume). The basic argument here is that what people find meaningful about themselves and their world is made manifest or expressed through language in the form of metaphors (Kenyon, Birren, & Schroots, 1991), narratives, (Polkinghorne, 1988, this volume), stories (Randall, this volume), or autobiography (Birren & Birren, this volume; De Vries & Lehman, this volume).

The characterization of human nature as personal existence provides a jumping-off point for the discussion of existential aspects of personal storytelling. The most basic point to be made here is that we are storied or narrative beings (Ruth & Kenyon, this volume). As Carr (1986) notes, "There is nothing below this narrative structure, at least nothing experienceable by us or comprehensible in experiential terms" (p. 66). This means that not only do we have stories to tell, but, importantly, we *are* stories. Further, as Bruner (1987) notes, "we become the autobiographical narratives by which we tell about our lives" (p. 15).

This view is in contrast to the work of such authors as Mink and Ricoeur who argue that the narrative form is an explicit recapitulation of the structure of everyday experience and action (Carr, 1986). From this point of view, narratives, like metaphors themselves, provide an "as if" account of "real" life and what is "in fact" experience (Schroots, Birren, & Kenyon, 1991). Narratives and lifestories, therefore, impose on events a form that they themselves do not have. Stories are window-dressing or something incidental to our knowledge. Further, personal storytelling represents such things as wishful thinking, a desire for coherence, or an escape from reality–or perhaps spinning one's wheels.

From the existential-philosophical point of view outlined here, the reverse is the case. Narratives and stories *are* the way the world is for us; they represent human reality, reality as it is for a situated, embodied, and self-creating being. Literary narratives are more self-conscious and technical renderings of experience. However, the bottom line is that stories are lived before they are told (MacIntyre, 1984; Polkinghorne, this volume). Similarily, human activity in other areas such as science can also be viewed as culturally, socially, and individually created stories.

There are a number of important features of personal storytelling. First, our perspectival nature inevitably implies that, like me, my story also exists in a situation. My story is a story from a particular point of view; moreover, this point of view changes with time, experience, and the very telling of my story, as I create, discover, and am created by my world. This means that our story, and our journey, is to some extent, opaque (Kenyon, 1991). We cannot and do not see or know all there is to know. As Polkinghorne (1988) points out, "We are in the middle of our stories and cannot be sure how they will end; we are constantly having to revise the plot as new events are added to our lives" (p. 150).

Further, understanding a life story is never complete. The whole story is being looked at from the point of view of one part; it is not yet over. Similarly, the story of another is not the whole story, since that story itself is part of a larger historical story. Therefore, neither an autobiography nor a biography is ever complete (Carr, 1986). One could say that death brings an end to a life but not to a lifestory, which continues on in other persons or in a culture. It is not possible to arrive at the final truth about a life (Ruth & Kenyon, this volume). Nevertheless, we know ourselves and others and we establish our identity by learning about lifestories. As part of the quality of opacity (and contingency) built in to our story, human beings do not always know the origin of events or what they can and should hold themselves responsible for. Human beings struggle with the distinction between accidents and those events that are a result of the nature of the protagonists (Schafer, 1983).

Another reason for our incapability of complete understanding of a lifestory is that, as existential beings, we are unique. At some point, we are not like anyone else. Still, our stories are *genre-lizable* (Randall, this volume) and, in this regard, lives can be discussed in more general terms, as can be seen, for example in the work of Ruth and Oberg, Heikkinen, De Vries and Lehman, and McAdams in this volume. However, even though the station stops on our journeys may be similar (Kenyon, 1991), our stories are never exactly alike.

In addition to this, we are not one story, but stories. That is, it seems unlikely that we, as Polkinghorne (1988), for example, argues, "make our existence into a whole by understanding it as an expression of a single unfolding and developing story" (p. 150). We are private or economic stories, inner stories, public stories, physical stories, family stories, emotional stories, and cultural stories. These many stories reflect the four dimensions discussed at the outset, and they are not necessarily partial stories that all fit in to one overarching narrative with a neat beginning, middle, and end. Often, the various stories run parallel and can only be said to be one story in the sense that they all belong to the same person. For this reason, in human terms, a detailed biography or life history does not necessarily make a good story (Carr, 1986). There would appear to be no *one* story to tell (Gergen & Gergen, 1984; Randall, 1995). Wallace (1992) points to the same conclusion in a study in which people were asked to "just tell their story." There were no ready-made lifestories; rather, the story emerged as a function of a specific interpersonal context (see also Ruth & Kenyon, this volume).

We are many stories in another sense. That is, over time we are part of stories that often do not easily blend into an overall coherence; one example is the case of divorce or the loss of a spouse, followed by remarriage, or in the case of a basic career change. There is an interesting feature of *guided autobiography* (Birren & Birren, this volume) that supports this view. It has to do with the different aspects and experiences that show themselves or do not show themselves in a minimally directed storytelling process. At one time a person will highlight and reflect on particular experiences, at another time they may be absent from their story. This can be disconcerting to some people when, after the fact, they realize that they did not consider a death or some other trauma, or a major positive event for example, their marriage. Yet, this also corroborates the idea that meaning and the coherence of a life is not an all-or-nothing phenomenon (see also Reker & Wong, 1988).

In my view, this is the aspect of openness, the moment of creativity in human life. Further, it is easier to see such moments when the agenda is not set, a priori. This means that when someone is simply given the opportunity to explore their autobiography without an explicit focus on specific major life events and not for therapy, then this existential dimension becomes visible. What becomes visible is the process by which the I, today, continues to create the person that I was, and am, yesterday. This is a powerful argument for a theory of personality that contains both continuity and change over the lifespan. It also provides grounds for optimism concerning the teleology of human nature. An unending journey may be preferable to an undesired end, despite its vulnerability to existential dizziness (Kenyon, 1991).

Third, although the notion of personal storytelling suggests that we are involved creatively in the content of our stories and that we become the stories we tell ourselves and others, this does not mean that we can become any story we want or change the plot at will. As Alheit (1992) points out, biographies comprise both emergence and structure. There are limitations due to the fact that human beings, following Jean-Paul Sartre, are a "mix of facticity and possibility" (Maddi, 1988, p. 183). We are free to create other stories; in other words, we make choices. However, "our sense of what is possible is intertwined with what we perceive as given, and the dynamic balance between the two gives our lives its particular flavor" (Maddi, 1988, p. 183). The term "facticity" here refers to the elements of the *stories we are* that include the stories we tell (and live) about ourselves, as well as the social, cultural, structural, interpersonal and biological "themes" that characterize personal lifestories (see also Mader, this volume; Ruth & Öberg, this volume).

This point is elucidated in the following annotated quotation by Alheit (1992):

> Biographical action is guided by socially pre-given developmental patterns, needs them and cannot escape their constraints, but it is not absorbed by repetitive action. Experiences and action patterns acquired in the biographical journey do not simply add up. Qualitative leaps, breaks, surprising fresh starts, moments of emergence and autonomy happen. (p. 190)

As social, or more precisely, as intersubjective or interpersonal beings, my story is only partly my own. That is, there is the inner, being-for-itself part of my story, and also the outer, being-for-the-other dimension. In other words, while I have an inner life or inner aging (Kenyon, 1988), as a related being, parts of my story are constituted by a social, linguistic, physical, and interpersonal environment. To be co-author of my story (Ruth and Kenyon, this volume) means to be aware of what I create, and what I may discover about the larger aspects of myself, individually speaking.

Ontologically, this means that we already *are* partly each other's stories. Stories are expressed on the basis of a "we," not an "I." The paradox is that the "I" has a crucial role to play in my making the story my own. Another way to say this is that we are shared solitary stories.

AUTHENTICITY

The discussion by authors such as Moody (1993) and MacIntyre (1984), asking whether an authentic lifestory is one that is individual or modern, or tribal or nonindividualized, sets up an inappropriate exclusive disjunction. Moody (1993, p. xxxv), for example, is concerned that "we now have no grand narrative that would legitimate individual sacrifice in the name of a greater good" (p. xxxv). On the one hand, as Alheit (1992) notes, "meaning is less and less guaranteed by the individual's unquestioned sharing of culture and society; its creation is left to the people themselves who are structurally overloaded. (p. 195)" Yet, on the other hand, meaning and authenticity are not achieved by simply enrolling in a course or a series of courses on autobiography, wherein the effort is being made to simply make up a convenient new individual lifestory to last a few months.

The notion of authenticity here does not reflect a specific version of a lifestory that would be a true (MacIntyre, 1984) or genuine story, as opposed to a false or inauthentic story. Such a quest breaks the hermeneutic circle, which is a fundamental element of personal storytelling and the entire enterprise of biography (Ruth & Kenyon, this volume). The notion of a true story implies that someone knows the truth. But we have argued that none of the characters in the story of human existence has the entire script. This situation has prompted the remark that "the narrative situation is ineluctably ironical due to the disparity of understanding between what the narrator, the characters, and the audience each know about the story" (Randall, 1995, p. 195).

Therefore, whether we live according to a more individualized story or a tribal, traditional story–for example, a particular religious tradition–an authentic lifestory is one that still must be made one's own. Our obligation to ourselves and to others is not to follow this or that story, but to acknowledge the inevitability of accepting and choosing that our story belongs only to us. That is, authenticity refers to the process of becoming aware of one's story and making it one's own, as Florida Scott-Maxwell (1986), for example, has pointed out.

In this respect, we might consider Sartre's (1956) rendering of bad faith a masterful description of modernity with its attendant alienation. However, it also represents perhaps a search for authenticity, an effort to arrive at a viable being-for-itself, being-for-the-other relationship. This search is not completed by a relinquishing of the being-for-itself in the name of a larger picture or set of values that has no personal meaning. Inauthenticity is having one's story; authenticity is being one's story. Nevertheless, Moody (1993) correctly warns us that in the postmodern era, *having* a story and *doing* your life review could become a technique for enlightenment or a new religion to replace traditional value systems and institutions, that is, the "flavor of the month."

The key to the understanding of an authentic or meaningful life in this context is the intersubjective situation wherein I am a self-aware being who exists in a social-interpersonal setting. My story as a person is already larger than my individuality. Yet, my involvement in a larger group reflects this phenomenological situation, in that although I find myself in a larger situation, I am still responsible for my belonging there (Heidegger, 1962; Sartre, 1956). What is important for a storied being is whether I am participating in the unfolding of my story or only drifting along, having it written for me. Further, I am responsible for my story, but only as a co-author. I am not locked in by my facticity, but neither am I to blame for it all; not everything is possible.

TIME

> What has passed is gone, what is past is yet to come. (Attributed to Martin Heidegger, by Victor Frankl)

The discussion thus far lays to rest the stereotype that was common until recently concerning the almost pathological nature of such things as reminiscence (Coleman, 1986) . On the contrary, the argument in this inquiry would conclude that such processes, in some form, are a given in human nature, and an integral aspect of identity and meaning in life.

In the case of older persons, personal storytelling does involve a considerable past dimension, a past life, including patterns of meaning or stories constructed earlier on. However, that past is being reconstructed creatively in serving the present (Coleman, 1986). People ascribe present meaning or express present metaphors of past events. As De Vries (1990) notes, in this sense, "individuals do not exist in the past, the past exists in individuals" (p. 26). Even the oldest old, although they must adjust to the limited number of years left, are still *living* time with a present, past, and future. These dimensions are continuously interlocking and have meaning (Agren, 1992). Joyce Horner (1982) describes the situation this way, in referring to her fellow nursing home resident: "I don't think anyone old is *afraid* of death, though many, including Mrs. B., who will be 108 on Monday, may want life to go on" (p. 16).

From this perspective, lifestories are a storehouse of experience and become very important because, in one sense, the past exists *only* as it is remembered and created and re-created in the interaction with present and future experiences and the meaning, interpretations, and metaphors ascribed to those experiences. According to Schroots and Birren (1988), "the psychological past and future are *constructions*, experienced as a series of presents (p. 11)." Human existence and action therefore consist, in agreement with Carr (1986), not in overcoming time, not in escaping it or arresting its flow, but in shaping and forming it. Human time is configured time. Nevertheless, the time that is configured is not arbitrary. The future that is projected is not simply a picture of what might be, but our very being (attributed to Martin Heidegger by Victor Frankl; Sartre, 1956). It is a future that we are already, that is based on this present and a past.

A further aspect of time that is relevant to present concerns is that there is an inner time and an outer time. Further, the time which we live includes both physical (outer) and psychological (inner) time (Achenbaum, 1991). In one sense, human nature is being-in-time, but not being-of-time, objectively speaking, in that there are individual experiences and perspectives of time, and those time perspectives may change over the lifespan. Our experience of time is therefore subject to the same dialectic or tension between the inner and outer, or in Sartrian terms, being-for-itself and being-for-the-other. The reference here is to such things as social time or social clocks (Neugarten & Hagestad, 1976; Schroots & Birren, 1988). According to this view, people judge themselves to be on-time or off-time in their life course. The crucial issue, from the point of view of personal storytelling, is the analysis of the creative ways that people interact with this outer clock. It must be dealt with and is part of human experience, part of my being-for-the-other, but only a part of it. It is the inner experience of time, which is highly personal, that tells us more about the nature of time, and the nature of aging (Ruth & Oberg, this volume). From this point of view, we are both participants in and surveyors of the temporal flow; both characters in and tellers of the stories constituted by it (Carr, 1986).

The significant differences between inner time-aging and outer time-aging are highlighted in an analysis by Schroots & Birren (1988) in which they discuss the claim by Butler (1963) that *life review* is a universal outcome of later life which is associated with approaching death. This rendering of life review makes it a phenomenon of outer time-aging, on a par with the social clocks just discussed. This is because from this perspective age guarantees an awareness of finitude (Munnichs, 1966). And second, it is assumed that the prospect of death in later life makes you lose a sense of the future, a future perspective. The sense of the immediacy of death therefore initiates a life review process (Kastenbaum, 1983).

Such a view of the past and of time implies that, as human beings, we are locked in by our earlier experiences and by a particular view of death; in a word, that we are determined entities. As Plank (1989) explains:

> We commonly accept this essentialistic view of the past as a thing or a series of events which happened once and for all in a specific way and which we, as historians, as witnesses in court, or merely as ordinary men who must live with what they have done, can grasp by a careful perusal of our memories or appropriate archives and documents. (p. 33)

This assumption of exclusive determinism may also be viewed as a story and may be partially our own creation, a cultural and even possibly a cohort phenomenon.

Further, the consideration of this issue calls into question the basis of a number of scientific theories in gerontology. One can ask, for example, whether continuity theory is about aging per se, or whether it reflects a cohort or cultural, period effect which is based on a widespread belief in a linear view of time that created a "bondage to the past" (Plank, 1989). There are significant differences in an understanding of aging based on chronological time or variations of physical time, on the one hand, and psychological or inner time on the other hand. Recent research supports this claim. Webster (1994), for example, reports that, in a number of recent studies, age is not a significant predictor of reminiscence frequency. If life span samples are employed, the expected triggers of reminiscence mentioned above are not evident.

The argument presented here is intended to indicate that the investigation of personal storytelling highlights a definition of time that has inner and outer dimensions, as we do ourselves. Further, this definition of the experience of time allows for the possibility of ontological freedom, or of the possibility for fundamental movement and change in aging. To sum up, personal storytelling is a present phenomenon that involves a past and a future; an interpretation in the present which may reflect a reinterpretation of the past in light of present circumstances (Kaufman, 1986), and future projections.

PERSONAL STORYTELLING AND MEANING-VALUE

> I found it difficult not to feel that if only we are offered a hospitable space in which we can tell and re-tell our story however we wish, then, through the story-telling process itself, we open ourselves to whatever measure of clarification or healing for which we happen to be ready at the time. (Randall, 1995)

Although it was argued that ascribing meaning through lifestories is a fundamental aspect of human nature, it is, nevertheless, the case that many older persons subscribe to negative stereotypes and images of aging (Philibert, 1968). However, rather than assuming that this is a natural outcome of aging, as sometimes occurs, the present discussion points to a different conclusion, namely, that the older person's self-creating, meaning-giving or storytelling dimension is possibly frustrated or dampened by habituation (Kastenbaum, 1980; Kenyon, 1988). This means that through pressures to conform or an atrophy of self-reflection, an older person is working with outdated or negative metaphors, or in terms of old stories; old in time and old in reference to self.

According to Prado (1986), over time people find particular narratives or stories to be very effective; however, this can lead to *perspective narrowing* and masquerade as rigidity or an inability to learn. As Bruner, (1987) notes, "The ways of telling and the ways of conceptualizing that go with them become recipes for structuring experience itself, for laying down routes into memory, for not only guiding the life narrative up to the present but directing it into the future" (p. 31). The problem here is that the past effectiveness of particular metaphors and stories might preclude a search for new images and plots, even as the circumstances of the traveler and the voyage have changed (Kenyon, 1991). But such a condition is really the result of doing something too well over a long period of time, to the point of counterproductiveness (Prado, 1986). Therefore, what is needed here, and what can be provided through storytelling, is access to new stories, new wrinkles in established patterns; in other words, new sources of meaning.

The importance of storytelling becomes particularly evident when one considers the social structural constraints to the creation and discovery of viable personal stories in Western society, a society that continues to be essentially ageist in its character. As Plank (1989) notes, there is a fate prepared for older people by nearly every aspect of American society (I would say Western society). This fate, brought about by such practices as mandatory retirement, inappropriate institutionalization and paternalistic social policy, results in a situation in which an older person's being is standardized or homogenized. Many older people resign themselves to an outer image of aging, since they cannot maintain an open relationship between the person they are inside, the personal dimension of their story, and the part of themselves that is outside, the social and structural stories. Such a relationship is necessary to an intersubjective being. In other words, we have a basic need to tell our stories and have them listened to in a nonjudgmental environment.

In contrast, in many instances,

> The self, then, can be seen as something that resides in the arrangements prevailing in a social system for its members. The self in this sense is not a property of the person to who it is attributed, but dwells rather in the pattern of social control that is exerted in connection with the person by himself and those around him. This special kind of institutional arrangement does not so much support the self as constitute it. (Goffman, 1961, cited in Plank, 1989)

The important point here is that this self that comes to be constituted from the outside, and to which many older people are resigned, is the result of a particular set of circumstances. For example, for Rosenmayr (1982), the continued internalization of socioeconomic disadvantage and the gradual acceptance of low standards depresses expectations and reduces or extinguishes aspirations. This amounts to self-induced social deprivation, and is particularly evident in old age. There are many conditions that suggest that Western society "is highly susceptible to the hazards of pathological narcissism. These hazards are undoubtedly exacerbated as people move into their later years" (Bressler-Feiner, cited in Mader, 1991).

Paraphrasing Mader (1991), this pathological narcissism is the result of the combination of, on the one hand, various losses associated with aging, and, on the other hand, the lack of viable new meaningful self-images that can be expressed and given support in the older person's lived experiences. Creating new stories and creating a self requires a dynamic between the for-itself and other people (Plank, 1989). Problems arise when our experiences are being "storied" by others, or ourselves in a way that does not represent our lived experience. In this situation, there is too much facticity and too little sense of possibility. Possibility can bring wonder, openness, feelings of well-being, happiness, gratitude towards life, and a view of life as an ongoing *journey,* and hope.

The foregoing discussion points to a need for more research and reflection on the nature and dynamics of inner aging, being-for-itself, or the inside story, and how it relates to outer aging and the public story. Ontologically, it is possible to be capable of authentic (Carr, 1986; Heidegger, 1962; Kenyon, 1991; Sartre, 1956) behavior to some degree or another with respect to one's aging, as in other spheres of human life. Consequently, it is not necesssarily natural to be reactive, nor is it necessarily the case that human beings are caught in a vicious circle of bad faith (Sartre, 1956) with respect to their aging. That is, it is not the case that people are deceiving themselves and others as to their ability to create new *storyotypes* (Randall, this volume) vis á vis their own aging, in various situations, and therefore denying or avoiding the reality of the situation. As discussed earlier, the question regarding authenticity becomes one of reality for *whom*.

In modern Western society, storytelling is often not a naturally occurring experience, nor is it commonplace for a person to take the time to listen and tell one's story to oneself or to another, to reflect on one's aging and life. For most people life is a matter of doing, achieving, producing, and consuming, with very little opportunity for being. Borrowing from McAdams (this volume), much attention is placed on agency and very little on communion. Moreover, socially acceptable life stories are often restricted to such things as social activity, ego-strength, and a realistic view of the world (Tornstam, 1989). Rest and silence are anathema to many people. In contrast to this, in later life rest and silence are often imposed on a person and sometimes radically, through various forms of loss (Horner, 1982). The occurrence of these events can either be opportunities for despair or opportunities for a transition to being; an opportunity for existential-spiritual growth, a natural part of the lifespan that involves sometimes radical changes in the meaning of such things as work, the body, and even the self (Kenyon, 1992; Tornstam, 1989).

The transition to being includes the notion that a person has an opportunity to explore their dimension of being-for-itself. The very act or *perceptual turn* of viewing one's life as a story can lead to detachment and, as a result of that detachment, enhanced personal meaning. Another way to say this is that through personal storytelling and story-listening one can increase one's sense of possibility (one can give oneself a break) as part of utilizing one's capacities for imagination, symbolization, and judgement (Maddi, 1988). This suggests that providing opportunities for telling one's story is important. Moreover, it is not a question of requiring that we all undergo some established form of therapy. What is required for most people is a rather unstructured but supportive environment where no particular therapeutic plot is projected upon us (Birren & Birren, this volume; Randall, 1995; Schafer, 1983). We need more approaches that encourage one to find one's own directionality (Maddi, 1988).

The activity of personal storytelling can result in a basic acceptance of one's life. This acceptance may or may not reflect what Erikson (1963) for example, refers to as ego integrity–if this is to be understood as a cognitively loaded notion of wisdom–or a truly coherent life narrative. That is, while such an outcome of wisdom and integrity is a possible end point for human development (Holliday & Chandler, 1986), for many people the situation probably reflects a somewhat different perspective. For example, acceptance might simply be something like *it was real* in reference to one's life; whereas for Erikson there appears to be more of an emphasis on a kind of Nietzschean necessity of one's life, with no substitutions (Erikson, 1963; Kaufman, 1986).

Erikson's rendering of this state of affairs reflects possibly a more developed phase of self-reflection or spiritual development; however, there is a significant benefit to be had for many people who simply come to *own* or to be aware of their lives in this more basic sense. The essential claim here is that, to borrow from Socrates, the examined life is worth living. Perhaps this distinction is more a matter of degree than of kind; nevertheless, it is a vital issue in considering both what we can expect with respect to our own lifestory, and also in the context of listening to other people's stories in the context of research and intervention in gerontology. (Ruth & Kenyon, this volume).

In agreement with authors such as Carr (1986), "coherence seems to be a need imposed on us whether we seek it or not, things need to make sense. We feel the lack of sense when it goes missing. (p. 97)" As we have discussed throughout this chapter, the will to meaning is a given in human nature. However, this does not imply that the *stories we are* need to add up in the end, that our lives as discussed earlier must be seen to fit into a grand narrative. Consider the following:

> "good" lives and "good" stories are both presumed to have a beginning, a middle and a definite ending (Ricoeur, 1977); later life becomes the testing ground for the success of our personal and collective search for narrative integrity. Preparation for what is expected to be a "good" death, with its attendant record of accomplishment in life and satisfaction with life as lived, is believed critical for the maintenance of morale in later life. (Cohler, 1993, p. 116)

To repeat an earlier remark, a detailed biography does not necessarily make a good story. To highlight the problematic character of this quotation, one need only point to the discussion thus far regarding the conditions of personal existence, including its opacity, its singularness in important aspects, its constant *en route* (Kenyon, 1991) character, and even its ironic and humorous features. That humor is highlighted in the perhaps Sisyphyean attempt to bring closure to a life, to control it, to wrap it up neatly.

A personally meaningful and authentic lifestory is not only created, it is also discovered. One makes an effort and hopes for a basic sense of coherence and viability. This coherence is established out of periodic confusion, incoherence, and chaos (Carr, 1986; Riegel, 1976). Moreover, sometimes it is a case of how some event or action fits in to the existing story, and other times one realizes that the question is now "what is the story." In a highly suggestive remark that deserves further attention, Tornstam (1989) points to the notion that there are leaps in our experience, and that consequently my new story may not be continuous with my old story.

Tornstam (1989) goes so far as to argue that in certain views and traditions such as those of Jung and Zen Buddhism, a person would not only *not* find coherence with their earlier story, but not be particularly fond of it, as the earlier story reflects a more narrow or egotistical way of life. For example, perhaps a certain degree of integrity then leads to increased generativity and viewing oneself as a larger being with strong desires for communion and participation. (for a discussion of generativity see McAdams, this volume). In this case, one's earlier personal story of independence and a focus on individualism would not necessarily be viewed in a positive light and therefore not reflect a felt coherence in this sense. This discussion raises another important issue: the teleology of human nature. That is, our life story is significantly a matter of how we are different as unique persons, but it is also a matter of how we fit into the larger picture. One can suggest that life as story involves a dialectic that is the basis for the development and realization of meaning, spirituality, and well-being in a life, as one moves toward an increasingly authentic lifestory.

The adumbration, or suspension of this process can occur and our story then becomes counterproductive, confused, and separated from the larger picture. The journey is temporarily interrupted or takes a problematic direction. However, the key is that if we view ourselves as a story, change is possible, towards increased authenticity, presence and communiton. As with the earlier discussed varieties of human interrelatedness, stories may reflect anything, from a need to be loved or a fear of *ontological abandonment* (Gergen & Gergen, 1984), to altruism, compassion, and wisdom. Moreover, several of these qualities may characterize our stories at any one time; for example, the loss of a job coincident with a new relationship. For these reasons, Cohler's (1993) well-intended interpretation, as with overcognized interpretations of Erikson, may not reflect an accurate phenomenological description of coherence, and may place inappropriate, inordinate, and counterproductive demands and expectations on aging *human* beings. The meaning-value of personal storytelling may be at least as much a matter of intuition as it is of logic, both in terms of our own story, as well as in our ability to understand another's story. (Although the above quotation by Cohler is employed to make a particular point, it should be noted that, for example, Cohler & Cole,[this volume] discuss the complexity and subtlety of the process of storytelling and story-listening.)

Erikson (1979) himself refers to this idea when he suggests that wisdom is reflected in a dynamic balancing of integrity and despair, which one hopes will be in integrity's favor. Another example is the discussion of Einstein's lifestory by Weiland (Cohler & Cole, this volume) in which Einstein states that although one may think that he looks back on life with serene satisfaction, *things are really not so bright*. These interpreations are significantly different from what sometimes appears to amount to a demand for an answer to one's life. Given our basic human condition, one could argue that a lifestory could possess too much coherence and be inauthentic in the sense that it is a story that I have, but not a story that I am. As a situated being, I am always inside a story anyway; therefore, I cannot know or tell the story exhaustively. Nevertheless, I can still authentically choose my story, tell it, listen to it, and to some extent change it. I can do this alone and I can do it with others. Persons can cocreate each other because we are significantly each other's stories, by our nature itself. We cannot know the story exhaustively, neither my version of me, nor your version of me, nor my version of you. And yet, communication and coherence are possible and can be enhanced. In this respect, the more aware we are of our stories, the more we can listen with compassion and be present to another and to ourselves.

CONCLUSION

The foregoing investigation of personal storytelling suggests that there is an open-endedness, flexibility, or to quote Riegel (1976), a *workability* to human aging. We can and do, to some extent, self-create. Further, we can, in many cases, re-story our lives or at least parts of them (Randall, this volume). And, since we are co-authors of our stories, we can *be* for each other, professionally and interpersonally; we are in any case, authentically or inauthentically. At this time, we do not know very much about the extent to which a person's sense of possibility or inner story is capable of adapting to, obviating, and transcending various deleterious biological and environmental constraints, or, in other words, losses, that occur during various phases of a long life. Such phenomena or outcomes as wisdom, authenticity, acceptance, and the attainment of meaning in life may be a more common outcome of human aging than has been thus far acknowledged in the field of aging, and could be more common with appropriate intervention, and, in particular, intervention based on biography.

A final remark is that while we tend to discuss personal storytelling with respect to the situation of older persons, the meaning-value of personal storytelling is increasingly an important issue for younger and middle-aged persons, as our lives become increasingly bureaucratized and corporatized, and as we face high divorce rates and unemployment. In such an environment, opportunities for mutual acceptance and nonjudgmental support through listening and being present are indispensable, as we cannot remain healthy without a viable being-for-itself and being-for-the-other relationship, or a viable inner-outer story. Nevertheless, storytelling is, in the end, a choice and should not be unethically imposed on anyone.

3

Emotionality and Continuity in Biographical Contexts

Wilhelm Mader, Ph.D.

There is one basic conviction among researchers who investigate the life course of men and women in different stages of their lives by using a biographical approach: A biography as a personal construct and a personal evaluation of a life course brings about the necessary and desired coherence and structure without which the connection between an individual and his or her culture would break into pieces. It is the biography which connects the individual and their life transitions with the culture a life has to be lived in. Taking this for granted and as a starting point (Ruth & Kenyon, this volume), the following contribution tries to outline the special role and function *emotionality* plays within these intricate and by no means mere cognitive processes of constituting the coherence of a life by creating a biography.

A biography, regarded as a personal evaluation of a life, encompasses and uses emotional patterns which not only have their own story, logic, and development, but also function as a basic grid in evaluating a life, in embodying the discontinuities of a life course into the continuities of a biography. Therefore, this contribution is directed towards the development of theoretical foundations for a tentative theory of an emotionality-continuity-nexus and its consequences for views on aging and age.

The inquiry starts with a general introduction to some problems and reasons for the fruitfulness of developing such a tentative theory (Section One), then outlines my understanding of "biography" and argues that a hidden consequence of societal modernization and detraditionalization for the elderly in our civilization is their growing dependency on their biography and its construction (Section Two). Section Three deals with theoretical and terminological issues of emotionality, Section Four with those of continuity. Both sections will discuss some relevant publications and research. These guiding categories and an explicit tentative theory of an emotionality-continuity-nexus in Section Five shall prepare the ground for the debate and application of such a theory on questions of aging in Section Six.

1. THE PROBLEM

In an essay on Thomas Mann's literary development we can read:

> Quite moving also to observe how unwavering are Thomas Mann's inclinations: no-one praised in old age who would not be loved by the young. His horizon widens steadily, his eyes catching sight of ever new mental landscapes, his feelings, however, not registering what the twenty-year-old had not experienced. Plato, Storm, Chamisso had been his comfort as a grammer-school boy. Then, after twenty, shaken by Schopenhauer, Nietzsche and Wagner, his belief in them stays with him over and along all the conflicting experiences he was obliged to undergo during the dictatorship. When he was twenty-five, Thomas Mann had formed his view of the world, however his works scan the European horizon. (Siedler, 1991, p. 63)

The key sentence indicating the scope and guiding question of the following considerations is "his feelings, however, not registering what the twenty-year-old had not experienced." This statement implies a far-reaching, debatable, and momentous hypothesis regarding biography and aging: Socially preset and individually acquired patterns of emotional sensitivities, established in early adolescence and early adulthood (McAdams, this volume), work as structurizing organizers (biographizers) of further experiences during life's future course and, with increasing age, turn into self-maintaining self-referential systems. Expressed in methodological terms, emotionality can be seen as a unique and personal configuration of an elderly human being, and increasingly, as an independent variable which explains other phenomena, and not just as an accompanying reaction to various states of later-life experiences.

On the one hand, these and similar assumptions build the framework for an inquiry into a debate of a general hypothesis regarding the life-long coherence and interdependency of patterns of behaviours, coping strategies, and patterns of thinking. On the other hand, the specific question this paper tries to answer is: In what way are emotionality and coherence dependent on each other during a life's course? In what way (if at all) are biographical continuities due to basic emotionalities (emotionality-continuity hypotheses)?

Answers to these questions, and possible applications to phenomena of age and aging, require some preliminary work. An important requisite is the establishment of precise terms of reference. The categorical framework for dealing with emotionality and continuity must be clarified (Sections Three and Four). But bear in mind that there is no intention at all to disregard the crises, upheavals, and reorientations in individual lives. Of course, there are breaks, discontinuities, and branching points in every life course. But by this subtle process of evaluating a life course, the life story, "the story I am" (Kenyon, this volume) transforms, even breaks, discontinuities and branching points without denying them a deeper significance. In addition, the concept which I am going to suggest looks at aging as a continuously ongoing developmental process and does not intend to foster a deterministic view by stressing continuity patterns. Continuity is regarded as an outcome of the unavoidable process of biographizing the life course.

"We can only reconstruct the logic of historic breaks and discontinuities, of wars, catastrophes, and revolutions, once we have understood people's need for continuity among all these discontinuities" (Alheit, 1993a, p. 388). Especially for the elderly, it seems to hold true that it is the biography which connects and shapes their lives in a society which falls apart into subcultures, milieus, lifestyles, and generations. Hence, some remarks are required on "biography" and how it functions in modern societies.

2. BIOGRAPHY AND MODERNIZATION

Angyal (1972) understood the biography of a human being as a "time-Gestalt." The most known presentation form of such a time-Gestalt, but not at all the only one, is telling stories, that is, the narrative format in which the gestalt ("emplotment," as Polkinghorne, this volume, describes it) is not only a story. Moreover, the story builds a container and resource of life-long accrued "capital." Within a given social space with its resources, openings and shortcomings, a unique story provides a frame in which a man or a woman can recognize himself/herself, which he/she can live with and by which he/she can draft meaningful anticipations and perspectives of his/her future life. It includes a logic of sequences and it encompasses the unrealized possibilities of a life, the unlived life.

An existential task of high complexity has to be solved by the lifelong and never-ending construction of such a biographical gestalt. It is built in a continuously ongoing process of balancing and synchronizing individual and societal dynamics and conditions. Hence, every biography at any point of one's life encompasses manifold conflicting tensions, which can be regarded as dialectical structures which the biographizing process has to balance: a time-space tension, a subjectivity-objectivity tension, a singularity-collectivity tension, a self-regulation-alienation tension (internal vs. external locus of control), a construction-reconstruction tension, a past-future tension, and a continuity-development tension.

But more important than this general description of what a biography is and how it works (many authors have described this process in similar words) is the investigation as to why creating such a unique biography has become a salient existential necessity in modern times. Not every known civilization obliged human beings to develop a very personal and individualized curriculum vitae which one has to present and to exhibit if one wants to take part in social life, the labor market, and so on. Traditional societies shape the life courses of their members more by socially preformed and standardized stages, passages, or traditions. In a traditional culture, a person knew what he or she had to expect when her or she grew old. The horizon of anticipation was set up socially for the elderly, too. The growing dependency on a shaped and presentable biography, however, emerged as an inner psychic and an outer societal condition of modernity. Social scientists who researched the development of social milieus and lifestyles (Beck, 1986; Karl, 1991; Vester, Oertzen, Geiling, Hermann, & Muller, 1992) epitomize their findings in terms of "pluralisierte Klassengesellschaft" (pluralized class society), "Enttrayditionalisierung" (detraditionalization) and "Individualisierung" (individualization).

Particularly with regard to the elderly, one has to face the fact that modern societies do not provide traditional patterns, milieus, and subcultures as a sufficient basis for a meaningful life in aging and which meet the different needs and stages of a life after work with its heterogeneity and which sometimes lasts more than 30 years (Kenyon, this volume; Mader, 1991;Young & Schuller, 1991). Although today growing old has become a mass phenomenon (that is why the elderly have become a social issue), there is no societal pattern which connects the aged among each other, in relationship to other generations, and in relation to one's former life. Gerontological research itself has reinforced this dynamic of modernity. One very remarkable consequence of exactly the *success* of classical gerontological studies is the fact that being older itself has increasingly lost its value and power as an explanatory category for numerous phenomena of aging.

Phenomena *in* old age are less and less considered as being results *of* old age. The findings of longitudinal studies repeatedly have proven the importance of interindividual differences in phenomena of aging, thus leading to a biographical approach with curiosity and the hope of deriving explanations as to the extent to which phenomena of aging are sociocultural or biographical constructs. Hand in hand with this discovery of individuality, on the one hand, and the detraditionalization of life worlds, traditions, and milieus, on the other hand, the elderly are forced to live on their biographically accrued capital; economically, culturally, and socially. Seniority itself, for instance, is not alive and well in modern civilization. To put it in a nutshell: The elderly depend on the resources of their life course. These resources basically are contained in their biographical construct. This might be represented in a told and repeated story, or might be represented and contained in home as a place, as Rubinstein, Kilbride, and Nagy (1992) claim. However represented, it must be considered as a serious source of capital:

> Homes are places where families grow and develop; they are safe havens; they are representations of feelings, either real or desired; they are investments; they are embodiments of both our individuality and our sense of community; their message, like a code, can be deciphered and read by others. The home, too, acts within the context of a domain of behavior that may be labeled rituals of the self such that those important elements of decor that are portrayed help organize memories and personal history (biography). (p.80)

The past as embodied in biography is the capital of the elderly as it is the future for the young. From this point of view, the growing interest of social scientists in research on biography in our century reflects a deeper fault line and need of modernization: we need to know about biographies as a resource of modern life, as hidden agendas and structures of modern societies.

Amazingly, another phenomenon seems to contradict this depicted scenario at first glance. Many new institutions, organizations, and associations have emerged to meet the needs of the elderly: third age universities, political parties, special insurance, specialized travel agencies, and adult education for the elderly (preretirement courses). The individualization process is paralleled by a standardization of the process of aging. Institutions function as standardizers of the manifold openings of life after work, as school or work standardizes life passages before work. But what does the increasing institutionalization of aging mean with regard to biography? Societies are accustomed to responding to issues of social order by establishing new institutions for those who appear as a problem to the social order. So these new institutions as organizers of a more or less amorphous and vaguely organized phase of life function as vicarious biographical patterns, as substitute biographies, or as integrating structures of a society. From a biographical point of view, the question arises whether the elderly are urged to create some sort of "patchwork" biography and to mask their real life stories (Featherstone & Hepworth, 1991). This turns out to be an emotional issue as well.

However, as the leading question of my inquiry is specifically the role and function of emotionality in the biography-creating process and its relation to continuity, I have to continue this thread first, and I will come back to an interesting relation between emotionality and modernization later on. The focus of my inquiry in the next two sections will be to depict some terminological issues concerning these guiding categories.

3. THEORETICAL AND TERMINOLOGICAL ISSUES OF EMOTIONALITY

The multitude of aspects in theory and research on emotionality requires us to provide distinct definitions within a clear framework. As Charles Cofer states in his comprehensive article in the *Encyclopedia Britannica* (1986) on human emotion and motivation.

> Emotional processes thus are characteristically complex, and there exists no theoretical frame that counts for all aspects without contradiction. There are difficulties even in framing a simple definition. (p. 347)

In view of this difficulty, the scientific core issue will therefore be restricted to the question of whether the concept "emotion" ought to be applied only to narrowly defined acute psychophysical reactions, episodes, and states, limited in time, or whether it could also be used advantageously for specific basic dispositions that do not easily fall into a better category.

Averill (1988) countered N.H. Frijda's (1986) thesis that emotions are occurrent (ongoing) reactions, with his own antithesis, namely, that emotional states are episodic dispositions. He stressed that "emotional episodes often last for hours (for example, in the case of anger) or even months (in the case of grief) without a response necessarily occuring throughout the period" (p.85). The range of my emotionality-continuity hypothesis is even wider. We must posit that there are "emotional states" that codetermine and survive whole periods of life, indeed the total life span, and which are therefore fundamentally significant for an understanding of the aging process as well as in handling old age. Mandl & Huber (1983) and Lamb (1987) use "mood" instead of "emotion" for these permanent frames of reference. Averill pleads for a Copernican revolution in studying emotions which would concentrate on higher and more complex levels of mental activities, social norms, and behavior patterns. In the end he is looking for a revised concept of emotion beyond the traditional scope, the one centering on 1) specific behaviors which are, 2) complex enough in themselves and going along rule-like with specific psychosubjective experiences and 3) a somatophysiological stimuli. This triad is usually called the "emotions proper." The classic example of fight-flight behavior, with its emission of adrenalin and similar bodily states, experienced as anxiety or anger, is often used as a prototypical example of emotions (Elias, 1991; Kraut, 1986).

In a different context, however, Frijda and Swagerman (1987) have fundamentally linked the function of emotionality with the idea of a "disposition:"

> Emotions are part of the system's concern realisation provision. By "concern" we mean the system's dispositions to evaluate events or internal conditions as desirable or as undesirable. The presence of such disposition, and of means to meet them or safeguard them, is essential to an independent self-organising system. Emotions, we say are part of a system for realising concerns (see Frijda, 1987, for a fuller discussion). They are parts of the mechanisms that do the detection of opportunities and threats; they do, as we shall discuss, the "relevance appraisal". They do the detection of whether or not something can be done about it and, roughly, what; they do the "context appraisal". In addition, they signal the appraisal outcomes to the system as a whole and to its action control and plan construction provisions in particular. (p. 237)

Hence, "relevance appraisal" and "context appraisal" would be the decisive tasks Frijda and Swagerman (1987) allocate to emotion as a dispostion. This is an answer to the question of whether emotionality could also be understood as a disposition. Self-referential systems, such as human beings, use emotions for self-regulating processes. Relevance and context are assessed and fed back.

Elias (1991), whose theory will be examined later, within the "continuity" concept, assumes, "emotions to stem from a connection of learned and non-learned processes." (p. 349) His term is "process dispositions" (p. 347) to characterize the genesis and effectiveness of emotions in human evolution:

> In the human context the concept of nature has to be re-defined. Perhaps one can start from the demonstrable fact that it is possible to distinguish between two types of structures which deserve to be called natural. There are, on the one hand, structures which are completely inaccessible to change as a result of stored and remembered experiences – that is, as a result of learning. There are also, on the other hand, natural human structures which remain dispositions. (Elias, 1991, p. 110)

The concept of emotionality will keep in view such "process dispositions" which are subject to change and development (humans are natural and cultural beings), but are so fundamental that they mold and influence learning and behavior to an increasing degree in later life.

The qualitative process of emotion in real life itself could well be described with the help of W. Wundt's three polarities: *Lust–Unlust* (pleasure vs. displeasure), *Lösung–Spannung* (tension vs. release), *H.Beunruhigung–Erregung* (calm vs. excitation) (Wundt, 1913, p. 91). It is among these dichotomous psychophysical, experiential processes that everyday life context appraisals take place where emotionality seems to have its dominant realm. Such appraisals are not free from tensions and disturbances, do not at all go along in harmony with those norms and values which form attitudes, beliefs, and the world-view to which humans subscribe. Intense conflicts may range between these two levels of practical and ideal norms, and sometimes they can only be "resolved" by various defense mechanisms such as displacement or compensation (in Freud's terms).

As early as 1941 Andras Angyal (1972), in his personality theory pointed out:

> We consider the feeling tone of emotions as the experience of the state and of the situation of the person under the aspect of value. The biological situations are constantly evaluated by the organism from the point of view of their significance for the life process. The emotional tone is the experience of such significance. It should be clear, however, that in emotion the significance of the biological situation is not experienced in thoughts and judgements, but in a very intimate and immediate manner, as joy and sorrow, depression and elation, or quite generally as various shadings of pleasantness and unpleasantness. (p.71)

As mentioned above it was Angyal who defined biography as a time-Gestalt.

The consideration that emotions contain appraisals of everyday perceptions and actions would lead to far-reaching queries. Are emotions, in the final analysis, perhaps perpetual states without objects, without intentions, or are they intentional (that is, intrinsically always directed towards something)? In brief, must we ascribe intentionality to such a process disposition as we do with regard to thinking? Put differently, can dispositional emotionalities act intentionally and in a goal-directed manner or are they just the basic "coloring" and background mood of biography? Since this question concerns the linkage of emotion and cognition (Mandl & Huber, 1983), or of emotion and communication (Fiehler, 1990), it is a worry not only to philosophers (like David Hume in former times or Max Scheler in our century who based value systems and ethics essentially on emotions), but also to current empirical research into emotions.

The linkage of emotion and cognition is actually debated with regard to the question of whether emotions and feelings do have a cognitive content *eo ipso* (in themselves) or are perhaps just lifelong neighbors. R. Kraut (1986) and R. Lamb (1987) have advanced subtle and penetrating arguments. Kraut starts from the widespread knowledge that there is no fear (feeling) unless there is a dangerous situation (cognition). An ideal type case would be that, "Under optimal conditions an agent does not fear lions without also believing lions to be dangerous: under optimal conditions an agent does not feel indignant towards Jones unless he judges Jones to have violated a legitimate expectation" (Kraut, 1986, p. 649).

In discussing the difference between emotion and feeling Kraut ascribes intentionality to emotion, but not to feelings. His thesis is that in the end, although emotions are "high-order states" and feelings "lower level items," there is no principal difference between emotion and feeling, and that both comprise a "context," a reference to perception as a constituent and not added later through rational analysis (see also Lamb, 1987). Kraut's conclusion is that

> We shouldn't have tried to put feelings in context; the context is already in the feelings. Therein lies the key to a successful identification of emotion with feeling and to providing a plausible alternative to cognitivist accounts of emotion. (Kraut, 1986, p. 652)

Following this very plausible thesis, one implication would be that dispositional emotions not only have a context but would also constitute one. Context can mean many things. For instance, the effectiveness of a context can appear as pure cognitive *choice* at branching points (Birren & Birren, this volume) for one's own life. Someone analyzes the circumstances, draws a consequence, and makes up his or her mind. But the context of such a choice encompasses also a multitude of emotional patterns: love or hate in choices of relationships; trust, mistrust, shame, self-esteem in choices of a career; feelings of belonging or of being a stranger in choices of a milieu or life world. Emotionality thus seen as a content-oriented constituent of contexts would indeed help to create even cultures (nationalities) and biographies, an assertion in stark contrast to the one held by Piaget that emotionality only supplies energy for action, but possesses no cognitive structures (Mandl & Huber, 1983).

After these terminological questions, let me summarize the characteristics of a new conception of emotions which does not contradict the traditional narrow concept of emotions as reactive psychophysical states, but which puts it in a wider horizon of self-regulating biographical processes in which emotion is understood as, similar to language, a *process disposition* with its own *intentionality* directed towards values and a valued future (see also Randall, this volume). It is experienced as a psychophysical subjectivity (such as pleasure vs. displeasure, tension vs. release, calm vs. excitation) and includes a cultural *structure*. Intentionality, subjectivity, and structure characterize the process disposition which will guide my further considerations.

4. THEORETICAL AND TERMINOLOGICAL ISSUES OF CONTINUITY

The following highlights several theoretical and terminological problems with respect to continuity by using *three* widely differing approaches, those of Albert Bandura, Norbert Elias and Erik H. Erikson.

Continuity and Chance (Albert Bandura)

Albert Bandura (1982) starts with a certainly correct statement which he would probably also use for an assessment of Thomas Mann's characterizations mentioned before: "One can always find linkages between early and later endeavors as, for example, between pursuit of scholarship in childhood and professional careers in adulthood" (Bandura, 1982, p. 747). Ergo: he who looks for continuities will find them. But this does not explain anything. Then he tries to support his core thesis that "chance encounters play a prominent role in shaping the course of human lives," with examples meant to show that "some of the most important determinants of life paths often arise through the most trivial circumstances" (p. 749). The accidents and incidents that lead two people to meet, lead one to find a job, or a husband or wife, are described in great detail, and hardly anybody would deny the grave consequences of such chains of events for a person's biography. His illustrations are events called chance constellations.

Chance encounters are, according to Bandura, opposed to deliberate plans, and in that sense the famous brick dropping from the roof, after decades of winds and storms, the very moment when I leave my house after being retained by a phone call, hitting me and causing a lifelong handicap, and this influencing my future life, may well serve as an example of chance causality and a subsequent biographical "continuity." At first glance, Bandura's approach seems to contradict the approach pursued here. However, the important theoretical point, for Bandura, seems to be the following:

> There are two psychological processes by which the products of early development can foster continuities in behavioral patterns. One process operates through selection of environments. After people acquire certain preferences and standards of behavior, they tend to select activities and associates who share similar value systems, thereby mutually reinforcing preexisting bents. (Bandura, 1982, p. 747)

The striking feature of Bandura's core thesis (chance encounters and chance events play dominant roles in life's paths) is that his entire argument really runs counter to it. He draws on a wealth of aspects and considerations which all show that modes of perception and dealing with such chance events shape the paths we take and not the chance event itself. The chance event may be part of the conditions of life's course, it may itself generate changeable conditions, but it neither generates continuity, nor explains it. The mechanisms used by Bandura himself in order to describe our coping behavior in the face of chance constellations under constraint tend to rely on intrahuman sources for the generation of continuity.

Bandura's psychomechanisms for the explanation of the genesis of continuities are, for example, the mutual reinforcement of preexisting bents, the reciprocal influence of persons and social factors (in other words, reciprocal, stabilizing dynamics), affectional involvement, value preference and self-evaluative standards, images of reality and belief systems that take on self-perpetuating properties. The heart of Bandura's concept of mechanisms is one where chance events and chance encounters are nevertheless converted into the continuity, identity, and stability of a life's course: "Knowing what factors mediate the impact of chance encounters on life paths provides guides for how to foster and safeguard valued future" (Bandura, 1982, p. 754). But what a "valued future" is belongs to the context of human existence and must itself be "generated", and is not pregiven.

Bandura does not elaborate how and why these mediators develop and function as conditions of continuity. They are all presupposed, after people acquire certain preferences and standards (Bandura, 1982). A fundamental answer to the how and why of human continuity is given by Norbert Elias.

Continuity and Evolution (Norbert Elias)

Elias's process and evolution sociology posits a fundamental difference between animals and humans. The evolutionary shift from animal to human happens when a being's existence depends on learning.

> The learning potential of humans had grown to such an extent that they, and they alone, came to be totally dependent on learned forms of knowledge for their dominant form of communication and for their orientation in the world (Elias, 1991, p. 109). This obligation to learn also extends to emotion as a means of finding one's bearings. Some of these means are, according to Elias's theory, so important that they must be learned very early in life
>
> . . . when the natural process of maturation creates as it were the strongest possible natural disposition for learning them. The capability for speaking and for understanding a language is one of the several instances of this kind. That of loving and responding to love is another, the capacity of regulating oneself according to learned social standards, of controlling one's drives and emotions, a third. (Elias, 1991, p. 112)

Elias points out that these path-finding or process dispositions are acquired in a "love and learning" process. Emotions have as basic a function for human interrelations as human language. If emotions, however, are fundamental codirectors of relationships, then they are necessarily also of all the cultural and civilatory aspects of human nature. If, also, these basic pathfinding means are learned similarly as early as language (and "mother tongue" is the model for the later learning of a foreign language), then continuity comes into human life, individually and collectively, via learning; and learning, also, is that which makes possible change and innovation in the history of people and humankind. Elias has developed this approach "for continuing continuity and innovation" (Elias, 1991, p. 105).

Continuity and Identity (Erik H. Erikson)

Another aspect of continuity, exploring. the individual psychosocial history, is that outlined by Erikson in *Childhood and Society* (1963). Erikson proposes stages of identity formation, with early adolescence having the psychosocial task of laying the foundation for a first, fundamental identity (against the danger of role diffusion). According to Erikson (1963,) "The sense of ego-identity, then, is the accrued confidence that the inner sameness and continuity prepared in the past are matched by the sameness and continuity of one's meaning for others" (p. 261).

In our context it is important to note that Erikson proposes a strictly *interactionist* definition of identity, avoiding and rejecting any idea that identity could possibly be restricted to an internal entity. The internal continuity corresponds to an external continuity out there in everyday, sociocultural life, and with it the development of continuity stretches into the individual's relationship to society. Individual development, crises, and life's journey as a whole can only be mastered on the background of such an experience of continuity. In addition, according to Erikson, the developmental crises of a human being basically are centred on a struggle for emotional dispositions which will become the basis of further steps; for example, trust vs. distrust in the first stage of early childhood, or shame and doubt in the second stage. As with Elias (1991), this approach requires continuity as a condition for innovation and further development.

Another interactionist approach has been elaborated by Bengtson (1989). Society itself has, of course, every interest in promoting continuity among successive generations:

> There is biosocial continuity across generations, seen in genetic and social similarities between parents and children. Despite change in both participants and social

> environment, the inertia of tradition does persist through the decades, as seen even in the rapidly changing world of science (see Cohen, 1985; Kuhn, 1962). Historical comparison suggests more stability through time in groups and societies, for better or worse, than we often acknowledge (Allen, 1952). Social continuity is attempted most directly in the efforts of the older generation to transmit and preserve. Upholding a social order they have created, perhaps struggling to preserve positions of power, the ancient regime has attempted to enhance continuity of social order in the face of generational succession and innovation. (Bengtson, 1989, p. 26)

Here again we see the biosocial web of continuity and innovation in the tension-laden succession of generations. Let me now summarize the terminological characteristics of a new conception of continuity: Continuity is a surface phenomenon, a necessary resource for the behaviour, thinking, and feelings of people, of interacting and communicating generations and cultures living together, so that, in comparing and "re-cognizing," they accrue confidence in "generalized others" (G.H. Mead 1969, p. 280) and they find their individual uniqueness.

5. THE EMOTIONALITY-CONTINUITY-HYPOTHESIS

Within such a general inquiry and its diversity of research tasks, there is a specific task when emotionality (as cause and explanation) simultaneously produces its own continuity (as effect and descriptive phenomenon). If an older person assesses their life as a good or bad, as a bitter or sweet life (Ruth & Öberg, this volume) it seems to mean emotional continuity. The earlier review of emotionality terminology should have clarified that emotionality fundamentally constitutes social relationships. Emotionality is a relationship category and will, therefore, also manifest itself as a relationship phenomenon. If, in theoretical terms, emotionality is a twin concept incorporating etiological and phenomenological aspects, then the intriguing question arises if and how patterns of emotions determine and mold a life during its social intercourse and thus contribute to a unique profile and a biography.

Such an inquiry would certainly dissolve any linear cause-effect schema of emotionality and continuity and favor a dialectic one; for it is evident that continuities themselves can generate emotionality, and vice versa. The older one grows the more continuity itself becomes a value of its own. The phenomenon that the elderly like to stick to their familiar situation even if the circumstances have changed negatively shows that continuity is associated with a highly valued positive emotion which can hinder a choice to change and to improve the objective life circumstances (Rubinstein et al., 1992; Tuchschmidt, 1988).

A metaphor from human physiology might highlight the complex problem of how both emotionality and continuity function and control each other: The upright posture of human beings has become one of our characteristics. It is an outstanding phylogenetic and ontogenetic phenomenon of continuity among the species. Such an upright posture, however, requires an organ (labyrinth, cupula organs of the semicircular canal, macula organs) known as sense of equilibrium which adjusts our spatial position according to the earth's gravitational field. This sensor tells us where "up" is, or "down," or "upside down." By analogy, I should like to call human emotionality the sense of balance, the social sonar for positioning us in the force field of cultural values, norms, expectations, and stereotypes through relevance appraisal and context appraisal. This emotional sense of balance contains the basic rules we need for the control of our social space.

Couched in theoretical terms and again referring to Elias: fundamental patterns of basic emotions, socially preset and individually acquired in early "loving and learning" (Elias, 1991), feed back to the thinking, judging, deciding, acting human being as to whether an actual state or possibility is desirable or not (using pleasure - displeasure; release - tension; excitation - calm as triggers). In practical terms, they signal (via anxieties and collywobbles) what a social situation means, whether we can or must see ourselves as an accepted member of our community or as a stranger. They keep us in (e)motion until we have found a more convenient social space after fight, flight, or negotiation. They also tell us what an adequate response would be in accord with the standard cultural expectations. Everybody scans the horizon for a favorable position. Basic emotionality is like a searchlight in a crowded social twilight, focussing eventually on a temporary resting place.

This disposition to trigger explorations can lead to innovations, even though the final aim is to find a preferred position in a social space in accord with emotionality's code, and continuity goes with it as a necessary consequence of the psychosocial balancing fact: Not every social balance will be experienced as pleasant or desirable. Being a public figure may be a pleasure to some, an abhorrence to others. The aim is not fixed as if emotions would tell us to do this or do that. The sense of balance is a homeostatic sonar. It keeps us on the move towards the code's signal "favorable." But this is exactly the overall goal of a biography. Emotionality reacts to individual, to social, and to societal conditions and situations.

A consequence of such a procedure is a repetition of those behavioral patterns and problem solutions which have proved successful or reasonable, and these repetitions become continuities, routine phenomena. In biographical terms, these patterns are called plots, themes, metaphors, or stories (Kenyon, this volume; McAdams, this volume; Polkinghorne, this volume; Randall, this volume). As a therapist I am often confronted with the "human phenomenon" that people cling tenaciously to detrimental behaviors with repetitions and repeat performances as a consequence. Continuities are surface phenomena which can thus be described phenomenologically. Continuities in biographies, history, and culture are, therefore, a phenomenon indirectly attained through a quest for a favorable place in social space. The repetitions themselves are part of the classical interactionist approach as defined by Erikson.

Averill (1984) has used a different metaphor, the ancient folklore of Theseus' ship, to elucidate continuities in human life:

> Men are like sailors who must rebuild their ship on the open sea, never able to dismantle it completely and to reconstruct it from the best materials, but forced to replace one board after another until nothing is left of the old wood, but still the "same" ship is there (or is it?). (p. 34)

This basic emotionality has been acquired in real-life social circumstances (as the organic sense of equilibrium had to integrate the earth's gravitation into its structure and functioning). It comprises both a "knowledge" of human reality (about trust and distrust) and an "image" of the human potential (designs and future). Peter Alheit (forthcoming) has recently tried to capture this biographical structure and dynamic with slightly different terminology:

> What is important is the finding that our basic feeling–that we can dispose relatively independently over our own biographies–does not necessarily conflict with the fact that the greater part of our biographical activities are either fixed to a large degree or require various processors to initiate it. It therefore appears plausible that the "feeling" is not actually an intentional action scheme at all, or a consciously desired biographical plan, but instead a kind of hidden "meaning" behind the alternating processual structures of our life course: the doubtless ubiquitous, but strategically not always available *intuition* that for all the contradiction, we are still dealing with "our" lives. We entertain this unique "background idea" of ourselves not in spite of, but precisely because of the structural limitations imposed by our social and ethnic origins, our gender and the era in which we are living. (p. 6)

Alheit talks of "mentalities," "habitual action," "prescriptive forms of knowledge," to give theoretical wording to such a hidden curriculum. Where in the aging process and in old age can we make out this hidden curriculum?

THE EMOTIONALITY-CONTINUITY HYPOTHESIS IN RELATION TO OLD AGE AND AGING

It is an everyday belief (a stereotype) that older people repeat their actions, cling to proven behavior, enjoy their habits, and feel irritated by changes in their enviroment and daily routine. Even though this view is inappropriately stereotypical, we are here looking for a more fundamental explanation of the often noticed repetitions in old-age behavior and thinking, with a view to discussing the difficulty and meaningfulness of opening up truly new horizons to aging people. There is a scientific interest in the explanation, understanding, and clarification of the meaning and function of repetition in old age.

To begin with, let us look into some approaches and their theories of how to conceptualize the internalization of these basic emotional patterns which, during a lifetime, eventually can become a constant in the aging process. One group of theorists and researchers are so-called social constructivists. Averill is one of them (see also, Fiehler, 1990, Malatesta & Izard, 1984). The social constructivist answer is: "Emotional schemata are the internal representation of social rules and norms" (Averill, 1984, p. 25). It is true that they do not take basic emotional patterns to be innate or determined by experiences in early childhood; they concede a potential for lifelong development. But the gist of their approach is the import of rules for emotions (their manifestation and their interpretation) from the social world outside, which in turn determines the emotions themselves. Social constructivists, therefore, cannot avoid the continuity problem. "There is continuity, and it is not possible to say at any given point in time that the infantile emotion has ended and the adult emotion has come into being" (Averill, 1984, p. 37).

It is somewhat surprising that Averill does not draw the (obvious) conclusion that a theoretical requirement to absorb basic rules of emotionality (including, above all, their manifestation and interpretation) from the social environment in early childhood will itself induce a process of continuity. Rules are set to facilitate and orient behavior. They must include a margin of flexibility to allow for various situations, but their basic goal is situation-independent stability, thus assuring safety and security: the world becomes recognizable and predictable. Rules bring continuity into social life. A healthy development must make a child recognize messages from relevant others. Rules must be decodable so that, for example, a mother's or a father's smile signals an emotionality (joy, acceptance, closeness, nonaggression) and can reliably be integrated into the child's own behavior pattern. A child would go mad if a smile would need a different interpretation for each different situation and block the development of an overarching code or emotionality pattern. The rule itself is the foundation of a lifelong continuity formation. Averill (1984) himself has described such general rules of emotionality in great detail, and so has Fiehler (1990).

Social constructivists do not appear to risk the step Elias took: emotional ground rules are acquired quite early, similar to language acquisition, and they are efficacious right into old age. They evidently even seem to imprint and to color lifestyles. I should now like to give some examples of such emotional patterns.

One of the most interesting and widely discussed questions in our culture is the gender difference and its influence on the shaping of emotions. Although a wide range of literature deals with gender differences and emotion, I prefer to illustrate the emotionality-continuity-nexus and the phenomenon of repetition by sharing some experiences from my psychotherapeutic practice.

Well-educated and emancipated women, having analyzed their own socialization and role in society, often describe observations like these: they feel a certain bias and a need to keep their own ideas and decisions to themselves and to support those of others and grant them precedence. Instead of adhering to their own judgements, they feel a readiness and an inward state to deal with other people's topics and problems instead of their own. Such a scenic constellation (against their own reasoning and understanding) would cast them again and again as a "fellow traveller" in the usually male gravitation field staged either by the man or even by herself. Not only do they note their own critical self-assessment, but also the emotional effort of taking their own themes and problems seriously, of putting them into the center of concern (see also the devoted, silenced way of life in Ruth & Oberg, this volume).

At the same time these women recognize an opposite tendency with regard to children and others who need care: a tendency and willingness to be thoroughly concerned with the care and handling that adolescents need. Even the delegation of certain tasks to a husband or a man is tinged with an overarching responsibility retained for the general run of things. In contrast to men, they see themselves as the final point of reference, even when and where a dependable agreement had been reached (and was kept). And, in the end, this is the way they are used by men and children.

Both tendencies taken together evidently describe a classical and simple stereotyped role of feminity that, also evidently, cannot be corrected by rational insight and exhaustive countervailing efforts. The continuity of such a pattern running through a biography up to old age is most clearly visible in the nursing of elderly parents, almost exclusively provided by women, and in their corresponding turn to their daughters. Increasingly, I observe biographies of women who bring up their offspring (mostly alone) and who take over the care for their older parents nearly at the same time when their adult children have left home. And even when these women eventually leave their homes and go into a residential home for the elderly they stick to this "leitmotif" of their lives, as Voges and Pongratz (1988) found out:

> We also observed that the former leitmotif was adapted via substitution of roles. Many women who struggled for their families all their lives looked for activities within the facility which allowed them to transform the leitmotif from the family area to the public domain. The efforts of active grandmothers who are always on the road to those members of the family who need them most, also conform to this pattern. (p. 81)

Another phenomenon, reported by women teachers, belongs to the same complex. Schoolgirls on a lower educational level confronted with career decisions usually have clear fantasies about their (future) family and vague ones about their career, and including a fantasy of how to handle the connection between the two. Schoolboys, however, have clear career fantasies, vague ones about a future family, and usually no fantasy of how to handle the connection between the two (or their fantasy delegates this realm to being the woman's concern).

If, however, in our society these phenomena are understood as basic emotional patterns of femininity (and a corresponding one of masculinity), then we can see why the real-life gender relationship is curiously unaffected and stays in its customary mold, despite all formal equal opportunity acts, and despite all critical-emancipatory enlightenment. The regulation of internal gender relations is perhaps founded more on such emotional patterns than we were hitherto prepared to accept. The true discrimination against women happens in emotionality with its long cultural history and will only be modified step by step.

Research shows (Dannhauer, 1977; Fagot, Leinbach, & O'Boyle, 1992) that basic gender patterns are founded already among 2- to 4- year-olds:

> We have found that four-year-olds, like college students, sort items in metaphorically gender-stereotypic ways (Lienbach & Hort, 1989); the results of this study place the beginning of these metaphorical associations with gender prior to age 3. Children, even at these early ages, may have begun to connect certain qualities with males and other qualities with females. Confirming the relation between gender labeling and gender stereotyping also supports the notion that even very young children's gender notion is schematic, that its bits and pieces are not acquired in isolation but assimilated into a schema built around the theme of gender. (Fagot et al., 1992, p. 229)

In a comprehensive inquiry into gender-specific differences, Dannhauer (1977) points out that the empirical material clearly shows, amongst other things, that there is a progressive differentiation in gender from kindergarten to adolescence, but only in adolescence can a recognizable difference be obtained from rich characteristics and data (whereas few data would permit significant gender ascriptions on the kindergarten level). At the same time, however, the distributors of self-ascriptions within the same gender decrease. In other words, gender difference as a basic pattern is established during the early years up to age 15 or 20.

The following might shed some further light on this issue: "Content-oriented research repeatedly mentions the quite different, even opposing socialization of boys (aggression) and girls (adaptation); indeed aggression and adaptation are the established key variables for gender differentiation" (Dannhauer, 1977, p. 179). This difference is significant at an early kindergarten age. Dannhauer, whose study was done in the former GDR, followed and proved the theoretical thesis that a child takes over "in the course of ontogenic development the active gender role which, internalized, appears as psychical gender difference" (Dannehauer 1977, p.183). In interpreting his data, however, he is obliged to pay tribute to the socialist ideology by trying to prove that "under socialist societal conditions gender-specific differences are more and more weakened." (Dannehauer, 1977, p. 183) The data themselves tell a different story. Following Norbert Elias (1991), I regard such phenomena as socially pregiven patterns of emotions, individually acquired, then self-regulating.

A further remarkable illustration of the relation between emotionality and the personal evaluation of a life course as it is represented in narrative formats can be drawn from the studies of Ruth and Öberg (this volume). The main aim of this Finnish study with those who were born between 1905 and 1915 (the generation of the wars and the Depression) was to find out how life was reflected in the narratives of the elderly. The typology which the researchers adopted more or less employs emotional categories in characterizing the personal evaluation of the interviewees: the bitter life, life as a trapping pit, life as a hurdle race, the devoted silenced life, life as a job career, and the sweet life. (Only the type "life as a job career" avoids an emotionally loaded description. I assume that reflects also the narrative formats of the job careerists themselves.) If one understands this typology not only as a classification by the researchers but also as a reflection on the narratives themselves, the findings suggest that the personal evaluation of a life arises from a very personal emotional point of view.

If I look at the characteristic description of each type in more depth, I observe that the emotional points of view (from "bitter life" on the one hand to "sweet life" on the other) are paralleled by a shift from an external locus of control on the one hand to an internal locus of control on the other. This means that an older person assesses his or her life by combining an emotion and a conviction about being, or not being, in command of their own life. In order to illustrate this hidden connection between emotionality and locus of control, I shall focus on some short examples. In Ruth & Öberg's study the bitter life is evaluated as, "I haven't been able to make any decisions. Life has made the decisions for me." Life as a hurdle race with a good outcome in the end is evaluated, for example, as "No one is commanding me and forcing me to go out head over heels in the middle of the night." The devoted silenced life, "I've certainly been some kind of driftwood. Pushes from here and there, things that happened and have taken me in a certain direction. Without my own co-operation." The sweet life, "One doesn't get good health free, if one doesn't care for oneself."

Many authors in gerontology stress the importance of locus of control in later life (de Vries & Lehman, this volume; Featherstone & Hepworth, 1991; Rubinstein et al. 1992). If I grasp the relation of locus of control and assessments of life as reflected in biographical narrative formats as a serious hypothesis, I find a very remarkable undercurrent relation between the structure of the narrative constructs of these elderly persons, on the one hand, and the above mentioned structure of modernity on the other. The "match" is this: One of the most important tasks which an individual in modern societies is supposed to achieve is to grow up to be a person with a highly stable *internal* locus of control. Self-responsibility is the corresponding value; life as a sequence of choices is the corresponding biographical pattern which people use to describe their lifestories. This normative pattern of modernity obviously structures the personal evaluation of a life and is reflected and embodied in the emotional tones of the stories we are (Kenyon, this volume; Turski, 1991). Life is worse in cases of prevailing external locus of control and better in cases of prevailing internal locus of control.

The emergence of continuity in an individual life exactly depends on the same roots of modernity. Self-responsibility as a must in modern societies depends on an individual internalization of precisely the social pattern which forces an individual to structure their life as a sequence of individual choices. Emotional patterns are part of social patterns. Looking back, was it good or bad, a bitter or a sweet life? Every culture prescribes how one has to feel or to manifest feelings, not only in given circumstances but also in basic assessments. Thus, the necessity of internalization covers emotional prescriptions as well. The seemingly paradoxical effect of such individual internalization of socially pregiven patterns of emotions is that, on the one hand, individuals are in synchrony with their cultural environment (this is the core of Erik Erikson's identity concept) yet, on the other hand, they gain a certain distance and independence from their social environment. This possibility of internalization assures that they need not react in a reflex-like manner to any change.

Internalization provides internal continuity, distance (perhaps freedom) from the external world, and synchrony to a certain extent at the same time. In this context, the elderly seem to adhere increasingly to this internal continuity and to be distanced from the external. But they are less forced to synchronize the tension between living from their internal resources and their external circumstances. The danger is that they are "free" in the sense of unrelatedness or separation (see also Kenyon, this volume). They have, as some of them say, "outlived" themselves, implying that the synchronization between actual environment and their individual pattern of sensitivity has broken down.

The more the actual relationship between an older man or woman and his or her environment reduces (by death of beloved persons, loss of work, or decreasing ability to move), the more the necessity of synchronizing environment and biography gets lost. A gap emerges, and nearly automatically there emerges a recourse to familiarities in order to fill the gap. In consequence the importance of the biography attained increases. Repetitions are the indicators and fulfillers of this new state of self-regulating processes. Repetitions serve as important upholders of identity. The dependence on these fulfillers increases in modernity. The significance of sharing the experience of a life from one generation to another seems to decrease. It seems as if the modern debate on aging is a substitute debate on dying and death in a secularized world in which the process of meaning is more and more left to the individual and in which the knowledge and experience of the elderly does not really count.

The writer Hermann Hesse (1877–1962) graphically expressed the internalization of this relation between societal structure and biographical construct in his personal evaluation of life, when he was 76:

> Old people's modes of experiencing are something else; here I may not and must not allow myself any fiction or illusion and shall stay with my factual knowledge that a younger or even adolescent human being has no idea at all of old people's experiencing. Basically, they do not experience anything new, they have long since got their allotted share of primary experiences, according to what befits them adequately. Their "new" experiences, becoming rarer and rarer, are repetitions of what had often been experienced and happened several times, are a fresh varnish on an apparently finished painting, covering a stock of old experiences under a thin new layer, one layer on top of ten or hundred earlier ones. And yet, they mean something novel, and although they are no primary experiences, they are genuine ones, for they become, amongst others, and every time, encounters and appraisals of oneself. Occasionally the idea struck me, this thirst for rambling and globe-trotting, this hunger for a new, unknown, for journeying and the exotic, known to all but the unimaginative, particularly in their youth, could also be a hunger for oblivion, for covering up pictures of former experiences with as many fresh ones as possible. The inclination of old age, however, with its firm habits and routines, its repeated returns to the same landscapes, people and situations, would then be a hankering for recollections, a never-ending need for memory's

> self-assurance, and perhaps also the desire, the faint hope that this treasure-chest of memories might even be enlarged. (Hesse, 1990, p.164)

From this graphic description of a complete individuation in old age, with its implicit meaning, we can bring out why older, even confused people, still create stability by returning to their childhood, and experience emotional continuity even when their cognitive stability (for example, by reason of senile dementia) is crumbling. "They are coming into their second childhood," as the former rural saying goes. But by no means is this a pure anthropological fact. It is also an issue of modern societies. In contrast to this view, Featherstone and Hepworth (1991) who dealt with postmodernity and the life course hold a view of more relatedness in later life:

> It is therefore important to have some sociological understanding of the theorization of the social construction of the life course in order to address the question of old age. Old age can only be understood in relational terms to (a) a discussion of the grounds for accounting for other stages of life; (b) a discussion of the previous life of the old people which acts as a background and context for their expectations and experience of old age; and (c) the relation of old people to other generations following behind who may have their own cultural priorities which point towards either a "caring" or "stigmatizing" attitude towards the old. (p. 387)

To conclude, the present inquiry suggests that a fruitful area for future research consists of a detailed analysis of the role and significance of the emotionality-continuity nexus as a biographizer throughout the life span and, in particular, in later life. Emotions may constitute a basic component of our understanding of aging and our efforts at intervention and the amelioration of quality of life in a postmodern society.

4

Studying Older Lives: Reciprocal Acts of Telling and Listening

Bertram J. Cohler, Ph.D. and Thomas R. Cole, Ph.D.

Understanding particular lives over time has become the subject of renewed controversy within the social sciences. Reconsideration of the goals and methods of human science study has placed renewed emphasis on the concrete and irreducible interplay of collective history and personal experience as factors shaping our knowledge of lives over time. For example the social constructionist perspective, which focuses attention on the relationship between person and society, has led to renewed interest in the study of lives, either through personal documents such as autobiographies and diaries, or through lifestories recounted in more or less formal interview situations (Polkinghorne, this volume; Ruth & Kenyon, this volume).

Contributions from areas as diverse as literary theory, ethnography, social psychology, and psychoanalysis all have suggested that neither lives nor texts can be understood apart from a complex interplay of participants. Indeed, no lifestory can be studied apart from the joint construction of teller and listener. Whether the survey research interview or a physician's interview with a patient, the story which emerges from particular conversations is a joint construction of each participant. If the story is a joint construction, then the intents and sentiments of each participant are essential in understanding this jointly constructed narrative. In particular, the experience of the listener or reader reciprocal to the telling or reading becomes of decisive significance for the story which is the product of this collaboration.

While there has been some discussion of the dialogic process of telling and listening (Bakhtin, 1986; Good, 1994; Ricoeur, 1971), there has been much less study of the manner in which wishes and feelings reciprocally elicited in listener or reader might contribute to the lifestory. Perspectives from within psychological anthropology and psychoanalysis suggest that this overlooked dimension of listening requires more detailed study. Nowhere is this dimension more urgently needed than in study of late life. Western European and particularly American society has long valued youth over age. The study of middle and later life has been a source of anxiety for scholars in disciplines ranging from literature to medicine. While understanding the source of this anxiety may enhance the study of lives over time, it may also make it more difficult. Listening to the life story of a much older adult may elicit complex feelings, ranging from longing for an ideal parent to anxiety or disgust. For example, younger listeners and readers sometimes find it difficult to hear or read about issues related to loss of function and the experience of dying and death. These concerns and problems inevitably affect the manner in which the lifestory of older adults is told, and are further enhanced when the older adult is suffering such personal distress as depression or shows evidence of such cognitive change as early stage dementia.

This chapter considers issues related to telling, listening to, and constructing the lifestory and focuses on the dialogic and socially located nature of the discourses known as lifestories, life histories, or biographies (Bakhtin, 1986). Our discussion is informed by discussions within ethnography focusing on the relationship between informant and ethnographer, and by recent psychoanalytic perspectives regarding the use of the past as constructed in the collaboration between analyst and analysand. To date, there has been little systematic and detailed consideration of issues related to the study of aging and the life history. Some exemplary initial efforts in this area have been reported by Johnson (1976); Cole and Premo (1986); Blytheway (1993); Humphrey (1993) and Berman (1988, 1994). The present inquiry expands on earlier discussions of such issues as recounting a life history as a story about the past, and the problem of making sense of this story. The listener of the life story uses empathetic understanding of this story, informed by a culturally constructed, shared understanding of the use of time and history, and a parallel life history which provides the basis for the process of vicarious introspection as a result of which we are able to understand others (Jackson, 1992; Kohut, 1959, 1984; Poland, 1993; Schafer, 1959; Stolorow & Atwood, 1992).

THE LIFESTORY: MAKING SENSE OF THE PERSONAL PAST

Over the past decade, there has also been particular interest in the concept of narrative, or schemes according to which we emplot meanings in lived experience (Bruner, 1986, 1990; Polkinghorne, 1988). Within contemporary society, maintenance of a sense of coherence or personal integrity, making sense of unpredictable life changes, is essential for morale and positive well-being (Antonovsky, 1987; Gergen & Gergen, 1983, 1986; Handel, 1987; Kohut, 1977; McAdams, 1990; Palombo, 1992, Schafer, 1980, 1981; Wyatt, 1963, 1986). Individuals maintain a sense of personal continuity or integrity by means of a continuing narrative or story which provides a present understanding of the course of the remembered past, experienced present, and anticipated future; all within a linear account which corresponds to the organization of time within our own culture (Cohler, 1982; Freeman, 1993; Polkinghorne, 1988; Ricoeur, 1977; Schafer, 1980, 1981).

Lifestory as a Personal Document

Narrative may be differentiated from such other accounts as chronicles, which present but do not order events. Narrative is intrinsically concerned with ordering experiences, particularly those unanticipated, generally adverse life-changes or "epiphanies" (Denzin, 1989a, 1989b) which disrupt the expectable order of experience. The lifestory is a narrative of a particular kind, one which unites disparate elements of a presently experienced life within a text which is coherent and at least potentially followable by others (Ricoeur, 1977). While there has been much discussion regarding lifestory, life history, and personal narrative, there has been little clarification of these related concepts. The lifestory represents a narrative told or recorded, reporting on one or more presently remembered events presumed to have taken place over time, organized in a manner potentially understandable by listener or reader.

The lifestory is a narrative precisely because it represents a discourse of a particular kind, organized with a potential listener or reader in mind and with an intent, often implicit, to convince self and others of a particular plot or present ordering of experience, rendered sensible within the understanding of coherence shared by speaker and listener or reader as participants with a particular culture (Denzin, 1989b; Titon, 1980). Denzin (1989a, 1989b) notes that these accounts represent narratives of lived experiences of some duration in which the act of constructing a story turns a person into an author (see also Randall, this volume). Concern with the integrity or coherence of a life, reflected in a lifestory of a particular kind, may be one of the few universals across cultures. An important aspect of being human is to search after meaning embedded in experience, and to recount these experiences in told or written form (Sarbin, 1986). (See also Kenyon, this volume).

Personal Circumstances and Lifestory

Narrative as represented by the lifestory does not make any assumptions regarding the reality of past events, but is concerned solely with what Erikson (1968) has termed "actuality" or the subjective experience attached to the interplay of particular life circumstances. For example, recounting experiences from his youth, the genetic epistemologist Jean Piaget (Bringuier, 1980) recounts a part of his lifestory in which it is said that he was nearly kidnapped while on an outing with his nursemaid who received a monetary reward for thwarting the kidnapping. Later discovery that this event never took place but was recounted by the nursemaid in an effort to account for money stolen from the family does not change the actuality (Erikson, 1986) that for a part of his life the nursemaid's tale and her heroism become a part of Piaget's own story of his experienced past. The meanings inherent in that encounter have become part of his own effort after meaning.

The significance of the past for understanding the present has become a major issue of concern within history and the social sciences. Reacting to the logical empiricist agenda for historical methods as means of formally testing propositions (Hempel and Oppenheim, 1978; 1942; Kolakowski, 1972; Popper, 1968), some contemporary historians (Gallie, 1968; Mink, 1966; White, 1975, 1987), have suggested that the important issue is not the reality of the Battle of Waterloo, but rather the place of that event in the present understanding of the subsequent course of history to the present time.

This issue of the reality of the past has also emerged within psychoanalysis and psychology. From the time of Freud's (1897, 1906) initial discussion of the reality of the seductions remembered by his analysands to the present time, psychoanalysis has struggled with the problem of the remembered and recollected past (Novey, 1968; Schafer, 1980, 1981; Spence, 1982; Wallace, 1985). Indeed, Schafer (1980, 1992) has suggested that the story of the personal past constructed within psychoanalysis must be understood principally from the perspective of the present relationship between analyst and analysand; the reality of the events recalled are of less significance than their place within a presently co-constructed account of the analysand's life.

A similar issue has been posed for the study of autobiographical memory within cognitive psychology. Recent discussion of memory has suggested that persons organize recollections about the past in order to maintain a coherent account of their lives. This discussion has generated the important insight that persons continually reorganize their memories about the past as a consequence of both earlier and later experience. The significance of this perspective on autobiographical memory has been highlighted in recent trials and media discussions of childhood sexual abuse. Loftus and her colleagues have raised significant questions regarding the accuracy of adult recollections of childhood abuse, and have expressed concern regarding assumptions underlying court testimony of a necessary association between adult experiences and childhood memories (Loftus, 1993; Loftus & Kaufman, 1992).

THE LIFESTORY OF THE HUMAN SCIENCES

The life history or lifestory, first systematically employed in Thomas and Znaniecki's *The Polish Peasant in Europe and America* (1918–20), has long played a significant role in social science inquiry (see also Ruth & Kenyon, this volume). Constructing the life history to document the impact of emigration, including the social dislocation accompanying passage from the Old World to the New World, Thomas and Znaniecki relied primarily upon the exchange of letters among family members and showed that, while other adults were able to find consociates (Plath, 1980) in America and a sense of community which fostered maintenance of traditional values, younger generations were less fortunate and felt adrift.

Over the past half century, psychology and sociology have embraced logical empiricism in a search after certainty in understanding wish and conduct. This program readily embraced the concern within philosophy with formal logic in an effort to enhance the experience of rationality in the study of lives. However, across the past decade, there has been a dramatic reconsideration of this so-called logic of discovery applied to the study of person and society. Experimental study has provided at best ambiguous findings which account for little of the variation in observed phenomena. Cultural study has shown the extent to which a means-ends rationality applied to the study of lives may be better understood as a distinctively Western ethnophilosophy than as a rational-scientific approach to the study of personal and social life.

Within our own society, studies ranging from Mannheim (1928) and concern with the sociology of knowledge, the Frankfurt school of critical social theory (Marcus & Tar, 1984; Fay, 1987) to Foucault and contemporary observational study (Latour, 1988; Lynch, 1993) have demonstrated the complex interplay between programs of study and present social context. From this perspective, it is difficult to study any phenomenon of personal and social life without a detailed consideration of present social forces interwoven with the problems to be approached through presumably logical empirical study (Bertaux, 1981; Rosenmayr, 1982; Elder & Caspi, 1990).

The philosopher of science Rorty (1980) has questioned whether the assumptions of a natural science approach to the study of human conduct will ever succeed, and pleads for renewed assessment of this tradition as normative inquiry within the human sciences. Rorty (1985) argues instead for a shift from concern with accuracy and "validity" of scholarly study within the human sciences to a focus on issues of meaning and coherence. Rychak (1988) has noted the importance of distinguishing between rigor in a mode of study and the positivist reductionism associated with much of the study of personality and social life across the past fifty years. Mishler (1986, 1990) has questioned the very foundation of the turn towards survey research and other modes of experience-distant inquiry. Mishler notes that this tradition makes assumptions regarding the presumed lack of relationship between the interviewer and respondent, and a replicable or reliable mode of inquiry which is contrary to the reality of the research interview. From the perspective of the present discussion, assumptions underlying the presumed value of the survey research interview cause the loss of the interviewer's experience or the respondent's story, which is particularly significant in the study of lives over time and in context.

Listeners and Tellers, Readers and Texts: Reflexive Study in the Human Sciences

Taken together, these revisionist perspectives have led to a shift from a natural science to a human science approach to the study of social life. This human science perspective, founded on a tradition of study best portrayed by the 19th century social philosopher Dilthey (1976) points to the possibility of a human science mode of study, founded on systematic study of persons and lives and concerned with issues of meaning and coherence rather than the assumptions of logical empiricism focused on concern with significance or validity (Polkinghorne, 1983, this volume). However, while sharing with the older human science tradition a concern with narrative or story, human science inquiry emerging across the past decade has also focused on the problem of creation of meanings within both texts and lives, and with the particular contribution of listener or reader in the process of making sense of these accounts.

At first, study based on a human science model had been undertaken by criticism, symbolic anthropology, and psychoanalysis. An alternative to a natural science mode of inquiry in the human sciences has been provided by psychoanalysis and anthropology which, as Foucault (1970) has noted, jointly provides a new method of study within the human sciences. The new perspective preserves the richness of particular lives though detailed, empathically informed study of lives over extended periods of time within the psychoanalytic interview. Consistent with Mishler's (1986) critique, this mode of inquiry features the relationship between interviewer and informant as central to the goals of study.

Over the course of the past decade, in fields ranging from developmental psychology to literary study, there has been increased appreciation of the "jointness" or dialogic perspective which is inherent in the study of lives. Particularly as founded in the work of the Russian psychologist Lev Vygotsky (1934), the Russian literary theorist Bakhtin (1986) and the interpretation of their work by Todrov (1984), Wertsch (1985, 1991), Kozulin (1990), and Wilson and Weinstein (1992a, 1992b), the dialogic perspective has emphasized the extent to which any account is necessarily co-constructed by the participants. Implicit in Mishler's (1986) discussion of the interview, this concept of both social life and text as founded within a social context suggests that there can be no lifestory apart from the particular collaboration between narrator and listener, or reader and text, apart from the matrix of their shared telling and listening.

Within psychoanalysis, there has been increased emphasis upon the concept of intersubjectivity (Stolorow & Atwood, 1992), as initially founded in phenomonologists such as Scheler and Husserl, and elaborated by Schutz (1940/1970) (see also Kenyon, this volume). While this concept emphasizes the extent to which psychological processes are founded within a relationship, the concept of intersubjectivity focuses primarily upon personal psychological processes, and the particular experience of self and others as founded in the child's earliest experience of the mother. In contrast, the more inclusive concept of dialogic process stresses not only the social foundation of thought but also the extent to which continuing social life modifies all thought as a function of the life with others. Within anthropology, this tradition of study has been portrayed as "reflexive," taking into account the ethnographer's experience of the situation (Meyerhoff, 1982), while in psychoanalysis a similar approach has been characterized in terms of "counter-transference," which is actually a misnomer for a process in which the analyst's experience of the analysand's account through a process of "vicarious introspection" becomes the focus for the analyst's understanding of the situation and the interpretation which is subsequently posed (Kohut, 1959/1978).

The disciplines of social and cultural anthropology have been based primarily upon reports by lone ethnographers in the "field," generally far from home in a foreign culture marked by primitive living conditions and little contact with the larger world. The sense of isolation from a familiar world is often enhanced by problems in speaking languages lacking dictionaries or the possibility of advance instruction. This sense of isolation and disruption of the familiar has tended both to focus attention upon the ethnographer's contribution to the process of study, and to highlight the significance of interpreters who stand between self and informant, and upon the relationship of self, interpreter, and particular key informants who are believed to characterize particular aspects of the culture being studied.

Enactment and Understanding: A Dialogic Perspective

A decisive advance in this concern with reflexive inquiry in ethnography occurred with the publication of Branislaw Malinowski's (1967/1989) posthumous diary based on his work in the Trobriands. Malinowski uses his feelings as a guide in his ethnography and, while highly critical of the specifics of Freud's formulation, his use of the method of psychoanalysis bears out assumptions regarding the relevance of the thoughts and sentiments of the investigator to the subject matter being studied (Crapanzano, 1977). Malinowski's diary has critical significance for method of study, not only in anthropology, but also more generally within the social sciences and humanities. Other field work has been carried out in the same reflexive perspective, albeit more explicitly informed regarding the significance of the ethnographers's wishes and fears reciprocally evoked by those studied. Inronically, considering Malinowski's suspicions regarding psychonanalysis, his diary points the way towards a psychoanalytic ethnography and, more generally, a psychoanalytic approach regarding the study of lives over time (Briggs, 1970; Crapanzano, 1980; Riesman, 1977; Rosaldo, 1993).

Freud's signal contribution may be less in a particular theory of function and mechanism in the study of mental life than a method for understanding lives. Derived from the incest taboo present in all cultures (Parsons, 1952), Freud's (1900/1958, 1910a/1957, 1910b/1957) concept of a "nuclear neurosis," or fundamental wish to possess the parent of the opposite gender, remains a much-abused (by proponents and opponents alike) yet essential contribution. Freud maintained that the intensity of this wish leads to a continuing search for satisfaction which is opposed by social reality in the form of a demand for repression of this wish. However, partial satisfaction of the nuclear wish may be attained in a disguised form through a compromise formation which both provides partial satisfaction yet meets the demands of social reality. Included among these compromise formations are dreams, slips of the tongue and other unintended actions, psychoneurotic symptoms (hysteria and the obsessional neurosis), creative activity or sublimation, and efforts at enactment through experience of self and other which has been termed the transference neurosis.

Within the analytic situation, the fact that the analyst is not a person involved in the analysand's daily life provides a point of attachment for partial satisfaction, in disguised form, of the nuclear wish. The process of psychoanalytic treatment is designed to provide an interpretation of this nuclear wish experienced anew in the here-and-now of the psychoanalytic situation and, through recognition of the nuclear wish, to diminish the power of this wish in everyday life where repetition may lead to conflict, frustration, and disappointment in experience of oneself and with others (see also Mader, this volume). From this perspective, the significance of Malinowski's (1967) diary is the recognition of the power of field work to evoke the nuclear wish anew within the person of the ethnographer. Indeed, at least until the end of the First World War, the experience of "primitive" culture, with different norms regarding expression of sexual wishes, appeared particularly likely to elicit countertransference-like enactments. This is evident both in Malinowski's diary and in Mead's (1928/1975, 1930/1975) fascination with the peoples of Melanesia. Viewed through Western eyes, a very different expression of sexuality among these people suggested a lack of conflict regarding sexual expression and the absence of nuclear neurosis, which contrasted markedly with the burdens of Western civilization (Dwyer, 1977, 1979; Freud, 1930, 1961).

Kohut (1959/1978, 1971, 1977, 1984) has reformulated the continuing impact of childhood across the adult years in terms of an expectable lifelong effort to recreate the comfort and caring associated in a nonspecific manner with the years of infancy and early childhood. Kohut argues both for the experience of shame and disavowal, as well as guilt and repression, as an important sector of personality, and also for the study and interpretation of these "transference-like" enactments of idealization, mirroring, and experience of merger or twinship. These enactments are important responses, both to expectable life changes such as retirement and to unexpected adversity, such as personal illness or the illness or loss of beloved family members. Again, Malinowski's diary reflects these "transference-like" enactments in his longing for comfort from family and close friends during his ordeal in the field. The activity of calling upon or evoking memories of past care and comfort was able to sustain Malinowski through difficult times of trying to understand a culture different from his own.

The extension of the concept of transference from its original understanding as the transference of the psychic energy associated with the nuclear wish to include longing for childhood security and coherence suggests the need for some more general concept. Most recently, the concept of enactment has been proposed as a more inclusive concept in a number of clinical and theoretical reports by Jacobs (1986, 1991), McLaughlin (1991), Chused (1991), and a panel report of a meeting of the American Psychoanalytic Association (Johon, 1992). Based on Jacob's (1986) discussion, emphasizing the effort to satisfy unconscious (Oedipal) wishes outside of awareness, the 1989 panel emphasized both the dramatic quality of enactments and also the extent to which these dramatizations determine the response of the other to the situation.

The significance of the analyst's capacity for self-observation as the foundation of the "analyzing instrument," following Freud (1900/1958, 1912/1958) was initially portrayed by Isakower (Jaffe, 1986; New York Psychoanalytic Institute, 1963a, 1963b) in terms of the significance of the analyst's continuing attention to their own experience as a source of information regarding the psychoanalytic process. This capacity for self-observation, elaborated by Gardner (1983, 1993) and by Jacobs (1986, 1991) may be the most essential contribution of psychoanalysis as a method of study within human sciences. Continuing self-observation on the part of the analyst within the discourse of the psychoanalytic process (Bakhtin, 1986; McLaughlin, 1993; Smith, 1993) is the foundation of the capacity for empathy as the means of "tasting" (Fliess, 1944, 1953) the experience of the other through vicarious introspection (Kohut, 1959). It is also an essential element not only in gathering information for a life history, but also in the subsequent study of both ethnographies and personal documents or lifestories transcribed and rendered as texts (see also Ruth & Kenyon, this volume).

This "double dialogic" perspective, in which the reader's present understanding of the text is informed by vicarious introspection founded on the "tasting" of the text, is essential in understanding the foundations "reader-response" theory within criticism and the human sciences (Freund, 1987; Good, 1994; Iser, 1978; Mattingly, 1989; Phelan, 1989; Rabinowitz, 1994). The interplay of empathy as vicarious introspection founded on the analyst's own presently understood lifestory, enacted not only within the context of the psychoanalytic situation, but also in gathering and interpreting ethnographies and stories, is an important next step in the study of both lives and texts. Chused (1991) and McLaughlin (1991) have reformulated the concept of transference within the larger perspective of enactment, recognizing the extension of the concept of enactment as transference in the most extended sense of that term expressed in terms of the experience of relationships with others.

The experience of others out of awareness is characteristically expressed in action which has the additional significance of the impact of this action upon others. Underlying the formulation of this concept is recognition that we emplot all relationships with meanings based on the totality of experienced life circumstances, and enact these meanings in fantasy, word, and deed. These meanings include the variety of ways in which persons experience others, not only in the realm of competition but also as a source of sustenance, comfort, and solace (see also McAdams, this volume).

Countertransference and enactment. Just as each person enacts a variety of culturally prescribed intents in fantasy and actuality, within the therapeutic situation, the therapist reciprocally enacts intentions based on a particular lifestory. While the interpretation of such transference represents a part of the analyst's activity, the therapeutic activity of psychoanalysis involves far more than such a limited view of therapeutic activity. Enactments are an essential aspect of all relationships across the course of life in which the past is ever recreated within the present. The extent to which these enactments facilitate or hinder therapeutic activity is largely a function of the analyst's capacity for continuing self-inquiry which fosters increased awareness regarding these enactments, enhancing capacity for empathetic understanding or concordant identifications, rather than interfering in the process of experiencing the analysand's lifestory as told within the psychoanalytic interview.

Just as with the analysand's enactment in word and deed of experiences taking place across a lifetime, the analyst's response to the analysand's material reflects the analyst's own lived experience. Those aspects of the analyst's own experience not previously the subject of self-inquiry and understanding, presently out of awareness, may be reciprocally evoked by the collaboration between analyst and analysand. The analysand's bid for a mirroring or idealizing relationship may lead to the analyst's own feelings of lowered self-esteem and of being unworthy of such emulation. The analyst's own analysis and continuing attention to experienced response to the anlaysand provides a method for attaining enhanced awareness and understanding of enactments (Gardner, 1983, 1993; Smith, 1993). Personal therapeutic analysis is necessarily incomplete and enactments are inevitable, particularly as a consequence of work with the more troubled analysand. These persons are particularly capable of evoking intense counter-enactments and are frequently transferred to other therapists or modalities because of the anxiety which they evoke (Burke & Cohler, 1992).

Enactment, identification, and empathy. The analyst's enhanced awareness of the analysand's lived experience within the analytic collaboration may lead to a counterenactment, including the more narrowly defined countertransference responses which are reciprocal to the analysand's transference neurosis. However, enhanced awareness of the analyst's own lived experience may lead to enhanced empathic response. As Kohut (1959) has observed, empathy is a method of study which may be used in a variety of contexts, from interrogation to psychotherapy, and represents a method of study which is distinctive of the human sciences. The extent to which enactments reciprocally evoked within the person of the analyst as a response to hearing the analysand's lifestory lead to impasse, or interfere in the distinctive mode of listening which characterizes psychoanalysis and psychoanalytically informed inquiry, is related to the analyst's capacity for continuing self-inquiry. Enactments are an inevitable aspect of human relationships: fruitful questions regarding enactment involve bringing them to consciousness within the clinical process and in studying the lifestory.

The evocation of a variety of meanings of others for oneself is intrinsic to all relationships. Indeed, there is no "other," apart from one's own present experience of that other in terms of our own lived experience. The issue of self and other is one of particular sensitivity within the human sciences. Much recent discussion within anthropology and psychology (Clifford & Marcus, 1986; Rosaldo, 1993) has questioned the assumption of the "other" existing apart from our particular construction of the other. Dialogic perspectives pose the question whether there can ever be an other existing apart from oneself, and whether the construction of the other, as in fascination with "primitive" lives although instructive for our own culture, is but a representation of the other constructed by ethnologists living within particular cultures at particular points in time. One dramatic example of this perspective is Margaret Mead's (1930/1975) fascination with the relative lack of conflict among Samoan youth regarding issues of sexuality which represented an other constructed within a Puritan culture.

The use of one's own vicarious introspection (Gardner, 1983/1987, 1993; Kohut, 1959; Sonnenberg, 1991) or empathy provides a means for transforming meanings evoked by this "essential other" (Galatzer-Levy & Cohler, 1993) into enhanced understanding of oneself and maintenance of the capacity for bearing the lived experience of another (Poland, 1993). The danger lies here: in the complex ways that the anxiety evoked by sensing the experience of another may transform the other's evoked significance into enactments which are detrimental to enhanced understanding in the consulting room, field work, or constructed text. Clearly, continuing self-inquiry over time is essential in maintaining awareness of counterenactments and taking advantage of the experience of another as a means of fostering enhanced understanding.

As the fundamental method of clinical psychoanalysis, the capacity to "taste" or experience and interpret the variety of enactments within the clinical situation facilitates personality change through bringing previously unacceptable sentiments and intents into awareness and thereby making them available for potential change. Freud's (1900/1958, 1912/1958) original concept of "evenly hovering attention" implicitly assumed an experience-near collaborative process similar to that more thoroughly explored by Schafer (1959), Kohut (1959/1978, 1971), and Schwaber (1983), rather than the more experience-distant and scientistic role so often assumed as the ideal for psychoanalysis. Described by Kohut as vicarious introspection, this cryptic description was later extended by Schwaber (1983). Optimally, the analyst is attuned to the wishes, thoughts, and feelings of the analysand as a consequence of a process of listening to the analysand's narrative, experiencing the pain and joy of the analysand's life world, and fostering the analysand's enhanced self-awareness through integration, organization, and focus of this narrative, leading to an "interpretation" which further extends the analysand's range of self-observation and capacity for self-inquiry.

As a consequence of the detailed clinical and developmental study of the past decade, enhanced by the contributions of literary theory, we now recognize that this process of empathetic listening, attuned to the analysand's narrative, does not take place in a vacuum and that, clearly, the analyst's experience is of a jointly constructed actuality or dialogic actuality (Erikson, 1968/1976; Schafer, 1980, 1981). Winnicott (1953, 1960) has well portrayed the manner in which the child constructs an actuality based both on the reality of the person of the caregiver, and the child's construction of caregiver attunement. At the same time, the concept of intersubjectivity fostering experience of attunement of child with caregiver (Kohut, 1977), as portrayed in the developmental study of Trevarthan and others (Cohn & Tronick, 1987; Stolorow & Atwood, 1992; Trevarthan, 1980, 1989; Trevarthan & Hubley, 1978), may not sufficiently recognize the inherently social nature of this activity.

The impact of the work of Vygotsky (1934) and, most recently, Bakhtin (1986), has been to emphasize the inherently social nature of all thought which is dialogically or jointly constructed within shared discourse. The dialogic process leads to the rewriting or refashioning of such narratives as that of the analysand over the course of that collaborative work which leads to the creation of a new narrative as a consequence of the analysand's life story enacted anew within the context of the analytic process. Placing the activity of analyst and analysand within a dialogic context suggests first that any lifestory (re)constructed across the course of an analysis reflects a shared construction of two participants.

Analysand and analyst jointly contribute to the presumably new lifestory which is constructed across the course of the analysis and which permits the analysand an enhanced sense of personal congruity and vitality, as contrasted with the analysand's life at the beginning of the analysis (Schafer, 1980, 1981, 1992). In the second place, analyst and analysand, as any teller and listener, live within the constraints of the larger social order. The nature of the lifestory presently constructed within analysis differs in a significant manner from that which would have been told at the inception of psychoanalysis in America, or that at the conclusion of the Second World War.

Finally, the psychoanalytic lifestory, as any lifestory, is a performance in which telling is a mode of acting. Just as in the telling of lifestories more generally, gesture and speech, recognition of audience, and other aspects of performance are an intrinsic element of the lifestory which is both told and acted (Meyeroff, 1992; Meyeroff & Ruby, 1982). Teller and listener each bring a history of meanings of experience across a life-time; each has a varying capacity for self-inquiry, which is associated with variation in the capacity to listen to others without experiencing such dysphoric sentiments that listening becomes particularly painful. As a result of collaborative inquiry, by the completion of the analysis, the analysand has acquired many of these same attributes and becomes both a different and more reflexive listener and teller.

CONCLUSION

Inspired by the expectation that the social sciences conform to the model of experience-distant inquiry characteristic of the natural sciences at the turn of the century, ethnographic study was transformed from travelogue into scientific monologue. Accompanying this formation, the author's voice was replaced by the rational authority of the observer. Clifford (1986) has suggested that efforts by Radcliff-Brown and other structuralists to carry out field work in which the voice of the ethnographer was silent led to crisis within in the systematic study of culture. Reflecting larger social changes across the past two decades, cultural study has realized a shift of perspective. This perspective has been marked by the elimination of a concept of "self" and "other" in ethnographic and other cultural study. Rather, there is increasing recognition that the other is deliberately constructed in study ranging from the recent resurgence of interest in "multiple personality disorders" to ethnographic accounts of presumably "primitive" cultures. It is the ethnographer and the text which creates the other in the narrative which is told regarding these experiences.

Recent ethnographic, clinical, and biographical study has also been marked by the recognition that each of the participants, whether a life, culture, or text, becomes a participant in a jointly constructed story. There can be no ethnography or text apart from the continuing, changing, relationship between teller, informant, patient, or reader, and the narrative or text with which there is a relationship. The dialogic immediacy of this relationship is marked by increased focus on interpretive study of accounts; field work, clinical study, and joining with a text, whether a report of field work or a literary work, represents a real relationship between ethnographer and some others. This relationship is an intrinsic element of the narrative account, and must be studied in a systematic manner, in order that interaction becomes transcript in the form of fieldwork notes, and that these field notes represent narratives which may be studied using means more generally available within criticism.

Finally, it must be recognized that changing historical and social context dramatically alters the focus of interpretive inquiry over time. Whether the text be the report of field work or a transcript or other literary work, changing perspectives both in theory and in the larger society lead to quite different perspectives on listening or reading over time. The significance of both clinical interview or initial ethnographic study and the study of culture as text is undertaken within a particular milieu and cannot be understood apart from such context. The nature of interpretation changes over time; the significant interpretation is that which provides a presently coherent account, and one which presently provides the most complete and convincing reading of either culture or text. While it may be important, from one perspective in criticism, to know the author's intent in the telling or writing, from another perspective, this authorial intent may not be germane to the present interpretation of the work which is always read in a particular context (see also Ruth & Kenyon, this volume).

These perspectives have yet to be applied systematically to the study of the lifestories of older adults, as told and textualized, or as represented by such personal documents as diaries and letters (Berman, 1988, 1994; Blytheway, 1993; Cole & Premo, 1986-1987; Johnson, 1976; Peterson & Steward, 1990; Runyan, 1982, 1990; Stewart, Franz, & Layton, 1988). In ethnography, cultural studies, and literary criticism, the premier effort in this direction is Marc Kaminsky's (1992) pioneering critique and appreciation of Barbara Meyerhoff's ethnographic essays on aging. It is important that we explore this "blurred genre" of case history, life history, and biography, recognizing both the potential and difficulties posed by such a study (Cole, in preparation; Meyerhoff, 1992).

Scholars are increasingly exploring lifespan creativity through biographical accounts of writers, scientists, and politicians (de Vries & Lehman, this volume; Wyatt-Brown & Rosen, 1993). The intersection of literary gerontology and lifespan psychology has made it clear, in Steven Weiland's words, that "aging can no longer be considered an afterthought in biographies. Readers of biographies can discover in accounts of the subject's last years the same interest in developmental values typical of biographical attention to youth" (Weiland, 1989, p. 191). We learn surprising things about great figures; in Ronald Clark's biography of Albert Einstein, for example, we hear Einstein talking to a friend toward the end of his life, "You seem to think that I look back upon my life's work with serene satisfaction. Viewed more closely, however, things are not so bright. There is not an idea of which I can be certain. I am not even sure that I am on the right road" (cited in Weiland, 1989, p. 193).

To a large extent, aging represents a mirror in which we see reflected our own hopes and fears of a lifetime. Biographer and society alike see in aging the pain inherent in evaluating a lifetime's achievements. All of these issues which are posed for either ethnograph or biographer emerge with enhanced clarity in the study of older life. Nowhere is this more clearly evident than in Erikson's (1969) report on the central character of Bergman's movie *Wild Strawberries.* There can be little doubt that Erikson saw in Dr. Borg a parallel to his own life and the effort to review his own attainments in the light of advancing age. Just as with Borg, Erikson portrays a struggle between art and science, and between scholarship and this-worldly passion. Erikson enacts anew with the film as text his own parallel concerns and is then able to reflect on these concerns and to use them empathically as a means of understanding the complex world of Bergman's protagonist.

Within our culture, we search within aging for a sign of unusual wisdom and find that "old" and "wise" may not be equivalent. Our own anxiety regarding aging may be one reason that so few detailed studies have been undertaken of older lives. It is apparently particularly difficult to maintain an empathic stance in ethnographic or biographical study of later life. Even as sensitive an observer as Meyerhoff, although able to write with appreciation regarding the activist stance adopted by the community she studied when confronted with activity on the Venice boardwalk which interfered with their lives, still saw in her own wheelchair-bound existence towards the end of her life a real parallel with her older informants. Aging need not be understood in bifurcated terms, as either enhanced infirmity or enhanced wisdom; reflexive biographic and ethnographic study can be important in extending our understanding regarding issues of continuity and change within lives over time.

ACKNOWLEDGMENT

The authors wish to thank Byron Good, Cheryl Mattingly, and Marc Kaminsky for their work which has made this paper possible. Some of the ideas in this paper were first presented at the Biannual meetings, Society for Psychological Anthropology, Montreal, October, 1993.

5

Narrative Knowing and the Study of Lives

Donald E. Polkinghorne, Ph.D.

Narrative knowing is a fundamental mode of understanding by which people make sense of their own and others' actions and life events. When people know about an event or action narratively, they grasp it as contributing a part to the conclusion of a larger life episode. People can relate their narrative knowledge of an event by including, in a storied account of the larger episode, a description of the contribution the event made to that episode. One approach to the study of lives is to use people's narrative accounts as data. In studies using people's narrative accounts, narrative knowing underlies the subject's production of data. It does not, however, necessarily underlie the type of knowing researchers employ in analyzing the data. Most often researchers use a paradigmatic type of knowing to analyze the data. That is, researchers use a paradigmatic type of knowing to analyze descriptions of what subjects have known narratively.

Narratives that people relate about their own, rather than others', life episodes or lives is of particular interest for the study of lives. Subjects' narrative accounts of their life episodes provide an especially rich and "thick" source of data for the study of lives (Ruth & Kenyon, this volume). They are particularly useful for the study of meanings that people have attributed to the happenings and actions that make up their lives (Kenyon, this volume). Through narrative knowing people come to understand the significance of past choices and events in relation to "how things turned out" (Ruth & Öberg, this volume). One way people have of arranging their experiences into meaningful units is to gather together single events into larger episodes. Individual actions and happenings, such as making out a grocery list, getting in the car, and driving to the store, are identified as parts of the episode of going shopping. A person's entire life can be viewed as the collective whole of the various episodes in which they have engaged. When people understand their lives narratively, they see the events of their lives as playing contributing and consequential roles in bringing about a conclusion or denouement of a life episode, and the total of their life episodes as the parts that make up their whole lives.

People produce narratives as an ordinary way of making sense of how certain events interacted to produce a particular outcome. This narrative way of knowing by composing actions and events into a story is one of the cognitive operations people use to give coherence and order to their experiences. Narrative composing operates by employing a plot or storyline to configure events and actions into an episodic whole (Randall, this volume). In this way the meaning of these elements is derived from the recognition of their part in a systemic whole, a life episode. Although the word *narrative* has other acceptable meanings, in this chapter I will be using *narrative* exclusively to refer to a storied linguistic production of a person's emplotted configuration of life events into episodes or a whole life.

The use of people's narratives as the data for the study of lives is a relatively recent development in the social sciences. The effective analysis of data in narrative form most often requires the use of qualitative procedures to explicate the themes and motifs of the stories. Historically, the human disciplines adopted their methods and research procedures from those developed by the physical sciences for studying the physical world. The human disciplines assumed that this approach was the only one that could produce valid and applicable knowledge. The traditional approach emphasized the use of data that could be publicly observed and measured, as well as analytic procedures based on statistical operations. Nonquantified data and qualitative analysis were avoided. The appreciation of the possibilities of studying lives through qualitative examination of narratives has had to wait until developments in the philosophy of science and the emergence of cognitive science. Recent studies (for example, Josselson & Lieblich, 1993; Thomas, 1989), using data in narrative form and analyzing them with qualitative procedures, have increased our understanding of the sense and meaning people give to their actions and life events (see also Ruth & Kenyon, this volume).

The purpose of this chapter is to examine the attributes of narrative data and how they are used in the study of lives. I believe that by clarifying the characteristics of narrative knowing and its expression in stories people tell about their lives, researchers will be aided in gathering and analyzing narratively generated data. The first section of this chapter inquires into the nature of narratives and the cognitive processes that produce them. The second section explores the study of lives using narrative data and compares this approach to those using other types of data.

CHARACTERISTICS OF NARRATIVE DATA

Narrative data are expressions of subjects' constructions of understanding that are the result of narrative cognitive operations. The study of narrative knowing, and cognitive operations in general, is taking place in a different philosophical context than that which informed earlier studies in the human disciplines. Thus, to situate the exploration of the characteristics of narrative knowing, this section begins with a review of this changed philosophical context. Next, I introduce the general characteristics of narrative knowing by contrasting it to operation-paradigmatic knowing. This is followed by a more detailed explication of narrative knowing as a reflective composition that draws from a prereflective form of *prenarrative* comprehension. The section concludes with a consideration of the various communication forms through which narrative understanding is expressed.

The Context for Understanding Narrative Data

The growing recognition of the importance of studying narrative knowing for the social sciences is taking place within the context of a more general change in the beliefs that have determined what methods and procedures are deemed appropriate for the study of the human realm (Toulmin, 1972). This more general change has been described as a movement from a positivist understanding of knowledge generation to a postpositivist understanding (Kvale, 1992). The movement is represented by a complex of positions that together challenge some of the traditional assumptions of social science. Within this complex, two contentions are particularly significant for understanding the place of the study of narrative knowing in a postpositivist social science. One of these is that, by its nature, the social realm includes the subjective experiences of people; a second is that experience is a production of an active mind in interaction with the world.

The first contention called for expanding the notion of what were considered legitimate realms for scientific study. The received view of the social sciences was that cognitive processes were not publicly observable and, thus, not available to scientific study. This position followed from the adoption by the human disciplines of views developed by the physical sciences in their traditional study of the material realm. The growth of the physical sciences preceded that of the social sciences and set a trajectory of how all scientific knowledge was to be developed (Giorgi, 1986).

The research procedures of the physical sciences were designed to produce a "true picture" of the material realm. Because this realm is presented to humans somewhat inaccurately through sensory perception, research methods were constructed that would produce knowledge statements that described the world as it "actually" existed, independent of its altered appearance in human experience. The focus of scientific investigation was on what was to be known (that is, the objects and the relations among them), not on the knower. The strategy was to remove any effects of the knower on the known in order to cleanse knowledge of any influence of the subject. An implication some drew from this approach to knowledge was that reality itself consisted only of what could be known through the procedures refined by the physical sciences. This physicalist assumption left no place in what was considered a reality for the experiences of human subjects. The postpositivist contention rejected this assumption that reality consists only of physical things. They held that reality is made up of both human experiences and material elements.

Several inferences for social science issue from the notion that reality is composed of the thoughts and feelings of people as well as material things. First, experience should not be dismissed as an unreal epiphenomenon shadowing an ultimately physical reality. Rather, experience is an authentic realm in its own right and needs to be included as an area of study by disciplines that aim to understand human conduct and practice (see also Kenyon, this volume). Second, experience is an emerged reality with its own essential properties that are not necessarily isometric with the material realm. Thus, the understanding of experience requires models and terms derived from the study of experience itself. Third, access to the experiential realm differs from access to the material realm. The material realm presents itself in a somewhat public manner in that several people can acknowledge the appearance of the same physical object. The physical sciences have used this characteristic of the material realm to define its notion of objectivity; that is, knowledge is held to be objective if several people report the appearance of the same object. The experiential realm does not present itself in a publically direct manner. It is directly knowable only to the individual who is the experiencer.

The experiential data a researcher collects are several times removed from the actual flow of experience. Because we have direct awareness of only one experiential flow, our own, collecting information about the experiential realm presents several problems. On the one hand, the act of reflecting, by researchers on their own experiences or by subjects on theirs, effects a change in awareness.

The initial nonreflective, direct engagement with the flow of experience (the object of study) is itself transformed by the reflective stance involved in attending to one's experience. On the other hand, to report to another what one has experienced requires that the experience be described in a language. The verbal or written report is not a duplication of what was experienced; it is a translation of the complex flow of experience into a culturally conventional system of signs. The language system structures and orders the experience into its own network of available concepts.

The second contention follows from the attention postpositivist investigators brought to bear on the experiential realm. They found that experience is not simply a mirrored reflection of the world passively received by us in the form of imaged representations. Instead, experience displays a world in which structures and consistencies are recognized. We are not presented with a simple flow of diverse sense impressions, but with a world of relationships in which objects and events are understood as connected in various ways. Experience appears as already meaningful with perceptual images identified as instances of categories and concepts (Lakoff, 1987). Experiences are the products of an active body and mind in interaction with the world. We dynamically contribute to our experience of the physical environment, of others, and of ourselves. We are constructive agents who use our organizing and systematizing schemes to meaningfully understand the elements of our worldly interactions as parts of an interconnected whole. Also, experiential productions are not simply compositions of elements drawn from the present interaction with the world, but integrated displays that include recollections and imagined and anticipated worlds (Nagel, 1986).

This postpositivist notion that we human beings are active participants in the production of our own experience is a significant change from the idea that our minds are passive recipients and like "blank tablets" on which sensation writes. The view of the mind as passive was advocated by the British empiricists and served as a basic position of Western philosopy of science through the time of the logical positivists. The understanding of the mind as a noncontributing recipient of sense data was the ground for the notion that objective knowledge could be founded on the transparent reflections of the world that appeared in experience. In the late eighteenth century, Kant (1781/1965) heralded a new view of the mind as an active and organizing agent of experience. The notion that experience is the consequence of the constructive activity of the mind continued to gain adherents through the efforts of Husserl (1931) and other phenomenologists (for example, Schultz, 1973), and later through the research of Piaget (1952) on cognitive development. Still more recently this issue has been investigated through the re-emergence of the study of mental operations and perception by cognitive scientists (Bolles, 1991). Today, the view of the mind as active contributor to experience holds ascendancy among cognitive psychologists, educators, and philosophers of science. The postpositivist contention enlarged the notion of the real and made the previously neglected realm of personal experience a necessary area of inquiry.

These two contentions provide the conditions for understanding the characteristics of narrative knowing. In relation to the first contention, narrative knowing is an experiential reality and thus, awareness of its presence requires a different sensitivity than the awareness of physical objects. In relation to the second, narrative knowing is one of the mental activities that structures and orders elements of experience so that they appear in awareness as meaningful and related. In particular, narrative structuring presents awareness with life events and happenings coherently connected together into a storied gestalt. The purpose of narrative knowing is not to produce a representation of reality as it exists independent of the knower; rather, it is a display of a type of meaning that life events have for the experiencer.

NARRATIVE AND PARADIGMATIC KNOWING

Narrative knowing is a cognitive structuring process that provides an understanding of life events and actions by displaying their contribution to the conclusion of a life episode. There are other ways of knowing in addition to narrative knowing; that is, there are other types of cognitive structures and processes by which people organize and make meaningful their interactions with the world, others, and themselves. Bruner (1986), in his *Actual Minds, Possible Worlds*, has identified two major kinds of cognitive structuring activities, namely, paradigmatic and narrative.

> There are two modes of cognitive functioning [paradigmatic and narrative], two modes of thought, each providing distinctive ways of ordering experience, of constructing reality. The two (though complementary) are irreducible to one another . . . Each of the ways of knowing, moreover, has operating principles of its own and its own criteria of well-formedness. They differ radically in their procedures for verification. (p. 11)

Paradigmatic structuring is a mode of comprehension that produces knowledge about the kind of thing something is. In this mode, knowledge of something involves recognition of the category or concept it is an instance of. In the narrative mode of knowing, knowledge of something involves recognition of the part it plays in the interaction with other events in the conclusion of a human episode. Both paradigmatic and narrative cognition generate useful and valid knowledge. They are part of a human cognitive repertoire for reasoning about and making sense of the encounter with self, others, and the material realm (see Gardner, 1983).

Paradigmatic Comprehension

The primary operation of paradigmatic cognition is classifying a particular instance as belonging to a category or concept. The concept is defined by a set of common attributes that are shared by its members. General concepts can include subordinate concepts or categories (Strauss & Corbin, 1990). For example, the concept *furniture* contains the subordinate categories chair, table and desk. Paradigmatic cognition attends to the features of attributes that essentially define particular experienced items as instances of a category. This kind of thinking focuses on what makes the item a member of a category. It does not focus on what makes it different from other members of its category. Thus, the actual size, shade of red, or marks on the skin that make a particular apple unique are not of primary concern.

The classificatory function of cognition locates or establishes the category to which an item is a member. For example, in a grocery store a child points to a particular round, red object with a stem and asks, "What is that?" The parent responds, "That is an apple." Paradigmatic thought links the particular to the formal concept. In the realm of the particular, actual items are experienced in a different manner than is their conceptually assigned identification. The concept *apple* is not the same as an actual, material piece of fruit. The power of paradigmatic thought is to bring order to experience by seeing individual things as belonging to a category. By understanding that this particular item is an apple, I can anticipate and act on the knowledge I have of apples in general (Smith, 1989).

Paradigmatic reasoning is one of the primary methods by which we humans constitute our experience as ordered and consistent. It draws on cognitive networks of concepts that allow us to construct experiences as familiar, by noticing, that items have common elements, and to conceive of them as the same as or similar to each other. The conceptual networks are maintained and transported through local languages and are personalized through the history of an individual's experiences. The networks, however, are abstractions of or collections from the flow and flux of experience. By focusing on the qualities items share with other members of the same category, categories draw attention away from the differences in items of the same category.

The differences in shading that categorical items present in diverse contextual and temporal settings and the qualities that each individual item does not share with other members of its category are overlooked. Nevertheless, paradigmatic classification allows us to manage the uniqueness and diversity of each experience as if it were generally the same as or similar to previous experiences. The usefulness of paradigmatic comprehension is derived from its capacity to abstract items from the complex of appearances and to recognize their sameness or similarity to previous elements. We are able to learn a repertoire of responses to be applied in each conceptually identified situation.

The second kind of cognitive structuring, narrative, is not a replacement for paradigmatic knowing; rather, it gives an additional way of knowing that draws attention to the relationships among the elements of experience. In particular, it points to the temporal connections among our experienced events.

Narrative Comprehension

Mandler (1984) conceived of four types of cognitive structuring activity, for which she posits four operations; the categorical or taxonomic, the matrix, the serial, and the schematic. The first two of these can be understood as paradigmatic operations. In the categorical or taxonomic operations, facts are related according to a shared similarity of form, function, or other aspects; for example, taxonomic knowledge about an individual animal is created by locating it in a particular category, such as feline, through the size and shape it shares with other known members of this category. In the matrix operation, knowledge is organized through its identification as a member of multiple categories. Items are identified through the recognition of their membership in several linked categories instead of simply their membership in a single category.

The third and fourth of Mandler's types, the serial and the schematic, help locate and differentiate narrative knowing from the other types of comprehension. In serial knowledge structuring, the items are understood as meaningful in terms of their connection to one another along a unidirectional dimension. For example, the letters of the alphabet and chronologically ordered historical events are forms of serially organized knowledge. In her fourth type of cognitive operation, schematic structuring, elements are recognized as meaningful in terms of their participation in or contribution to a system whole or gestalt form. For example, three dots that do not sit on a straight line can be recognized as the angle points of a triangular figure. They can also be paradigmatically recognized as individual instances of the category *dot*. Whereas in categorical knowledge each entity is an instance of the class through which it is known (a particular round object is an example of the class *ball*), in a schematic organization the entity is known through its participation in the collection (the individual is known as a team member because knowing about the individual involves knowing the part he or she plays in the performance of the team; the individual him- or herself is not an example of the concept *team).*

Schematically organized knowledge can be related spatially, as when one collects and comes to know the aspects as parts of a spatial whole (a triangle, for instance), or temporally, as when one links together various events to make a story or a narrative. Historically, interest in schematic organizing principles has been focused on operations that display experiences of visual elements configured as gestalts. Narrative knowing is a type of schematic knowing that structures events and happenings as parts of a temporal gestalt or story. Unlike serial structures in which events are simply displayed as following one after the other without causal links, narrative knowing structures events by understanding them as mutually affecting aspects of a temporally extended episode which is marked off as having a beginning, a middle and an end.

Narrative cognition operates by configuring diverse elements of a particular episode into a unified whole in which each element is comprehended as a sequentially situated contributor to the episode's outcome (Feldman, Bruner, Renderer, & Spitzer, 1990). Changing, adding, or subtracting an element, or changing the sequence in which the elements occurred, produces a reorganization of the temporal whole with the likely effect of changing the outcome. In narration, events and actions are drawn together into an organized whole by means of a plot (Ricoeur, 1984). A plot is a type of conceptual scheme by which the contexual meaning of individual events can be displayed.

A simple story can illustrate the operation of emplotment; for example, "The king died, the prince cried." In isolation the two events are simply propositions describing two independent happenings, but when composed into a story, a new level of relational significance appears. Within a storied production, the meaning of the prince's crying is understood as a response to his father's death and the meaning of the father's death is linked to its effect on the prince. The plot provides the context in which the two events are meaningfully linked so that their comprehension includes their contribution to the whole episode. It is this relational meaning that is displayed when events are configured together through the operation of a plot.

The human propensity to emplot events as meaningfully linked parts of an episode was exemplified in experiments carried out by Michotte (1963). In conducting research on causality, Michotte asked subjects to describe the motion of colored rectangles that were projected on a screen. The subjects' descriptions unexpectedly took the form of emplotted stories. For example, "rectangle A's approach frightened rectangle B, and B ran away." Although narrative configuration appears to be primordially associated with the understanding of actions and life events of human beings (Bruner, 1986; Johnson, 1987; Mitchell, 1981; Ricoeur, 1984), the inclination to understand events as narratively related can be extended to animal behavior and inanimate movement (for example, to Michotte's moving rectangles). When applied to animal behavior, for example in fairy tales, narrative structuring tends to display the responses of animals as thoughtfully purposive, producing a seemingly anthropomorphized account of their conduct. Narrative structuring can also be applied to inanimate movement, for example, in the sequence of statements: "the tree was old and rotten; there came up a strong wind; then the tree fell." When used in this way the essential narrative notion of an acting protagonist is replaced by a passive object whose movement is caused by naturally occurring phenomena.

The capacity to produce and understand stories that incorporate personal emotions and purposes and interpret happenings and events appears to be mastered at an early age by children (Kemper, 1984; McAdams, this volume). Storied accounts are also found in nearly all cultures. Whether narrative competence is an innate human characteristic on the order of Chomsky's (1975) notion of deep structures or a socially learned skill, most humans have a predisposition to understand their own and others' actions through narrative configuration (Mancuso, 1986). For a discussion of the ontology of storytelling, see Kenyon (this volume) and Ruth & Kenyon (this volume).

People employ narrative knowing as a method for uncovering and identifying the meaning their life actions and events have in relation to the accomplishment or lack of accomplishment of their intended outcomes. Unlike paradigmatic knowing, which identifies events as instances of a category, narrative knowing displays meaning by showing the connections that hold among life happenings. Narrative knowing allows for the integration of a person's previous experiences, presently situated presses (Svensson, this volume), and proposed goals and purposes in a unifying story. It is a type of comprehension that attends to an actor's motivations and desires, as well as his or her publicly observable behaviors. Research that employs people's narratives as its data has access to the meanings and interpretations that have informed subjects' decisions and actions.

Prenarrative and Narrative Knowing

The narrative operation that produces a coherently emplotted story is a cognitive activity that involves reflective thought. Mandler (1984) writes that a fully developed narrative accounting begins with a setting in which a narrator introduces the characters, the location, and the time in which the story takes place. After the setting has been established, the story proceeds with one or more episodes, each of which has a beginning and a development. In the episode, the character, reacting to the beginning events, sets a direction and outlines a path to achieve an outcome. Each episode includes the outcome of the attempts to reach the goal and assumes that the attempts are understood as the causes that bring about the outcome. When the outcome has been given, the episode ends, and the ending links the episode to the whole story. After the whole series of episodes has been presented, the narrative includes ending portions that show that the episodes coalesce into one story .

Such fully developed narrative coherence seems not to present itself in our ordinary, unreflective, everyday lived-through experience. However, although we do not experience events at the time of their occurence as fully integrated parts of a plot, neither are they experienced as mere disconnected fragments following one after another. Lived-through experience is primordially structured and temporally ordered; events and actions already appear as contoured and linked sequences in which what has happened earlier can affect the present (Peterson & McCabe, 1991). Lived-through experience also draws on an inherent understanding that human actions differ from physical movements. Human actions appear in lived-through experience as purposeful consequences of human actors. Our unreflective, everyday experience of human conduct does not appear as disconnected and meaningless, but as already having the characteristics of temporal occurrences and directed actions. These characteristics give our primordial experience a *prenarrative quality*, that is, a prefiguredness that "constitutes a demand for narrative" (Ricoeur, 1989, p. 74).

This understanding that everyday lived-through experience has a prenarrative quality is a middle position regarding the narrative character of unreflective experience (Fell, 1992). On one side are those who hold that primordial experience manifests in a near narrative structure, for example, David Carr (Carr, Taylor, & Ricoeur, 1991) (see also Ruth & Kenyon, this volume). On the other side are those who maintain that experience presents itself originally as disconnected and fragmentary and that narrative ordering is an imposition on this primordial chaos (White, 1973). For those who hold the middle position (Kerby, 1991; Ricoeur, 1989), the knowledge presented by our prenarrative understanding of human conduct, on reflection, appears as unfinished. It calls for a reflective review that can consider the unintentional (as well as the intentional) effects of our actions, effects which at the time of the act we could not be aware of. The reflective review integrates the prenarrative understandings we had at the time of the happenings and actions with understandings that we have after the outcome of the episode to produce a fully articulated narrative.

Narrative knowing, then, is a reflective explication of the prenarrative quality of our unreflective experience; it is a drawing out of the story that experience embodies. The presence of unarticulated prenarrative experiences serve as a corrective or guide to the reflectively produced story. Not just any telling can authentically integrate a prenarrative into a legitimate account. The "felt meanings" of our prenarrative experiences serve to produce phrases and plots which more closely conform to our "pre-thematic" understanding (Gendlin, 1992). Narrative constructions must be continually adjusted until we are satisfied that they are adequate symbolic transformations of our lived-experience.

The retrospective nature of narrative knowing and human understanding has been described by hermeneutic philosophers. For example, Gadamer (1981) says, "All beginnings lie in darkness, and what is more, they can be illuminated only in the light of what came later and from the perspective of what followed (p. 40)". And Merleau-Ponty (1962), who presaged the hermeneutic observations, said, "[I understand my past] by following it up with a future which will be seen after the event as forshadowed by it, thus introducing historicity into my life " (p. 346).

As a retrospective process of attributing meaning to one's life events and actions, narrative is more than a simple recounting of one's life activities as they were experienced; they are newly created configurations. Several elements of narratives require them to be different from accurate reproductions of life as it was lived: (a) memory as reconstruction of past events, (b) the smoothing processes of gestalt-type configuration, and (c) the use of culturally available plots.

Memory as Reconstruction

In personal stories, narrative structuring draws experiential traces from memory. Memory is not a container of taped replays of life events. Recollection is a partial reconstruction of the past that attends to and connects memory traces according to the press of present needs and interpretations (Casey, 1987). Narrative structuring operates dialectically with memory to re-create past occurences in light of the emplotting task to produce coherence and closure. Thus, the recollected images that make up the retrospective story are not simple replications of the actual events as they originally occurred.

Narrative Smoothing

Life as lived is more diverse and disjointed than the stories we tell about it. Our daily lives consist in eating and sleeping, going to and from work, and running errands. Narratives are not simply a running description of videotape that includes descriptions of every moment of the time covered by a storied episode. Narrative structuring highlights and marks off from the flow of one's mundane daily tasks the happenings, thoughts, and actions that are needed to comprehend the way in which the storied episode unfolded. In life we are engaged in many projects at once, not all of which interlock into a significant episode. An event may be extraneous and irrelevant to one episode, but important for understanding another. A narrative production, in contrast to life as lived, usually concerns a single major plot, incorporating only the subplots and events that contribute to that plot and selecting out all irrelevant happenings (Carr, 1986).

In configuring a story of a life episode, narratives often omit details and condense parts ("flattening"), elaborate and exaggerate other parts ("sharpening"), and make parts more compact and consistent ("rationalization") to produce a coherent and understandable explanation (Cortazzi, 1993). Narrative, like the visual gestalt process, draws out from a background those elements which compose the patterned figure or plot that is the focus of attention. In addition, it operates according to a principle of closure in which incomplete figures are perceived as whole (Glass, Holyoak, & Santa, 1979) by the process of "smoothing" (see also Randall, this volume).

Culturally Available Plots

Meaning-giving interpretive plots are adapted from the repertoire of stories made available in one's culture. While a chosen plot needs to resonate with the prenarrative experiences on which it is based, it also functions dialectically to select for the told story those events and actions that were significant contributors to the story's resolution (Polkinghorne, 1991).

Narrative knowledge is not a simple recall of the past. Narrative comprehension is a retrospective, interpretive composition that displays past events in the light of current understanding and evaluation of their significance. While referring to the original past life events, narrative transforms them by ordering them into a coherent part-whole plot structure. Narrated descriptions of life episodes are not mirrored reflections of what occurred. Narrative structuring is an interpretation of life in which past events and happenings are understood as meaningful from a current perspective of their emplotted contribution to an outcome.

The creative and constructive character of narrative knowing allows for different stories about the same past events. The interpretive point of view that informed the first narrative retrospection can change over time and in different settings. The evaluation of the outcome and the significance of an element's contribution to the completion of an episode may lead to differences from one narrative articulation to another concerning the same happenings and actions. Thus, what is known narratively about a life episode from the perspective of the accumulated experience of old age may differ from the narrative knowing of the episode developed in midlife. For example, this is a common outcome of the process of guided autobiography (Birren & Birren, this volume).

EXPRESSIONS OF NARRATIVE KNOWLEDGE

The literature about narrative knowing recognizes a distinction between the content that is referred to in a narrative and the means by which the content is communicated. Chatman (1978) uses the term *story* to refer to the content or chain of events and the term *discourse* for the means of expression in which the story is communicated. The mode of discourse through which a story is expressed is not, however, neutral and transparent. The conceptual network of the symbolic system in which the story comes to expression dialectically contributes to the final articulated understanding given by the narrative. Also, the retrospective and reflective operation of narrative comprehension adapts already expressed plots to compose and configure an episode's happenings, events, thoughts, and actions.

The presentation of a completed narrative understanding of the meaning of a group of happenings requires expression. Most often the medium of expression is a natural language, although it could be dance, a series of gestures, or a mixed medium, such as drama or motion pictures. (These nonlanguage presentations of narrative knowledge, however, are usually derivatives from the original construction in natural language.) Narrative cognition processing may operate out of awareness, but whether a consciously or nonconsciously directed process, it moves dialectically to and fro from parts to possible wholes until a whole is generated that fits and gives sense to the parts. Prior to the resolution of the narrative process, potential integrating story lines are continually adjusted until they produce a gestalt which brings the parts into focus and displays them as meaningfully integrated. The result of narrative cognitive processing is a story that can be thought through signifiers of one's language. Fully formed narrative knowing is achieved when it reaches the threshold of articulation. The story may appear at first in a private self-telling and may be retained as a private understanding. At times a narrative understanding of an episode is only short-lived, and is dismissed or forgotten as not significant or as mistaken. The narrative may be shared by telling the storied interpretation to others or by making it public with the publication of the written account. If the story is committed to writing, as in an autobiography, it loses the fluidity of oral presentations and its capacity for ongoing revisions.

The storied content of narrative discourse I have been describing thus far is about episodes in one's own life. These are often the expressions of interest to the researchers studying lives. I believe that understanding the episodes of one's own life and those of others with whom one interacts is the primary and most basic use we make of narrative knowing. The same cognitive operations we use to understand our own past actions, however, can be applied to develop understanding of other situations. Closest to its function as a retrospectively con-structured understanding of self and others' actions is its use to construct imagined hypothetical stories as a means to plan one's future actions or to anticipate possible future actions of others. One can play out various stories drawn analogically on one's prior collection of storied understandings of the connections among actions and outcomes to assist in planning future action episodes (McGuire, 1990). The collection of stories is searched to find one whose outcome is similar to the one that a person wants to achieve or avoid.

Imagined hypothetical stories can also be constructed as fictional episodes of imagined characters in imagined settings. Fictional stories draw on our narrative understanding of the interactive and consequential effects of happenings in human lives. Hearing, reading, or watching a storied presentation about a person's movement through a life episode touches us in a way such as to evoke our emotions of sympathy, anger, or sadness. Fictional presentations not only engage and entertain, but they also increase our awareness of possible configurations to explain and understand our own and others' life episodes.

Narrative cognition can also be employed to understand historical episodes by retrospectively emplotting their events and actions into a story that gives a believable explanation consistent with our knowledge of human motivation and responsiveness to types of happenings. Narrative has been used to construct a story in which the protagonist is a group of people or an organization. Narrative is often used to construct a story that provides an account of how an outcome came about; for example, investigators have interviewed participants and examined documents with a purpose of constructing the "true" story of how the Iran-Contra affair happened. The purpose of many legal proceedings is to uncover the story that fully accounts for the diverse happenings and actions of the episode in question. Fictional and actual life-based presentations that want to depict life as fragmented and disordered can play against the expected coherence and unifying function of emplotment by telling tales which do not include a meaning giving plot, or in which the elements are so disjointed that the offered plot lacks the puissance to configure them into a consequential whole. The poignancy of these presentations derives from the contrast between their storylike appearance and the lack of conclusion and unifying emplotment.

Thus far I have explored the operation of narrative knowing and the type of knowledge it creates. In summary, narrative knowing produces a type of schematic knowledge about the relationship of parts to a whole and the whole to its parts. The kinds of wholes that are the object of narrative knowledge are the temporal episodes that make up people's lives. Narratives provide a systematic knowledge of the relationships among life events, happenings, motivations, purposes and actions. What one has when something is narratively comprehended is an interpreted understanding of the relationship of an episode's elements to one another and of their contribution to the outcome of the episode. I have proposed that narrative is a reflective composition that explicates the prenarrative component of primordial experience by bringing to it the ordering properties of the language and story grammars. I have also proposed that the base function of narrative cognition is to understand our own and others' life episodes. The narrative operations that serve to order and interpret personal experiences, can, however, be used for other purposes, such as producing fictional stories and formally investigating socially meaningful events. The next section will explore the use of people's narrative productions as data for the study of lives.

THE STUDY OF LIVES

Researchers studying lives can use various forms of data. Researchers are not limited, as in studies of the physical world, to data derived from observations. Unlike objects, humans can express themselves, and through their expressions humans provide information about how they are experiencing themselves and the world. Data in the form of human expressions give researchers studying lives a unique form of data not available in the study of nonhuman realms (Dilthey, 1988). Researchers can gather expressions of a subject's self-understanding through four basic categories of data; short answer, numerical, essay, and narrative. A data-gathering questionnaire illustrates these categories. Respondents can be asked to provide data about their subjective understandings in a short-answer format, for example, identifying the word that most closely describes their feelings about a job; in a numerical format, choosing a number on a Likert scale indicating the level of their interest in a topic; in an essay format, writing a paragraph on why they are interested in a position; and in a narrative format, a story of a life episode that resulted in their decision to pursue a career. When researchers want to study how people understand and make sense of their lives, it is most appropriate to use data in the narrative format.

Narrative data, like other types of self-report data, is a production of research subjects. But narrative data, unlike the other types of data, retain subjects' accounts of the temporal connections they have attributed to aspects of their lives. Narrative data contain the kind of information about lives that most fully manifests the uniquely human characteristics of temporal wholeness and purposeful action (Josselson, 1993). As described in the previous section, narrative data consist of stories people tell about their life episodes, or in some cases about ther lives as a whole. These stories relate how people understand the significance of things that have happened to them and of the things they have done. Thus, data consisting of people's narratives provide researchers with the richest and thickest source for explicating their subjects' understanding of their own lives.

The unique capacity of narrative data to exhibit the temporal dimension of human experiences makes it especially powerful and useful for understanding human lives. Heidegger (1962) has proposed that the primary dimension of human existence is time. Researchers engaged in the study of lives need to attend to the significance of the temporal dimension of human beings (Kenyon, this volume). They should make use of data that retain consideration of when something happens to or is undertaken by a person. An incomplete study of a life's temporal dimension can be based on data in the short-answer format, in which a subject answers the question "what happened next." These data can yield only a chronological ordering of the series of events that make up a life. But these short-answer data do not render an understanding of the meaning that these events have for the subject.

A more complete approach to the study of lives by attending to the temporal dimension of human existence requires narrative data. Narrative data allow the researcher to move beyond the mere listing of the chronological order of a person's life events. Studies based in narrative data can produce results that incorporate subjects' retrospective interpretations of events from the perspective of the time at which the data are gathered. The operations of narrative comprehension by which narrative data are produced show how subjects view events in their temporal relations to other events and to the episodic outcomes to which they were contributed. Narrative presents life events in their configured connectedness and relationship to an emplotted episodic whole.

Gathering Narrative Data

Narrative knowing is, first of all, a normal cognitive operation that produces an everyday retrospective understanding of the coherence and consequential relationships that make up human experience. People regularly seek to know the meanings of their life events through acts of narrative comprehension. In people's normal and ordinary narrative reflections, the topic of understanding is usually a particular life episode of limited duration and focused on a particular theme; for example, the travail of getting the children to bed the night before, as told in a story to friends. In these ordinary narrative enterprises, the person marks off from the flow of life beginning and end points between which the topic of the story took place.

Studies using narrative data can gather "naturally" produced stories by recording normal conversations. For example, Cortazzi (1993), in his study of primary teachers' ways of understanding their work, used "naturally" occurring stories from teachers' gatherings in staff meetings, conferences, and seminars. However, most studies generate and record stories through interviews. The occasion of producing a story for a researcher is a special and unusual occurrence of narrative reflection in people's lives. Subjects are asked to create a story, using what is a normally informal cognitive operation to generate data for a research study of lives.

Formal studies of lives usually take place within the framework of academically institutionalized traditions of knowledge development. These traditions call for researchers' public accountability of their procedures and for peer review and judgement of the acceptability of the results for entry into a discipline's body of knowledge. Academic investigations abstract formal procedures and methods from these everyday knowledge operations. These abstractions are meant to improve on the everyday cognitive operations by protecting researchers from error and bias.

The Co-Constitution of Narrative Data

The tradition calls for researchers to maintain a disengaged and formal relation with subjects, so as not to influence or affect in any way the data produced by subjects. Except when using "naturally" generated stories, researchers engage with subjects in assisting them in their construction of a reflective story about an episode in their lives. The resulting story, that is, the narrative data, is the product of the interactive conversation between the subject and researcher (Mishler, 1986; Ruth & Kenyon, this volume). The researcher's choice of questions and probes, as well as the changes in level of attentiveness, help shape the story told by the subject. The audience (in this case the researcher) and its responsiveness influence the telling of the story. The story that is told is a co-constituted production that occurs between the subject and researcher. With another researcher or with the same researcher at another time, the emphasis and shaping of the story may change.

Because the story is co-constituted, the relationship between the teller and audience (Cohler & Cole, this volume), or subject and researcher, affects the type and depth of the produced story. If the subject comes to trust the researcher as accepting and nonjudgmental, the teller may include embarrassing actions and socially incorrect interpretations in the story; such elements may be filtered out of the telling by a subject who feels the researcher is not trustworthy or accepting.

Narrative Data Differ from Factual Reports

The data created by subjects in their production of stories is not simply a recounting of past events, but a reflectively generated current interpretation of those events. Mishler (in press, p. 12) describes this characteristic of narrative data; "I take it for granted that the account produced during the interview is a reconstruction of the past, shaped by the particular context of its telling"(p. 12). The subject matter of narrative stories is not the "real" past, but the subjects' current retrospetcive interpretations of past events and actions. Subjects' stories contain references to "real" occurrences, such as the loss of a job, but the importance of narrative data is not the correctness of their factual references, but rather the significance placed on reported events, even if these events did not occur in the way they are described in the story. The report of a friend's slight may be central to the subject's subsequent actions, whether or not there was an actual slight. Storied knowledge is drawn from the subject's experience and understanding of events, not the understanding a third party would have of the events. A researcher's knowledge of an event that is left out of a subject's story, however, such as the death of a loved one, might be of help in the researcher's interpretation of the story.

Different stories can be told about the same events. Intervening life experiences may change a person's evaluation of past events. For example, a young man whose romantic relationship is ended by his partner may wonder how and why this outcome occurred. From the immediate perspective of this ending he may review his past actions and beliefs in terms of how they might have contributed to the eventual breakup. Actions taken and not taken, which at the time were not understood as significant for the future of the relationship, might now be re-understood as important parts of the storied meaning of the relational drama with its tragic ending. From the perspective of several years after the breakup, the relational episode may be reinterpreted as a positive developmental experience and be no longer seen as a tragedy.

The criterion for the significance of narrative data is not whether the events reported are "true" or "false," that is, whether they actually happened or not. Rather, the criterion is whether they are expressive of the subject's current assessment of their value and importance in contributing to the episode that is the topic of the story.

Life Reviews

In the formal study of lives using narrative data, researchers are often interested in having subjects produce retrospective accounts of their whole lives, that is, subjects are to construct an autobiography or life review. In the life review, the episode of narrative interest is expanded to include the whole of one's life (Ruth & Oberg, this volume). The beginning of the story is marked as one's birth and the ending as the present moment. Life reviews need not be undertaken by people only when they are subjects of a formal study. Most often they occur "naturally" when people are in crisis and faced with questions of their identity and life's meaning. Such crises sometimes move people to seek psychotherapy, where their life review is often part of the therapeutic work (Schafer, 1992). Some individuals engage in a formal written autobiographical review that they present for publication. McAdams (1985) holds that narrative life review is an ongoing operation that occurs throughout a person's life. He proposes that the type of coherence that reviews address vary according to one's stage of cognitive and life development. McAdams proposes that as we move through life the issues that threaten the coherence of our lives change. The developmental "re-writes" of our life story are not, however, created from "scratch." Each re-write incorporates earlier interpretations; for example, the underlying tone that is retained in each re-write is first established in the experiences of the early years of life. (see also Mader, this volume).

As part of a research group, I have investigated life reviews written by older people enrolled in a university class in autobiography. Very few of these life reviews have used a fully emplotted story to configure the events of their lives into a unified narrative whole. Most often these life reviews are a chronicle of narrated episodes that follow one after another. The individual episode often has a narrative quality and the episode's events are congealed into a unified temporal gestalt. The person's life as a whole, however, is not drawn together through a unifying operation of an overarching plot. The student's reviews display their lives as moving through a series of somewhat disconnected episodes but not with an integrative relationship among the episodes. The students were not instructed in narrative configuration, nor were they asked to engage in a reflective project that would end with a single story line that would tie the episodic threads together. Gergen (1991) suggests that the prenarrative experiences of contemporary life present the self as fragmented and with many conflicting identities. It may be that the search for a narrative plot that can provide unity of purpose and coherence for a life in contemporary Western culture requires greater effort than in a culture in which unifying plots are clearly presented to its members (Kenyon, this volume), It may also be that a person's prenarrative experiences may be so fragmented and disjointed that no plot can authentically join them together and the life telling does not coalesce into an emplotted story. Narrative studies of lives do not always produce descriptions of functioning emplotted stories that can serve as interpretive scaffolding for subjects' lives. Such findings are significant in themselves and worthy results of investigation.

ANALYSIS OF NARRATIVE DATA

Narrative data can be used in various types of research inquiries. For example, sociolinguistic inquiries can study narrative data to determine the social functions performed by stories; literary studies can delineate formal units that are used in composing stories; and psychological studies can seek to establish the cognitive processes that generate stories (de Vries & Lehman, this volume). The use of narrative data in the study of lives differs from other studies in that its purpose is to examine the ways people understand their lives. Thus, its interest is focused on the content of the story, rather than on the formal attributes of narrative constructions.

The results of a study of lives using narrative data can be simply a display of subjects' stories. At times these stories are so powerful they need no analysis or interpretation to provide insight into the ways people can understand their lives. Most often, however, researchers using narrative data in the study of lives employ qualitative analytic procedures to develop paradigmatic categories of kind of stories of life understandings that are apparent in the narratives gathered for their data. The results of this type of investigation can be the construction of a taxonomy of lives or the identification of the type of life each life story depicts, or both. Analysis of narrative data can also seek to find consistencies across the narratives and define the likelihood that certain elements will appear within stories that are members of the same category.

Ruth and Öberg (1992) provide an exemplar of a paradigmatic analysis of storied narratives. Their study was based on the life stories of 23 women between the ages of 75 and 85 living in Helsinki, Finland. The first group of subjects was gathered from respondents to an advertisement asking for people who would tell about their lives. Additional subjects were selected in order to include people from different social strata. Extensive interviews were conducted over several settings with each subject. The total amount of time spent interviewing each subject averaged 7 hours and 40 minutes. In the interviews subjects were first asked to tell their life stories, then they were asked to provide more detailed information about particular common themes in their life stories; that the researchers had decided were important to their project. The interviews were audio recorded and later transcribed. The transcribed text made up the data base for the study.

The procedures used in the paradigmatic analysis of the data are described by Ruth and Öberg (1992):

> The data were analyzed using the "Grounded Theory" method, that is, groups of qualitatively similar life stories were brought together in one category and they were labeled after the dominating qualities in the category. We found six different

> categories of ways of life among the elderly which were named "the bitter life," "the sweet life, " "life as a hurdle race," "life as a trapping pit," "the arduous working life" and "the silenced life." All 23 women interviewed could be found represented in the above-mentioned ways of life. The basis of this typification was the way the interviewees started and ended their stories, what turning points their stories included, how they overcame major changes in their lives, and how they interpreted and evaluated these changes. (p. 135)

The report of the study provides extended descriptions of each of the six ways of life. Further analysis involved examining the place of the categorized stories along a series of dimensions. For example, each category of way of life was inspected for its place on the locus-of-control dimension, as follows: The "bitter life" stories displayed an outer directed locus of control; the "life as a trapping pit" stories displayed the theme of loss of control over life and the "arduous working life" stories displayed an inner directed locus of control. Other dimensions used by Ruth and Öberg in their analysis included the self-image evinced in the stories, the evaluation of one's life as a whole, and the evaluation of one's old age (see also Ruth & Oberg, this volume).

Paradigmatic analyses of narrative life stories have also been used to determine into which of the predetermined list of categories the story fits. This type of study, instead of developing a taxonomy out of the collected narrative data, uses an already developed taxonomy to order the collected stories. One example of a pre-existing category system used to categorize stories is Frye's (1957) five-fold typology of story type, namely, myths, romances, high mimetic stories, low mimetic stories, and ironic stories. Closer to the study of lives are the category systems that differentiate personality styles. For example, Millon (1990) has developed a taxonomy of 13 personality styles. Using his system, life stories are analyzed for their position on three axes: pleasure-pain, passive-active, and self-other. It is the combination of positions on these axes that defines which category the life style depicted in a person's story would fit into.

Analyzers of narrative data need to draw on their own cognitive narrative operations to comprehend the data. Before narrative data can be coded or organized into paradigmatic categories, the stories need to be understood as stories. Understanding stories cannot be reduced to an algorithmic or technical procedure. To grasp the significance of the information expressed in narrative form, the researcher is called upon to undertake the to-and-fro movement from part to whole and whole to part that produces the understanding of systematically organized expressions. This type of hermeneutic process differs from approaches that seek understanding by dividing the object of inquiry into its parts and then examining each part individually. After the stories that make up the data are themselves narratively known by the researcher, then the search for patterns and themes across and within the stories proceeds.

A final type of study of lives associated with narrative knowing differs from those described above in that its data consist of personal documents and interview material rather than stories. The purpose of these studies is to produce a story about a person's life in the form of a biography. Instead of organizing storied data into paradigmatic categories, biographical studies oreganize data about a person into a narrtive. The researcher develops an integrating plot that displays the meaning of the happenings and actions of the subject's life. This type of research is designed to produce biographies such as Erikson's (1958) story of Luther's life and White's (1975) study of the three people who were the subjects in his *Lives in Progress*. Researchers may gather data about living subjects by interviewing them and people who knew them, and may search personal and public documents for additional information. Of course, with subjects who are no longer alive, studies must be based on information from people who knew the subjects or from historical documents or both. These data are used to inform and correct the researcher's construction of a biographical plot. In this type of study, the researcher becomes the author of a narrative biography containing a plot line that integrates and gives interpretive meaning to the happenings and actions of the subject's life (Polkinghorne, in press).

SUMMARY

The use of data expressing the narrative knowledge of subjects for the study of lives provides access to the retrospective meanings and interpretations people assign to their life events and actions. Narrative data make available to researchers views of people's lives that most fully represent the way in which they understand themselves. The use of stories to convey the reasons and purposes of people's actions reaches back to humankind's prehistory (Breisach, 1983). Changes in the philosophy of science have removed the barriers to the use of narrative data in the human disciplines. The recovery of stories for the study of lives provides researchers the opportunity to study lives from the point of view of those who live them.

6

Competence and Quality of Life: Theoretical Views of Biography

Torbjörn Svensson, Ph.D.

Among the qualitative methods of studying and understanding the aging process, the use of biographical material is both one of the oldest and one that, during the last few years, has drawn increased interest from scholars in the field of gerontology. By and large, qualitative methods have been given more attention as a means of investigating phenomenological or perceived aspects of the aging process. This important aspect of aging was for many years neglected or seen as nonscientific. Now that qualitative research in general and biographical methods in particular have become á la mode, it is important to find ways of using the research findings and understandings as productively as possible for furthering gerontological knowledge (Ruth & Kenyon, this volume). The protection of turf and the unwillingness to look at the same issue from more than one angle can lead to a cementing of old paths, rather than an opening up of new fields.

This chapter attempts to elaborate on the merits and specifics of biography and biographical methods in the context of a model of human competence. The purpose of this inquiry is to study aging and various qualities in life, which are the elements that constitute the meaning of competence. These qualities in life can be investigated on the basis of both quantitative and qualitative methods. That is, these methods are used to describe or analyze the same phenomena from different perspectives, in that they take opposing and complementary angles to investigate the same entity, human aging. In a way, it is like looking at a coin and trying to describe it from one side or the other. It is like "Yin and Yang," opposing but totally interdependent, where both are essential aspects of the same life and cannot be separated. It is futile and unfruitful to hold one perspective as being better or more correct, when they are really complementary and where both are needed to construct a full understanding of human aging. The value of qualitative methods is already well documented and indisputable, and the use of different methods is extensively presented elsewhere in this volume. The present chapter deals with the importance and difficulty of communicating the results of biographical studies in a research community that for long has had its base in a positivist paradigm. Health, for instance, is an aspect of life that is perceived and reported as a quality in life by many people (Clark, 1988; Larson, 1978). Different aspects of health can be studied both quantitatively and qualitatively. This has been done by using objective health measures and subjective health ratings or subjective health histories. The problem has been to provide a rationale for them, as adequate theoretical models have not been formulated (Jylhä, 1994).

The largest problem in attempting to integrate two angles of research, or at least to employ them as complements, is that of forming a common ground for communicating research problems and results. This objective can not readily be reached by striving for a common specific theory. Rather, it might be possible to find common ground in a higher order general theory that would be at a level that could be called the mezzo-level. A mezzo-level theory would have a general interdisciplinary character between the within-disciplines-theory level and the metatheory level. Such a theory in gerontology should be signified by its ability to cover the whole lifespan so as to be a theory of aging and not only a theory of the elderly. It should also cover biological, psychological, and social aspects of life. Apart from this, a good theory must also take into account the ever ongoing interchange with the environment that takes part during our lives. The theory would also have to permit of both qualitative and quantitative investigations without losing any of its explanatory power. If all this could be reached in one mezzo-level theory, the possibility of communicating results between disciplines and between researchers using different methodological approaches would be possible. The general theory would then allow more specific within-discipline theories to be formulated under the more general framework.

Human beings are born with certain capabilities that we can generally name competence, or competencies. Further, these competencies are expressed and developed in interchange with the surrounding environment, be it physical or social. To simplify the general aim of research in the field of gerontology, one could say that the purpose is to study the interplay between people's competencies and the environment, and how this is reflected in the quality of their lives.

This chapter is an attempt to discuss competence in individuals over the life span in relation to quality of life with special emphasis on the elderly. First, an ecological model of aging, initially developed by Lawton (1972, 1975, 1980) will be introduced and elaborated. The major benefit of having an ecological model as the theoretical base is that it accommodates the element of chaos that is, a priori, present in all ecological systems, and which is consistent with modern chaos theory as discussed by Prigogine (1979) and Schroots (this volume) and gerodynamics (Schroots & Birren, 1988). The different aspects of the model that concern biography and biographical methods will be indicated. Secondly, an attempt will be made to connect the ecological model with quality-of-life- issues.

AN ECOLOGICAL MEZZO-THEORY OF HUMAN DEVELOPMENT

With advancing age people face more and more losses and deprivations. Lawton (1972, 1975, 1980) has proposed a theoretical model for describing the interchange between human beings, especially the elderly, and the environment. The major components of this model are competence and environmental press. The model has its base in the works by Lewin (1951) and Murray (1938).

Lewin (1951) discussed the field in which human beings exist. He called it the "life space." This life space consists of the individual and the environment as it relates to him. Lewin stated that any scientist has to develop constructs and techniques to characterize the properties of the life space, so as to be able to understand human behavior in relation to environmental conditions. Lewin (1951) was the first to formulate the so called ecological equation:

$$B = f\,(P, E)$$

Behavior (B) is a function of the person variables (P) and the environment (E), where P and E are interdependent variables.

Murray (1938) described environmental press as stimuli possessing motivating qualities to activate individual needs. These stimuli are environmental entities that have some demand quality for the individual. Murray distinguished between objective demands, which he called "alpha press," and those construed or perceived by the individual, which he called "beta press." "Press" may be either qualitative or quantitative, and signifies something that is either harmful or beneficial to the well-being of an organism. Already at this point we can consider that the study of "alpha press" lends itself more to quantitative studies, while "beta press" is more appropriately studied through the use of qualitative and biographical methods.

"Competence," in Lawton's terms, is seen as characteristic of the organism, independent of factors outside the individual. Environmental press is a characteristic of the environment with demand quality for activation of an individual need. Competence represents, according to Lawton, a limited number of aspects that might be included in the person variables (P). He excludes needs, personality traits and personality styles from inclusion in competence. Those are treated as to be part of an interactional concept in the ecological equation, namely P × E. This leaves us with an equation:

$$B = f\,(P, E, P \times E)$$

In the ecological equation, behavior is the dependent variable. Lawton includes both the outward behavior and the inner affective responses. What is included in the concept of competence, which Lawton treats as equivalent to the P component, are biological health, sensory and perceptual capacities, motor skills, cognitive capacity, and ego strength. These classes of competence he sees as coming in an ascending order of complexity and dependence on the outer environment. He therefore sees it as more and more difficult to separate them from the interactional variables. Competence then, is defined as "the theoretical upper limit of capacity of the individual to function in the areas of biological health, sensation-perception, motoric behavior, and cognition" (Lawton, 1975, p. 21), here leaving out ego strength. This omission is probably due to its interactive character, although Lawton does not treat ego strength as part of the interactional concept, P × E.

In my view, competence cannot be treated as independent of factors outside the organism, as we know that environmental conditions do affect our organisms down to their genetic base. Furthermore, it is problematic to exclude factors like ego strength, motivation, and personality style from a person's competence. Theoretically, these aspects should also be included in the definition of competence. Lawton's concept of competence has also been criticized by Carp (1976), in that it fosters a negative view of competence in advanced age. Given the restricted view of competence taken by Lawton, since there are reductions in biological health, sensation-perception, motoric behavior, and cognition that are associated with advanced age, there is no possibility for growth in elderly persons. Although it is a matter of definition as to what competence is, most people would agree that growth in competence can be seen even in the elderly.

"Environmental press," in Lawton's terms, is defined as a stimulus or a context in the environment that is associated with a particular behavioral outcome in an individual. The environment is divided into four categories. The first element is the personal environment that consists of significant others. Second, there is the suprapersonal environment, which consists of the significant characteristics of the people in the close environment, such as the ages and socioeconomic status of those living in one's neighborhood. The third consists of the social environment constituting norms and values in the society in which the individual lives, and the fourth is the physical environment, or the hardware attributes of the outside world.

Lawton also makes an attempt to dimensionalize the physical environment. He presents three dimensions. The first consists of the phenomenal physical environment, which is the unique individual perception of the physical environment. The second dimension is the consensual physical environment, which is the shared consensus that exists about the physical environment, and the third is the explicitly physical environment, namely, the objective physical environment that can be measured.

In fact, the personal, the suprapersonal, and the social environment are only describing different levels of the social environment, rather than acting as separate constructs. Therefore, they ought to be treated as the social environment, with all that is included in that construct. On the other hand, the social environment ought to be treated along the same dimensions as the physical environment. In this way, we would have a phenomenal social environment, and an explicit social environment. The phenomenal dimension can be exemplified, for example, by the fear a person perceives when he or she is out walking at night. The consensual social environment could be the agreed-upon hostility in the neighborhood. The third dimension then would be the actual crime rate in the area. Biographical methods would be the natural choice for studying the phenomenological aspects of the social and physical environments, as quantitative methods would be for investigating the explicit aspects of the environment. In the consensual domain it seems that both qualitative and quantitative methods would be effective, depending on the question under study.

A summary of Lawton's ecological model appears in Figure 6.1, where behavior is a function of the individual's competence and the press exercised by the environment. The featherlike shape of the behavioral outcome is based on the assumption that the more competence an individual possesses, the less influenced he or she is by changes in environmental press and, conversely, the individual with reduced competence is more vulnerable to changes in the environment. This assumption is called the *docility hypothesis* (Lawton & Simon, 1968). The horizontal bold line in Lawton's model shows the individual's overall competence, which means that it is possible to characterize an individual by

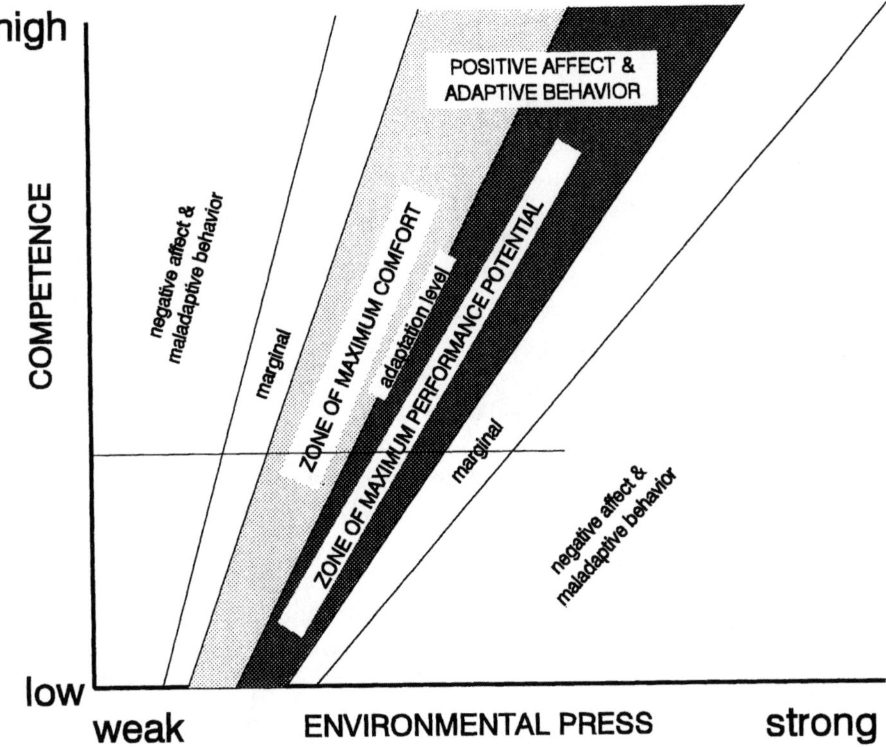

FIGURE 6.1. A schematic representation of Lawton's ecological model of aging.

means of a profile of biological health, sensation-perception, motoric behavior, and cognition.

Adaptation level represents a state of balance between press and the individual's health, sensations, perceptions, and cognitions. It is said to be the state where the awareness of stimuli fades away. A change brings about awareness. Lowered press results in the state of comfort and heightened press in a state of motivation and striving. Minor deviations from adaptation in either direction are evaluated positively by the individual. If the press is too high or too low, the individual will experience stress and discomfort. If the environmental press is either extremely low or extremely high, it will result in maladaptive behavior and negative affect, unless it is in a situation that the individual has chosen and has control over, such as in cases of peak performance.

Lawton states that change in competence can be brought about through either lowering or heightening the environmental press to a point where it represents a just noticeable difference from adaptation level. The individual will then adapt to the new press level. In cases of an optimally heightened press level, we will see the possibility for growth in competence. Notice, though, that competence in Lawton's terms is defined as consisting of biological health, sensation-perception, motor skills, and cognition. This would lead to a too restricted view of the possibility for growth in the elderly. What we would then have to discuss in many cases of elderly and in all but none of the elderly suffering from dementias, as their capacities in the aforementioned four areas are limited and progressively diminishing, would only be the possibility of social growth as a consequence of measures taken in the social and physical environment.

As pointed out earlier, Lawton has chosen to treat personality style and environmental cognition as an interactive concept, P × E, as they are interactive rather than intrapersonal. I propose that we treat personality, personality style, and environmental cognition as mediating variables, or in Lawton's terms, interactive, and part of the individual's competence. It is obvious that personality style, personality, and environmental cognition are the effects of the mutual interchange between individual and environment, but so are biological and cognitive factors, to some degree. Lawton is aware of the problem of not counting such things as social status and personality as competencies in his model, and suggests that they are treated as such when other adaptive behaviors are acting as the outcome variable. However, Windley and Scheidt (1980) criticize the omission of cultural-sociological factors, and indicate that this is a dialectical weakness in the theory.

In what follows, a revision of Lawton's theory will be presented. The objective of this revision is to include the social environment on the same grounds as the physical, and to widen the concept of competence to include mediating factors such as personality. The overall objective is to better explain growth and decline in competence resulting from the human interchange with both the social and physical environment. It is also important that the theory possess explanatory powers for the interchange between person and environment, irrespective of the age of the individual.

A REVISED ECOLOGICAL THEORY

According to the docility hypothesis (Lawton & Simon, 1968), the less competence an individual possesses, the more vulnerable he or she is, to change in the environment, and conversely, the more competent he or she is, the less influenced he or she is by change in the environment. This hypothesis is applicable to all human beings, probably to all living organisms, and can thereby be used to explain docility in all groups suffering from decreased competence. It means that it ought to be valid for all groups suffering from involutions of transient or permanent character, no matter what their age or handicap. The healthy, well-adapted individual with relatively good status can reach for important personal goals by using or even changing the environment. Individuals lacking resources in physical, psychological, and/or social competence are much more restricted in their ability to choose environmental conditions that support their striving for desired goals. They also have a lowered ability to change their environment, as too much energy is spent on overcoming and adapting to barriers in the environment. Therefore, negative changes in the environment are apt to have greater negative impact on these individuals. But it is also important to note that minor improvements in the environment produce a relatively more positive outcome in the "handicapped" individual than those with high competence.

In order to be able to include the interactions between person and environment in a definition of competence, a number of mediating variables have to be discussed. Parr (1980) discusses a model where person and environment characteristics interact through a set of mediators that moderate the effects on behavior. In agreement with Parr, these mediators consist of perceptions of the environment and include intrapsychic factors in an individual that result from the interchange between organism and environment as we grow and age, and which regulate our behavior and attitudes towards the social and physical environment. The mediators are really the effect of the mutual interchange between person and environment. Of course, the biological, sensational, motoric, and cognitive factors are also influenced by the environment, but they are not outcomes of the interchange itself. The ego would be a good example of this type of mediator, as it is an effect of the infant's interplay with the outer world according to the reality principle (Freud, 1911). In other words, it can be said that mediators contain internalized material, where environmental cognition rates highest in manifest content of processed external reality.

Lawton sees competence as reflecting an individual's upper limit capacity in biological health, sensation-perception, motor skills, and cognition. As has been pointed out earlier, this view of competence is too narrow. Competence as a construct reflects three different dimensions. First, there is the inner "true" competence, which will be referred to as covert competence. Covert competence, then, would be the upper limit of an individual's total capacity. The second dimension refers to individuals own perception of their competence, which will be treated as part of the set of mediators, as it is based on a personal evaluation of capacity in relation to the environment. Third, there is competence as perceived by the environment which will be referred to as overt competence.

The person and the environment interact on many levels. On a basic level, the organism, O, the genetic, physiologic, biologic human body interacts with the environment. So it does from birth, or even before, to the minute we die. On this level we can study the organism, as do physiologists, biologists, and others. We can also study the outcome of the interplay between organism and environment. Put in an equation it would read:

$$P = f(O, E)$$

where P reflects the person factors: biological health, sensation-perception, motor skills, and cognition. Growth and decline during our life concerning these factors are partly dependent on the environment, and we can study subjects like nutrition, hearing loss, body posture, and memory. At the next level we have the mediators resulting from the interchange between the P factors and the environment:

$$M = f(P, E).$$

As we can see, environmental factors influence growth and decline at every level and every level has its own representations in the study of human nature. At this level we study, as examples, personality factors, ego strength, orientation to the environment, both physical and social, and the individual's own perceptions of competence in different areas. These aspects of competence are those that are preferably studied through biographical and other qualitative methods. In particular, it is important to investigate how these aspects have developed over the life span.

Further, covert competence, seen as the maximum of the total inner capacities, would be represented by:

$$cC = f(P, M)$$

as both the person factors and the mediator's attributes to it. We can study the P factor and the M factor, as mentioned, for better or worse, but if we try to measure total competence we end up evaluating its overt representation. The overt representation cannot be studied free from environmental conditions. This leaves us with:

$$oC = f(cC, E).$$

Why substitute overt competence (oC) for behavior as described in Lawton's theory? What we have here is an ecological model that should be able to explain not only behavior, but also the total resources of an individual in their environment. Behavior is one aspect, and if we want to study some form of behavior, B will be the dependent variable in the equation. Other resources that can be measured as part of overt competence are social status and the number and quality of social networks. It is of importance also to note that the environment consists of both social and physical aspects. Both the social and the physical environment are divided into a phenomenal, a consensual, and an explicit representation. The phenomenal aspect of the environment is an internalized entity and thereby one of the mediators. The consensual aspect is a social environmental dimension, whether it is of social or physical origin. This is the case since it is based on a shared value among people, for instance, the common notion about what is to be considered a tall building. The explicit environment is always a physical entity, as it is measurable. The point here is that whether we look at the physical or social environment, it can be treated either as phenomenal, consensual, or explicit.

The life span ecological model, described in Figure 6.2, shows how overt competence and environmental press are related and that they have a history over the life span. The horizontal bold line signifies covert competence.

The dotted line describes the overt competence of an individual. In agreement with Lawton, an individual strives, as do all ecological systems, to adapt to the environment. This can be achieved either through personal change or by using one's resources to change the environment. As stated earlier, the healthy individual with high competence can more easily accomplish change in the environment to attain important personal goals.

The covert competence in the model can be seen as the potential abilities an individual possesses to master the environment or life space in which he or she lives. Overt competence is the competence an individual exhibits in a certain environment. It is important to note here that an individual can only exhibit competence up to the level the environment permits. It is necessary to attempt to infer covert competence by measuring the overt. An underestimation of covert competence constitutes a significant oversight. This is particularly the case with institutionalized elderly, where it is possible to observe one of the advantages of the revised ecological model. For example, when we register progress in social behavior, such as grooming as a consequence of change in routine in an institution, this can be explained by the unused potential in covert competence that was at hand (Svensson, 1984).

It is possible to criticize the positive value of adaptation which is advocated by Lawton. Diversion from adaptation level is rather the mother of change, either growth or decline. Consequently, what is negative is not the imbalance in the relation between person and environment, but the direction of the mismatch. However, lasting environmental press below adaptation level is negative to the individual, as it fosters inactivity and gradual decline, even though it may initially be perceived as relaxing and comforting. On the other hand, environmental press above adaptation level is positive, as it fosters activity and growth,

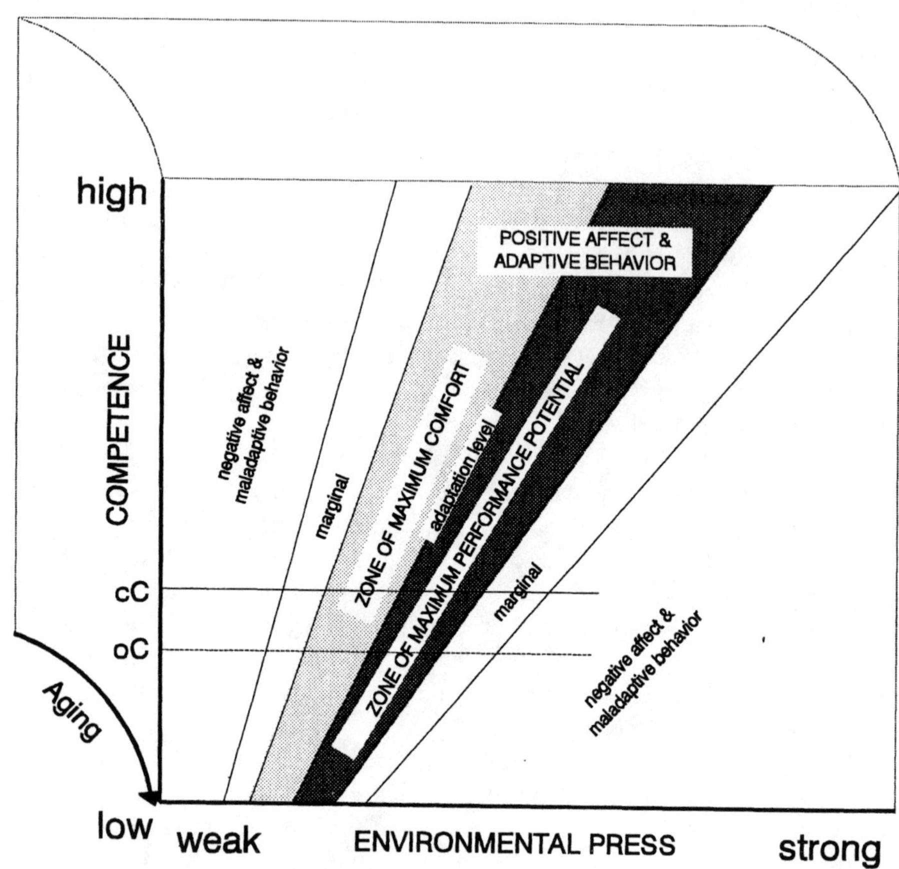

FIGURE 6.2. The ecological life span model.

as long as it does not exceed the limit and create overload and stress in the individual. To be in perfect balance would then only be viewed as a momentary state of rest. Thus, discrepancy is the prerequisite for growth. However, it should be noted that as a consequence of limited competence in a certain sphere, for example, ability to walk, a state of adaptation, or total match between press and competence would be preferred in that particular domain of the individual. In fact, it is not possible that the environment and competence match each other in every instance. It is probable that a discrepancy can be more easily tolerated in an area of minor importance to the individual, whereas that would not be the case in areas of great importance affectively, physically or otherwise.

The ecological life span model states that overt competence is a function of covert competence and environment, where the person factors and the mediators are constituting the covert competence. Overt competence varies from environment to environment and from time to time, while covert competence is rather stable in the short term. However, covert competence is, over the life span, influenced by changes in the individual's physical and/or psychic status, either positively or negatively. Further, it can be stated that covert competence decreases in all factors with advancing age as a function of the normal aging process, even if growth and stability in some areas can be registered in advanced age, for example, in such areas as verbal understanding and wisdom. There is, for example, agreement on the fact that, due to accelerated cell loss, decrement can be found, to a large or minor extent, in the total organism, affecting also the person (P) and mediating (M) factors. Losses can be registered, as examples, in sensory acuity, motor speed, intellectual capacity, decisionmaking, and information processing. Accelerated decrement in covert competence will also follow as a consequence of chronic illness.

A person can only be schematically described through this overall interpretation of competence. The fact is that we possess a number of competencies (see Figure 6.3), and they all have a history over our life span. The life span can be seen as a series of combinations of competencies and environmental press levels. In other words, each competence has a past as well as a present and a future. The life span perspective of competence and its relation to the environment, be it social or physical, is where biography and biographical methods have special value. Especially important is the possibility to describe the perception of competencies and how they are valued, that is, the meaning they hold to the individual. These perceptions are of great interest, as a person's competencies are the domains of life that are of importance when the individual evaluates his or her quality of life.

COMPETENCE AND QUALITY OF LIFE

Quality of life can be looked upon as a global concept that is intuitively understood and in some respect shared by people. Many definitions of quality of life have been proposed and there is only moderate agreement among them (Bearon, 1988; George & Bearon, 1980; Lawton, 1983; Maeland, 1989; Nordbeck, 1989; Siegrist & Junge, 1989). When asking individuals to evaluate their quality of life, the response is generally based on an evaluation of the whole life span (Ruth & Öberg, this volume). The answer is based on experiences from former and present periods of life, but also on an estimate of the coming life, on future expectations.

As there is agreement that quality *of* life is a global measure or concept, there is also agreement that it is built upon other concepts that have been described as

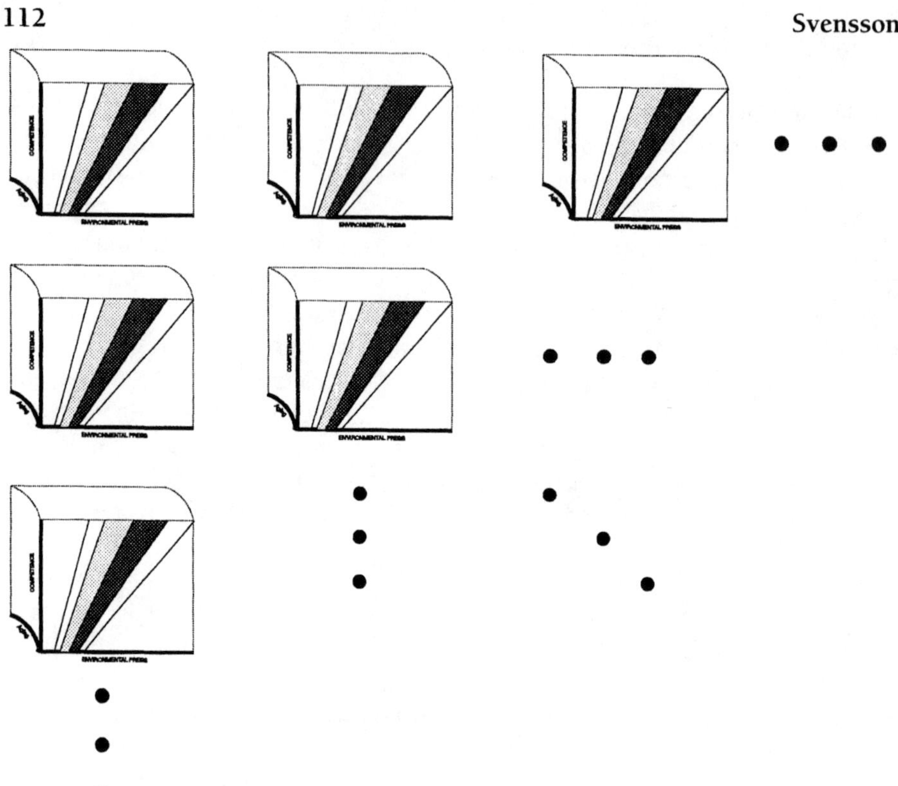

FIGURE 6.3. A multi-competence representation of the ecological life span model.

domains or attributes. It has been proposed that these domains are to be called qualities *in* life (Svensson, 1991). Qualities *in* life are the specific areas a person perceives to have meaning in life and that are vital to the ability to enjoy life. Qualities *in* life are also those areas where an individual shows a high degree of involvement. Both involvement and meaning are important for discerning what is perceived as a quality *in* life. Meaning in life, in particular, must be considered since it also involves a global evaluation of the entire life situation or life story including former, present, future, and perhaps even transcendent aspects of the individual's life content (Kenyon, 1989, this volume; Reker & Wong, 1988; Tornstam, 1989).

As just mentioned, several definitions of quality *of* life have been formulated and used. Svensson (1991, p. 258) proposed the following definition in which the contents of life are stressed. The overall quality *of* life was defined as "the global evaluation of the fulfillment of what is by the individual considered to be meaningful contents in life in light of former, present and future experiences and expectations of life" (p. 258).

This definition stresses the importance of the individual's own evaluations and perceptions. Nevertheless, it does not neglect the socionormative aspects of quality of life (Lawton, 1991), but rather points out that these are always filtered through and interpreted by the individual. Naturally, what is considered as a norm for what is good or bad in life has great impact on the individual's perception of his or her personal quality of life. However, what is crucial is that these norms only have relevance to the extent that they hold meaning to a particular individual. Irrespective of whether we study the individual or socionormative aspects of quality of life, biographical methods would be our first choice, as we are dealing with phenomenological representations and how they are evaluated by the individual (Ruth and Kenyon, this volume). It can also be noted that our perceptions of the environment form the contents of life. When it comes to studying the phenomenological aspect, but also the consensual, as well as the changes that have occurred over the life span, the best way to reach understanding is through the use of biographical material. For example, the consensual aspect of the environment would be well suited to be studied or understood through the use of autobiography groups in the way they are described by Birren and Birren (this volume).

It has to be noted that not only is it of importance to identify the different qualities *in* life and how they are perceived, but the relative importance of one quality *in* life as compared to other qualities must also be considered. Stability over time may exist at the global level of quality *of* life, while at the same time different domains, or qualities *in* life, may change in value, function, or importance, just as is the case with competencies. Individuals can make reevaluations of domains such that no change is seen at the overall level, while there may be major changes in and between the different qualities *in* life. It has, for instance, been demonstrated (Nordbeck, 1989) that there can be very little difference in quality *of* life between individuals with and without chronic pain, while at the same time there is a great difference in qualities in life between persons with and without severe chronic pain.

The foregoing example supports the assumption that a decline in one quality *in* life does not affect the global evaluation as long as certain limits are not exceeded. It also points to the effectiveness of coping and compensation in overcoming threats in a domain. It is possible that in some cases people devalue areas of life with high ascribed meaning or involvement and upgrade other areas in order to maintain the same overall quality *of* life. This means that the loss of ability or negative change in a particular domain, due to changes in competence or environmental press, and exceeding the limits of effectiveness of different forms of compensation and coping would have a negative effect on a person's perceived quality *of* life. This is under the circumstance that this quality *in* life is not ascribed less meaning or no meaning at all by the individual, who could then also relieve the threat by upgrading the degree of meaning of other areas in life. Of course growth in competence in a domain with high ascribed personal meaning would lead to a more positive evaluation of this particular quality *in* life and eventually give a higher perceived quality *of* life.

With elderly persons, especially the frail elderly, it is the inevitable negative decline along with the eventual possibility for positive change that must be emphasized. While profound change poses a threat to the person's perception of fulfillment and success, moments or lasting periods of stability produce positive feelings of accomplishment. According to the aforementioned definition of quality *of* life, it can be said that when an individual is evaluating his quality *of* life, he or she is also evaluating his competencies in different areas. These different competencies are the basis for, or at least some of the more important elements in, what has here been described as qualities *in* life.

In evaluating his or her quality of life, an individual must engage in some form of autobiographical process with the intention of evaluating and synthesizing the meanings and involvements that have been experienced so far. This information has to be related to the present situation and expectations for the future. As quality *of* life and qualities *in* life are phenomenological entities, as are the perceptions of underlying competencies, biographical methods are the best way of understanding and explaining how a person has experienced his or her life process, and how life, in his or her view, has added up to the present life circumstances that the individual manifests. By understanding the different competencies and meanings in life that a person has experienced, not only the life lived can be understood, but also how this life has affected the aging process and the present everyday life (Hagberg, in press; Ruth & Öberg, this volume). The use of biographical methods will also help us understand and describe the shifts in meaning in domains and between domains that are made through life to gain or maintain quality in life as we age.

DISCUSSION

This has been an attempt to present a theoretical model of human development and aging. This model might serve as a base for establishing a common "language" or set of concepts for communicating results and findings over the barrier that often exists between qualitative and quantitative research. Other attempts have been made to bridge this gap between paradigms. Eskola (1993) has suggested a model for the study of human activity where concepts and laws from the mechanistic-deterministic paradigm are integrated into what he calls the realistic paradigm. The core of the model is based on the assumption that in a given situation, when performing an activity, the actor, based on individual logic, evaluates outcomes, if X then Y, based on established laws and rules. This paradigm would then serve as a base for integrating the two different perspectives to better understand and communicate findings from studies of everyday life.

The model that has been proposed here is relevant both for qualitative and quantitative studies. To illustrate the model, one of the ways of life, *the bitter life,* presented by Ruth & Öberg (this volume) will be employed as an example. First, it can be noted that different competencies and the interplay with the environment, social and physical, are the sources from which lifestories have been derived. The dominating pattern in the individual in representing this way of life is the lack of supporting and rewarding relationships in the social environment, even in childhood, which creates low competence in the ability to build close bonds. This low competence has followed them through life, as many have stayed unmarried, and if married usually have no children. The low competence for building trust between themselves and the surrounding world has probably meant that they have often been experiencing excessive environmental press in situations where they had to relate to other persons.

Consequently, these "bitter life" persons have suffered from maladaptive behaviors and affective disturbances. Several have suffered from psychiatric disturbances and they perceived themselves as low in autonomy. As their competence was low in this vital area they described the environment as being hard, unfair, and sometimes mean, all examples of stress because of too high environmental press. As many of the "bitter life" subjects suffered from bad physical health and often for a considerable period of their lives, they were, according to the docility hypothesis, more vulnerable to heightened levels of environmental press. Even small increases in press level would mean that they found themselves facing a situation they could not handle, with accompanying stress. These individuals often described the turning points of their lives as negative. The different forms of illness and ailments, physical or mental, could naturally also have been recorded through different kinds of quantitative measures, as could the stress levels. Consequently, these results can be analyzed from a qualitative or quantitative perspective, using concepts from the same model.

As stated in the model, permanent low environmental press levels also have a negative impact on competence. It is also a fact that we both form and are influenced by our environment. That is, we create and are created by our world (Kenyon, this volume). One way for individuals to adjust to lowered competence is to make changes in the relation to the environment, so that they are not confronted with excessive press levels. The individuals in the "bitter life" reported that they lowered their expectations and standards, as examples, concerning marriage and social relations. In old age they perceive their poor health to be a barrier to an active social life. This is again consistent with the docility hypothesis. This would pose a particular problem for those with a permanent disability.

The barriers that these persons face in the form of environmental press are both from the social and physical world. The ability of these individuals to form social relationships is already low, as is the possibility for support to overcome these barriers. With the overload they are perceiving as they find themselves, more or less constantly in the zone of maladaptive behavior and negative affect, it is not surprising that they report anxiety, fear, and depressive mood. Again, these different states could also be quantified in different ways, but still be understood from the same basic theoretical mezzo-model.

When these individuals evaluate their lives and their different qualities *in* life, they express great dissatisfaction and thereby a low degree of life satisfaction. From their report and their preoccupation with the themes of social relationships and health issues it can be concluded that these areas are highly cathected and probably have a high ascribed personal meaning (Reker & Wong, 1988). As they have constantly throughout their lives experienced low competence in these qualities *in* life, it is hardly surprising that they feel that their quality *of* life has been low and stayed low. These areas are reported as important domains by most people and are not easily compensated for. In other words, it is highly probable that the individuals in the "bitter life" will rate them high in meaning but low in fulfillment. For this reason it is not surprising to find that, for instance, an adequate economic status in old age cannot change their general perception of bitterness and the low quality *of* life.

To sum up, the general suggestion that follows from the above example is that it is important to attempt to establish a common mezzo-theory for communicating qualitative and quantitative research using the same concepts. The study of phenomenological representations of competencies in their relation to the perceived environment over the life span, and how this is reflected in qualities in people's lives, is one side of the "truth" of aging that has to gain respect and equal worth through the employment of qualitative methods.

7

The Fractal Structure of Lives: Continuity and Discontinuity in Autobiography

Johannes J. F. Schroots, Ph.D.

> It is the pattern which connects.
> Gregory Bateson

"Every man is in certain respects (a) like all other men, (b) like some other men, (c) like no other man" (Kluckhohn & Murray, 1953, p. 53). The last term of this classic dictum seems to be an appropriate point of departure for the study of biography and individual lives. Translated in terms of aging, the dictum is even more appropriate, that is, the discipline of gerontology is concerned with learning (a) what is true of human aging in general; (b) what is true of group-specific aging, with groups distinguished by race, sex, social class, historical cohort, and so on; and (c) what is true of aging individuals (Runyan, 1982). However, what makes the dictum really appealing for a biographer/gerontologist is the suggestion of some order within each of the three levels, and the individual level in particular. After all, the study of order, structure, or pattern in individual lives is, or should be, the main topic of this volume.

At first sight, the lives of many aging individuals make a chaotic impression. There are so many details, experiences, and events, in brief biographical data, that it is notoriously difficult to create some order in the plethoric chaos. On closer consideration, however, the many details begin to make sense, as they are part of the puzzle of life, whose pattern become gradually visible, bit by bit, with each piece of the puzzle.

The purpose of this paper is to explore methods and techniques for the detection of patterns which connect the apparently unrelated events in individual lives, for it is the pattern which connects (Bateson, 1979). Following Allport (1962), these methods and techniques can be characterized as "morphogenic" (from the Greek *morphe*, form), which means essentially that they examine the development of patterned structures. As such, this chapter will be an extension of *"On growing, formative change and aging"* (Schroots, 1988). However, before introducing some morphogenic methods, it seems necessary to examine briefly the dynamics of development and aging.

GERODYNAMICS

The dynamics of aging, or gerodynamics (Schroots & Birren, 1988), results from an earlier conceptualization of ontogenetic psychology as the study of development and aging, which are conceived as two parallel but somehow related, ordered processes of change over the life-span of an individual (Birren & Schroots, 1984). Both development and aging have been placed in the perspective of general systems theory. The dominant metaphor in this theory is the human organism, hierarchically organized from many subsystems, such as cells, cell tissues, organs, and so on (Miller, 1978). The growth and development of living systems (organisms, individuals) are explained in terms of absorbing information and the free and continuous exchange of information at each level of the hierarchical organization. Senescence and aging, on the other hand, are explained in terms of increasing entropy (the second law of thermodynamics). Briefly summarized, general systems theory proposes that each living system shows two opposing tendencies: on the one hand, the tendency to maximum entropy, chaos, minimum differentiation, maximum disorganization, or death; and, on the other hand, the tendency to maximum negentropy, order, differentiation, organization, or life.

The ontogenetic view of development and aging from a general systems perspective bears some resemblance to Baltes' (1987) view of age-related changes as a joint expression of gains (development) and losses (aging) over the life span. The second law of thermodynamics teaches that there is an increase of entropy in energetic systems. In other words, a living system evolves from order to disorder. This means that changes in the individual toward increasing order with age are highly improbable. Development, however, implies increasing *differentiation* (gains, order) with age. As it turns out, both general systems theory and Baltes' gain/loss conceptions partially failed to describe the paradox of opposing tendencies, namely, the dynamics of development and aging (Schroots, 1990). A new theory was necessary to explain the paradoxical complexity of individual lives.

Living open systems such as the human individual are continuously fluctuating. Strong fluctuations in individual lives, as might be the case with increased age, do not fit well with the classical model of equilibrium thermodynamics developed during the 19th century. This model led to the introduction of thermodynamic concepts like entropy, dealing with processes near equilibrium for closed systems only. To solve the problem of fit for fluctuating, open systems in far from equilibrium conditions, Prigogine (1979) and his associates (Prigogine & Stengers, 1984) developed the so-called *chaos theory* (nonlinear dynamics) or theory of dissipative structures.

This theory postulates that a single fluctuation, or combination of them, may become so powerful, as a result of positive feedback, that it passes a critical level and shatters the preexisting form or structure. At this moment, termed the *bifurcation point*, it is inherently impossible to determine in advance which direction change will take: whether the system will disintegrate into chaos, or leap to a new, more differentiated order, that is, a dissipative structure. However, the more complex the structure is, the more energy it must dissipate or disperse in order to sustain its complexity. Thus, Prigogine's solution (1979) of the paradox of two opposing tendencies, that is, the problem of fit, is that order emerges because of, and not despite, entropy or disorder. Order can actually arise spontaneously out of disorder and chaos through a process of *self-organization*.

Prigogine and his associates (1979) demonstrated clearly that entropy is not merely a downward slide toward chaos and disorganization. Under nonequilibrium conditions certain systems run down while other systems simultaneously evolve and grow more coherent at a higher level of organization. In terms of nonlinear dynamics (chaos theory) aging can now be defined as the process of increasing entropy with age in individuals, from which *disorder and order* emerge. It should be noted, however, that according to the second law of thermodynamics, there is an increasing trend toward more disorder than order, which results, in the end, in maximum entropy or death of the individual. In other words, aging should be conceived, first of all, as a finite process of change. Borrowing from Jung (1953), this process is called *individuation*, as distinct from differentiation or development. The term "individuation" comes from the verb *individuate*, to form into an individual (from the Latin *individuus*, not divisible) (Schroots, 1990). In conclusion, it can be said that gerodynamics, that is, the dynamics of individuation or aging, relates to a finite series of changes toward increasing disorderly and orderly structures of increasing uniqueness.

BRANCHING MODEL OF LIFE

When older persons are asked to describe their life, they frequently use metaphors like the river or footpath (Vischer, 1961). The river symbolizes the stream of life and the footpath stands for the journey one makes from birth to death, when one alternately crosses the mountains and valleys of life (Schroots, 1991). Most metaphors of life have a basic pattern in common, that is, the branching point, which refers to another metaphor of life, the branching tree ("tree of life"). *Branching points*, turning points, transitions, or transformations, may be defined as those changes in the life of the individual which direct the life path distinctly, and which are separated in time from each other by one or more affective, important, or critical events, experiences or happenings (Birren & Deutchman, 1991). The branching point constitutes the root metaphor of the branching model of life, as shown in figure 7.1 (Breeuwsma, 1990; Schroots, 1988, 1994 a, b).

Shaped like an inverted branching tree, figure 7.1 reflects the hypothetical life span trajectories as well as the *de facto* trajectory of an individual. The individual trajectory may be conceived as a finite series of branching points, from conception (A) to death (G), which *de facto* differs from other trajectories.

Earlier, the term "birfurcation" was introduced, which literally means "the fact of dividing into two parts of branches". In other words; the term "bifurcation point" is identical with the branching point as defined before. Similarly, the dynamics of development and aging parallels the dynamics of the branching model of life. Expressed in gerodynamic terms, the journey of life can now be described by and large as follows: In the absence of fluctuations, the individual maintains a dynamic equilibrium, and moves through time in a straight line until emerging fluctuations direct the life path distinctly toward a higher and/or lower order structure. This description is illustrated in figure 7.2, where two life span trajectories are contrasted (Nesselroade, 1988, p. 21). Figure 7.2 also conveys the correlation between chronological age and mortality, in the sense that more and more of the later alternatives that uniquely define an individual's trajectory lead to mortality, or, in gerodynamic terms, to increasing disorderly structures.

Nesselroade (1988) uses the term *choice point* instead of branching point to specify the phenomenon in time which changes the direction or shape of the individual's trajectory and creates a branching tree in the topological sense, which differs from the tree that would have appeared had another choice been

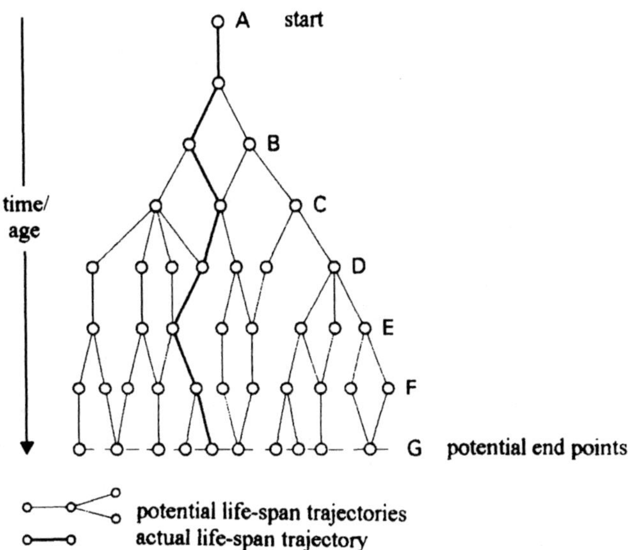

FIGURE 7.1. Branching model of life.

made (the individual trajectory in figure 7.1). If we view the individual, whether young or old, as an open system of irreversible relations both within the living system itself and in its personal and social relations with the surroundings, we can think of a choice point, whether the decision be made by the individual or forced upon him by outside circumstances, as a new orientation of the individual (Anderson, 1980).

The term "choice point" is used in a similar way as the term "branching point". Nevertheless, the latter term is preferred, since the word "choice" implies an individual act of one's own free will, and that is out of the question, when circumstances or aleatory factors change the direction of the individual trajectory. In this respect, Birren and Hedlund's (1987) observation should be quoted "branching points become branching points (choice points) by reviewing one's life rather than while they are actually occurring"; also, there is considerable agreement "between life events that participants felt were branching points and their statements concerning what made life meaningful to them" (pp. 406-407).

The problem of choice vs. circumstances and aleatory influences draws our attention to still another aspect of branching points, that is, the issue of *predictability* about the direction of the life path. Firstly, most people are hardly inclined to recognize that chance plays or has played a sometimes decisive role in the direction of their lives (Bandura, 1982; Mader, this volume). Secondly, the lower or higher order direction of a life path immediately after branching is

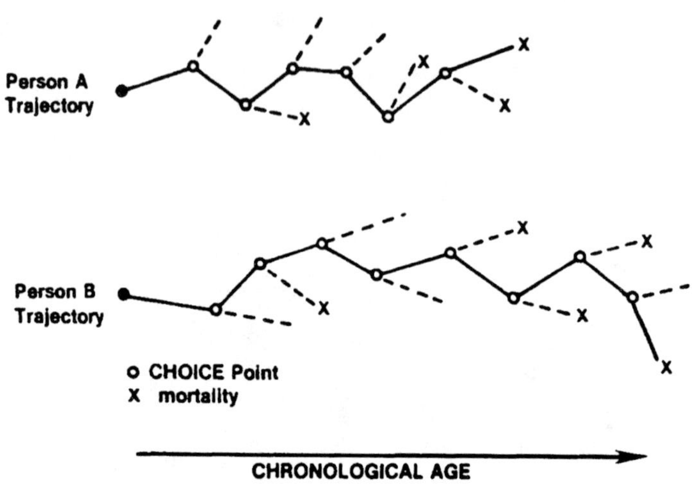

FIGURE 7.2. Life span trajectories.

predictable only to some extent, due to the nonlinear, chaotic nature of gerodynamics. In other words, the branching power of emergent fluctuations makes the specific life trajectory of the individual neither easily predictable nor easily controllable for interventionists. To this the Danish philosopher Kierkegaard might have added that life can only be understood backwards, but it must be lived forwards (Birren, 1987).

Finally, it shoud be noted that the two-dimensional branching model of life (fig. 7.1) is just a dim reflection of n-dimensional reality, that is, the branching tree of life, which grows and flowers and dies in n-dimensional space. In this *life space*, as metaphor for human autonomy, we are free to move, choose and act (Lewin, 1936). In principle, the branching tree of life reflects all human possibilities; in practice, however, there are numerous restrictions. The two-dimensional branching model, for example, demonstrates clearly that the number of possible life trajectories decreases with the number of experienced branching points (bifurcations, transformations). The precise possibilities and restrictions, however, are determined by historical, geographical, biological, psychological, and social factors, to name just a few determinants. At the *biological* level of the branching model, for instance, we might argue that with age there is a reduction of possible life trajectories, homeodynamic stability, and viability, or conversely, that there is an increase of possible morbidity and mortality trajectories, vulnerability, and predictability of future life paths. Thus, to put it differently, the biological life space pulls together and the degrees of freedom are reduced at successive branching points. From a *psychological* perspective, however, it is quite conceivable that branching points result in higher order structures and that the individual transcends biological limitations, so that the degrees of freedom for the individual increase instead of decrease and the psychological life space expands instead of shrinks. Be that as it may, the branching model of life, based on the dynamics of aging and development, seems to offer an appropriate starting point for the introduction of morphogenic methods and techniques.

LIFELINE INTERVIEW METHOD

Essentially, the morphogenic method to be presented has been developed on the basis of metaphors which people use to describe their life histories and expectations for the future (Schroots & Ten Kate, 1989). Particularly, the metaphor of the *footpath*, which stands for the journey one makes from birth to death, proved to be applicable for the development of a biographical assessment method, called Lifeline Interview Method or LIM for short. In a typical LIM session, a person is asked to place perceptions of his or her life visually in a temporal framework by drawing a lifeline. This life-line is the graphical, two-dimensional representation of a footpath with time on the horizontal dimension and affect on the vertical dimension, and which symbolizes the course of human life. With the help of this method one can elicit biographical information about affective, important, or critical events, experiences or happenings in a nonverbal, visual way. As soon as the lifeline has been drawn, the interviewee is asked to label each peak and each dip by chronological age and to tell what happened at a certain moment or during an indicated period. At the same time, the interviewer makes a verbatim report of what the subject views as the most important events in his or her life. Figure 7.3 shows the life-line of Mrs. K., a depressed 81–year-old-Dutch widow, with verbatim report below.

Verbatim Report of Mrs. K.

Past (0). I had a very happy childhood, that's for sure. When I was 16, I had to leave school (1). I suppose I was fortunate in being able to stay on even for that long, but I would have liked to have been a teacher like my eldest sister. She was allowed to continue her studies because the family didn't consider her suitable enough to help at home as I, being more practical, was made to do. My mother wasn't very strong, she had a weak heart, and therefore needed help. Because of her bad health, we were advised to move to the countryside. I continued helping at home, until I was 22, when I married (2). A year and a half later my husband contracted ulcers. Those days weren't too good. Well, we did have a lovely family (I had eight children of whom I am very fond), but my husband was often ill.

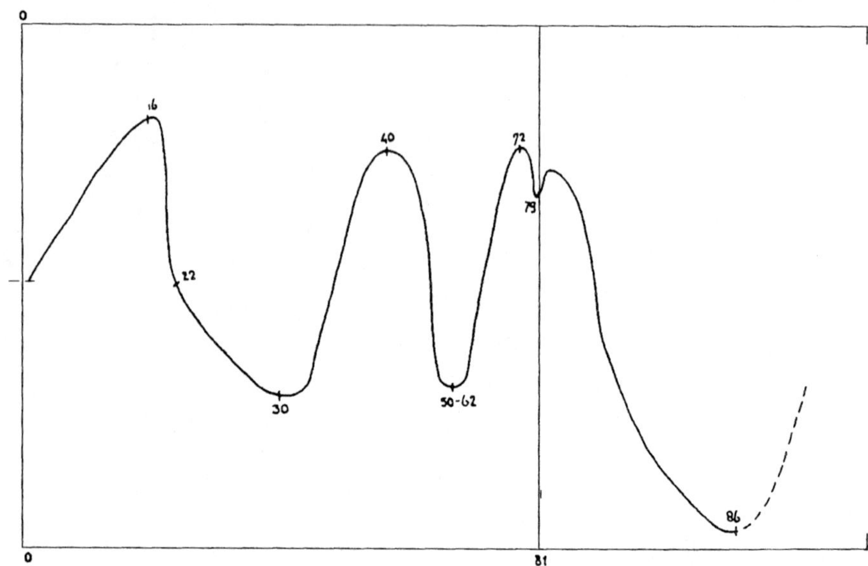

FIGURE 7.3. The lifeline of Mrs. K.

Because of this we had financial difficulties (3). When I was 35 the war started and the problems became worse. It can be considered a miracle that we all came through it so well. In spite of having to eat bulbs (etc.) we did manage to have a good meal a day. Two of my children were born during the war. Now I suppose you'll be thinking: "how could she have let it come so far in a time like that", but they weren't as clever then as they are nowadays. Anyway, we survived. After the war (4) my husband started to work again, you could consider this a highlight, but his health deteriorated. He had at least 10 operations (5) and when I was 62 he was taken into a nursing home. This totally confused him and 2 years later he died. One year later my eldest son died. Dreadful. I often thought "How will I survive?" But I have learnt from life: "You'll always manage somehow." My son died of lung cancer, he was only 42 years old. Shortly afterwards one of my grandchildren died, and also a daughter-in-law, she had a sudden fatal attack, while doing shopping. That time I went through a depressive period. Of course, I've had a good life, but I have been through some very hard times. You have to be grateful for life, after all there is no choice. I was 72 (6) when I moved to this apartment and things improved. I did a lot of traveling: Scandinavia, Russia, Israel, Egypt, Africa, etc. I really enjoyed visiting those countries, so why shouldn't I? Two years ago (7) I had dizzy spells, so I had to go to hospital for a month, but they couldn't find anything. A few months ago I started to suffer from something again. Now I'm really old. I find it difficult to accept this. I still want to do such a lot, but I'm not able to do anything. I have difficulties in walking and I'm afraid to travel. I have become so dependent on others. Life seems meaningless, except perhaps for my children who still come and see me, but they don't really need me anymore. I try to be interested in their lives, but it's extremely difficult and very trying.

Future (I). I haven't much faith in the future. I'm constantly afraid of my failing health. I also think of the end of the world. When I look around me and see what is happening to people: for money they seem to do everything. Apart from that, all they do is complain. And all those unemployed. No, I don't want to sound like a pessimist, but I hope that I, nor my children will have to live through it all over again (II).

One of the unsolved problems with regard to the content analysis of verbatim reports concerns the categorization of unstructured data in such a way that it can be analyzed statistically and significantly. To solve this problem Gergen (1988) and Wolf (1985) introduced a somewhat similar approach by using a story line method and life-line, respectively, in analyzing narrative structures and life reviews. In this regard Gergen (1988) notes that "Previous research using free-form responses to open-ended questions had proved difficult to transform into narrative forms because of the subjective nature of the data, and the complexity of trying to graph the narratives on to a two-dimensional space" (p. 103). This remark is in line with the quality of *self-structuring* of the LIM; that is to say, the interviewee, and *not* the researcher, categorizes and structures the data in terms of number of events, age, and affect. The self-structuring quality makes it also possible to analyze the interview data in terms of patterned structures (branching points) which reflect the events, experiences, or happenings in the life of the individual. Table 7.1 presents the summarized analysis of the above verbatim report in terms of age, branching points, events, and affect (for a full analysis, see Schroots & Ten Kate, 1989).

Generally, a hypothetical branching tree can be described as follows. At the beginning of the life-span trajectory, with birth, the individual is awaiting an as yet unknown but finite number of transformations (branching points.) As he or she moves through time and transformations occur, a patterned structure emerges that looks very much like a branching tree, composed of consecutive trunk segments or relatively stable periods of events, as well as moments of instability or branching points, from which branches of potential life paths originate, that is, unrealized directions in life.

As the above description of a branching tree clearly suggests, there is a problem in knowing how to describe patterned structures or the variation in patterns of, for example, branching trees. If we knew how to formally describe these patterns, then we would have some kind of "measure" for the life pattern of an individual. The morphogenic technique of fractal geometry seems to provide us with such a measure. For a clear understanding of the matter, it is necessary to discuss some principles of this new measurement technique.

TABLE 7.1 Summary of Verbatim Report

Age	Branching point	Event	Affect
		Past	
0	birth (0)		
0–16		childhood	+
		school	+
		teacher	+
		sister	+
		being practical	+
		mother	–
16	leaving school (1)		
16–22		move	–
		help at home	–
22	marriage (2)		
22–30		marriage	0
		husband	–
		children	+
		financial problems	–
30	crisis/war (3)		
30–40		crisis/war	–
40	end of war (4)		
40–50		husband	+
50	illness husband (5)		
50–72		husband	–
		son	–
		grandchild	–
		daughter-in-law	–
72	move (6)		
72–79		move	+
		traveling	+
79	illness (7)		
79–81		being ill	–
		being old	–
		Future	
81	future (I)		
81–86		no faith in future	–
		failing health	–
		black pessimism	–
86	death (II)		

FRACTAL TREE

Shapes and patterns such as coastlines, mountains, clouds, and branching trees are not easily described by traditional Euclidean geometry. Mandelbrot's (1983) fractal geometry, however, provides both a description and a mathematical model for many of the seemingly complex forms found in nature. The central concept in this non-Euclidean geometry is the *fractal,* a neologism from the Latin adjective *fractus* or the verb *frango*, to break into (irregular) pieces, to fragment. Mandelbrot's concept of a fractal extends our usual ideas of geometry beyond those of point, line, circle and so on into the irregular, disjoint, and singular. Classical geometry deals with regular forms having integer dimensions: 0 for a point, 1 for a line, 2 for an area, 3 for a volume, and so on. However, complex forms in nature are perversely non-Euclidean, as anyone who has tried to trace the outline of a tree can readily attest. Compared with smooth Euclidean forms, a fractal curve appears corrugated. A simple example is the so called Von Koch curve, shown in figure 7.4.

Beginning with a straight line of length Lo, the middle third of the line is replaced by two sections of length Lo/3, so that the new total length is Lo.4/3. For the next generation each straight line segment is replaced by four segments in the identical fashion so that the total length is Lo.(4/3)2. With each succeeding generation the length increases in the same proportion so that by the Nth generation the length Ln has grown to Lo. (4/3)n. As N approximates infinity, the Length Ln does also. Put in words, on closer examination, each curve is seen to be composed of smaller curves, and these in turn of even smaller curves. At each successively smaller scale more and more line fragments (or irregular structures) are revealed. Clearly, there can be no characteristic scale of length for such an irregular object: the smaller the ruler used to measure it, the longer the fractal line appears to be.

There is an expression that gives the length of the fractal line for each particular ruler or unit of measure (E): L(E) = LoE1–D, where D is the fractal dimension. For example, take a particular case, when E is reduced from 1 to 1/3 and the measure of L is increased by 4/3. Substituting the actual lengths in the expression, a little algebra gives the fractal dimension D=1.262, which is a measure of the irregularity of the structure. Generally, D must equal or exceed (the usual case) the topological dimension (0 for a point, 1 for a line). Thus, in the one-dimensional case of the Von Koch curve (figure 7.4) the value of the fractal dimension lies between one and two, D=1.262.

The above example illustrates three related properties of fractal forms: *heterogeneity* (variation, irregularity), *self -similarity*, and the *absence of a characteristic scale of length* (West, 1987). The last two properties need some explanation. First, fractals are those structures whose characteristic form or variation of form

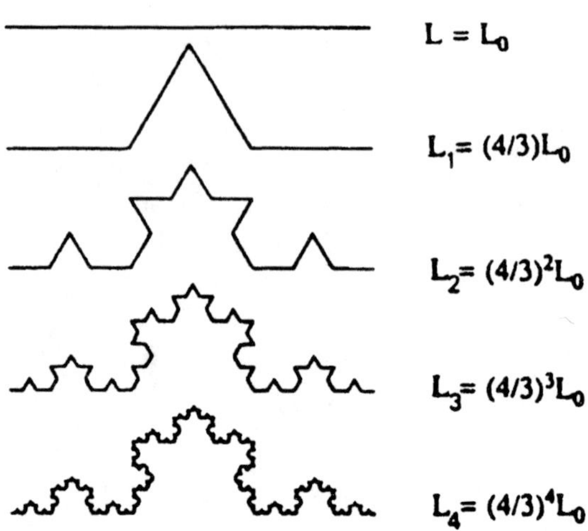

FIGURE 7.4. The Von Koch curve.

or degree of irregularity is the same through a succession of magnifications of scale. Second, fractals are generally those forms that follow simple rules of recursion, that is, undergo an iterative process by which a feature is changed generation by generation, in discrete steps. Given these properties, so-called "fractal trees" can be constructed. A well-known example is the tree of Pythagoras (figure 7.5), but more complex variations of fractal trees have been developed as well (Peitgen & Saupe, 1988).

In concluding this section, it can be stated that Mandelbrot's fractal geometry provides some new tools for quantifying nature's complex and irregular forms in terms of the fractal dimension D, particularly with respect to the description of branching trees.

FRACTAL LIFE

In the foregoing the dynamics of aging have been discussed. Gerodynamics lies at the root of the proposed branching model of life, which reflects emergent patterned structures in the form of a branching tree. Lifespan trajectories and branching trees are generated by means of the morphogenic Life-line Interview Method. Essentially, the generated patterns with their underlying dynamics represent self-constructed time series data in the form of so called "strange attractors" (Yates, 1987). They can be measured in terms of the fractal dimension D by means of the morphogenic technique of fractal analysis. Briefly summarized, branching trees form the fractal structure of lives, or "fractal life" for short.

The fractal structure of lives can be defined as typical patterns of stability and

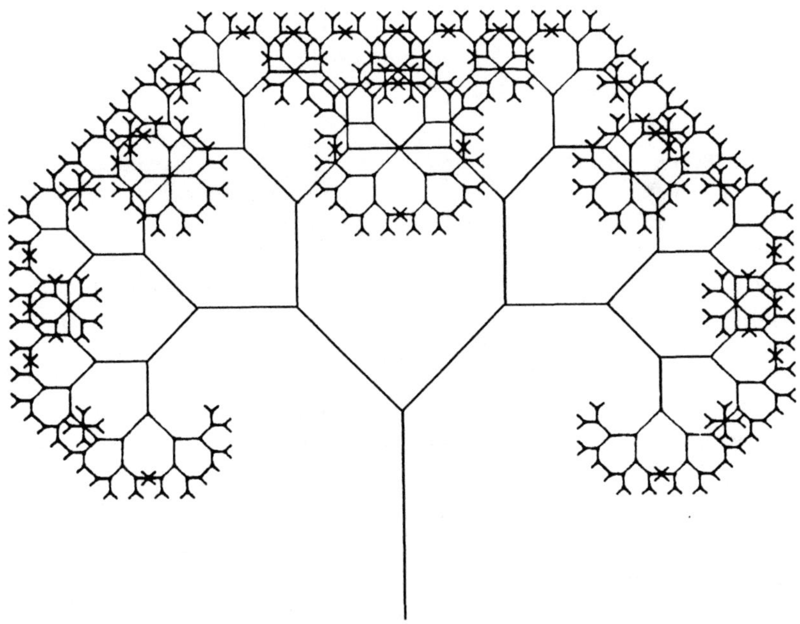

FIGURE 7.5. Tree of Pythagoras.

change in the form of a branching tree at the behavioral level of individual lives. By analogy with factor analytic studies of personality, it is conceivable that a psychomorphogenic typology of fractal lives will be developed on the basis of fractal analysis. Metaphorically speaking, these new fractal analytic types might be envisaged as autobiographical *icons* of life, which are both static and dynamic: static, because of the branching tree "graph"; and dynamic, because icons form the graphical representation of individual time series data.

Although the adjective "fractal" suggests a fragmented, crumbled, or discontinuous life, the meaning of the term *fractal life* is different, that is, it refers to the integrated structure or pattern of continuities *and* discontinuities over the life course. In this respect, the continuity of the person refers to the fractal property of self-similarity and the repetition of (branching) patterns of behavior (Mader, this volume). Discontinuity, on the other hand, refers to the property of branching and the issue of chance vs. choice. As such, the icon of fractal life transcends the ancient continuity/discontinuity problem, which can be defined as the maintenance of some unity of the person throughout life, even if this course itself is subject to abrupt changes (Back, 1987). This definition considers the underlying identity of the self throughout life as the essential concept, which integrates an individual's experiences across time. The quality of self-organization (gerodynamics), self-structuring (LIM) and self-similarity (fractals) refers to this *self-concept*, of which Markus and Herzog (1992, p. 110) have shown the importance for understanding fractal lives:

> Although people experience the same life events–marriage, parenthood, retirement, loss of a spouse, the onset of illness they respond to those events in highly divergent and idiosyncratic ways. The individual impact of a given event appears to depend not only on objective indicators of its severity or stressfulness, but on whether the event is importantly self-relevant and on how it has been interpreted and given personal meaning. It is how a person frames an event (e.g., is it a threat to my self-image or an opportunity to enhance my self-image?) that is significant. (The self-concept) is centrally implicated in all aspects of psychological experience– in emotion, well-being, and coping; in goal-setting, striving, motivation, and control; and in ability, efficacy, and competence.

At the beginning of this chapter, it was noted that the study of order, structure or pattern in individual lives is, or should be, the main topic in research on biography and aging. To this should be added that the ultimate goal is to discover how people organize the experiences of their lives into coherent, internally consistent patterns and thereby find meaning in their lives (Markus & Herzog, 1992). After all, it is the pattern which connects.

8

Narrating the Self in Adulthood

Dan P. McAdams, Ph.D.

We experience our lives as both actors in and observers of a series of multiply layered and overlapping events organized in time. As actors, we feel that we intend to do certain things, that we desire particular ends or goals toward which we strive, and that we wish to avoid certain other end-states, away from which we try to move. As observers, we are conscious of ourselves as actors in time. Consciousness and intention organized in time: these are hallmarks of normal human experience. In trying to relate that experience to another, in trying to explain the nature of that experience, to tell why we did what we did in a particular event or over a period of time, we naturally resort to narrative. We tell stories to explain our lives, to others and to ourselves. We tell stories because stories seem ideally suited to convey how a human or humanlike character, endowed with consciousness and motivated by intention, enacts desires and strives for goals over time (Bruner, 1990; Ricoeur, 1984).

In their own efforts to understand human behavior and experience, many social scientists have recently come around to *the story* to vitalize their methods and their concepts for the study of lives (Bertaux & Kohli, 1984; Cohler, 1982; Hermans & Kempen, 1993; Howard, 1991; Josselson & Lieblich, 1993; Kotre, 1984; Linde, 1990; Rosenwald & Ochberg, 1992; Ruth & Kenyon, this volume; Sarbin, 1986; Singer & Salovey, 1993; Tomkins, 1987). What Cohler (1994) calls the "emerging human sciences tradition" suggests that human lives "may be seen as stories told or read within the context of a particular time and with particular others as listeners or readers" (p. 137). Polkinghorne (1988) evokes the central message of this emerging intellectual movement:

> Our lives are ceaselessly intertwined with narrative, with the stories that we tell and hear told, with the stories that we dream or imagine or would like to tell. All these stories are reworked in the story of our own lives which we narrate to ourselves in an episodic, sometimes semiconscious, virtually uninterrupted monologue. We live immersed in narrative, recounting and reassessing the meanings of our past actions, anticipating the outcomes of our future projects, situating ourselves at the intersection of several stories not yet completed. We explain our actions in terms of plots, and often no other form of explanation can produce sensible statements. (p. 160)

One result of the move toward narrative is that social scientists now appear more eager than they did 20 years ago to explore nonconventional, qualitative methodologies that ask their subjects to provide accounts or tell stories about their own experience (Denzin & Lincoln, 1994; DeWaele, forthcoming; Franz & Stewart, 1994; McAdams & Ochberg, 1988; Runyan, 1982; Ruth & Öberg, this volume). An increasing number of social scientists employ "narrative" or "biographical" methods today, "life stories," "life histories," "personal accounts," and so on. Narrative, therefore, may refer to a particular way of collecting data (asking people to tell stories) or applies to the actual data obtained (the storied accounts they provide).

Beyond methodology, however, narrative can also refer to a *construct*, a psychological or sociological phenomenon which may be sampled or glimpsed via a given methodology but which is itself not perfectly synonymous with the storied data obtained. Thus, one may speak conceptually of a culture's myths (Campbell, 1949), a society's canonical narratives (Bellah, Madsen, Sullivan, Sandler & Tipton, 1985; Reich, 1987), an organization's myths and stories (Pondy et al., 1983), or an individual's internalized life story (McAdams, 1985), or life script (Tomkins, 1987). In my own lifestory model of identity, I conceive of an adult's life story as an internalized and evolving personal myth that functions to provide life with unity and purpose (McAdams, 1984, 1985, 1987, 1990, 1993). By employing narrative methods of inquiry, I obtain leads and hints concerning a narrated identity within. To perceive the vague outlines of *the* life story, the investigator must ask the subject to tell stories. The data on lifestories are people's storied accounts. But the data obtained from even the most successful lifestory interview is not precisely the same thing as the implicit, inner narrative that the adult has constructed over time to make sense of life in time, the personal myth that integrates the reconstructed past with the perceived present and anticipated future and provides life with that sense of unity and purpose that is so characteristic of mature adult identity in Western societies. This chapter focuses on narrative as a construct, a psychological structure in the minds of people, rather than merely as a method of psychological inquiry. It considers the function and shape of internalized and evolving adult life stories, traces some of their origins to early childhood experience, and briefly describes recent research exploring the lifestories constructed by adults who have distinguished themselves for a strong commitment to what Erikson (1963) has called "generativity."

THE NARRATING "I" AND THE NARRATED "ME"

What William James (1892) called the *self-as-subject*, the sense of "I" as a separate, continuous, and volitional agent, appears to emerge in the first year and a half of human life as the infant comes to apprehend "*that* I am" (Harter, 1983; Lewis & Brooks-Gunn, 1979; Stern, 1985). This "subjective self" (Hart, 1988) or "ego" (Freud, 1923) is not so much a thing or an entity within the personality as it is a process, perspective, or stance through which things are known (Blasi, 1988; Loevinger, 1976). Thus, the I may be profitably viewed as the process of synthesizing and making sense of things. Perhaps the most intriguing object of sensemaking for the I is the very self itself, what James termed the *self-as-object*, the "Me." The Me is the I's concept of itself. Hart (1988) calls the Me the "definitional self," but it most commonly goes by the name of "self-concept." Thus, once the I emerges as a process affirming "that I am," it begins the lifelong endeavor of reflecting upon "*what* I am." Beginning in the second year of life, the human being builds up a rudimentary self-concept (a Me), starting perhaps with a schema of the bodily self and moving eventually toward the construction of a verbal self, a self that can be *told* in words (Harter, 1983; Stern, 1985). Through tellings of various kinds, people (I) share themselves (Me) with each other. The Me is told, shared, and negotiated in a social context (Mead, 1934; Selman, 1976), and its development is marked by transformations in the tellings. A 6-year-old girl may describe herself as "Jessica's best friend" and "good at ice skating," whereas a 16-year-old may tell the Me by saying she is "extraverted," "heading for a career in acting," and "intolerant of people who claim that they know it all unless thay can make me laugh."

As the I matures through childhood and into adolescence, the Me it constructs and tells becomes progressively more complex and nuanced. For many adolescents and young adults in contemporary Western societies, the I eventually comes to demand that the Me be endowed with an *identity* (Berger, 1974; Erikson, 1959). To endow the Me with identity is to tell the self in such a way as to confer upon life a sense of *unity and purpose* (McAdams, 1985). For reasons that are no doubt physiological and cognitive as well as social and cultural, it is in late adolescence and young adulthood that many contemporary Westerners come to believe that the Me must or should be told in a manner that integrates the disparate roles they play, incorporates their many different values and skills, and organizes into a meaningful temporal pattern their reconstructed past, perceived present, and anticipated future. The I comes to demand that the Me be more than "what I am," more than a list of the self's many attributes and qualities. The I comes to demand that the Me tell "*who* I am."

"Who I am" is a psychosocial patterning that synthesizes synchronic and diachronic elements in the self in such a way as to suggest that (1) despite its many facets the Me is coherent and unified and (2) despite the many changes that attend the passage of time, the Me of the past *led up to* or set the stage for the Me of the present, which in turn will lead up to or set the stage for the Me of the future (McAdams, 1990; Mader, this volume). Life in time becomes meaningful to the extent that past, present, and future are organized by purpose and design (Charme, 1984; Sartre, 1965). Therefore, identity is a *quality of the mature Me*, a way of telling the Me in adolescence and adulthood so that the Me appears (to the self and to others) to be unified and purposeful. Children do not demand such a telling (and adults do not demand it of them); therefore, children do not typically have identities, in this sense. But unity and purpose *do* become problems later on. In addressing the problems, adolescents and adults come to "have" identities to the extent that they manage to create Mes that tell *who* they are, rather than merely what they are, and that provide their often scattered and disjointed lives with a sense of unity in the here-and-now and continuity over time.

What form do such tellings take? A growing number of theorists believe that the only conceivable form for a unified and purposeful telling of a life is *the story* (Bruner, 1990; Charme, 1984; Cohler, 1982; Hermans & Kempen, 1993; Kotre, 1984; Linde, 1990; MacIntyre, 1984; McAdams, 1985, 1993; Polkinghorne, 1988). In my own theoretical and empirical work, I have argued that identity is itself a lifestory. The I creates identity to the extent that a Me can be told in coherent, followable, and vivifying narrative that integrates the person into society in a productive and generative way, and provides the person with a purposeful self-history that explains how the Me of yesterday became the Me of today and will become the anticipated Me of tomorrow. The I narrates the Me as a story. More than anything else, identity is a good story.

In most all known cultures and throughout human history, it is likely that human beings have valued good stories (Forster, 1954). But it may be only within the last few hundred years or so, and perhaps primarily in the West, that human beings have come to demand of each other and themselves that their own lives be made into good stories. The problem of identity may be a modern

(Baumeister, 1986) and postmodern (Gergen, 1992) problem, most characteristic of middle-class Westerners living in industrial and postindustrial societies wherein people are expected to author their own lives as self-defining and individuating historical journeys (Cole, 1992) and projects (Sartre, 1965). While the Protestant Reformation, the rise of capitalism, the establishment of democratic institutions, and the Industrial Revolution were surely instrumental in fostering an individualist consciousness in the West between the 16th and 19th centuries, the concern for unity and purpose in the individual life seems to have grown even stronger in the last one hundred years, as Westerners have witnessed a great proliferation of occupational and ideological life choices. In addition, many social critics have lamented a growing alienation among 20th-century adults who, more than ever before, feel cut off from and have lost faith in those authoritative institutions that have traditionally bolstered self-unity and purpose (Lasch, 1979; Lifton, 1979; Mader, 1991). As Langbaum (1982) puts it, identity may now be "*the* spiritual problem of our time" (p. 352).

For scholars strongly influenced by recent intellectual trends identified with "postmodernism" and "deconstructionism," furthermore, identity has become so problematic that the very concept may no longer be tenable (e.g., Denzin, 1989; Gergen, 1992; Harre, 1989; Sampson, 1989). For example, Shotter and Gergen (1989) contend that selves are made through talk, by uttering words and putting forth symbols in a social context. But words and symbols are ultimately indeterminate, for their meanings shift as a function of time and context. Likewise, the self (Me) lurches from one meaning to another with each moment of discourse. Over time, tellings are collected and patched together into a montage or collage. The Me is rather like a bulletin board: each day the I tacks up something new, and over time the "look" of the board changes, randomly rather than by design. Because all texts are indeterminate, no single life can really mean a single thing. No organizing pattern or identity can be validly discerned in any single human life. Unity and purpose are too much to expect in the rapidly changing world of today, wherein the individual must juggle so many different roles and communicate with so many different people in so many different ways. The postmodern critique of the concept of identity would seem to suggest that no story, no matter how grand, would stand much of a chance in providing an individual life with unity and purpose. Writes Gergen (1992):

> Under postmodern conditions, persons exist in a state of continuous construction and reconstruction; it is a world where anything goes that can be negotiated. Each reality of the self gives way to a reflexive questioning, irony, and ultimately the playful probing of yet another reality. The center does not hold. (p. 7)

While Gergen (1992) and others have raised important issues about the problems of unity and purpose in the postmodern world, it would appear that most Westerners do nonetheless seek some kind of unity and purpose in their lives, even if their efforts are doomed to partial success at best. Deconstructionism notwithstanding, most people do believe that texts (the Me) have real authors (the I), and that the tellings they fashion are more than mere ephemeral utterances in discourse (Kenyon, this volume). The authorial I doggedly works to narrate the Me, seeking a valid story, amidst the surrounding narrative swirl, a story that will provide life with some semblance of unity and purpose despite the confusion that abounds.

NARRATION OVER THE LIFE COURSE

The development of identity over the life course may be divided into three very broad stages. In the first *premythic* stage, infants, children, and early adolescents gather material for the stories they will some day narrate about themselves. Identity is not yet a part of their tellings of the self, but they are still immersed in experiences that may have a significant effect in the long run on the stories they someday will tell to provide their lives with unity and purpose.[1] The second stage of identity proper, the *mythic* stage, runs from the point in adolescence or young adulthood when the individual begins to create a self-defining life story through most, if not all, of adulthood, during which time identity continues to be refashioned. A third, *postmythic* stage may occur in some lives, synonymous with Erikson's (1963) stage of ego integrity vs. despair, wherein the elderly person looks upon his or her life as something that has been and must now be reviewed or evaluated as a near-finished product, a story that may be accepted (integrity) or rejected (despair) but which can no longer be substantially changed.

Gathering Material

Infants and children are not actively creating identity, for their self-tellings do not require a consideration of life unity and purpose. But during the premythic stage, a wide range of experiences in family, school, church, neighborhood, and so forth may impact identity in the long run by providing narrative material to be used later on. Early experiences of attachment, for example, may ultimately have an effect on the *narrative tone* of adult identities. Ranging from blissful optimism (comedy and romance) to biting negativism (tragedy and irony), narrative tone is perhaps the most pervasive and identifiable feature of a life story in adulthood (see also Mader, this volume and Ruth & Öberg, this volume). Narrative tone speaks to the author's underlying faith in the possibilities of human intention and behavior. It reflects the extent to which a person believes that the world can be good and that one's place can be more or less secure within it.

Infants learn the first lessons of hope and trust played out over time in the early attachment bonds (Ainsworth & Bowlby, 1991; Erikson, 1963; Sroufe, 1988). The first formative influences on narrative tone may be traced to the earliest years of life, in which each person establishes a relatively secure or insecure attachment relationship with caregivers and begins the process of consolidating the sense of a subjective self. Secure attachment, therefore, may provide a positively toned resource for subsequent identity formation. It may help provide lives with hope and trust and promote an unconscious belief in the attainability of fervent wishes organized in time, a deeply ingrained assumption about life and narrative, suggesting that my wishful beginnings may lead predictably to happy endings. By contrast, insecure attachment may provide a negatively toned resource for identity. In the long run, it may color one's life story in more somber hues.

A second feature of adult life stories that may be partly traceable to the premythic stage is *imagery*. One businessman's personal myth may be saturated with the imagery of mounting acceleration: Life moves faster and faster each day, people race to reach the top, but they never get there. A mother may tell a life story filled with the verdant imagery of lush gardens, children blooming like flowers, lives reaching fruition in accord with nature's ways. The imagery of a story is determined by the word pictures, the sounds, even the smells and tastes the author summons forth, the metaphors, similes, and so on that provide certain kinds of stories with a distinctive "feel" (Randall, this volume). In the preschool years, children are cognitively predisposed to understand and appreciate the world from the standpoint of imagery. Preschool thought is fluid and magical, and often unrestrained by the dictates of logical reasoning (Piaget, 1970).

In play and talk, the child represents the world in symbols and images, but he or she does not insist that these representations remain true to logic or context. For the 4-year-old, Cinderella can be dead one minute and alive the next. She can perform actions that are completely at odds with her original narrative context (she can even be mean and nasty), for what appeals to the preschooler is the egocentric appropriation of the image–how the child can make Cinderella do what he or she wants the image to do. People begin stockpiling emotionally charged images for identity in their preschool years. Major sources for this imagery include family, peers, schools and churches, books, and increasingly the media. While most of this early imagery passes into oblivion, some of the most significant images and representations may survive into adulthood and become magnified to assume prominent positions in Me-defining life stories.

As children enter formal schooling and develop in the direction of increasingly logical and systematic thought, they come to appreciate stories as thematically organized wholes (Sutton-Smith, 1986). Older children implicitly understand that stories are about the "vicissitudes of human intention" organized in time (Bruner, 1986). Older children see stories as goal-oriented sequences, and they invest interest in the story's characters as a function of the desirability of the goals toward which the characters strive. A *theme* is a recurrent goal sequence in narrative (McAdams, 1993). Thus, themes convey motivation; they specify what a character in the story wants, needs, desires, tries to get. Two dominant thematic lines in many forms of Western narrative, including adults' self-defining lifestories, are power and love, or what Bakan (1966) calls *agency* and *communion*, respectively.

As children move through elementary school, they begin to comprehend themselves in terms of their own recurrent wants and desires organized in time (Kegan, 1982). Unlike preschoolers, their thinking patterns seem to be dictated less by the impulses of the moment and more oriented to future goals and plans. The systematic and organized quality of what Piaget (1970) called "concrete-operational thinking" in elementary school enables children to reason about the world in logical, cause-and-effect terms, expanding their understanding of how prior events lead to subsequent events over time. Thus, older children's understandings of themselves and of stories are couched in thematic, motivational terms. Furthermore, their own recurrent desires and wants may become organized themselves into relatively stable motivational dispositions, such as the agentic motives of achievement (McClelland, 1961) and power (Winter, 1973), and the communal affiliation (Atkinson, Heyns, & Veroff, 1954) and intimacy (McAdams, 1989) motivation. When they reach adolescence and adulthood, the organization of their characteristic desires will be reflected in the life stories they create.

Beginning the Story

Erikson (1959, 1963) was the first to identify adolescence as a prime time for the formation of identity. Chief among the reasons for the emergence of identity as a central issue in the teenage years, Erikson maintained, was the eruption of genital sexuality and its attendant changes in body form and emotional experience. Such dramatic changes usher in a period of questioning, Erikson suggested. Who am I now? I am not what I was before! What is next for me, now that I am no longer a child but not yet an adult? Social and cultural forces play a major role as well. In Western societies, people come to expect that adolescents will begin to shape their lives into some kind of pattern or design. Adolescents are expected to struggle with the ambiguities of their new ontological status; they are expected to begin thinking seriously about what roles they are going to assume in the adult world of work and families; they are expected to leave home soon, to begin lives "on their own."

Cognitive development also plays a critical role. Blessed now with what Piaget (1970) called "formal-operational thought," the adolescent can systematically address hypothetical problems and possibilities and can proceed logically from a verbally stated proposition to derive hypotheses to be tested for truth. "Who I am" may become something of an abstract puzzle, a search for the hidden "truth" behind the facades of daily life. The adolescent may come to reflect on his or her past and present and how they may or may not connect to a host of hypothetical futures. Further, he or she may come to reflect upon the process of reflecting. Approaching reflection from the standpoint of the knower who is able to understand the nature of things both real and hypothetical, the individual may strive to bind together, in reflection, the reality of the past and present with an imagined or hypothetical future. The construction of hypothetical "ideals" (Elkind, 1981)—ideal families, religions, societies and lives—may help launch the identity project. The adolescent discovers the striking contrast between realities of the present and past and ideals for the future. The contrast may stimulate a campaign of concerted and sometimes painful questioning of the present and past. The targets of questioning may be previously unassailable beliefs and values, as well as the significant persons who represent the sources of those beliefs and values. Berger (1974) summarizes the process:

> During the early years, the child has different selves and is not bothered by inconsistencies between them, by his lack of unity or wholeness. He may be one person with his parents, another with his friends, and still another in his dreams. The limitations of intuitive and concrete operational thought permit such shifting about and contradictions. . . . The idea of a unitary or whole self in which past memories of who one was, present experiences of who one is, and future expectations of who one will be, is the sort of abstraction that the child simply does not think about. . . . With the emergence of formal operations in adolescence, wholeness, unity, and integration become introspectively real problems. Central to the idealism of adolescence is concern with an ideal self. Holden Caulfield's preoccupation with phoniness is a striking example of this concern. He, and many young persons like him, become critical of those who only play at roles, who are one moment this and another moment that. This critical stance is taken toward themselves as well. Wholeness is, thus, an *ideal* conceived in late adolescence; a goal which may be pursued thereafter. (pp. 330–331)

By the time one has reached the teenage years, a great deal of to-be-narrated material has already been gathered, and some of the information and experiences from the past are now likely to influence markedly the particular tone, imagery, and themes that the lifestory will eventually reveal. In adolescence, it is finally time to begin putting things together into a narrative form. The adolescent may begin by consciously and unconsciously working through an *ideological setting* for the lifestory. An ideological setting is the backdrop of fundamental belief and value that situates the story within a particular ethical and religious location. A person's beliefs about truth, right versus wrong, God, and other ultimate concerns situate the action of the story in a particular ideological time and place.

With the advent of formal-operational thinking, the adolescent may begin to search for answers to abstract philosophical, ethical, political, and religious questions. Indeed, the consolidation of an ideological setting may be a central task of identitiy formation for many, though by no means all, adolescents (McAdams, Booth, & Selvik, 1981). It may be very difficult to construct a meaningful life narrative before the setting of belief and value is firmly established, as Erikson (1958) suggests in his analysis of the life of Martin Luther. Once established, however, the ideological setting generally does not change much. Like the geographical and historical settings of most stories, the ideological setting remains in the background, rarely questioned or examined seriously by the person after adolescence and young adulthood, and thus fairly resistant to change.

While the adolescent begins to formulate personalized beliefs and values, he or she is also likely to adopt, for the first time in the life cycle, a historical perspective on the self (Hankiss, 1981). Teenagers realize that childhood is now a thing of the past. For the first time in their lives, adolescents now have a history. In their minds, they *were* something before, and now they *are* something else. They seek to understand the meaning of what they were in the context of what they are now and what they may become in the future. As a way, then, of gaining perspective on the past, adolescents begin to sort through memories in order to highlight key events and major turning points in their percieved autobiography. In their private and public self-tellings, they now underscore high points, low points, turning points, and perceived beginnings and endings that stand out in bold print in their evolving life story. These *nuclear episodes* are chosen and reconstructed to create followable and convincing explanations of how the past gave birth to the present, and how the present may pave the way for the future.

Expanding the Story

The reconstruction of the past is always accomplished through the consideration of the present and the anticipation of what is yet to come. The aspiring medical student may choose as a turning point experience from her past the day she received her chemistry set. The young man who just broke up with his girlfriend may decide that an important memory from his past was the time the girl next door told him he was "conceited." He will give up on women for now. He will pour himself into his work. He will advance quickly in the company. He will create a story in which the disappointments of love are consigned to the bad old days. He will emerge victorious in the masculine world of ambition. He will prove the women wrong. In his new story, the rags of communion will give way to the riches of agency. Past disappointments in love will be magnified so that future successes in work will prove even sweeter than they might have had the story had a nicer beginning.

Moving from adolescence into young adulthood, the central task of identity formation becomes the creation and refinement of "main characters" in the lifestory. All stories have main characters. In a lifestory, the main character is also, in a sense, the author, the I. However, the main character may appear as a Me in a wide variety of forms. The various forms may be understood as main characters in their own right, semiautonomous agents whose actions and interactions define the story's plot. These main characters are *imagoes*. An imago is an idealized personification of the self that functions as a main character in the lifestory. Imagoes are one-dimensional, "stock" characters in the lifestory, and each integrates a host of different characteristics, roles, and experiences in the person's life. Imagoes are like little "me"s inside of Me who act and think in highly personalized ways. The concept of imago resembles the idea of "possible selves" (Markus & Nurius, 1986) or "ideal" and "ought" selves (Higgins, 1987), and it shares conceptual space with certain psychoanalytic ideas such as "internalized objects" (Fairbairn, 1952) and inner "states" (Berne, 1964), "voices" (Watkins, 1986), and "personifications" (Sullivan, 1953).

A person may see himself or herself as "the good boy (or girl) who never gets into trouble," "the sophisticated and intellectual professor," "the rough-around-the-edges working-class kid from the wrong side of the tracks," "the corporate executive playing out the American dream," "the worldly traveller in search of all that is new and exotic," "the athlete," "the loyal friend," "the sage," "the soldier," "the teacher," "the clown," or "the peacemaker." Each of these capsule self-definitions might qualify as an imago. Each might exist within a particular lifestory as an idiosyncratically crafted part of the self that shows up as a main character in many different parts of the narrative. A person's life story is likely to contain a number of different imagoes, most often between two and about five. (For a related discussion of complexity and biography, see de Vries & Lehman, this volume.) Each of the imagoes lays claim to a particular set of identity resources.

Imagoes are typically infused with some sort of moral meaning. Writes

MacIntyre (1984), "*Characters* are the masks worn by moral philosophies" (p. 28). Adults wish to create main characters that are, in some sense, good or valuable. Indeed, imagoes are partly scripted by culture, and they reflect the values to which a given culture aspires. In addition, imagoes often personify the narrative themes of agency and communion, providing models of power or loving action, or both (McAdams, 1984). As main characters in personal myths, imagoes provide a narrative mechanism for accommodating the diversity of modern and postmodern life. In seeking pattern and organization for identity, the adult in his or her twenties or thirties may psychologically pull together social roles and other divergent aspects of the self to form integrative imagoes, which themselves are larger and more personalized than particular roles.

Central conflicts and dynamics in one's life may be represented and played out as conflicting and interacting imagoes, as main characters in any story act and interact to push the plot forward. While postmodern life may insist that adults be many different things to many different people, that they enact a plethora of discordant roles, adults may be able to reduce the multiplicity by organizing the many roles and demands into a smaller and more manageable cast of lifestory characters. Creating a lifestory that contains a rich but finite source of characterization, a suitable cast of imagoes, enables the I to tell the Me in such a way as to convey the multiplicity of life while still remaining true to a unifying and purpose-giving script (Knowles & Sibicky, 1990).

In their twenties and thirties, then, many Western adults concentrate their identity efforts on the fashioning and refining of imagoes. As they enter the workplace, begin raising families, and become established in various sorts of communities, they make identity commitments to various social roles and they invest time and thought into making sense of their lives in terms of a delimited set of main characters. They are figuring out what it means to be "the caregiver," "the small businessman," and so on; they are pushing these idealizations as far as possible, exploring the many ways in which these characterizations of self can enrich their lives and their tellings of their lives. As one moves into midlife, however, subtle changes in story-making and-telling begin to appear.

First, midlife may usher in a new concern for *harmony* and reconciliation in the life story. Now that many different imagoes have reached their zenith of self-expression, it may be time to consider how the divergent trends and themes they personify may be reconciled or balanced. Indeed, the striving for balance in the middle-adult years is a prominent theme in lifespan personality theory (Fowler, 1981; Frenkel, 1936; Gutmann, 1987; Jung, 1961), though little empirical research has demonstrated such a trend. McAdams (1993) provides some initial data from lifestory interviews, suggesting that adults over the age of 40 seek harmony, balance, and reconciliation in their life stories by (1) crafting especially integrative imagoes that combine strong needs for power and love (agency and communion) and (2) identifying conflicts among different imagoes that they hope to resolve in future chapters of the narrative.

Second, midlife may focus one's storymaking on the creation of a satisfying *ending* for the narrative. Though men and women may be at the prime of their lives in their middle years, the social clock suggests that the end of life is closer to the present than is the beginning of life (Neugarten, 1968). In their forties, fifties and sixties, men and women in contemporary Western societies begin to consider in more detail and with greater urgency the problem of construing an appropriate ending for their self-defining life story. The identity task becomes the fashioning and telling of an envisioned ending for the personal myth that will tie together the beginning and the middle to create a narrative affirming unity, purpose, and direction in life over time. Not just any kind of ending, however, will do. It is not enough that the envisioned ending of one's lifestory weaves together threads of continuity and purpose in life. Ideally, it must also *produce new beginnings*. What middle-aged and older men and women often want in identity is a way to imagine and tell the ending such that, paradoxically, the story *does not really end* (see also Kenyon, 1991; this volume). Adults may seek in narrative an ending that enables them to attain a kind of symbolic immortality, generating a legacy of the self that will "live on" even after they are no longer living (Becker, 1973; Kotre, 1984; McAdams, 1985). As a result, adults are challenged in midlife to fashion what may be termed a *generativity script* (McAdams, 1985, 1993; McAdams, Ruetzel, & Foley, 1986). The generativity script is the part of the life story that concerns how the adult has and will continue to generate, create, nurture, or develop a *gift* of the self, to be offered to subsequent generations. The gift lives on; the ending gives birth to new beginnings; a legacy of the self is generated and offered up to others as the middle-aged adult comes to realize, in the words of Erikson (1968), that "I am what survives me" (p. 141).

As people approach and move through the midlife years of the forties, fifties, and sixties, they may become increasingly concerned with their own mortality and with what they will be able to leave behind after they die. As integrated and responsible members of society, they begin to define themselves in terms of the gifts they create and offer. Generating gifts in their own image, they refashion their identities to accommodate their developing sense of an ending. They recast, revise, and retell their own lifestories so that the past is seen as giving birth to the present and the future, so that beginning, middle, and ending make sense in terms of each other. In part, their identities become the stories of that which will survive them; how they were created so that *they* might create *it*, nurture it, and eventually let it go.

Types of Narration: The Generative Adult

The preceding section describes an idealized developmental course for the formation of identity across the lifespan. It is proposed that the making of the self through narrative follows a more or less predictable sequence, beginning in the derivation of narrative tone via the infant attachment relationships and culminating in the construction of a generativity script providing the life narrative with a meaningful and satisfying sense of an ending. One should not assume, however, that all lives follow the model articulated above. On the contrary, each individual's identity project has unique features to it, and no two people follow the same route in developing a unified and purposeful Me. While the process of storymaking will vary from one individual to the next, furthermore, the evolving narrative product, the lifestory itself, is unique to each individual. No two stories are alike; yet, there may be common dimensions upon which various stories may be compared and contrasted (tone, imagery, theme, characters), and there may be more-or-less common *types* of lifestories (Randall, this volume; Ruth & Kenyon, this volume; Ruth & Öberg, this volume). One might even expect that adults sharing certain common characteristics that make them part of a well-demarcated group, for example, eminent scientists, professional basketball players, women who have entered the professions after raising families, and so on, would construct and tell somewhat similar stories to define who they are. Thus, life stories may indicate not only how a given individual is unique and special but also how he or she partakes of a common set of narrative forms unique to a particular group or type to which he or she belongs (Carlson, 1988; de Vries & Lehman, this volume).

There are many ways to designate types in the study of persons. In recent research undertaken with colleagues and students, I have chosen a psychosocial categorization for delineating potential types. We have collected and examined accounts of lifestories from a group of adults who have distinguished themselves for their achievements in and commitments to promoting the next generation. These are adults who have excelled in the area of what Erikson (1963) first described as *generativity*. Among other things, generativity is the concern for and commitment to promoting the next generation, through teaching, mentoring, and generating life products and outcomes that aim to benefit youth and foster the development and well-being of those individuals and social systems that will outlive the self (Erikson, 1963; Kotre, 1984; McAdams & de St. Aubin, 1992). As a psychosocial construct, generativity is often viewed as being situated in the midlife "stage" of development (Erikson, 1963), and indeed research suggests that adults in their midlife years tend to score higher on standard measures of generativity than do younger and older adults (McAdams, de St. Aubin, & Logan, 1993; Ryff & Heincke, 1983). But generativity may also be viewed as a quality of living that can be manifest at virtually any point in adulthood. Thus, one may view generativity as an individual difference variable among adult lives, such that one may find many examples of highly generative young adults and, likewise, many in their midlife years for whom generativity is not an especially strong life theme.

We chose a sample of 40 highly generative adults, ranging in age from 25 to 70, from a group made up of elementary school teachers who have been recognized by their peers for excellence in their profession, and community volunteers who have been centrally involved in an organization dedicated to helping families and youth. In order to be eligible for the high-generativity group, furthermore, the teachers and volunteers had to score in the medium-to-high range on two paper-and-pencil measures of generativity that were validated in previous studies (McAdams & de St. Aubin, 1992; McAdams, de St. Aubin & Logan, 1993). As a contrasting sample, we chose a group of 30 adults, matched on age and other demographic variables, who were not teachers and not centrally involved in community volunteer work and who scored in the medium-to-low range on the measures of generativity. All 70 subjects were administered a number of psychological measures and were interviewed for 2 to 3 hours each, according to McAdams' (1985, 1993) lifestory interview. Interview protocols were transcribed and subjected to a wide range of intensive coding strategies.

The central goal of the study was to delineate consistent group differences in the lifestory interviews. In what ways were the lifestories told by highly generative adults different from those told by adults lower on generativity? Realizing that each lifestory is unique, are there nonetheless characteristic ways whereby highly generative adults reconstruct their lives that differ consistently from the ways in which lives are reconstructed and told by less generative adults, such as those in the comparison group? While such differences might be a direct product of contrasting life events and developmental influences characterizing the two groups, we prefer to conceptualize the findings as differences in narrative strategies. Highly generative adults may prefer certain kinds of stories about themselves, by virtue of their current commitment to generativity rather than simply as a function of having had certain experiences in the past. Thus, we prefer to view retrospective interviews as evidence of *current* reconstructions rather than clear windows into what "really" happened in the *past*.

The results of this work have begun to converge on a generic metastory that seems to characterize the accounts told by highly generative adults. While no single interview presents a "perfect fit" to the model, statistical comparisons suggest that the two groups differ significantly and markedly with respect to the extent to which they manifest the themes that make up the model. The generic model bears some similarities to what Tomkins (1987) calls a *commitment script*, and some of the findings reflect case data garnered by Colby and Damon (1991) in their investigation of the lives of "moral exemplars." The research suggests, therefore, that amidst tremendous diversity in life storytelling, there appears to be at least one rather compelling, perhaps exemplary, way to narrate the generative life, among the contemporary Americans interviewed for this study.

The story told by the highly generative adult often begins with a tension established in childhood between a sense that I am special and lucky in some way, even though I may not be completely happy or content, and a contrasting sense that certain other people are much less fortunate. Highly generative adults are more likely than their less generative peers to point to a particular supportive relationship with another person, or a particularly powerful institutional influence in childhood that singled them out for special, positive treatment. They are also more likely to say that they were acutely aware of suffering, tragedy, and injustice at an early age. In essence, they were singled out for a blessing while others were suffering. As a result of this tension between being blessed and seeing the suffering of others, I come to believe that I have been *called* to service in some sense, that it is my personal destiny to do something good because I am blessed and others are not. The concept of a "calling" has been identified by Weber (1958) and associated with Protestantism and the rise of capitalism and by Campbell (1949) as a theme in the myth of the hero. Highly generative adults suggest the same kind of phenomenon in conceptualizing their lives as a mission or destiny that, in some sense, is justified by something larger than themselves. While this idea sometimes has a religious flavoring, the highly generative adults do not always couch it in religious terms. Indeed, there are no group differences in religiosity in the study.

The notion of a calling results in the development of a personal philosophy of life to which I swear a kind of allegiance. As time goes on, I remain steadfast in my beliefs about what is good and right. Highly generative adults prove to be much *less* likely than those in the contrasting sample to say that they ever doubted their fundamental beliefs. Contrary to expectations that might come from humanistic and existential psychology (Maslow, 1968; Sartre, 1965), highly generative adults suggest that they rarely have struggled with doubt and uncertainty concerning what is right and good and what they should be doing with their lives. Rather, they tend to be "true believers" in some sense, and they suggest that they have pretty much always been that way.

Over time, I repeatedly encounter suffering and confront numerous obstacles and bad events, but these I turn into good outcomes, or else they are transformed by me, by fate or luck, maybe by God, though I do not have to be especially religious to develop this kind of narrative. Turning bad into good is a distinctive narrative form in the stories of highly generative adults, to which is given the name *redemptive experience*. Redemptive imagery appears again and again in some of the great cultural stories and sacred myths centrally associated with generativity. For example, the ultimate progenitors for the Israelite people, Abraham and Sarah in the Book of Genesis, must endure many long years of childlessness (bad) before they are given their son Isaac (good). The Israelites must wander 40 years in the Wilderness (bad) before they are able to enter the Promised Land and claim their rightful destiny as the chosen children of God (good). In the mythology of ancient Greece, the generative goddess of fruit and fertility, Demeter, must endure separation from her daughter, Persephone, who descends to the underworld (bad: winter), before she can enjoy the reunion with her beloved when she reascends in the spring (good).

My story celebrates caring, dialogue, and intimacy, and perhaps because of this, and because I value myself as one singled out to do important and good things with my life (a forceful agent, a powerful source), I find that I cannot do and be it all; I cannot experience agency and communion to their fullest, together. The tension between agency and communion, power vs. love, is especially problematic in the lifestories of highly generative adults. It is a kind of motivational ambivalence, and it contrasts in a peculiar way to the ideological certitude that these same people show. In some stories the motivational ambivalence seems to undermine the subject's best generative efforts. In other stories, the tension between power and love provides opportunities for growth and individuation and may even enhance generativity further.

Highly generative adults narrate stories in which they move into the future with both confidence (in the realm of ideology) and frustration (when it comes to motivation: power vs. love). Nonetheless, their stories underscore their commitment to humanistic goals for themselves, their families, and their society. While the rest of us may see things as getting worse and worse over time, the highly generative adult seems to stick in narrative to what Erikson (1963) called a "belief in the species." Things do grow and blossom, even as suggested in the generative metaphors and similes that animate the stories they tell. Some things do get better. There is progress amidst the setbacks and the suffering. And I can make a difference.

CONCLUSION

Psychologists have just begun to catalogue in a systematic way the different kinds of stories adults tell in order to provide their lives with unity and purpose. A great deal of intensive, descriptive research needs to be done, in order to categorize and classify the rich assortment of narrative forms and contents to be found in lifestories and to delineate the developmental processes that go into the making of narrative over the life course. My colleagues and I have recently focused our inquiries on the lifestories of especially generative adults because we believe that these narratives are both psychologically intriguing and sociologically noteworthy for their potential to promote the social good. Campbell (1949) has written that "it has always been the prime function of mythology and rite to supply the symbols that carry the human spirit forward, in counteraction to those other constant human fantasies that tend to tie it back" (p. 11). Like the religious and cosmic myths that humankind has created across the ages, the best kind of personal myth, the exemplary Me, can carry something forward about humankind that is worth preserving and improving.

Thus, the stories that adults make and tell to provide their lives with unity and purpose are not mere psychological musings, but instead influence deeply the stories and the lives that other people make, for better or for ill. And those stories give rise still to others, in a continuous process of individual and cultural evolution. From one generation to the next, people find meaning and connection within a web of storymaking, storytelling, and storyliving. Through lifestories, human beings help to create the world they live in at the same time that it is creating them.

ACKNOWLEDGMENT

Preparation of this manuscript was aided by a grant from The Spencer Foundation.

9

The Complexity of Personal Narratives

Brian de Vries, Ph.D. and Allen J. Lehman

The complexity of personal narratives is derived from many sources. This complexity is attested to, in part, by the multidisciplinary attention it has received. As Ruth and Kenyon (this volume) have identified, autobiographies and other personal narratives have been the tools found in the empirical toolchests of many different disciplines operating within diverse theoretical frameworks. Ethnographers and cultural anthropologists, for example, have reported on individuals and people(s) in their cultural and historical context through the stories they tell of their lives. Historians have excavated and reconstructed epochs and eras from the diaries and personal accounts of individuals whose lives are presented in such text.

Psychologists have operated in parallel, in their attempts to account for the ways in which individuals experience their lives, using narratives and life stories as evidence of cognitive organization. For example, Epstein (1973) and Greenwald (1980), following Kelly (1955), suggested that individuals interpret the experiences of life just as scientists adopt models or paradigms to interpret experimental data, confirm "hypotheses" and preserve the integrity of theoretical constructs (Kuhn, 1970). Gergen and Gergen (1983), Cohler (1982) and others have described the personal narrative as the most internally consistent interpretation of the presently understood past, the experienced present, and the anticipated future, revealing the psychological basis for sequences of actions over time.

Further evidence of the complexity of autobiographies and other personal narratives has resided in its empirically derived multidimensionality. Researchers have most frequently concerned themselves with when such personal storytelling occurs and the outcome (or "why"s) of such an enterprise. For example, life review is seen to be a major psychosocial task and process of old age (Coleman, 1986; Erikson, 1968/1976; Webster & Cappeliez, 1993), initiated as a response to the inevitable losses associated with aging (Buhler, 1933) and by the awareness of approaching dissolution and death (Butler, 1963). Attesting to the adaptive nature of autobiography and life review, Birren and Deutchman's (1991) summary of the empirical literature cited the following gains: renewed self-confidence, elevated self-esteem, and increased self-understanding; reaffirmation of a sense of continuity and bridges to historical times; renewed motivation and increased energy; new skills for newly identified demands; increased generativity and future orientation; adaptation to life circumstances; and contributions to cognitive functioning (see also Birren & Birren, this volume).

The above dimensions reflect the temporal and psychosocial aspects of autobiography and other personal narratives. Equally relevant are the finer dimensions that reflect their *content* (what is said) and *construction* (how it is said). For example, the content of autobiographies has been examined in terms of life themes (Birren & Deutchman, 1991; Csikszentmihalyi & Beattie, 1979), life meaning (Hedlund, 1987), ways of life (Ruth & Öberg, this volume), life's plots and characters (McAdams, 1985) and important relationships (Mathews, 1983). In contrast, limited effort has been invested in the understanding of the construction of autobiographies, with McAdams (1985, this volume) representing a notable exception. As linguistics have long recognized, however, "what is said" and "how it is said" are two distinct aspects of communication (Dinneen, 1967).

This is the broader framework for the task we have undertaken in this chapter. We look at one specific dimension of this construction, namely, *structure*, a dimension well represented by a cognitive style construct characterizing how the structure of an individual's thought is manifested in the verbal materials he or she produces. This construct is called *integrative complexity* (and hence the clever play on words in our title). It is the goal of this chapter to introduce integrative complexity and review the empirical research in ways that are relevant to the study of autobiography, concluding with suggestions for future research.

INTEGRATIVE COMPLEXITY

Integrative complexity is a direct descendant of Kelly's (1955) personal construct theory (Suedfeld, Tetlock, & Streufert, 1992). Its focus is on how thought is structured independent of content: how individuals organize and synthesize information about the objects and events of their worlds. Following Kelly, the complexity lineage proceeded through conceptual systems (Harvey, Hunt, & Schroder, 1961), conceptual complexity (Schroder, Driver, & Streufert, 1967), and interactive complexity (Streufert & Streufert, 1978) to integrative complexity (Baker-Brown, Ballard, Bluck, de Vries, Suedfeld, & Tetlock, 1992; Suedfeld, Tetlock, & Streufert, 1992). This evolution may be briefly represented as a move from stage and trait emphases to a relative focus on state characteristics, one in which complexity is seen to vary as a function of intrapsychic and social forces. This most recent emphasis does not reject the previous trait perspective; rather it holds it in abeyance in favor of studying the state (Suedfeld, Tetlock, & Streufert, 1992).

Methodologically, this evolution was accompanied by the broadening of materials appropriate for complexity coding. That is, initial studies used the Sentence or Paragraph Completion Test (Schroder et al., 1967), a semiprojective and time-constrained measure in which participants completed a number of sentence stems (that is, wrote paragraphs) addressing important domains of the decisionmaking environment. More recently, studies have used archival, narrative and other open-ended documents and materials prepared for a variety of purposes and under a variety of circumstances. For example, research has examined the integrative complexity as derived from the writings, speeches and communications of political figures (Suedfeld & Tetlock, 1977; Tetlock, 1985), Supreme Court justices' opinions (Tetlock, Bernzwieg, & Gallant, 1986), magazine editorials (Suedfeld, 1980), experimental attitudinal thought protocols (de Vries & Walker, 1988), thematic essays and interview transcripts (de Vries, Bluck, & Birren, 1993; Pratt, Hunsberger, Pancer, Roth, & Santolupo, 1993), and personal letters (Porter & Suedfeld, 1981). Patterns of findings from these diverse data sources are summarized in what follows.

Complexity holds, as its basic premise, that in any written or verbal material of "sufficient length," an individual is providing the manifestations of the structure underlying thought. The basic scoring unit of complexity refers to a section of material that focuses on one idea; usually, but not always, this scorable unit consists of a single paragraph. Integrative complexity is defined in terms of two cognitive structural variables: differentiation and integration. Differentiation refers to the perception of different dimensions and/or the taking of different perspectives when considering an issue. Integration refers to the development of conceptual connections among differentiated dimensions of the stimulus and/or among differentiated perspectives about the stimulus. It follows that some degree of differentiation is a necessary, although not a sufficient condition for integration.

Integrative complexity scoring proceeds on a 1–7 scale. Scores of 1 indicate no evidence of either differentiation or integration. The author relies on unidimensional, value-laden, and evaluatively consistent rules for processing information. Scores of 3 indicate moderate or even high differentiation but no integration. The author presents at least two distinct dimensions of judgement, but fails to consider possible conceptual connections between these dimensions. Scores of 5 indicate moderate to high differentiation and moderate integration. The author notes the existence of conceptual connections between differentiated dimensions such as the identification of a superordinate category linking two concepts, or the creation of a novel product. Scores of 7 indicate high differentiation and high integration. A general principle provides a conceptual framework for understanding specific interactions among differentiated dimensions. This type of systemic analysis yields second-order integration principles that place in context, and perhaps reveal, limits on the generalizability of integration rules that operate at the scale value of 5 (see Table 9.1 for examples of the above scores). Scores of 2, 4, and 6 represent transitional levels in conceptual structure.

As might be predicted, the coding of complexity is itself a complex task, primarily because it does not rely on simple "content-counting rules" of the sort common to content analytic approaches. The coding system, as the construct itself, focuses on structure rather than content; there is no built-in bias for or against any particular position. The complexity of a person's thought on an issue is not determined by the specific beliefs he or she endorses, but by the conceptual structure underlying the positions taken. Moreover, it is not always "better" to be more complex. The complexity coding system does not rest on assumptions concerning the logical, pragmatic, or ethical superiority of any particular school of thought. Nor is complexity English-bound: the scores of English translators do not differ from the scores assigned to the same passage in the original language (Suedfeld, Tetlock, & Streufert, 1992).

The empirical relation between complexity and autobiography is surprisingly indirect, framed in an analysis of personal documents from a variety of sources and written under a variety of conditions. The review that follows is organized around the findings and issues of complexity and the "who"s, "what"s, and "when"s of storytelling, that is, individual attributes (including gender), life experiences (life events and stressors), and age, respectively. In descending order of prevalence, these have been the primary variables most frequently and empirically linked to complexity. These are constructs that do not fall under the exclusive purview of integrative complexity, however. That is, sizable literatures exist in which individual attributes, life experiences, and age are represented with autobiographical accounts; these representations open each of the following discussions. We will conclude by drawing from this review and applying

TABLE 9.1 Examples of Integrative Complexity Scores at Levels 1, 3, 5, and 7.

Score	Examples
1	Life can present you with either a seemingly endless supply of hardship or an abundance of comfort; life is the hand of cards you are dealt.
3	Life offers both the hardships of loss and misfortunes as well as the comforts of family and friends.
5	Life includes the experience of both hardship and comfort producing an appreciation of the value of the moment; life is what you make it.
7	The experience of life's hardships and comforts fosters an awareness of both the value and impermanence of the moment; all of these influence and are influenced by the meaning we make – which is further negotiated over time and through interaction with others – and manifested in our autobiographies.

integrative complexity both conceptually and empirically to the area of autobiography and aging.

PERSONAL NARRATIVES AND COMPLEXITY: THE INFLUENCE OF INDIVIDUAL ATTRIBUTES

Personal narratives may be seen as windows into individual lives, offering a vantage point from which to see, among other things, how meaning and understanding have been constructed and/or reconstructed. Such materials are shaped, at least in part, by underlying personality and individual attributes. For example, psychobiographers, as part of their efforts to understand and describe individuals, have explored personality attributes represented by and manifested in the personal documents of famous people (McAdams & Ochberg, 1988). Erikson's psychohistorical method, so often ignored by developmentalists, "provides a triune synthesis of personal ego identity, one's cultural context, and the historical zeitgeist" (Green, 1989, p. 84). His psychobiographies of Martin Luther (Erikson, 1958) and Mahatma Gandhi (Erikson, 1969) are perhaps the best known examples of such psychosocial descriptions of individual lives. Subsequently, and more recently, Stewart, Franz, and Layton (1988) found evidence of Erikson's themes of identity, intimacy, and generativity in their analysis of the life of Vera Brittain, a British feminist and pacifist writer. The motivational themes of achievement, affiliation-intimacy, and power were reported by Winter and Carlson (1988) in their analysis of Richard Nixon's life. With a larger and more representative sample, McAdams (1982) found high intimacy and power scores in narratives written on autobiographical memories of specific peak experiences.

In a different but related stream of conceptual and empirical work, orientations toward the self have been explored in autobiographical material (de Vries & Shannon, 1992; de Vries & Watt, in press; Pratt, Pancer, Hunsberger, & Manchester, 1990). These efforts largely follow from Gilligan (1982) who discussed the concept of two perspectives on the self: a separate and objective self and a connected self. Separateness, most evident in the self-perspectives of men, tends towards impartiality, objectivity, and distancing the self from others; connectedness, most evident in the self-perceptions of women, tends towards interdependence, subjectivity and care, and responsiveness to others (Lyons, 1983). Preliminary investigations by Lyons (1983) have substantiated these conceptual claims with a lifespan sample of 16 men and 14 women. Along similar lines, Gergen and Gergen's (1993) examination of popular autobiographies (e.g., film stars, athletes) revealed that women tended to disclose more about emotions and relationships and discuss multiple life themes such as family and work, whereas men's autobiographies focused more on the pursuit of single goals. In a study designed to explore differences between women's and men's retrospective accounts of close relationships, Ross and Holmberg (1992) found that women, as compared to their husbands, reported more affective descriptions of events.

These reports suggest that manifested in the stories we tell of our lives are important aspects and dimensions of, as well as orientations toward, ourselves. As broad domains, these have also been affiliates of complexity; for example, complexity has been correlated with a host of individual attributes, including political and social ideologies, attitudes and traits, intellectual competence, and educational pursuits/attainment, as well as religious and moral beliefs. Furthermore, complexity has also been correlated with a variety of perspectives on and orientations toward the self. The accounting of these associations forms the basis of the following paragraphs.

The relation between complexity and political ideology is perhaps best characterized in the context of the value pluralism model (Tetlock, 1984). The model posits that adherents to ideologies in which two or more principles are equally and highly valued are under greater cognitive pressure to consider issues in more complex terms (reflected in more complex reasoning about the issue) than are advocates of ideologies that place a greater weight on only one value. For example, Tetlock (1981, 1983) and Tetlock, Hannum, and Michelletti (1984) explored the speeches of United States politicians and their reasoning about political issues. They found that politicians who held more moderate or liberal orientations (tending to highly value both social equality and economic freedom) reasoned in more complex ways than politicians of conservative orientations (tending to predominantly value economic freedom). Similarly, Tetlock (1984) found that British politicians' interpretations of policy issues varied in complexity depending on political ideology: extreme conservatives and extreme socialists had lower complexity levels, while moderate socialists revealed higher levels of complexity. Along similar lines, de Vries and Walker (1988) examined attitudes about capital punishment and their relationship with complexity. They found a curvilinear relationship between attitudes toward capital punishment and complexity level. Individuals holding extreme "pro" attitudes (valuing law) or extreme "con" attitudes (valuing life) reasoned in less complex ways than individuals holding moderate attitudes (valuing both law and life).

Schroder, Driver, and Streufert (1967) examined the relation between complexity and both authoritarianism and dogmatism and found moderate negative correlations in each pairing. These relations are not unexpected, given the presumed rigidity of information processing inherent in such personality styles (see also Pratt et al. 1992). Similarly, researchers have examined levels of complexity in relation to intelligence and education. For example, with a sample of university undergraduates, Suedfeld and Coren (1992) found that complexity scores were positively associated with mental abilities in the domains of verbal intelligence, crystallized intelligence, and divergent thinking. Similarly, Pratt and colleagues (1992) found that WAIS-R vocabulary scores were positively predictive of complexity scores in the discussion of religious issues. Schroder and colleagues (1967) found low to moderate correlations between complexity and educational attainment. Pratt, Diessner, Hunsburger, Pancer, and Savoy (1991) found complexity to be positively associated with education in their life span sample of women and men. de Vries and Walker (1986) reported a similar finding with their sample of primarily young adults.

Religious beliefs have also been explored in association with complexity. In a series of five studies, Hunsberger and his colleagues examined the relationship between religion and complexity (see Hunsberger, 1991, for a summary). Evidence from preliminary investigations was equivocal, with the initial study finding only a low positive correlation between religious quest (striving to comprehend religious and existential issues) and complexity of responses to the existential material. Subsequent studies found correlations between complexity of particular sentence stem responses (existential and traditional issues) and religious orthodoxy. Religious fundamentalism was moderately negatively correlated with complexity of discussions about dilemmas on abortion, and a loving God. Methodological problems (low inter-rater reliabilities) may have accounted for some of the variability in the findings and failures to replicate. More recently, however, Pratt and colleagues (1992) found that Christian orthodoxy was a negative predictor of complexity in their examination of reasoning about religious and philosophical issues.

Other researchers have explored the role of complexity in moral reasoning and related areas. Moral reasoning, based on Kohlberg's (1984) moral stage model, as revealed in discussions about capital punishment issues (de Vries & Walker, 1986) and real-life moral dilemmas (Pratt et al., 1991), was positively associated with levels of complexity. Pitts, Walker, Chandler, and Lehman (1992) examined stages of faith development (Fowler, 1981) and found a moderately high correlation between stages of faith development and the complexity of written materials addressing issues of relationships, commitments and values, and religion.

Complexity has also been examined in conjunction with Gilligan's (1982) and Lyons' (1983) self-orientation concepts of connectedness (interdependence and subjectivity) and separateness (independence and objectivity). de Vries and Shannon (1992) examined the complexity of individuals' self-evaluations (discussion of "Who am I?") and found that, independent of gender, individuals who scored higher on the measure of connectedness also revealed higher complexity scores. Similarly, Pratt and colleagues (1990) found that individuals with more connected self-concepts reasoned about relationships and the self in more complex ways than individuals who were more separated. However, the evidence for the relationship between gender and complexity is equivocal. Hunt and Dopyesa (1966) found women to score higher in complexity, while others found men to be higher in complexity (Suedfeld & Bluck, 1993; Suedfeld & Piedrahita, 1984). Other researchers have found no gender differences (de Vries et al., 1993; de Vries & Walker, 1988).

Identity has also been examined in terms of complexity. Slugoski, Marcia, and Koopman (1984) examined the relation between complexity and the four ego identity statuses charted by Marcia (1966, 1976). Marcia coded identity statuses by way of responses to probes about sex, sex-role behaviors, occupation, political ideologies, and religion. Slugoski and colleagues (1984) found that individuals in the "high" identity statuses of achievement and moratorium had higher complexity scores than did "low" ego identity status individuals (foreclosure and diffusion). Similarly, Sullivan, McCullough, and Stager (1970) examined Loevinger's (1966) measure of ego development and found a moderate correlation with complexity. In an examination of ego functioning processes (Haan, 1977) and individuals' writings on religion, relationships, and commitments and values, Pitts and Lehman (1994) found mature, "coping" mechanisms (e.g., objectivity, empathy, concentration, and sublimination) positively correlated with complexity and immature, "defense" mechanisms (e.g., rationalization, regression, denial, and repression) negatively correlated with complexity. This suggests that lifestories, including the identities and other individual attributes embedded within them, may be further understood by examining the structure underlying and organizing the substance.

PERSONAL NARRATIVES AND COMPLEXITY: THE INFLUENCE OF LIFE EXPERIENCES

Butler (1963) has most often been credited with establishing empirical interest in the construct of life review and described it as "a naturally occurring, universal mental process characterized by the progressive return to consciousness of past experiences," the nature and outcome of which "are affected by the lifelong unfolding of character" (p. 66). Central to this definition is an understanding of the nature and forces shaping life, such as previous experiences and their meanings, and life events, and their effects. Cognitive effort is expended to achieve and maintain an ordered account of life (McAdams, 1985) and changes to the lifestory arise, in large measure, "as a consequence of normative or expected life events and eruptive or unexpected and, generally, adverse life events" (Cohler, 1982, p. 206). As Bruner (1987) has suggested, "we become the autobiographical narratives by which we 'tell about' our lives" and such life narratives "achieve the power to structure perceptual experience, to organize memory, to segment and purpose-build the very 'events' of a life" (p. 15). As identified by many authors including Birren and Hedlund (1987), Bruner (1987), Cohler (1982), Gergen and Gergen (1983), McAdams (1985), and Runyan (1982), the interpretation, reinterpretation, and eventual integration of the salient events of a life is the essence of a coherent personal narrative (see also de Vries, Blando & Walker, in press; Kenyon, this volume; Polkinghorne, this volume; Ruth & Kenyon, this volume).

The foregoing cognitive activities of structuring, organizing, and integrating are well articulated in the framework of integrative complexity. Moreover, the explicit involvement of these activities in assessing the ways in which life events are understood has been frequently described in the complexity literature. Such descriptions originated in the examination of stress on integrative complexity. For example, in an innovative archival analysis, Suedfeld and Tetlock (1977) examined speeches and diplomatic communications of leading decisionmakers written prior to international conflicts, including the Moroccan Crisis, World War I, the Berlin Blockade, the Korean War, and the Cuban Missile Crisis. They found that the complexity of the communications declined as the crisis turned to war, whereas there was an increase in the complexity of documents associated with those crises that were resolved peacefully or in compromise. Similar results were reported in the archival research of Suedfeld and Rank (1976) as well as Suedfeld, Tetlock, and Ramirez (1977).

The effects of war-related stress are not restricted to international decisionmakers, however. Governmental and military leaders evidenced comparable patterns of complexity in response to the stresses of war (Ballard, 1983; Suedfeld, Corteen & McCormick, 1986) as did other aristocratic and socially influential individuals (Porter & Suedfeld, 1981). A particularly intriguing study performed by Suedfeld (1980) examined the complexity of editorials in the *Bulletin of the Atomic Scientists* (a journal founded by scientists involved in the development of nuclear technology and shocked by its potentially disastrous applications) in relation to the hand of the "Doomsday Clock" (the *Bulletin*'s measure of impending nuclear war). As the hands of the clock moved closer to midnight, the complexity of the editorial decreased. "Presumably, the integrative level of editorials is influenced by the perception of the seriousness of world events that affect the likelihood of nuclear war" (Suedfeld, 1980, p. 121).

This "disruptive stress effect" (Suedfeld & Bluck, 1993) has also been seen with stressors other than war. For example, Porter and Suedfeld (1981) analyzed the personal correspondence of five famous authors and found that complexity was negatively related to illness and positively related to civil unrest. That is, adverse (and therefore stressful) changes in health were characterized by lower levels of complexity, while periods of civil unrest characterized higher complexity. This reduction may be a consequence of such factors as fearing for one's life, threats to one's values, economic hardship, or even the simplistic and rigid way in which information was presented, inhibiting an open and flexible interpretation of events.

Suedfeld and Bluck (1993) examined changes in complexity in relation to positive (e.g., major accomplishments, marriage, birth of child) and negative life events (e.g., illness, death of significant other) of 30 prominent individuals living primarily in the 19th and 20th centuries. The scores of complexity were derived from random samples of correspondence from periods immediately preceding, during, and following the events as identified in published biographies. The results revealed that positive events had no effect on complexity; in contrast, complexity levels rose from before to during the negative event and fell thereafter. This pattern was particularly true for men. This finding differs from the accumulating research evidence in the political decisionmaking studies suggesting decreases in complexity accompanying negative events. Suedfeld and Bluck (1993) account for this discrepancy by suggesting that personal events differ from larger societal events, for example, war, along dimensions of perceived control, the immediacy and sorts of decisions required, the balance between emotional and cognitive influences, and the anticipated duration of the crisis. The authors speculate that the sex difference is representative of the different coping styles of women and men; that is, a problem-solving focus, perhaps more characteristic of men, might be reflected in a greater investment of effort in information processing.

This use of biographical data in the assessment of complexity associated with stress in general or particular types of events is, in an interesting juxtaposition, archivally concurrent: stress and events are identified in one source (the published biographies of prominent individuals) and compared to the complexity as derived from an independent source (the posthumously published private correspondence). Biographies (and particuarly autobiographies), as explored in this book, are more frequently perceived in an hermeneutic framework; that is, one in which the emphasis is on the individual's construction and/or reconstruction of life from the perspective of the present. This interpretation, more in line with the life review construct, has yet to be fully explored using the integrative complexity construct (see de Vries et al., in press-b).

PERSONAL NARRATIVES AND COMPLEXITY: THE INFLUENCE OF AGE

Age and biography have been long-term conceptual associates; Buhler (1933), Butler (1963), Erikson (1976) and others have written about the life review as a task of the later years. This alleged age specificity of life review has recently been questioned, however (Kenyon, this volume; Thornton & Brotchie, 1987). Webster and Young (1988), for example, proposed that life review is an ongoing, dialectical process and that individuals of all ages regularly rewrite their autobiographies in the service of identity maintenance and enhancement. Supporting such a proposition in a preliminary way, Weenolsen (1986) found that age was unrelated to frequency of life review. Merriam and Cross (1982) found that younger and older adults (identity developing and synthesizing periods of the life course, respectively) reminisced with similar frequency and more than middle-aged adults, a finding at least partially corroborated by both Hyland and Ackerman (1988) and Webster (1989). These conceptual and empirical accounts suggest that life review is perhaps better understood as a life span process and not confined to the later years (e.g., Webster & Cappeliez, 1993).

Parallel discussions of development have been noted in the complexity literature. Initial writings on the relationship between complexity and age (e.g., Harvey, Hunt & Schroder, 1961) asserted increases in complexity during childhood and adolescence with relatively stable levels throughout the adult years. Early development was seen as highly dependent on training and upbringing and could be arrested at any one of the developmental levels if the proper conditions for progress were not met. This developmental orientation was abandoned with the explicit recognition of the interactive nature of environmental and dispositional factors within information processing (e.g., Schroder et al., 1967; Suedfeld, Tetlock & Streufert 1992).

Correspondingly, empirical evidence is equivocal on the association between chronological age and complexity. Porter and Suedfeld (1981), for example, reported a significant, positive relationship between age and complexity in an archival, pseudolongitudinal study of 19th- and 20th-century eminent authors. Eminence insured the presence of reliable biographical material. The data for this study comprised the posthumously published personal correspondence for each novelist in 5-year intervals (following Simonton, 1977). Suedfeld and Piedrahita (1984) reported no relation between complexity (again, as assessed in the published personal correspondence) and age in a similar archival, pseudo-longitudinal sample of deceased men and women from the 18th and 20th centuries who were considered eminent to the point of having had several biographies written about them. De Vries and colleagues (in press-b) and de Vries and others (1993) also reported no age differences between the young, middle, and older adults in their samples who, respectively, discussed the events of their pasts and wrote on their ideas about the experiences with death and dying. In contrast, Pratt and colleagues (1990) found negative association between age and complexity in a cross-sectional sample of younger and older adults, which they tentatively attribute to specific task demands.

In two separate studies, however, the influence of age on complexity has been somewhat more pronounced when age is identified not as time since birth but as time yet to live, that is, in the context of terminal drop (Kleemeier, 1962; Riegel & Riegel, 1972). Suedfeld and Piedrahita (1984), in particular, replicating the serendipitous findings reported in Porter and Suedfeld (1981), examined changes in complexity in the published correspondence written by individuals in the 10 years prior to their death. Seudfeld and Piedrahita found a significant decline in complexity in the 5 years preceding death. Among those for whom death came suddenly, there was no gradual decline during the 9 years prior to death, but a sharp average decline in the last year of life. The authors ponder if impairment of information processing capability is causally related to some forms of death or, provocatively, if reliable changes in complexity could be used to predict death as it has been used to predict the outbreak of armed conflict (Suedfeld, Tetlock & Ramirez,1977). The flexibility and versatility of complexity, particularly in the presence of archival and narrative materials, makes possible a response to such musings.

COMPLEXITY AND AUTOBIOGRAPHY

Autobiographies, personal narratives, and lifestories of all sorts may be characterized along several dimensions, including the timing of such stories (in a lifespan context) and the consequences of such storytelling, as well as by both content and construction or structure. The greatest proportion of the empirical efforts of psychologists has resided in trying to understand when such stories are told and the benefits of such storytelling. Less is known about the content that is revealed, and what has been relatively neglected is an understanding of the structure underlying this content. Complexity, a cognitive style construct characterizing the manifestations of the structure of individual thought, offers an avenue to begin to examine that structure and its associates and concomitants. The foregoing review has presented complexity in association with individual attributes, life experiences, and age, all significant facets or issues of life stories and personal narratives (and the life review in particular). Our task now is to package these issues more formally into an understanding of structure in the context of autobiography. This concluding section undertakes this task and is organized around an understanding of complexity as both product and process (dependent and independent variable).

Complexity as Product

Reviewed in the sections above are examples and analyses of complexity as a dependent variable. This "state" approach to complexity (Suedfeld, et al., 1992) has apparently received preferred status in the most recent empirical literature. Complexity is seen to vary, for example, as a function of personal and societal stress or turmoil, as well as illness and nearness to death. These analyses suggest that, in prospect, we may be able to predict important psychosocial events in an individual's life from the ways in which he or she presents information; alternatively, in retrospect, perhaps we can better understand the conditions of an individuals' life from the ways in which he or she has framed the relevant discussion. Perhaps the untold stress or psychological closure manifests itself in discussion form.

As such, complexity may be seen as an indirect assessment of the ways in which an individual is coping with the circumstances and events of a life. Broadly framed within this coping and the interpretive perspective, de Vries and colleagues (1993) examined individuals' representations of death and dying (as applied to the self, another, or in the abstract) as part of a Guided Autobiography exercise (see Birren & Birren, this volume; Birren & Deutchman, 1991; de Vries, Birren, & Deutchman, 1990, in press-a). They found that death was represented both more frequently and in more complex ways than was dying, and they attributed this difference to familiarity and experience: "Life holds more constant reminders of the loss of a loved one than the process by which that loss occurred" (de Vries et al., 1993, p. 370). Implicit in this interpretation is that the discussion of issues within an individual's realm of consideration is represented by greater complexity, the outcome of more extensive thought.

de Vries and colleagues (1993) also found that discussions of death and dying as applied to the self or in the abstract were presented in more complex terms than were the discussions of death or dying of a significant other. They suggest that although "another's death is a more frequent experience than one's own and may be a more frequent thought, it is also the substance of bereavement, grief, and mourning" (p. 371). The concomitant stress and emotional turmoil may serve to harness the complexity levels with which it is discussed. In contrast, the comparability of death and dying discussions relevant to the self or in the abstract may rest in the view that thoughts of our own death (or the process by which this death arrives) are almost by definition abstract or hypothetical and somewhat emotionally removed. Perhaps this relative emotional distance manifests itself in elevated complexity. The implications of these findings are that areas of greater relevance and personal significance (including distress) are represented in structurally different ways and are important dimensions to consider in examinations of personal narratives (see also Svensson, this volume).

Recently, de Vries and colleagues (in press-b) adopted a more formal and pointed analysis of the structure of the life review construct. Participants in their research included equal numbers of young, middle-, and older-aged women and men who identified the events of their past and then rated these events on a series of dimensions. Participants were also interviewed regarding their subjective evaluation of those events (a narrative life review), the transcribed discussions of which were coded for integrative complexity. Results indicated, perhaps not surprisingly, that those in middle and later adulthood identified a greater number of events than did those in early adulthood. For all participants, positive events outnumbered negative events by a ratio of three to one, and with minor exceptions, men and women of all ages also rated their events as high on dimensions of intensity, responsibility, adjustment, and anticipation. Greater complexity was associated with events rated as low on adjustment (implying continued and sometimes implicit effort at understanding and/or acceptance of the event, a Zeigarnik effect), responsibility (implying that those events not of an individual's own doing may require greater cognitive effort), and anticipation. This latter finding perhaps supports Neugarten's (1970) assertion that unanticipated events are the ones most likely to introduce dissonance, the resolution of which results in greater complexity. In addition, greater complexity was associated with events rated as more intense and negative, perhaps requiring, in retrospect, some cognitive effort on the part of the individual in the search for understanding and meaning. These patterns were found for men and women of all ages, except on the latter two dimensions for women in the oldest age group, similar to Suedfeld and Bluck's (1993) study, suggesting some provocative and subtle age and sex distinctions in life review construction.

What are the information processing consequences of storytelling, and life revew in particular? Amidst the waving of cautionary flags, a fairly extensive and growing literature exists testifying to the positive consequences of life review and the autobiographical process (Burnside, this volume; Coleman & Gearing, this volume; Kenyon, this volume; Randall, this volume; Ruth & Kenyon, this volume). Birren and Deutchman (1991) have summarized much of this empirical literature (as previously described) and identify gains in areas relating the self (understanding and esteem), time perspective, motivation and energy, adaptability, and cognitive functioning. Clearly, these acquisitions have information processing (i.e., complexity) correlates, most pronounced in the latter examples. Birren and Deutchman (1991) write, for example, that "memories of prior experiences enter consciousness together with their past and present emotions" which provide "material for synthesis and integration of past with the present" (p. 19). This is more than a similarity in language; both are suggesting a change in the underlying structure of the ways in which information is processed. This represents fertile ground for subsequent research.

Complexity as Process

Complexity may also be seen as an independent variable, along the lines of its "trait" roots (Schroder et al., 1967). That is, the characteristic ways in which we process information are associated with opinion extremity and a host of attributes, as previously reviewed. Such characteristic processes are also likely to exert their influence in the ways in which lives are reviewed or stories are told.

In particular, complexity may predict the shape or form of the story being told; for example, complexity may be associated with the ways in which events are identified or what becomes an event. To examine this intriguing hypothesis, we reanalyzed some of the data previously described (de Vries et al., in press-b). Specifically, we examined the relation between complexity and the total number of events identified by the 60 participants of the study. For each participant, a complexity score was derived from a measure of self-evaluation (responses to the identity question, "Who am I?") completed prior to the identification and explanation of the events of a life. We created three groups of scores on the complexity measure to reflect meaningfully different levels of information processing (as previously described). Scores of 1 and 2 comprised the group labelled "low differentiation" (n = 22); scores of 3 comprised the group labelled "high differentiation" (n = 25); scores of 4 or greater comprised the group labelled "integration" (n = 13). The strong curvilinear relationship found between the number of life events and these complexity groups is presented as Figure 9.1.

This interesting finding not only attests to the executive function performed by complexity, but also serves as a sort of construct validity for the various

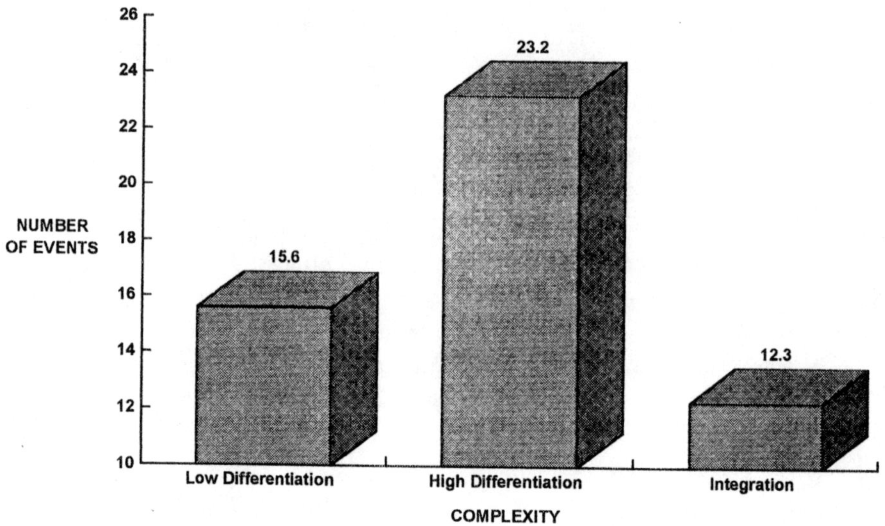

FIGURE 9.1. The relationship between the number of life events and complexity groups.

scoring levels. One would expect that simplistic information processing (e.g., "x or y") would be associated with a smaller overall pool of items than would more highly differentiative processing (e.g., "x and y"). More integrative processing (e.g., "xy"), alternatively, might incorporate a greater number of these parts and pieces into some overarching or synthetic whole. For example, one older participant, whose self-evaluation complexity score fell in the third group, identified a total of six life events. One event was labelled "conversion to Catholicism" and contained several job experiences, two changes in dwelling, a marriage, and a divorce. Nevertheless, she explained that although these "sub-events" were of importance, their true relevance laid in their service of the superordinate event. They were embedded in some hierarchical structure, this in integration.

Watt and Wong recently have proposed a reminiscence typology delineating six categories or types (Wong & Watt, 1991). Indicative of integrative reminiscence is the acceptance of one's life and resolution of past conflicts and negative life events. Characteristic of instrumental reminiscence is the recollection of, and drawing from, past plans, goals, and difficulties in order to address current problems. The function of transmissive reminiscence is to transfer one's legacy and cultural heritage. Indicative of escapist reminiscence is the glorification of the past and condemnation of the present. Obsessive reminiscence is characterized by ruminations about problematic and unresolved past experiences, often housed in feelings of guilt. Narrative reminiscence reflects a descriptive recollection of the past. Wong and Watt (1991) found both integrative and instrumental reminiscence to be associated with successful aging (i.e., mental and physical well-being).

Perhaps there are also structural correlates of these types of reminiscence, some of which may also be associated with successful aging. For example, the integrative and intrumental types of reminiscence might be most frequently found amongst those whose characteristic complexity levels are higher. In contrast, lower complexity is expected to be associated with escapist and narrative reminiscence. Developing a structural framework that is coherent and extends through time requires greater complexity than does a structure that is either value-laden or purely descriptive. Transmissive reminiscence may be associated with more simplistic or complex structures, depending on the extent to which the audience is considered in the presentation. Similarly, obsessive reminiscence may be simple or complex if it is mired in guilt on the one hand, or highly scrutinizing and vigilant on the other. These and other interesting biographical hypotheses derived from an individual difference vantage point on integrative complexity await empirical attention.

CONCLUSION

This chapter presented integrative complexity, a cognitive style construct characterizing the structure of individual thought as manifested in verbal materials, in the context of personal narratives. The relevant empirical research was reviewed highlighting the interface of complexity with other salient aspects of personal narratives, namely, individual attributes, life experiences, and age. This review brought to the foreground an understanding of complexity as an analytical tool (an independent or dependent variable) in the study of autobiography and identified provocative areas for subsequent research.

Implicit in this review, however, has been the uncovering and/or highlighting of several other issues of interest to researchers in the field of biography. For example, biographies may be characterized by both their content and construction, each revealing unique messages and together revealing a more holistic image of the life being reported. Furthermore, using complexity as a lens through which biographies are examined offers a rare opportunity to question and target the defining features of biographical content. The identification of individual attributes (or personality), experience and events, and age (or time) attests to the naturalness of complexity in this enterprise. Finally, complexity, particularly as applied to narrative documents in the creative research of Suedfeld, Tetlock and others, also fosters an awareness of the vast range of materials that are biographically relevant and prime for exploration. Couched in terms of what and how we report on both the particulars and generalities of our lives are evidence of who we are and how we think. Integrative complexity offers a language and a tool for organizing and understanding this valuable information.

10

Ways of Life: Old Age in a Life History Perspective

Jan-Erik Ruth, Ph.D., and Peter Öberg, Ph.D.

The primary objective of this study was to describe the ways of life of Finns from the generation of "the Wars and the Depression." A second objective was to describe and understand how the life lived is reflected on and gives meaning to old age. The more detailed research questions included the following. (1) How does a way of life originate and which factors affect its maintenance? (2) Can changes appear in ways of life, and what is the impact of sociohistorical versus personal events in forming ways of life? (3) Are there some especially hard and problematic ways of life, and what are the origins of such ways of life?

The data in the study consisted of taped and transcribed life stories, thematical questions on the life lived, data on life at present, and perceptions of the future. Participation in the study was voluntary and the interviews were conducted in the respondents' homes. A group of 37 strategically selected older men and women constitute the group of respondents. The data analysis was based on the constant comparisons principle of the grounded theory method (Glaser & Strauss, 1967). The credibility of the results is addressed by negotiations aiming at consensus between the researchers and a group of experts partaking in a larger Scandinavian study on the same topic (Waerness, Ruth, & Tornstam, 1993).

In this study the concept "*way of life* "was adopted rather than "*life style*" because the latter connotes a totally self-chosen mode of living. We define "*way of life*" as the strategy that an individual uses in order to utilize those resources and possibilities that social background, education, tradition and the economy have created" (see Weber, 1947). Ways of life are to be understood as theoretical constructs which illuminate and do not directly reflect empirical reality, and which make it possible to structure the data in a logically consistent manner. The intention of this hermeutically oriented study is to create concepts and describe life patterns among a group of contemporary older persons, however, inferences regarding ways of life in the population in general are neither appropriate nor possible on the basis of this research design.

THE STRATEGIC SAMPLE AND THE COLLECTION OF DATA

The study focused on urban individuals living alone in Helsinki, representing the older old portion of the population between 73–83 years of age. The respondents were selected to represent occupations that, theoretically speaking, allowed for different degrees of freedom in steering careers and the life course in general. Included in the sample were "careerists," representing persons from leading positions and public administration; "entrepreneurs," that is, persons with private practices or private enterprises; "employees," such as office clerks and factory workers; and "women from a generation past," representing housewives or daughters at home (see Höjrup, 1984).

The generation studied was born between 1905 and 1915 and as such they had experienced the Civil War as children, the Depression as young adults seeking employment, the Winter War, and finally, the Continuation War (1939–1944) when beginning their family life. According to Roos (1985a,b, 1988) this generation has been called "*the generation of the Wars and the Depression.*" Typical experiences for Finns of that generation were: poverty, separation from family in childhood and possibly living in an orphanage, the death of a parent, interrupted schooling, difficulties in finding employment, shortage of goods, and periods of illness. The lifestories presented below partly verify but also alter this picture, especially in the case of the urban middle and upper-class individuals in the study.

Participation in the study was invited through announcements in several newspapers, one published by the Social Insurance Institution in Finland, which is available to all retirees. Letters to former Finnish "Who's Who" persons, a group who did not spontaneously volunteer to participate, completed the sample. Previously married and single retirees were chosen, because of our interest in studying how an aging individual coped with life without the resource of a spouse. Furthermore, urban elderly were chosen, because that way of life has become increasingly more common.

Altogether 37 respondents participated, 23 women and 14 men. The respondents were interviewed in their homes, in most cases on two visits. Various kinds of data were collected from interviews averaging 7–1/2 hours in length and ranging from 4 to 16 hours. An open, subjective life history was conducted at first followed by a semistructured interview concerning central life themes. A description of an ordinary day in old age, as well as demographic data on the life lived, was also attained. In the life history interview, the respondent was given the role of the subject of the story, who autonomously decided what should and what should not be included. The respondent also decided how and in which order the elements in the story would be told (see Roos, 1988).

METHOD OF ANALYSIS

The data were taped and transcribed, producing approximately a total of 2,200 pages of text. From these a summary text of 4–7 pages per respondent was made. The objective was to condense the data to a manageable length, saving as much as possible the everyday explanations of life in the original data, that is, the self-understanding of the respondents of their everyday world (Alasuutari, 1990; Gergen, 1988). All data were computerized, with many checks on the original expressions and the context in which they occurred in different stages of the analytical process. Original statements of the respondents that were used to illuminate abstractions produced by the analysis could easily be identified in this database.

Attaining a more abstract understanding and description of the data was the departure point of the analysis. The data were approached through the research questions set up for the study. The main question concerned which patterns of life, or "*ways of life*" were discernable in the data material. Related questions concerned how a way of life develops and which factors maintain it. Other questions pertained to the influence of personal and sociohistorical life events in forming and maintaining ways of life. The lifespan perspective was central here in that we were interested in how the life lived was reflected in older age and how an optimal or dysfunctional old age could be interpreted in a life history perspective.

First, with inspiration from the grounded theory method (Glaser & Strauss, 1967; Strauss & Corbin, 1990), the most startling case in the data and the contrast case were searched for. These proved to be two linear stories, one of misery and one of happiness. According to the dominant qualities in the stories, these ways of life were labeled "the *bitter life*" and "*the sweet life*". Analysing further stories, the typology was then supplemented with two discontinuous accounts of life, "*life as a trapping pit*" and "*life as a hurdle race*". At the end of the analysis the typology was completed with two gender-specific ways of life, "*the devoted*", "*silenced life*" and "*life as a job career*". The typology and the characteristics for each way of life will be discussed in detail in what follows.

The analysis was based on analytical induction (Birren & Hedlund, 1987; Denzin, 1970, 1989a,b) whereby the theoretical way of life model (the typology) had been defined and redefined through analyzing every case until all cases had been considered and were consistent with the model. When "deviant cases" occurred during the process of analysis, they were seen as important tests of the credibility of the typology. From those cases that did not fit, new cues concerning the reformulation of the model could be attained. In this manner, the analysis progressed as an inductive spiral where the ways of life, their determinants, characteristics, and the case material were processed in the minds of the researchers until the typology gained its final form (see Eckert, 1988). Bertaux & Bertaux-Wiame (1981) used a similar method which they called a process of *saturation*.

In the first stage of the analytic process, an understanding of the life lived as a whole was attempted. The impression created by the text, and the connotative meaning that was derived from it was very important. Every respondent was gradually categorized according to a specific way of life, and grouped under a specific way of life label (Glaser & Strauss, 1967). In the next step of the analysis, the way of life that had been found was deconstructed. This was an attempt to check in more detail the denotative meaning of what was expressed and to extract central dimensions characterizing the ways of life (Strauss & Corbin, 1990). The dimensions can be seen in Table 10.1.

The main questions and testing of ideas for validating the results have been applied to the transcribed texts. Thus, questions concerning the importance of marriage and children, for example, were posed to all available data sources (the life story, the theme interview, and accounts of an ordinary day). These different data sources neatly complete a puzzle that otherwise would have shown missing pieces, but in some cases produced contradictory information and paradoxical statements (Rubinstein, 1988). These contradictions were accepted as part of the life world of the respondents and of their ways of telling their stories (Kvale, 1977, 1989). Attempts were made to interpret these statements in the context in which they were produced, but the ultimate principle for understanding their meaning was interpretation against the picture that was created of the respondent's life as a whole, i.e. the *emplotment* of the story (Polkinghorne, 1988, 1991).

TABLE 10.1 Ways of life among elderly Finns living alone

Analytical Dimensions:	*Ways of Life:* The Bitter Life	Life as a Trapping Pit	Life as a Hurdle Race	The Devoted Silenced Live	Life as a Job Career	The Sweet Life
Life begins	with misery & losses	neutrally/with difficulties	with despair & Losses	neutrally	neutrally	as a sweet dream
Relations to parents	negative & losses	distant/tight & loveless	positive/ losses	good/ bad	good/ losses	good
Marriage	unsatisfactory	good & childless/ unsatisfactory	bad, with alcoholim & illness	none	background support/ work companionship/ never married	very satisfying
Children	none/few	few	many	none	many/none	(very) many
Human relationships	negative & problematic	negative & problematic	earlier negative, now positive	rich/ a loner	rich social life/ a loner	positive & rewarding
Subjective health	bad; life-long health problems	bad; a central problem	good, in spite of some earlier problems	very good throughtout life	good/relatively good throughout life	very good throughout life
Locus of control	outer directed	lost control over life	regained control over life	outer directed	inner directed working life	inner directed
Self-image	the suffering one	the loser	the fighter	the altruist	the careerist	the happy one
Evaluation of life	not as expected	partly not as expected (now)	partly not as expected (earlier)	not as expected/ partly as expected	as expected	as expected
Old age	depression & isolation	depression & isolation	satisfied	satisfied	satisfied	content & happy
Perception of the future	gloomy	gloomy	positive	bright,irrespective of circumstances	positive	positive
	Demographical Description:					
N	8	4	8	3	8	6
Women	5	3	7	3	1	4
Men	3	1	1	0	7	2
Widow/er	3	3	5	1	4	5
Separated	1	1	3	0	0	0
Never married	4	0	0	2	4	1
Blue collar	6	1	5	1	0	0
White collar	2	2	0	2	5	6
Entrepreneurs	0	1	3	0	3	0

ON THE EPISTEMOLOGICAL NATURE OF WAYS OF LIFE

The ways of life identified in this study are to be considered as *ideal types* as set forth by Weber (1949). Weber built on the tradition of Kant, stating that "concepts are primarily analytical instruments for the intellectual mastery of empirical data and can be only that" (Weber, 1949, p. 106). Concepts become ideal types, and as such are not represented in complete conceptual purity in empirical reality. In other words, ideal types are rational, indisputable thought images (*Gedankenbild*), which illuminate reality *as if it were logical*. We know, however, that "life with its irrational reality and its store of possible meanings is inexhaustible" (Weber, 1949, p. 111). (See also Kenyon, this volume; Ruth & Kenyon, this volume.)

Weber observed the relationship between concepts and reality, and emphasized "the danger that the ideal type and reality will be confused with one another" (Weber, 1949, p. 101). While in content analysis we classify the empirical material according to given concepts, the ideal types are abstractions of a higher order of empirically grounded qualities. However, they cannot be used mechanically to classify individual cases. This is not a problem, and we can compare them with other ideal type concepts, such as individualism/collectivism, or introversion/extroversion, which are intellectual tools for understanding reality, but which have only relative and restricted validity.

We have thus created ideal types of ways of life through abstraction and by emphasizing certain elements that are essential for each type. However, types are always object-specific, or as Weber (1949) says, "in the cultural sciences concept construction depends on the setting of the problem" (p. 105). Moreover, "the concepts are not *ends* but are *means* to the end of understanding phenomena" (p. 106). Hence, ways of life are not to be seen as a final *result as such*, but rather as a way of structuring and understanding phenomena in relation to aging. In the present case our aim is to illustrate how different ways of life in old age form an integrated part of the whole life span, and how certain ways of life end up in a problematic rather than positive old age.

A CONCEPTUAL MODEL OF WAYS OF LIFE

The Bitter Life

The first way of life which emerged from the data (or was "lifted up" by the researchers) was named *"the bitter life."* The story describing this type of life started with hardships and problems. Those individuals representing this way of life lacked rewarding intimate human relationships, and the turning points in life were described as negative. They were often unmarried, or married but without children. In their stories they did not describe themselves as persons who were autonomously guiding their life course. Many of them were born in the countryside. Most of them belonged to the working class, and some to the middle class, according to their occupation later in life.

In many respects life for these *suffering ones* did not turn out the way they wished, often because of illness, both physical and mental. Even a reasonably good economic situation in old age did not turn their lives around. The experiences of life in old age were still gloomy, even depressive, as was the perception of the future. The feeling of alienation that these respondents expressed was tied to feelings of being different, outcast, or socially unsuccessful. Consider the following:

> I can't get rid of the feeling of not being like others. Worries and bitterness it has all been since childhood.

> I haven't been able to make any decisions. Life has made the decisions for me.

> My life has just been mistakes. I'm really unsatisfied with my life, but I can't change it, either.

This way of life somewhat resembles what Hankiss (1981) in a study of ontologies of the self calls "self-absolutory," a strategy used when present hardships are seen as mere reflections of earlier childhood problems. According to the way the respondents of the bitter life perceive their selves, there is a conflict between the self and the others. The world at large is seen as hard, unfair, even mean, and personal suffering is caused by forces out of control of the respondents. This way of life also shows some similarities to "the victims" in Saarenheimo's (1989) Finnish study on old age and mental health. In this study the victims tended to blame fate for the hardships they had encountered in life. The victims seemed to constantly derive reinforcement for their self-victimization and their depressive mood.

Many of the "*bitter life*" respondents had endured long periods of severe illness in their lives, in some cases resulting in permanent disability. Because of this, they lowered their standards for a possible spouse or decided to stay unmarried. Even in old age, poor health is seen as a barrier to an active social life and as a cause of the anxiety, fear, and depressive mood they often find themselves in. The fact that there are no longer any possibilities for working is also experienced as a terrible state of affairs. For example:

> I do not have a good time. I start panicking in my loneliness. Not until now have I really felt my retirement, it is disgusting. There is no meaning in this kind of life . . .

Life as a Trapping Pit

The "*life as a trapping pit* "way of life often started with emotional problems in relationships with parents, although in some cases life started "neutrally." Persons from all social strata can be found in this way of life. Marriage was problematic in many cases, but there were also a few rather good marriages. Usually the marriage was childless, however. A downward social mobility constituted a trap in this way of life for some respondents from an upper-class background.

Many respondents describe how they, just when life looked at its best, suddenly were trapped, and the traps occurred for some repeatedly throughout the life span. The last trap was the illness of a spouse, followed by their own illness which they did not successfully cope with in old age. Because of these negative turning points, life did not turn out as expected.

A typical account of childhood experiences is:

> What a child really needs is love. I got a roof over my head, food in my belly and a proper home. But there never was any motherly love, no affection.

Whereas in the bitter life, there were health problems throughout, in the trapping pit the illnesses struck later. A male respondent described the illness of his wife:

> We never got a single happy day together in retirement. I was shocked when caring for my wife on her death bed. The cancer situated in the large intestine. The large intestine was removed and they had to pierce a hole here (in the stomach). And it all came out (the feces) from this opening and everything was poured out in the bed and I cared for her here. I changed the sheets and it all was poured out once more, within some minutes. There the whole thought (of sex) was stupefied, it vanished.

In this way of life there is a feeling of an earlier inner control of life that was lost. The loss of spouse or health in late life constituted part of the lost control. Even the self-image reflected this predicament in feelings of a lost youth and a lost vitality.

> I see an old man, a really old man (in the mirror). Earlier I was much more active, but no more. The steps are getting shorter . . . Now you get phlegmatic, you lose interest.

The days are considered rather trivial in old age for these respondents, and they stress their illnesses in their stories. Old age is described as gloomy, and a further disengagement from the world is projected into the future.

Some common features of this way of life and Hankiss's (1981) "compensatory strategy" can be found, even if these two types do not exactly overlap. The person with a compensatory strategy balances a gloomy present with memories of a bright past (Hankiss, 1981). The reasons for the mishaps of today are projected onto circumstances outside the respondent's control. In this study, however, the reasons for a good life turning bad are tied more to life events, "trapping pits," and the contrast between now and then is not produced through an idealization of life passed.

Life as a Hurdle Race

In the way of life, "*life as a hurdle race*", the impact of sociohistorical events are very visible (for a contrary view, see Kaufman, 1986). Rural living conditions in childhood formed both the value structures and the life-world (Schutz, 1967) for these respondents. The sociohistorical events pertained to circumstances, such as an execution of a father in the Civil War, the absence of a male or the death of a spouse during the wars, the evacuation of the family to other parts of the country, or the hard life because of severe economic problems.

However, in this way of life successful coping with hardships was followed by a feeling of worth and self-respect in old age. A woman states that her life initially did not turn out as she wished because of poverty, lack of education, and the necessity to emigrate to the capital in search for a job. But in old age she still says:

> Bitter am I not. I got a rich life this way, too. I'm not bitter even if I didn't get there where I strived for. In spite of it all I'm quite content. T'was not until in Helsinki that I really started to live.

The things that gave life meaning came later in life for these respondents. In "life as a hurdle race", the unwanted twists of life were actively coped with and life ended well. The respondents felt proud of their heroic struggle, of never giving up. The odds were against them, but as heroes in their own lives they fought and won the battle.

Good health in old age seems to be a prerequisite for this way of life. Occasional periods of illness have been overcome and some repression has to be used in defense against these negative memories by the respondents, most of whom were women. For example:

> Then I got married. For a year my husband's health was good, but then he got ill. This was an extremely hard and unpleasant time. During the Winter War his feet

> froze to his boots, that started polio and he got the feet amputated. This is nothing nice (to tell), concerning my family. You would gladly forget about it all. It is all over now.

In "life as a hurdle race" there was an outer locus of control to start with, but later the respondents gained an inner control of life. This was often the result of effective coping with problems, as described earlier. But in some cases, unpredicted turning points (like the death of a spouse), which could be interpreted as negative, actually turned their lives around in a positive way, as for those women who were mistreated by their aggressive and heavily drinking spouses.

> My life turned out to the better, when I was left alone. Now I am happy.
>
> I felt like a big dictator had died. I felt like a bird turned free from the cage.
>
> I always went on with my life. Never fell into any pit. I never bent from the hardships I saw.

Old age is experienced as a good time; the relationships with children and grandchildren are rewarding, as well as the freedom from former difficulties–spouse, poverty, or war. The future seems rather bright. In another study including younger Finns, Roos (1985a,b) described a way of life that is similar in many aspects: a life with rural background, often guided by outer events, but well handled through effective coping. Both positive and negative experiences were included in this way of life. The "life as a hurdle race" is also similar to "the antithetic strategy" (Hankiss, 1981) whereby a childhood of hardships teaches one to fight for a better adult life. In spite of bad odds, the respondents created a better life for themselves by never giving up.

The Devoted, Silenced Life

The "*devoted, silenced*" way of life was exclusively a female phenomenon. These women usually had a working-class background but later in life ended up in middle-class professions. They got there through stages of being maids for academic families, as caregivers to their relatives' children, or (in most cases) to their own parents. Life is experienced as guided by others in a devoted, silenced life, and because they were unmarried and childless the women never really got the life they hoped for. Relationships with their parents were often ambivalent, but they made serious efforts to adapt to their circumstances and devoted their lives to the care of others.

> It was all given, perhaps my mission in life. But I'm still not satisfied with that mission, or with my life, but there was never no choice. The main meaning in my life was caring for my active father for twenty years. It's how I was, otherwise I can't find any meaning with my life.

Taking the needs of others into account often resulted in giving up their own goals and pursuits. For these caretaking, altruistic women, outer forces turned their lives around; they were never active agents in directing life's flow.

> I've certainly been some kind of driftwood. Pushes from here and there, things that happened have taken me in certain directions, without my cooperation.

The respondents adapted to life events partly by lowering their own aspiration level (see Tornstam, 1987) and they ended up rather satisfied with life in old age. A good life was described as silent, ordinary, and honest, where the well-being of other human beings was taken into consideration. It is a life with Christian values and temperance.

In old age contentment arises from the absence of caretaking duties and a freedom from living up to the expectations of others. Good health and a reasonably good economic situation add to this "everyday contentment." The future seems quite bright for these women, who always seem to find a way of adapting to the circumstances.

> I will live here (in the service flat) as long as it is all right. Then I won't complain if I have to move to a hospital. I have always felt at home where I have been situated.

The respondents with a devoted, silenced life expressed no special plans for the future. With a humble heart, following "God's will," these women will continue to fulfill the expectations that are put on a "decent woman," according to the behavioral expectations of their time. This way of life shows some common features with the type of personality integration that Saarenheimo (1989) calls "the always adaptable". Individuals in this category have a life strategy which has shown an adaptation to others, to an extent that partly hampered their own growth as an adult, and in becoming independent agents in their own lives.

Life as a Job Career

"*Life as a job career*" is mainly a way of life for middle-and upper-class men from an urban environment. In the primary analysis, this way of life was labeled "the arduous working life," but the label was altered because of its misleading connotations (see Ruth & Öberg, 1992). The life story of these men is linear, even straight, and it often takes the form of a curriculum vitae. The respondents tell of their several jobs and their commissions of trust. Most of the turning points in life are job changes. Managing directors and professors tell of their lives according to their achievements. Even the social network of friends and colleagues is presented according to the titles they hold or the achievements they have made.

These careerists have either stayed unmarried, or they have been married to a spouse that served them well, staying in the background. When telling about their lives, they stress career matters, and family matters take second place. In some cases the spouses or children are not even mentioned, if not specifically asked about.

> Work has to be done. My work has mostly been the important thing (in life). Primarily it has been my work.

The distinction between private and public matters is stressed by most respondents. This can be seen in the thematic interviews, where the respondents use the terms *most persons* or *the aged* when asked about matters concerning the life lived. In many cases repression is used by the respondents, as evidenced in very general, seemingly philosophical answers to personal questions. The marking of distance can even be seen in the way the interviewer is received into the home. He is invited only to the study or sitting room, seldom shown memorabilia from family life (such as photographs of children or grandchildren), but in some cases is shown pictures of prominent persons in society whom the respondents have met. The following discourse evolved between the researcher (Q) and a managing director (A):

Q: What major moments of joy have there been in your life?
A: Well, do I have to start thinking about those again. There have been some for sure. One moment of joy was when I was received by the Minister of Economy while visiting Sweden. Not everybody could state that in the year 1960.
Q: What major moments of sorrow have there been in your life?
A: Nobody can do without those, yes.
Q: What have they been?
A: When I lost my father, to start with . . .
Q: Have there been some other sorrows?
A: There are always sorrows tied to others. It's said: Bear the burden of each other . . .
Q: Were there some other major losses in adult life?
A: Uhuh, remember your own faults and forget those of others. I won't accuse anybody of anything.

The respondent even in old age shows the autonomy he has always been used to, and he will actively decide what life experiences will be made public and which will not, even in discussions concerning the image of the Self. Being needed, important, and valued by others or society in general can be seen in expressions like "the contributions I made to society and my country," "my literary enterprise," or "my contributions during the war."

The life stories project a person with a firm grip on life, an inner control that is extended well into old age. There is still a sense of continuity concerning the job career in subscribing to professional journals and accepting new leading positions in retirement associations or other interest groups. This can, in some cases, be considered as positive, but in others as a somewhat manic defense against the awareness of aging. Some respondents still attend to the extended family of former employees, who are evidently still needed to sustain the self-image of a careerist.

> I stroll along there from time to time (in the company building) because they like to meet their former boss, reminiscing how well things were during my time.

Life as a job career resembles a way of life that Roos (1985a,b) has labeled "I'm doing well, perhaps too well, am I not?" Good control in official spheres of life is characteristic of this way of life, but positive experiences from the private sphere are scarce. Thus, a construction of facades is used as a defense for peekers behind the "wall of happiness." Two of Saarenheimo's (1989) integration types of personality show some common features with life as a job career, namely "The architects of one's own fortune" and "The guardians of their own borders." The former had received their life satisfaction from leadership roles in job-related activities. By splitting "those frail, complaining oldsters" and "we able, active ones" into two separate categories, they retain a good morale, or a defense against depression in old age.

The Sweet Life

Most of the "sweet life" respondents tell stories about a good start in life, a rather happy marriage, and many children and grandchildren. Life has been fulfilling and self-actualizing within many arenas; family life, work, and leisure. Throughout life, an active engagement in life can be seen. The life story mostly starts like a beautiful dream:

> What do I remember from childhood? Sunshine days, as every kid does.

In retrospect, life seems to have turned out just as wished, even without delineated life goals and plans. Most developmental tasks concerning family and work get a positive, even exuberant evaluation.

> My life has been so colorful and rewarding. My wife was great, blessed, gifted, has given birth to six super gifted children. My life has been filled with assignments. I loved my studies . . . I am quite happy to be a physician, happy over my life companion. Now I have got a beautiful home, and I would like to enjoy it for some more. And my (new) partner (fiancée) who is so fervently good with me. So, I'm curious about life.

The sense of inner control over life is even projected to the health area. By adopting a healthy life, perceiving situational medical problems as "natural" or "minor," and actively seeking proper care, good health was guaranteed. This concerns the health status of the spouse, too. A woman with a manic-depressive husband states that he still, on the whole, did not have any severe medical problems, and since he was the depressed one, she did not see why she should suffer from it.

The feeling of firm inner control over life and effective personal coping can be seen in many statements. If fate intervened, it was mostly in a positive way.

> I would say, that the main architect (of life) has been me. But you have to admit, that in one way or another you get the support of others, too, living a long life.

A well webbed social network constituted a natural support system throughout life. If there were some marital problems, these are not stressed in the accounts, but the subject is the way problems were overcome. As part of the coping process there seems to be a basically optimistic stance towards life. Life was described as "a piece of cake." For an aged woman, the loss of the spouse was not stressed, but the good time they had together before the husband's death.

Even in old age the respondents follow their positive life script (McAdams, 1993). They recognize their own aging, but they still feel young for their age. For example, one male respondent recognizes an old man's face in the mirror, but he feels at the same time that the face shows a refined, cultured contour. Even in old age, there are expressions of being not only content, but happy. There is also often a sense of being important and privileged. These respondents have had, and still have, the capacity to create and retain relationships and social arenas and to be special in a crowd where the majority seem to be victims of external forces (Roos, 1985a,b).

> Even seen from the view point of the republic, I must have made an impact.

The "sweet life" in old age consists of engagement and having a good time. Like the lived life, even the future seems quite bright. A solid economy, many children and grandchildren, and activities of different kinds keep these respondents active. In the "sweet life" there is no anxiety concerning death, either, in spite of the belief that life does not continue after death. The "sweet life" has been described in two other Finnish studies in ways resembling our findings. Roos (1985) calls this way of life "a harmonious, really happy life;" its characeristics are autonomy and effective coping. No barriers are built between the formal and informal, because there seems to be nothing to hide. Characteristics include good education or social background that produces competence (Svensson, this volume), a rewarding family life, and a blend of interests.

Saarenheimo (1989) called a type with a similar way of adapting to life "the flexible," showing an openness to life experiences and the way of stressing the positive aspects in the life lived. A constructive dependence on significant others is also mentioned by Saarenheimo. Hankiss (1981) terms this type of biography a "*dynastic strategy*", in which a successful life in middle age is but a reflection of an even happier and grander childhood. In these biographies, Hankiss says, there can be seen an attitude of "we are special and superior." Some prominent Finnish writers have also expressed in their life stories a kind of "family superiority" as the reason for creative output later in life (Ruth, 1989).

WAYS OF LIFE BY CLASS, SEX AND TIME

The foregoing ways of life did not follow any strict social class boundaries, even though some central trends could be detected. The "*sweet life*" and "*life as a job career*" were mainly ways of life of people with urban background, in upper or middle-class families, and with little vertical social mobility. The respondents generally had leading positions in professional life. "*Life as a hurdle race*" and "*the devoted, silenced life*" were represented by people from a rural or working-class background with certain upward social mobility. This occurred even though the respondents themselves did not experience their lives as being very much different from their parents' lives.

"*The bitter life*" and "*life as a trapping pit*" crossed over class boundaries. These respondents had both rural and urban backgrounds and represented all social classes. These ways of life cannot be understood without considering other characterictics, such as illness or problematic relationships, which often affected people's lives early on. Typically in these ways of life, problems continued, or even increased, towards old age. Of importance is the finding that the effects of material resources did not erase the problems the respondents experienced.

The described ways of life were not unambiguously divided according to sex.

Only the *"devoted, silenced life"* was typically female, while *"life as a job career"* was mostly a male way of life. However, certain typical male–"versus"–female features could be detected in the life stories when considering how the narrator presented her/himself.

In women's life stories one can see clear traces of their socialization as caregivers. The women from working-class and rural families learned their role at home where their mothers raised them, or when they entered the labor market as maids. They were expected to put other people's needs before their own. For the women raised in middle-or upper-class families, who had close contact with both parents in childhood, the caregiver's role came later on as they set up families and often, at that point, discontinued their own careers. As women told their stories they often expressed themselves in the plural form "we", which reflected their roles as caregivers and emotional leaders in the family.

It seems obvious that the *"devoted, silenced life,"* was cohort-bound. This way of life, as well as the role of housewife, represented most of the female respondents as least at some point in their lives. It was formed because of social structures and norm expectations in former times. This has changed, as more and more women have entered the labor market and public caregiving has been developed.

The men's life stories reflected a more active narrator in control of his own life. The socialization of men as careerists and supporters was especially evident in life as a job career, in which life consisted of work performances and the family was merely a background setting. In the careerists' world, the concept of family was sometimes extended to cover employees, colleagues, and other representatives of the social network. In *"the sweet life"*, the men combined successfully, and in a rather modern way, the roles of supporter, lover, and father. When the wife died, these men had developed new love relationships in old age.

Bearing in mind the urbanization and modernization processes in our society, the ways of life anchored in urban middle-and upper-class backgrounds will probably become more common. Therefore, the cautious projection we dare to make is that the ways of life of *"life as a job career"* and possibly even "*the sweet life*", will be shared by more and more people in the future.

Predicting the future is always risky, however. According to Wittgenstein (1922), the future can never be fully anticipated or explained by present day conceptualizations. Another prediction ventured by Roos (1994) is that two central elements in future Finnish ways of life will be reflexivity and ambivalence. How future ways of life are connected to these postmodernistic constructs remains to be seen.

THE IMPORTANCE OF THE SPOUSE

We worked with two contradictory hypotheses concerning the significance of living unmarried for old age. On the one hand, the unmarried would have been a more exposed group among the elderly, because they lacked the resources of a spouse, for example, during illness. On the other hand, we could assume that the unmarried had a greater continuity in their lives, because they did not need to experience the illness or death of a spouse.

We found certain support for both of these hypotheses, the main trend being that the respondents, quite unexpectedly, managed their lives very well, even without a spouse. In "the bitter life", we could find an exposed group of elderly people living alone. Illness often filled their lives, they felt themselves lonely and depressed, and some of them expressed a death wish.

However, we found several groups of elderly who had gradually adjusted to solitude, had chosen it by themselves, or had been able to compensate for it in old age. These people had survived the deaths of their close ones, had gone on with their lives, any maybe even found new relationships (as in "the sweet life"). Or perhaps they had found themselves at ease with living alone and experienced an everyday contentment in old age (as in "the devoted, silenced life"). Or, they were still actively participating in various social activities, maintained contact with old colleagues, and made new acquaintances (as in "life as a job career").

Many respondents did not ever want any new intimate partners in old age. One explanation for this, common for both men and women, was that their marriage had been so good they could not consider a new one. They did not want to destroy the memory of the old spouse, or they thought they could never find anyone as good. A contrary explanation was that they had had such a negative experience from the first marriage that they did not want to repeat the same mistake. The unmarried men and women, who did not want to marry earlier in life, did not want it in old age either.

Of those wanting a new relationship, men were usually more positive about the idea. Their explanation was the companionship and care marriage provided for them. The men in our study who had new relationships, however, lived in open relationships, living separately and unmarried. For the women who did not want a new relationship, the explanation was basically the same as for men who wanted it, namely, caregiving. The women were careful not to end up in a caregiving situation again, especially with an aging and sick man.

TIMING, LOCUS OF CONTROL AND COPING

One of the results of this study was that certain generally used theoretical concepts in gerontology and social psychology seemed to assume a new meaning. Our analysis showed, for example, that for the respondents the concept of *timing* had a different meaning than what was generally assumed in the research literature (Neugarten, 1968). For the respondents, being "on-time" did not necessarily depend on whether the events or turning points had occurred at a point defined by society, or at a point typical of "a normal life cycle" (For a further discussion of biography and time, see Kenyon, 1991, this volume).

In "the bitter life," many major events in life had happened at the wrong time. People also felt they had been affected by harsh events, that their lives often turned towards a more negative direction. In "the sweet life," however, events came at the right time. Life events were assessed as positive, and respondents themselves actively created opportunities in their own lives. The consequences of a turning point were important in that if the consequences were positive, people experienced the event as happening at the right moment.

Furthermore, it seems obvious that the concepts of timing and *locus of control* (see Rotter, 1966; Schaie & Willis, 1991) have a connection. If individuals had an inner control over their own lives, turning points came at the right moment. Here it can also be seen how the life lived, "life as a whole," affects the interpretation of separate life events in the phenomenological analysis of life in retrospect. In the life cycle perspective we can see how the locus of control can dynamically change during a lifetime. This was manifested in the life as a hurdle race, where the respondents did not experience an inner control over their lives until old age.

The case was reversed in the life as a trapping pit. In spite of good control early in life, the respondents felt they had lost control as they had aged. These findings indicate that there is no "typical aging pattern" concerning locus of control (see Schaie & Willis, 1991). For some people control increased, and for others it decreased. For a third group of people, the experienced degree of control remained more or less constant throughout life, as in "the bitter life" and "the sweet life."

There are seldom any "typical" or "uniform" features of the aging process applicable to all older persons. This idea is further confirmed when we study the coping mechanisms people use in controlling their lives, the defense mechanisms they use in order to avoid awareness of problems, or even what kind of picture they create of themselves during their lifetime. Every way of life was *de facto* characterized by divergent *self-images* of the respondents. In "the bitter life" we saw "*the sufferer,*" in "life as a trapping pit" we saw "*the loser,*" in "life as a hurdle race" "*the fighter,*" in "the devoted, silenced life" "*the altruist,*" in "life as a job career" "*the careerist,*" and in "the sweet life" "*the successful.*"

Much in the same manner, people in different ways of life employed divergent *coping strategies*. In "the sweet life", people had an attitude that they were special and privileged. They felt they could control their lives and create life, and they felt optimistic. Favorable external circumstances and psychological mechanisms, such as rationalization, intellectualization, and positive outlook, helped the respondents always to emphasize the positive things in life.

In "life as a hurdle race", people succeeded in mastering illness and other problems, and they managed to integrate earlier difficulties in life with a good old age. Even though people admitted that life did not always turn out the way they wished, they experienced old age as the best time of their lives. Their strength consisted in never giving up. These life stories showed that an idyllic depiction of past difficulties was not a general pattern in the retrospective reports.

In "life as a job career", life was guided mainly by the career, the primary goal in life. Social skills helped to create contacts and networks, which further supported this goal. These achievement-oriented people were seldom affected by any other aspect of life on a deeper level. The family was more of a background for the career than a social or interpersonal arena in itself. Denial and certain chronic defenses obviously contributed to the fact that problems never intruded on the respondents in a threatening way, not even in old age.

In "the bitter life" and "life as a trapping pit," old age became one of life's main tragedies. External hardships, together with unsuccessful coping with illness, economic problems and difficult relationships, led to feelings of alienation and depression. The illness of old age gave the respondents a constant confirmation of the victimized position they held. Disease bled their life force and predicted their death. The respondents used a certain amount of projection and they easily blamed others, or fate, for the problems they experienced.

In the "devoted, silenced life," which did not always turn out as expected, the respondents still managed to reach a serene satisfaction in old age. This was explained by favorable external circumstances, as well as by freedom from restraints and caregiving responsibilities. Adaptability bordering on self-sacrifice always made adjustment seemingly easy. This adjustment, however, took place at the expense of individual growth and provided a life that was, to some extent, unlived.

CONCLUSION

It can be stated that our analysis showed that two of these ways of life produced *a problematic old age*; "the bitter life "and "life as a trapping pit." "The representatives of these ways of life experienced old age as a time of health problems, powerlessness, and an inability to control their lives. The life histories depicted them as losers, suffering stigmatized individuals, who had lost their life force and who had negative expectations about old age.

The other ways of life showed various ways of achieving *a good old age.* "The sweet life" was characterized by a good childhood with satisfactory economic conditions, and good relationships gave life a positive tone from beginning to end. People in this category felt they could control their lives and master their misfortunes. Life as a job career was centered around professional performance, and family was secondary. The career offered satisfaction during adult life for these men, and engagement in work or other activities continued in old age.

"Life as a hurdle race" was described as a life that began with difficulties but, with the assiduity and perseverance of the respondent, ended happily. In the lives of these respondents it could clearly be seen how external, sociohistorical events affected the beginning of life. At the same time it could be seen how inner factors, that is, coping, were a way to regain inner control of life. In "the devoted, silenced life", the last of the good old age types, life had consisted of taking care of others and that caregiving had guided the respondents' lives. Even in old age a streak of unselfishness could be detected in these women. The professional lives of these women had been favorable and in old age they could, with the benefit of a relatively good economic situation, enjoy their new freedom from caregiving responsibilities.

In addition to the differentiated aging patterns, the analysis showed that gerontological knowledge based solely on current circumstances is not adequate. The physical, psychological, and social functional capacity are explained by the circumstances in childhood, adolescence, and adult life. Aging must be seen as a continuation of an integrated process, starting with earlier life, where the life lived gives meaning to old age (see also Öberg & Ruth, 1994).

11

Experienced Aging as Elucidated by Narratives

Riitta-Liisa Heikkinen, Ph.D.

> Meaning and time constitute a distinctive, individual texture of life in which the historical and cultural landscape provide the horizon.

THE NARRATIVE SELF

The identity of the self is constructed in and through the story, the narrative that runs from beginning to end, from birth to death of the self. This narrative, as a story that proceeds through consecutive events, cannot be anticipated, but is nonetheless the telos of a life (Kusch, 1988). The narrative is a concept of crucial importance in any attempt to understand how we know ourselves, each other, and the world around us. By telling their story, people can reach down into themselves as well as reaching each other (Kenyon, this volume; Ruth & Kenyon, this volume).

Charles Taylor says that our interpretations of ourselves partly constitute our stories (Taylor, 1977). In other words, we "create" ourselves by and in the process of storytelling. Internal speech often accompanies our "doing" in life. We tell ourselves (or, more precisely an internalized other) what we have done, and how we anticipate and justify our acts (Kusch, 1988; Taylor, 1977).

With respect to lifestories and time, Samuel Beckett has shown in his play *Krapp's Last Tape*, how both the past and future are beyond our reach. The same, alas, may apply, at least in part, to the present. One way in which we can try to uncover past and present stages of the individual's life is to examine documentary material produced by that individual. When we want to understand and interpret people and the events that have been important to them personally, we can interview them or study written accounts they have produced.

We look at our past through the present, which is the present we share with others; there exists no present that is not permeated by the future (Kenyon, this volume). Our relationship to the future changes as we grow older, as the future grows shorter. Nevertheless, Martin Kusch (1988) notes that the question of "who I am" always presupposes the question of "who will I be." Polkinghorne (1988) says that in Heidegger's analysis of temporal experience, the most profound level of understanding is the realization that one's personal existence is coming to an end. This realization elevates the experience of personal time to a unity in which the past, the present, and the future and one's existence are seen as a whole, a single episode. The narrative story is the mode of meaning construction that displays various experiences with time.

For some years now I have been convinced that the narrative approach can help to provide privileged information about a dimension of human reality that could not be approached by other means. One key reason for this is that the narrative form makes it possible to combine feeling into knowing (Barthes, 1984; Mader, this volume).

The narrative method seems to be a promising tool with sufficient sensitivity for a meaningful study of aging experiences. An interesting opportunity to utilize the method for this purpose was given to me in the context of a cohort study of 80-year-old residents of Jyväskylä, a small town (pop. 66,000) in central Finland. The study looks at a picture of aging that unfolds from 20 tape-recorded narratives by 10 men and 10 women (Heikkinen, 1993).

The purpose of this chapter is to shed light on the process of aging, that is, to find a story of aging on the basis of 20 oral narrative stories. At the same time, the intention is to uncover some of the meanings and experiences that are attached to aging. Further, the interest of this inquiry is in continuity, in the sameness of the individual over time, from one point in time to another (Mader, this volume). The question is whether the self or self-perception changes with time. Although every individual has a unique frame of reference, the interesting question is whether there are similarities in the way people experience themselves and their relationships with others and with the surrounding world (see also Ruth & Öberg, this volume).

GATHERING DATA ON THE NARRATIVE SELF

We sat in my study, myself and my narrator, with a tape recorder on the table. I opened the conversation by saying that "We know quite a lot about the facts of aging, but we do not know enough about how you, elderly people, actually experience aging. Could you tell me something about this?" The following examples describe how the study got under way:

A: I don't really know where to start . . .
Q: You can start wherever you like.
A: Hm, it will take me quite a while if I go all the way back to my childhood, but I could start from when I retired. Is that alright?
Q: Yes, that's OK, start from there and we can go back to your childhood when we see.
A: Yes, erm. When I was, I had just turned 60 in January when my husband died and then they started giving me this family pension and erm . . . I was in this situation that we had our own house and—it wasn't very big but plenty for two people, comfortable . . . (continues as a life-story involving grandchildren, children, husband, illness, husband's illness, husband's job, own childhood and school). (Narrator 1)
A: I don't know. I've been fortunate enough to stay fit and well, I don't really see aging as any problem, and I always say that, because I'm, my face all wrinkled and generally I'm beginning to feel my posture is beginning to go, so I say that you're allowed at this age to—I mean you don't have to be like you're 21 do you . . . (story continues in close connection with life and memories). (Narrator 3)
A: Yes, well we at least, we were left alone—my mother was only 37 when she died and I was the oldest and I had a sister and a brother. My sister was 3 years old when my mother died. (Narrator 12)
A: Yes, well I was born, it was almost 80 years ago when I was born, or that's what my mother said, but they sent me to school, so there was 10 of us, 7 brothers and 3 sisters. My father was quite young when he lost his capacity for work and we children were supposed to go to school. (Narrator 18).

Given the short amount of time available, it is impossible to include everything that has happened in one's life in a single narrative. Instead, the narrator will select and order the information in accordance with his or her current self-understanding. A lifestory is not produced in and into a social vacuum, but it always contains an element of human interaction. This fact has a major impact on the final shape of narratives (Ruth & Kenyon, this volume).

It is hard to translate feelings, impressions and memories into coherent sentences. The hesitation we hear as the story advances may be due to difficulties in finding the right words, or to the storyteller's reluctance to disclose the most intimate things about his or her life. The amount of information imparted to the listener may also depend on what the storyteller believes the interviewer is expecting to hear. The reactions of individuals in situations of social interaction vary considerably. While some may want to find out what the interviewer's intentions are and want to agree as far as possible with his or her opinions, others may pour out their internal world without any concern for the speech situation, its form or terms (Siikala, 1984). Contextual and motivational factors influence the whole narration process. People also seem to act and operate on the presumption that they experience the same, common world and depend on this assumption of "shared understanding" (Heikkinen, 1988; Skinner, 1975) in their interactions. This may lead to misunderstandings between teller and listener (Cohler & Cole, this volume).

The focus here is on the way in which the individual sees and experiences his or her own aging, the aim being to collect spontaneous accounts of 80-year-old people. The narrative method is a process of running through the past once again; it is a description of experiences that takes shape as a continuum of choices at different levels (Siikala, 1984). As language is unable to convey all the special characteristics of individual experience, the process of narration is in itself an interpretation. When I asked my interviewees to tell me about their aging, most of them started by making this point and then proceeded to talk in more general terms about their lifestories. Some narrators started from their childhood or from their active years at work. Some narratives took on an episodic structure. By selecting past incidents and by arranging them into a narrative, the storytellers engaged in a process of biographical reasoning.

By taking on the narrative function, the interviewee provides us a representation of a world which will give coherence to the narrative only if he or she is capable of organizing it as a narrator (Burgos, 1988). This requires that, so long as the narration continues, the world projected by the narrative has to be relatively autonomous with respect to the real world that the interviewee shares. According to Burgos, this projection is primarily a product of the interview situation which expresses and delimits it in time and space. It seems inevitable that in the course of a qualitative study, where individuals are asked to become informers or witnesses, a strong subjective relationship develops between the researcher and the interviewee or informant in a study (Burgos, 1988).

The autonomy, in turn, is probably the result of gentle questioning as the researcher participates in the process of production only as a supporter. When it is time to transcribe these statements, it becomes evident that the questions can be omitted without adversely affecting the coherence of the narrative (Burgos, 1988). The autobiography makes sense and constitutes an almost independent whole that is not disturbed by the logic of the questions. The "fragments" become elements of a narrative. The essential unity is built by the person whose story is directing the narration, placing the elements of the world in a chronological sequence leading up to the point of narration (Burgos, 1988).

The way the story unfolds, the way it is understood, and the way it is remembered are all influenced by several factors that are related both to the participants and to the situation in which the story is told. The attention of the people present is drawn in different directions by momentary wishes, needs and preferences, by situational intentions and objectives, and by norms, values and attitudes internalized (Burgos, 1988). Some of the things that are said may be very personal and indeed, unknown to and unshared by the researcher (Siikala, 1984).

In this study, the storytellers set out to describe their stories of aging at the specific request of the researcher; they told their stories in order to satisfy the researcher's request. The multiplicity and complexity of the narrator's goals and life situations may influence the way in which the story takes shape. A narrative is a personal story, an expression of personal experience; it unfolds in conversational interaction. The researcher should adopt "the pleasure of listening" attitude, trying to listen and understand rather than ask questions (Burgos, 1988). For both parties, the actual context provided by the interview situation seems to disappear temporarily when the narrative is being told. It is obvious that an unequal, or as Goffman (1972) says, asymmetrical relationship exists at the beginning of the projected oral narrative, since the initiative comes from the researcher who knows what he or she is expecting. However, it is the narrator who should become "the master of the game" (Burgos, 1988) and the very form of the story captures both the narrator and the researcher.

Titon (1980) stresses the difference between life history and life story: a story is created, whereas a history is discovered. The study sometimes reveals a lot about the narrator's motives and about his or her internal and external life. In describing who he or she is and how he or she became what they are, the narrator also works to strengthen their own identity (Titon, 1980).

The perspective on the past takes shape from the vantage point of the narrator's present situation (Kenyon, this volume). The things disclosed are selected or may be selected through the narrator's current interests (Siikala, 1984). For example, in this study I paid special attention to the "absence"of one narrator; towards the end of the interview, I asked him whether he had something on his mind. He said he was going to the hospital immediately after the interview to find out whether the growth he had was malignant. A very current and real concern prevented this person from investing all his concentration in the interaction.

Siikala (1984) refers to the comments by Labov and Waletzky (1966) and Kohli (1986) on the referential and evaluation function of the narrative. The referential function comprises the description of past events in chronological order, while the evaluation function relates these things to present time, that is, the purpose is to demonstrate to those involved in the narrative situation what the stories actually mean. According to Siikala (1984), it is from the evaluative elements of lifestories that we can draw inferences with regard to the narrator's personality and personal experience.

Ricoeur (1981), in turn, says that every narrative combines two dimensions in various proportions, one chronological and the other nonchronological. The first of these he calls the episodic dimension, which characterizes the story as an entity constructed out of events. The second is the configurational dimension according to which the plot construes significant wholes out of scattered events (see also McAdams, this volume; Polkinghorne, this volume; Randall, this volume).

ANALYSIS OF THE MATERIAL

In this kind of research, data collection and the processing of data are closely interwoven. Ideally, interpretation of the data begins in the course of the interview; the interviewer should try to be as sensitive as possible to the subtle and alternative meanings that flow from the narrative (Wahlström, 1992). It is essential that from the stage of data collection onwards, the researcher is keenly aware of his or her relationship both to the subjects of the study and to the data. In the interview situation the researcher's relationship to the material is immediate and experiential; but at the stage of reading the transcripts, it becomes more mediated and conceptual (Wahlström, 1992). All these factors influence the narrator's stories of aging, and provide direction for the interpretation of lifestories.

In the analysis of research material, each narrative was examined separately as an independent entity. Slowly, as the researcher reread the transcribed stories, their logic and arguments, their tensions and perspectives began to surface. In the analysis of the corpus of narratives, the objective was first to conceptualize the phenomenon at hand and to uncover within that phenomenon a general qualitative form. As the analysis proceeded, a conceptual model of the experience of aging began gradually to unfold (Heikkinen, 1993).

This study is grounded in phenomenological premises, which broadly means that the individual is approached within the experiential frame. As the analysis advanced, the goal was to penetrate through people's layered notions and conceptions and to uncover genuine, original experiences of aging and its meaning (Laine, 1993). Further, the goal was to reach a theoretical understanding of aging at the level of meaning formation.

As the researcher moves in her process of interpretation from knowing to not knowing and back again, a hermeneutic spiral is created which carries forward the interpretation; that which is already understood transforms into a preconception which furthers the interpretation of that which as yet is uninterpreted (Wahlström, 1992).

IN SEARCH OF THE CORE THEME

The conceptual tools emerging from the content of the narratives make it possible to *find the findable* within the material (Walhström, 1992). The most important conceptual "building block" emerging from this study was what was termed the "boundary conditions" for aging. The boundary conditions attached to aging in the experiential narratives, such as deteriorating health, the deterioration of the senses (particularly eyesight and hearing), frailty, pains, impaired memory, and loss of human relations (particularly the loss of a spouse through death), were negative in terms of their content. I have termed these "boundary conditions" *vulnerability* factors (Heikkinen, 1993). The word "aging" seemed to carry negative connotations for the 80-year-old narrators. The boundary conditions of aging imposed limits on people's degrees of freedom (Schroots, this volume), made it harder for them to cope independently, and often undermined togetherness. On the basis of the substances or meanings attached to aging, first a model of the boundary conditions of aging was constructed, followed by a conceptual model of experienced aging (Heikkinen, 1993; Yates, 1991).

The contents that were produced by the narratives on the core theme of the study indicated that even though these 80-year-old people were older people, they did not seem to be living "an old age existence;" they were living their lives just as anybody else. If they were not experiencing problems in everyday life and life in general, the narrators I talked with said they did not realize that they were living the stage of life that we call old age (Heikkinen, 1993; Kaufman, 1986; Kenyon, 1991). For example:

> No, not really, I wouldn't say I've noticed that I'm old yet. I still look after myself and arrange all of my errands for myself. I was in hospital some time ago and they came over from the social welfare and said that I can go over for meals at the service center if I want to. But I've managed all on my own. I've even gone over to mind my grandchildren when they're all at work, and go over to pick them up from school and, so I mean I can't say that I'm feeling old really. I feel perfectly well and healthy, if I compare myself with other people I know and who are still much younger than I am. They are in a much worse shape they are (laughter) (Narrator 7).

The personal experience of aging does not automatically translate into a certain number of years: "and I just can't believe I'm 80 now, I just have this feeling personally" (Narrator 14). When aging is described in terms of the passage of time, it is not possible experientially to capture what the process consists of (see Kenyon, this volume).

THE MEANING OF AGING

In looking at experiential aging, we are in effect looking at the meaning(s) of aging. Experiences of aging find expression in the set of positive and negative meanings that individuals attach and ascribe to the process. This set is built up on the basis of each individual's unique life history. People's experiences develop and unfold in interaction with the environment (Svensson, this volume) and are therefore closely intertwined with the system of values prevailing in the culture of the community and society in which they live. The following description, which contains numerous references to meanings of life, is a response by one of my narrators to the challenge of talking about aging.

> I was a housewife; we had three children and my husband he went to work and he always wanted to have his supper ready when he came home, so that there's no point in me going to work. And we had a house of our own so there was plenty to do all year round. I worked myself and the husband it was the same with him, he required a lot of me because he was working late into the night, and there was no problem, I mean even for him when he retired, there was always plenty of work around the house and I would help him and that's how it went, I didn't even notice that I was getting older. All my life I had the, I've been able to do my work and I've had no health problems at all, so there's not much I can say to you about aging. The children were there and they grew up. Then they, three of them there were, they left home and we were left there just the two of us. But we still carried on with the work and stayed at home most of the time, we never went into any clubs or things like that. I did go to church, mind you, and when the children were small I took them as well, especially for Christmas, so they know what it means. And that's how it went. Well then my husband fell ill, but—well that meant there was quite a lot of work for me, it was diabetes, and you always had to be on your guard and, but I was healthy, so I really can't say very much about getting old and I've always been a modest person, and my children they're real darlings, and they always come round to see that I've got everything I need, like now they come round almost every day, so that no, I'm not lonely at all, although I'm now living here on my own. But it was a real shock when my husband died, it would have been our golden wedding in January but then in July he slipped away. It's four years now, but it was really awful when I was left alone. I had to face the winter all by myself, it was that horrible cold winter, I had so much work to do, but I must say that I thank God that I had that work to do, that helped me pull through those weeks and months (trembling voice). I knew that I was alone and if there had been nothing to do, if it had been like it is here now, nothing to do but just sit around this flat, I suppose they would have to put me away, because I tend to be quite nervous, a silly old one I am (recovers). But anyway I loved the work and our home was so important to me; we built it ourselves and then; but then I thought that I can't stay in a four-bedroom house all on my own and heat the

> whole place, we heated it with stoves, there was so much work to do that we decided to sell the place. And the flat I got was really nice, I was so pleased with the flat, that when my daughter got married she had lived in these same houses. Exactly the same kind of flat, I looked after her son and it was all so familiar to me in the sense that, but I have to say that you have to be quite a lot on your own in those houses, I mean they don't even say hello the people who live above you, but about this old age, I don't know, I do often think of what it will be like the day when I go. I mean it's always on your mind and when you are living on your own like this, you wonder what's going to happen, that's why you, hmm. So life has just been what it is, one day after another. I can't really say anything about getting old, I've always been so healthy and I haven't really had to think about it. (Narrator 20)

Meanings and values are always reorganized and readjusted with aging (Dittman-Kohli, 1990). A good example is provided by health, which takes on an extremely important meaning with increasing age as a guarantor of independence. The social world, our common and shared existence, is an inevitable fact to all of us and thereby carries an "unconditional" meaning, even though the meanings of human relations may change as life goes on. For elderly people, significant others are important sources of strength and support, and (as is indicated by the story above) they provide a significant content to their existence as well as a feeling of continuity into the future.

Aging brings an increasing respect and understanding of the value of life. The difficulties one has experienced in earlier life may also be reinterpreted and thereby possibly acquire a positive meaning. It also seems that with increasing age people develop a clearer understanding of life itself as a source of meaning of life. The following provide some examples of how the elderly people I talked with described their thought and feelings about life's meaning in relation to themselves, to each other, and to the world in which they live.

RELATIONSHIP TO ONE'S BODY

The phenomenological framework adopted in this study to explore people and their aging problematizes the assumption of Cartesian traditional philosophy that the human being is divided into two domains, the spiritual and the bodily (Laine, 1993). Our approach is to look at the human individual as a single, complex being. The reference here is to the indivisibility of experience. Even though our elderly narrators had to some extent adopted in their own speech practices the distinction between the physical and the psychological, there were also many discourses which transcended that dichotomy. In keeping with the phenomenological frame of reference, the human individual is approached in this study as a creature living his or her existence within the world, within life itself; he or she is not a self-enclosed subject confronting the external world (Laine, 1993).

The existential analysis of the French phenomenologist–existentialist Merleau-Ponty (1962) deals with the spatial and motor patterns of the body. Merleau-Ponty says that existence consists of our mode of existing our body. The body, has two aspects which change into one another; the body that is not noticed and the body that is noticed (Merleau-Ponty, 1962). The normal life of the body is hidden; we are not able to perceive it. We live our existence as a body in fatigue, in illness, when we eat, and so on. When we grow old our body changes; we get tired more easily, we have symptoms more frequently; and so the body is noticed more frequently. According to Merleau-Ponty, the body is the basis of situatedness, the means by which we have a perspective on the world (see also Kenyon, this volume). The body is not a subject, but it is a vehicle by which I am a subject in the world, and the means by which a world is possible. The weaker the body becomes, the worse it will be as a "vehicle." The dependency that follows physical and mental impairment is a frightening and unpleasant thing to some older persons. As bodies, we live in the field of the present and in the constant presence of the past. In the presence of the body we also anticipate the future.

> I really and truly hope and pray that I can manage to keep myself physically and mentally in such a shape that someone will just find me when I die. I'd like to fall over like a tree. I can't stand the idea of lying around in the hospital or a nursing home and have someone push me around, my senses still there. You'd be better off not knowing. (Narrator 14).
>
> My legs and hands are still perfectly all right. And I still go out for walks, like half an hour a time just to cheer myself up. You know, so that I could carry on for a few more years, so that I could take care of myself while I'm still alive. You know, I would not want to give in. I know there are all these people who would take care of me, but I could not stand the idea of being bed-ridden. (Narrator 2)
>
> Otherwise my legs have been all right, but for a year or so I've had this illness and I have no longer been able to go walking, I can't walk a lot—and I used to do long walks, one and a half even two hours a day. I would love to go out walking but I can't because of my illness. But I do my exercise; this condition requires exercises; I do them every evening. They're just for the upper part of the body. So you start thinking that even though you have seen healthier days, you don't really notice it, even you've grown much older, but somehow, it's like hard to believe am I really that old (laughter). (Narrator 6)

The body not only enables us to perceive but it also allows the world to exist (Kirk, 1986). "Our own body is in the world as the heart is in the organism; it keeps the visible spectacle constantly alive, it breathes life into it and sustains it inwardly and with it forms a system" (Merleau-Ponty, 1962, p. 203). So while the body is a means with which we perceive a world, it also creates and maintains a world; it constitutes and regulates a world (Kirk, 1986).

Our bodily, sensuous relationship to the world is an indivisible wholeness. We gain our own bodiliness, "my" body, with life experience; our body becomes familiar as we live with it. The changes that occur in values and in espoused meanings also reflect the changes that happen in the way we experience our body.

RELATIONSHIP TO "I"

What do our 80-year-old narrators think about when they talk about their aging self, when they say "I"? How do they experience themselves, how do they perceive themselves, how does the "I" appear and manifest itself? The following excerpts provide examples of a wide range where sameness and change constitute an experientially indivisible life.

You Do Change

> Well I think I would say at least that you become more understanding and that you develop a more positive attitude, I mean I don't carry on any more like I used to when I was younger, the troubles we had felt so much harder and, but somehow, you can't say that, that I've actually become an angel or anything, the best person in the world, but I do think about things a bit differently than when I was young; more positively—and I've tried to tell this to other people, to younger people that, there's no point in stopping in your tracks and crying over spilt milk, that this is the end of everything, that life is so hard and this must end and this is coming to nothing. (Narrator 1).
>
> I think that you do change—it does affect your state of mind and things like that, someone might become a bit more irritable and like you never seem to be satisfied with things. And I'm sure there are various things, other things, that you're less active—of course you are and erm, yet it definitely does bring changes. I dare say we all change. I wouldn't say otherwise but I do try to (laughter). I don't want to be very bitter or mean or anything, but I mean it does make you slower and you're not as eager to leave as you used to be and it takes a bit more time and thought before you set off and go out. (Narrator 12)
>
> I've noticed that when you were young you had all sorts of dreams and daydreams and that sort of things. You liked to dream up things but nowadays there's nothing to think about. You tend to get a bit more religious and start to think that there is this heavenly father, mine is the father who is in heaven, and you still

> don't consider yourself religious. It's perfectly true though that you begin to think about these things of eternity. It didn't really mean anything when you were younger and at confirmation school you thought that, you thought that there was too much of this religion, but now you need it all. (Narrator 15)

The Unchangeable in Change

> No, there've been no changes. I feel just like I would amongst younger people, I don't feel older at all. It's quite amazing really, someone said this to me, especially my old lady who says that old age doesn't affect me. I'm very, I have a great sense of humour and; So you have it, but there are these effects, like you're not like younger people there; feelings are still like a younger person's. (Narrator 13)
>
> Well I can't say I've noticed anything that—well of course that the only thing is that when you were younger you were a bit happier, and perhaps had more of a temper, but there haven't been any other real changes. (Narrator 4)

Old Age Changes You

> Although you, although you try and erm, but it's like that old age begins to change you, and you can't keep up with everything that you should. Old age quite simply, it becomes natural. You no longer care and then you get to the stage where you no longer care so much about seeing other people and you actually feel physically ill when you have to, when you have visitors and you have to talk so much you feel, oh I do hope they leave (laughter) (Narrator 8).
>
> I feel that you just gradually slow down, stop and slow down, you think about things more. Yes and I write a lot of letters. I have many people I write to and erm, when it all quietens down and there's nothing to do, like hobbies or activities like I used to have, I mean that's quite natural that eventually you stop . . . but I can't say it's negative change, on the contrary (Narrator 9).

Every I is an I with a nature, not a "pure" I. This is reflected in our narrator's view of change. Reflective comments on one's changes are complex and rich in their variety, just as life itself. A certain continuity is an important precondition for the unity of a person, for experiencing oneself as I. Indeed, many narrators say they are exactly the same person they have always been. Sameness and selfness go hand in hand, but things begin to show up differently in light of the life lived. Something is gained, something lost. Some of my elderly narrators were annoyed and embarrassed by their declining memory. It made everyday life harder, made them feel insecure. Loss of memory is also distressing because it threatens the very continuity of the self and the world; someone or something is erased out every now and then.

> I don't think, I don't think otherwise I've changed very much but I must say that my memory is going and then that, how should I put this, it's harder to keep up with things, it's impossible to; and I mean it must be that with your memory going and but you do get more humble, yes that happens quite a lot (Narrator 19).

Changes are often brought about by such things as accidents, fortunate coincidences, or major upheavals (Krohn, 1990). But aging is not a major upheaval; there is no dramatic turn. What comes later is distinguished from what went before simply by the fact that it is different in terms of certain qualities of relationships. The experience of aging consists very much in an experience of difference, in the recognition that you are somehow different from what you were before and you see things differently than before. The changes that come with aging are often invisible changes. A visible change is a change for others as well; "others" are mirrors that always follow you, wherever you go. Attitudes of the environment towards aging commonly reflect expectations of difference.

EXPERIENCING OTHERS

Experienced Changes in Others

> Elderly people today are much more energetic than earlier, when I was a child old grannies like me today, they were so slow and hunchbacked. Not today. They've got so much to do nowadays, there are all sorts of things to keep them busy and occupied. It was work really, you learned to work even as a child and it's been, it hasn't been; I would say that I've been fortunate enough to have my health, I've worked all my life very hard; well of course they didn't actually kill you with domestic work, but even so there were heavy demands there (Narrator 8).

Describing the Younger Generation

> It's really, they're always in such a hurry. I mean I've been watching them in the countryside and seen people coming from work and then as soon as they, they all have cars now and as soon as they get out of work they're in a rush to play golf or squash or whatever, they're always in a hurry. But when we go up there we try to take things a bit easier, we try not to spoil everything by being in a hurry. When we're up there for two weeks there's plenty of time, and we have to spend a lot of time inside and then there's always all sorts of new things and you can easily spend your time doing various things, the time whiles itself away very nicely (Narrator 10).
>
> But sometimes when you hear young children who are growing up, like my grandchildren, sometimes I tell them when they're complaining about their clothes,

do you know that if you had just one dress or one pair of trousers, you wouldn't be making such a racket, you should have seen the sort of life your grandmother had. My daughter always tells me off and says I shouldn't always nag at them, these young people don't like being told off. But I do feel they should understand that, that they may still have to face more difficult times in life. But I suppose we all go along and live our lives our own ways (Narrator 2).

People do not live in a void; they live in society, in a social system, and it is within this system that they have to identify themselves. It is that very same social system that is the source of any morality we can imagine (White, 1981). The values of elderly people and their morality have been internalized in an historical and cultural situation that was very different from the situation today. They are now trying to cope with new values espoused by a new society; some are lost and somewhat critical about the way of life and general attitude of younger generations. White (1981) suggests that narrativity, expecially in factual storytelling, is intimately related to if not a function of, the impulse to moralize reality (see also Randall, this volume). Apparently the evaluative function of storytelling also implies a certain measure of critical reflection that focuses on difference and adds firmness to the picture of life-world experiences.

Navigating through the world of good and evil, people rely on their moral perspective (von Wright, 1963); they could not survive without the guidance. People who have lived a long life easily recognize the moral changes that have taken place in human culture. The changes they see may cause a sense of aggravation, perhaps even uncertainty about the future.

You need to set some limits, you should start to teach them as soon as they're old enough to understand. If you give them rights then they also must have obligations, yes, exactly. You musn't be too hard and say they aren't allowed to do anything, but you do need to have a certain order. You know, that there's some sense: And, when they say that we old people, that we tend to romanticize the good old days and that, but I must say that today, the youth in our days, it was all very different from what it is today. We didn't go around painting walls and, well of course we did have our drawings but these things today, they're absolutely horrific. Somehow they just don't seem to care (Narrator 12).

. . . in the end of course life is very short, isn't it. Even though there's so many, I think it's a pity that young people in this day and age, how, why is it that they destroy their lives . . . their way of life is all wrong, it causes so much harm and damage that I really feel sorry for them. I always pray for these people, dear God try to open their eyes, how lovely it would be if these people could live their lives in happiness; yes well I did go to the dances when I was younger, and a good dancer I was, but there was nothing else to it because it was that sort of life. And I think it is important that young people live an active sort of life; and even in

> towns nowadays there's so much they can do, to choose a good life style and there are all sorts of opportunities, but I suppose there's just nothing you can do about the way things are today, but if you do ask for help from upstairs you'll certainly get it (Narrator 1).

THE EXPERIENCED WORLD

Every individual has his or her own frame of reference, his or her own life experiences. At the same time, however, being members of the same culture and the same age cohort, our narrators also seemed to share the way of perceiving themselves and the surrounding world. We must assume that underlying the similarities of our experiential worlds there lies a common "root foundation" which in turn (Krohn, 1990) makes possible shared experiences and shared understandings. Shared understandings, a certain similarity in people's values and attitudes, were perhaps most clearly reflected in differences of way of life and fundamental values in relation to younger generations. This is also the case with respect to experiences of financial security during retirement in comparison with the situation of one's own grandparents and parents. The longer the shared distance covered in life, the more there is to share.

> I sometimes can't help laughing when my daughter calls me up and says that it's laundry day, and says I don't have the time for all this because it's laundry day. And I say oh dear me, two grown up people and automatic washing machines and all you have to do is hang them up to dry afterwards, yes it is a strain isn't it (laughter). We went down with the neighbors, they had this place down by the lake, not on the lakeside but nearby, we went down the hill and there was the lake and the H's had a sauna there and that's where we did our laundry. There was no laundry room. We just had two of these tubs in which we scrubbed our clothes. A brush and, there wasn't even a washboard in those days when I went down for the first time to do our washing. Yes, so we scrubbed and scrubbed on the floor and then went down to the lake to rinse the washing, even in the winter Mr. H used to keep a hole in the ice so that we could go and rinse our washing. So I always tell these young people, I mean my skirt was frozen all the way to my waist when we came back from there. It wasn't just my fate, it was the fate of all the other people as well, all adults. It is quite wonderful now that, I mean I have now been able to do my laundry with a washing machine and had other people do my laundry, it's my heart; I really can't cope with heavier things. I'm not saying that; I'm not saying that I envy these people or that I'm bitter about the past. It was all so natural. You didn't know of anything better so you couldn't ask for anything else. We then got running water at home and all these conveniences, even though there was never any real luxuries, just the normal life of working-class people (Narrator 1).

> Yes of course, life is not a bed of roses, no one's life is, but I would say that if these people today, if they had to cope with the kind of situations that we old people have, you can be sure they would turn their backs and just leave. You wouldn't have that in our days, the only option we considered was to adjust. Today, what with women highly educated and independent, they're no longer dependent on a husband in the same way women used to be. In earlier times if you hadn't any education like me, I worked in the kitchen in Sortavala for 6 years, and then got married, and you know you were dependent on the husband's pay packet, you were dependent, there was nothing. I mean you had no education except what you learned through the job, but today people; today women are in a much better position in that they're independent and have the energy to look after themselves and they no longer have to accept everything, if the marriage doesn't work out. So you have the freedom to walk out (Narrator 8).
>
> I've been thinking that with a little bit of energy and enterprise you can go a long way nowadays, if you're talented and if you want to, I myself would. I would imagine that as long as people keep trying; obviously there are people who are still having some difficulty and finding it difficult to solve their problems, but I mean obviously it can't be the same for all can it? But I mean you'd get quite far just by wanting to, under these circumstances, but when I was a child others had to get on. And I've got this far haven't I: I'm 80 now (Narrator 14).

EVALUATING LIFE

The process in which the individual reflects upon aging and relates about his or her experiences to other people, in this case the researcher, is essentially one of evaluating life. The individual's relationship to him- or herself and to the surrounding world changes during the course of life. The change experienced by my narrators makes them redefine, in light of their life experiences, themselves as well as their relationship to each other and to the surrounding world. Many of these narrators said that is it much easier to put things into perspective with increasing age and life experience. The high value and appreciation of life itself comes across very clearly.

The narrators who had best succeeded in balancing the Janus-faced life, who felt that the gains and losses in life had balanced each other out, could perhaps best be described by such words as acceptance, experience, reflectiveness, flexibility, and good humor. One cannot overemphasize the importance of continuity (in human relations, in the living environment, in everyday life) and of good health for a good aging (Heikkinen, 1993).

I concluded the conversation with my narrators by asking them what had been the best thing in their life. This is what one of them said:

> Best thing . . . I've noticed that when people talk about happiness; happiness is just a short moment, you may be somewhere and think that oh, I'm so happy now, but as soon as you notice this, your happiness is gone. It's important that you don't notice it, but if you look back and think about real things, rather than this sort of short feelings, then, the best things have been my children. I only have one son of my own, but he's perhaps too dear to me, I mean I've made some mistakes bringing him up, yes. And so I would say that this has been a good thing in my life. I mean a thing like that, there are lots of good things and if you'd start making a list of them and I mean there's nothing wrong in looking back at good things in your life, but the problem is that this also tends to bring back all the problems and other things you've had to suffer. When I was a child we were short of almost everything, at that time. Finland was really a developing country, I mean it was under foreign rule and we weren't even independent. It is only since independence that life started to improve for ordinary people. And erm, in material terms, I don't know, one could go on for ever, but I don't know whether this story really makes any sense. Yes and of course at work; I was a primary school teacher, there were many beautiful things and many good things and inspiring things about it, but then there were also many unpleasant things like, well of course I had a good job and I had nice colleagues and nice neighbours, so that in that sense it was all very positive. But obviously work is, has both its good sides and bad sides for all people (Narrator 15).

CONCLUSION

The purpose of this chapter was to shed light on the process of aging, to find a story of aging on the basis of 20 oral narratives. At the same time, the intention was to uncover some of the meanings and experiences that are attached to aging.

In their discourses concerning experienced aging, the narrators integrated the past and the present. Elements were selected for the stories according to each narrator's own criteria, according to what they felt and thought was meaningful and important. Their shared cultural understanding of the world also played a role in those choices (Ruth & Kenyon, this volume).

Everything about the self is part of the same narrative; it is a narrative about one's relationship to oneself, to others, to the world, to the past, present and future. It is a narrative of the changes that have taken place and associated values and meanings; changes that have unfolded with life experience. It is a narrative of changing and of not changing. The Finnish novelist Leena Krohn (1993) says that "we remain the same stream even though its bed is embraced by new water that keeps flowing by" (p. 82).

The narrative format directs the narrator to the past and present time. However, the future is also included, because the present carries the key to the future. The human individual who exists in the world always looks forward because the horizon of meaning in life lies ahead in the future. The individual's existence is an existence as a life project (Klemola, 1991). For elderly people, concerns about the future, about the chances of existence (Heidegger, 1962) are present more than for younger people. Even though it is very difficult to capture the passage of time in experiential terms, the future perspective, future "projects" grow shorter. (For a contrasting view of biography and time, see Kenyon, 1991, this volume).

The verbalization of one's own experiences is no simple task; as Polkinghorne (1988) says, experience is accumulated in the storyteller's mind in detached clusters that are tied together by narrow threads of plots. What has been disjointed at a certain level in the narrative is most often joined later. Loose ends are tied up. The narrative form constituted the human reality of elderly Finnish narrators into wholes, manifested human values, and bestowed meaning on life (Polkinghorne, 1988).

The narrative method provided an opportunity to study the aging individual in a living relationship to the world, within everyday life, as a "whole" human being. For the researcher, it was an intriguing process to follow and subsequently to analyze the storytelling and the material that accumulated. In conveying images and experiences of aging, the researcher faced the same continuous choices as the narrator. The semantic richness of the narratives was quite fascinating. Meaning and time constituted a distinctive, individual texture of life in which the historical and cultural landscape provided the horizon. The descriptions of experiences of aging can be summarized in the following way: Narrative is simply there like life itself (Barthes, 1984).

12

Beyond Life Narratives in the Therapeutic Encounter*

Kenneth J. Gergen, PhD.

When aging adults seek psychotherapy they have a story to tell. It is frequently the troubled, hurt, or angry story of a life or relationship now spoiled. For many it is a story of loss that conspires against their sense of well-being, or the loss of desire for life itself. For others, the story may concern unseen and mysterious forces insinuating themselves into life's organized sequences, disrupting and destroying. And for still others it is as if, under the illusion of knowing how the world is or ought to be, they have somehow bumped up against physical deterioration or other realities for which they are unprepared. They have discovered some awful truth of finitude that bleeds all past understandings of cogency. Whatever its form, the therapist confronts a narrative, often persuasive and gripping; it is a narrative that may be terminated within a brief period, or it may be extended over weeks or months. However, at some juncture the therapist must inevitably respond to this account, and whatever follows within the therapeutic procedure will draw its significance in response to this account.

* The present chapter is derived from an earlier treatment in Gergen (1994).

What options are available to therapists or counselors as they now respond to the relational scenario? At least one option pervasive within the culture, and sometime used as well within counseling, social work, and short-term therapies, may be viewed as advisory. For the advisor, the client's story remains relatively inviolate. Its terms of description and forms of explanation remain unchallenged in a significant way. Rather, for the advisor the major attempt is to locate forms of effective action "under the circumstances" as narrated. Thus, for example, if the individual speaks of being depressed because of personal handicaps, means are sought for reestablishing efficacy. If the client is rendered ineffectual because of grief, then a program of action may be suggested for overcoming the problem. In effect, the client's lifestory is accepted as fundamentally accurate for him or her, and the problem is to locate ameliorative forms of action within the story's term.

There is much to be said on behalf of the advisory option. Within the realm of the relatively ordinary, it is most obviously *reasonable* and most probably effective. Here is the vital stuff of quotidian coping. Yet, for the more seriously chronic or deeply disturbed client, the advisory option harbors serious limitations. At the outset, there is little attempt to confront deeper origins of the problem or the complex ways it is sustained. The major concern is in locating a new course of action. Whatever the chain of antecedents, their existence simply remains unchallenged, often continuing to operate as threats to the future. Further, little attempt is typically made to probe the contours of the story, to determine its relative utility or viability. Could the client be out of synchrony with the social environment, or defining things in a less than optimal way? Such questions often remain unexplored. In accepting "the story as told," the problem definition also remains fixed. As a result, the range of possible options for action remains circumscribed. If the problem is said to be failure, for example, the relevant options are geared toward reestablishing success. Other possibilities are thrust to the margins of plausibility. And finally, in the chronic or severe case, the location of action alternatives too often seems a superficial palliative. For one who has been frustrated, struggling, and desperate for a period of years, for example, simple advice for living may seem little more than a whispering in the wind.

In the present offering two more substantial alternatives to the advisory option will be explored. The first is represented by the most traditional forms of psychotherapy and psychoanalytic practice. In its reliance on various neo-Enlightenment assumptions dominant in the sciences of the present century, this orientation toward client narratives may be viewed as *modernist*. In contrast, much thinking within the *postmodern* arena, and more specifically postmodern constructionist, forms a powerful challenge to the modernist conception of the narrative. In doing so new modes of therapeutic procedure are opened.

THERAPEUTIC NARRATIVES IN THE MODERNIST CONTEXT

Much has been written about modernism in the sciences, literature and the arts, and this is scarcely the context for thorough review. (See, for example, Randall, 1940; Berman, 1982; Levenson, 1984; and Frisby, 1985.) However, it is useful to consider briefly a set of assumptions that have guided activities in the sciences and the allied professions of mental health. For it is this array of assumptions that have largely informed the therapeutic treatment of client narratives. The modernist era in the sciences has been one committed, first of all, to the empirical elucidation of essences. Whether it be the character of the atom, the gene, or the synapse in the natural sciences, or processes of perception, economic decisionmaking, or organizational development in the social sciences, the major attempt has been to establish bodies of systematic and objective knowledge.

From the modernist standpoint, empirical knowledge is communicated through scientific languages. Narratives are essentially structures of language, and insofar as narratives are generated within the scientific milieu they can, on the modernist account, function as conveyors of objective knowledge. Thus, the narratives of the novelist are labeled as "fiction," and are considered inconsequential for serious scientific purposes. People's narratives of their lives, what has happened to them and why, are not necessarily fictions. But, as the behavioral scientist presumes, they are notoriously inaccurate and unreliable. Thus, they are of limited value in understanding the individual's life, and far less preferable than the empirically based accounts of the trained scientist. As a result, the narrative accounts of the scientist are accorded the highest credibility, and are set above and apart from the homespun stories of everyday life and the markets of public entertainment.

The mental health profession today is largely an outgrowth of the modernist context, and shares deeply in its assumptions. And too, these same assumptions are often applied to research and therapy with the aging population (see for example, Verwoerdt, 1981). Thus from Freud to contemporary cognitive and psychopharmacological therapists, the general belief is that the professional therapist functions (or ideally should function) as a scientist. By virtue of such activities as scientific training, research experience, knowledge of the scientific literature, and countless hours of systematic observation and thought within the therapeutic situation, the professional is armed with knowledge. To be sure, contemporary knowledge is incomplete, and more research is ever required. But the knowledge of the contemporary professional is far superior to that of the turn-of-the-century therapist, so it is said, and the future can only bring further improvements. Thus with few exceptions, therapeutic theories (whether behavioral, systematic, psychodynamic, experiential/humanist, or biochemical) contain explicit assumptions regarding a) the underlying cause or basis of pathology, b) the location of this cause within the client or his/her relationships, and c) the means by which the distress or pathology may be eliminated. In effect, the trained professional enters the therapeutic arena with a well-developed narrative for which there is abundant support within the community of scientific peers.

It is this background that establishes the therapist's posture toward the client's narrative (see also Cohler & Cole, this volume). For the client's narrative is, after all, made of the flimsy, homespun stuff–replete with whimsy, metaphor, wishful thinking, and distorted memories. The scientific narrative, by contrast, has the seal of professional approval. From this vantage point we see that the therapeutic process must inevitably result in the slow but inevitable replacement of the client's story with the therapist's. The client's story does not remain a free-standing reflection of the truth, but rather, as questions are asked and answered, descriptions and explanations are reframed, and affirmation and doubt are disseminated by the therapist, the client's narrative is either destroyed or incorporated, but in any case replaced, by the professional account. The client's account is transformed by the psychoanalyst into a tale of family romance, by the Rogerian into a struggle against conditional regard, by the attachment counselor as a tale of overdependency, and so on. It is this process of replacing the client's story with the professional's that is so deftly described in Donald Spence's *Narrative Truth and Historical Truth*. As Spence surmises,

> [the therapist] is constantly making decisions about the form and status of the patient's material. Specific listening conventions help to guide these decisions. If, for example, the analyst assumes that continuity indicates causality, then he will hear a sequence of disconnected statements as a causal chain; at some later time, he might make an interpretation that would make this assumption explicit. If he assumes that transference predominates and that the patient is always talking, in more or less disguised fashion, about the analyst, then he will "hear" the material in that way and make some kind of ongoing evaluation of the state of the transference. (p. 129)

Such replacement procedures do have certain therapeutic advantages. For one, as the client gains "real insight" into his or her problems, the problematic narrative may thereby be removed. The client is thus furnished with an alternative reality that holds promise for future well-being. In effect, the failure story with which the client entered therapy is swapped for an invitation to a success story. And, similar to the advisory option outlined earlier, the new story is likely to suggest alternative lines of action—forming or dissolving relationships, operating under a daily regimen, submitting to therapeutic procedures, and so on.

Within the professional story there are new and more hopeful things to do. And too, by providing the client a scientific formulation, the therapist has played his/her appointed role in the family of cultural rituals in which the ignorant, the failing, and the weak seek counsel from the wise, superior, and strong. It is often a comforting ritual to those who will submit.

Yet, in spite of these advantages, there is substantial reason for concern. Major shortcomings have been located in the modernist orientation to therapy. The scientific community has long been skeptical of the knowledge claims pervasive in the mental health professions. As it is held, mental health practitioners have little justification for their claims to knowledge of pathology and cure. Critics have also inveighed against traditional forms of therapy for their excessive concern with the individual. As it is argued, such theories are blind to the broad cultural conditions in which psychological difficulties may be lodged (Kovel, 1989; Mader, this volume). Feminist critics have grown increasingly vocal in such attacks, noting that many "female disorders" are inappropriately traced to the female mind and are instead the outcome of the oppressive conditions of the female in society (see, for example, Hare-Mustin & Marecek, 1988). Others have been deeply unsettled by the pathologizing of the profession. From the modernist standpoint, deviant or aberrant behavior is typically traced to deficient psychological states, and it is the task of the mental health profession, like the medical profession, to identify and treat such disorders. Yet, in accepting such assumptions the profession acts so as to objectify mental illness, even when there are many alternative means of interpreting or understanding the same phenomena (Gergen, 1994).

Over and above these problems, there are additional shortcomings in the modernist orientation to client narrative. There is, for one, a substantial imperious thrust to the modernist approach. Not only is the therapist's narrative never placed under threat, but the therapeutic procedure virtually ensures that it will be vindicated. In Spence's terms, "the search (within therapeutic interaction) can be infinitely expanded until the (therapist's) answer is discovered and there is no possibility of finding a negative solution, of deciding that the (therapist's) search has failed (p. 108)." Thus, regardless of the complexity (de Vries & Lehman, this volume), sophistication or value of the client's account, it is eventually to be replaced by a narrative created before his or her entry into therapy and the contours over which he/she has no control.

It is not simply that therapists from a given school will ensure their clients come away bearing beliefs in their particular account. By virtue of the bounded ontologies, the ultimate aims of most schools of therapy are hegemonic. All other schools of thought, and their associated narratives, should succumb. In general psychoanalysts wish to eradicate behavior modification; cognitive-behavioral therapists see systems therapy as misguided, and so on. Yet, the most immediate and potentially injurious consequences are reserved for the client. For in the end, the structure of the procedure furnishes the client a lesson in inferiority. The client is indirectly informed that he or she is ignorant, insensitive, or emotionally incapable of comprehending reality. In contrast, the therapist is positioned as the all-knowing and wise, a model to which the client might aspire. The situation is all the more lamentable owing to the fact that in occupying the superior role, the therapist fails to reveal its weaknesses. Almost nowhere are the fragile foundations of the therapist's account made known; almost nowhere do the therapist's personal doubts, foibles, and failings come to light. And the client is thus confronted with a vision of human possibility that is as unattainable as the heroism of cinematic mythology.

The modernist orientation suffers as well from the fixedness of the narrative formulations. As we have seen, modernist approaches to therapy begin with an *a priori* narrative, justified by claims to a scientific base. Because it is sanctioned as scientific, this narrative is relatively closed to alteration. Minor modifications may be entertained, but the system itself bears the weight of established doctrine. To the extent that such narratives become the client's reality, and his or her actions are guided accordingly, life options for the client are severely truncated. Of all possible modes of acting in the world, one is set on a course emphasizing ego autonomy, self-actualization, rational appraisal, emotional expressiveness, detachment, and so on, depending on the particular brand of therapy selected. Or to put it otherwise, each form of modernist therapy carries with it an image of the "fully functioning" or "good" individual; like a fashion plate, this image serves as a guiding model for the therapeutic outcome.

This constriction of life possibilities is all the more problematic because it is decontextualized. That is, the therapist's narrative is an abstract formulation, cut away from particular cultural and historical circumstances. None of the modernist narratives deal with the specific conditions of living in ghetto poverty, with a brother who had AIDS, with a grandchild who has Down syndrome, with an arthritic hand, and so on. In contrast to the complex details that crowd the corners of daily life, which are indeed life itself, modernist narratives are nonspecific. They aspire toward universality, and on this account, say very little about particularistic circumstance. As a result, these narratives are precariously insinuated into the life circumstances of the individual. They are, in this sense, clumsy and insensitive, failing to register the particularities of the client's life engagements. To emphasize self-fulfillment to a woman living on welfare and with a husband who has Alzheimer's disease is not likely to be beneficial: To press a retired attorney for increased emotional expressiveness in his daily routines is of doubtful assistance.

THERAPEUTIC REALITIES IN THE POSTMODERN CONTEXT

The literature on postmodernist culture is rapidly accumulating, and again this is an inappropriate context for a full review. (For further reading on postmodernism see Connor, 1989; Foster, 1983; Gergen, 1991; and Rosenau, 1992.) However, it is useful to emphasize a single contrast with modernism, one of central significance to the concept of knowledge, science, and therapy. Within the postmodernist wings of the academy major attention is now devoted to the process of representation, or the means by which "reality" is set forth in writing, the arts, the news, and popular media. As it is generally agreed, there is no means of arraying all the events in the "real world" on one side and all the syllables of the language on the other, and linking them in one-to-one fashion, such that each syllable would reflect an isolated atom of reality. Rather, in the case of writing, each style or genre of literature operates according to local rules or conventions, and these conventions will largely determine the way we understand the putative objects of representation. Scientific writing, then, furnishes no more accurate a picture of reality than does fiction. The former accounts may be embedded in scientific activity in a way that the latter are not. However, both kinds of accounts are guided by cultural conventions, historically situated, which largely determine the character of the reality they portray. Narrative accounts are not replicas of reality, but the devices from which reality is constructed. All accounts of the world, mythical, scientific, mysterious, are guided by historically and culturally based conventions (Kenyon, this volume; Polkinghorne, this volume; Randall, this volume).

This reconsideration of representation does not thus reduce the importance of scientific narrative. Rather, in two major ways it shifts the site of its significance. First, rather than such narratives retaining the status of "truth telling," thus claiming to be predictive aids to survival, they gain their importance as constitutive frames. That is, such narratives constitute reality as one kind of thing rather than another, as good or evil in certain respects as opposed to others. And in doing so, they furnish the rational grounds or justification for certain lines of conduct as opposed to others. Thus, if we believe with sociobiologists that human action is primarily governed by genetically based urges, the way we carry out daily life is likely to be different than if we believe, with learning psychologists, that people's actions are infinitely malleable. Each account, once embraced, invites certain actions and discourages others. Scientific narratives gain their chief significance, then, in terms of the forms of life they invite, rationalize, or justify. They are not so much reflections of life already lived as they are progenitors of the future.

The postmodern shift from the object of knowledge to its representation also relocates the grounds for justification. On the modernist account, scientific descriptions are the product of single individuals, scientists whose patient skills of observation yield insights for all. Individual scientists, then, are more or less authoritative, because they are more or less knowledgeable about the world as it is. From the postmodern perspective, the factual warrant is removed from the scientist's narrative. The scientist may "know how" to do certain things (what we might call, for example, "atomic fusion"), but the scientist does not "know that" what is being done *is* "atomic fusion."

What, then, gives the scientist the right to speak with authority? In the same way that the conventions of writing permit things to be said in one way and not others, so the social conventions of the scientific community bestow on its members the right to be authoritative. That is, the scientist only speaks with justifiable assuredness within the community of those who honor those particular ways of speaking. Or, to put it otherwise, scientific representations are products of the community of scientists, negotiating, competing, conspiring, and so on. Within a postmodern frame, what we take to be knowledge is a social product.

Such arguments form a major challenge to the modernist orientation to therapy. At the onset they remove the factual justification of the modernist narratives of pathology and cure, transforming these accounts to forms of cultural mythology. They undermine the unquestioned status of the therapist as scientific authority, with privileged knowledge of cause and cure. The therapist's narratives thus take their place along side the myriad other possibilities available in the culture, not transcendentally superior, but different in implication. By the same token, significant questions must be raised with the traditional practice of replacing the client's stories with the fixed and narrow alternatives of the modernist therapist. There is no justification outside the small community of like-minded therapists for hammering the client's complex and richly detailed life into a single, preformulated narrative, a narrative that may be of little relevance or promise for the client's subsequent life conditions. And finally, there is no broad justification for the traditional status hierarchy that both demeans and frustrates the client. The therapist and client form a community to which both bring resources and from which the contours of the future may be carved.

Although these various critiques cast a pall over the modernist adventure and its accompanying optimism, from the ashes of deconstruction new conceptions of therapy, counseling, and social work are slowly taking form. These alternatives have benefitted much from constructivist writings, phenomenological explorations, and hermeneutic inquiry in the social sciences, and as well from such domains as poststructuralism, feminism, symbolic anthropology, and rhetorical study elsewhere in the academy. Many of the chapters of the present volume reflect these developments (see especially chapters by Kenyon, Polkinghorne, Cohler and Cole, Mader, and Ruth and Kenyon). In my view, the postmodern impulse is most fully reflected in writings and practices often termed social constructionist. From a constructionist standpoint, human meaning is a byproduct of relationships. Ontologies, conceptions of value, theories of causation, social inferences, and the remaining rudiments of intelligibility by which we carry our life have their origins in human interchange. This orientation has informed many of the arguments of the chapter thus far. However, it may be helpful to underscore several of its chief consequences and implications for therapy.

FROM MENTAL TO SOCIAL PROCESS

Traditional therapies typically work at plumbing the depths of client subjectivity, for example, the client's experience, cognition, construals, meanings. In contrast, for the constructionist the emphasis shifts to the more accessible domain of client discourse. The pioneering work of Watzlawick, Beavin, & Jackson (1967) on the pragmatics of therapeutic language has had a major impact on the therapeutic field. However, this work, like many of its grandchildren (see, for example, Efran, Lukens, & Lukens, 1990) has also placed a strong emphasis on individual conceptual or cognitive processes. Constructionist writings, in contrast, deemphasize or bracket concern with individual construal and focus concern on language as a microsocial process. How is life being framed, what words are selected, what is their impact?

New analytic concepts now make their way into the therapeutic arena, concepts of metaphor, metonomy, narrative form, and the like (see, for example, Kenyon, Birren & Schroots, 1991). And with such concepts, new questions and new modes of therapeutic departure are invited. The concern shifts to "the ways in which a plurality of perspectives are coordinated into coherent patterns of interaction, each potentiating and simultaneously constraining particular forms of action" (McNamee, 1992, p. 191) A therapist may ask whether elements of a given self-description can be incorporated via metaphor or metonomy into a new form of account. Are there alternative narratives that make equally good sense of the facts of life as given? Can a marginalized voice within the discourse be given room for greater articulation? Can the content of a couple's arguments be bracketed ("ineffective ways of putting things"), and attention directed to the conditions that invite argumentative forms to be adopted? What are the means of effectively deconstructing and reconstructing client reality? We shall return to these issues later in the chapter.

TOWARD EQUALIZATION AND CO-CONSTRUCTION

The modernist view of the therapist as superior knower has been challenged by constructivist writings (Mahoney, 1991). Yet, for most constructivists the therapist remains independent of the client(s), "observing patterns," and from this remote and implicitly superior standpoint attempts to "perturb the system" of the client. However, from the constructionist standpoint, the therapist's loss of authority is in the forefront; the traditional hierarchy is dismantled. Instead, the therapist enters the arena not with superior truth about the world, but with modes of being, including a range of languages. Nor are these modes of being, life forms, inherently superior to those of the client. They are not model ways of life. Rather, they are modes of life that, together with the client's actions, may engender useful alternatives for the client. As commentators increasingly put the case, the therapist is placed in the position of collaborator, a co-constructor of meaning.

FROM DIAGNOSTICS AND CURE TO CULTURAL RESPONSIBILITY

Within the modernist view the attempt of the therapist is typically to locate the illness and destroy it: diagnosis and cure. The medical model of disease remains robust. However, as the emphasis shifts to the linguistic construction of reality, illness and problems lose ontological privilege. They cease to be "there" as constituents of an independent reality, and take their place among the array of cultural constructions. Thus, one may speak of problems, suffering, and alleviation, but such terms are always considered to index a reality only from a particular perspective. There are no problems beyond a culture's way of constituting them as such. On the one hand, such a conclusion suggests first that the process of diagnosis, or "locating the problem," is unnecessary. Indeed, the very existence of nosological categories and illness labeling adds incrementally to the cultural sense of enfeeblement.

Equally problematic is the yoked concept of "cure." If there is no "illness" in nature, then what counts as "cure"? Yet, questioning at this level sends ripples of anguish across the profession. For if the concept of cure is sacrificed, so is the function of therapy placed in question. If there are no problems, in reality, and no solutions, then how is therapy to be justified? Why should people seek therapeutic help, why should one enter the profession, and why should people be charged for the services? Surely, in principle, discussion of such questions is unbounded. However, in the final analysis we cannot escape culture, remove ourselves to ask how we should act in a world that is unconstructed. We may continue to play out the rituals in which we accept others as having real pain, and for which there are real cures, or we may locate or develop alternative realities. However, we cannot live outside any constitution of the real. There is, then, no knock-down argument against "treating problems" and making claims for "cure" and therapeutic "progress." Added from a constructionist perspective, however, are reflexive and creative dimensions, an acknowledgement of the contingent nature of one's constructions, a critical sensitivity to their possible effects, and an openness to generating alternatives. In effect, one is thus goaded to consider the implications of one's actions, their outcomes and implications from other standpoints, and the potentials inherent in other endeavors. In the broader sense this is to acknowledge one's membership in the broader culture, one's continuing participation in the multiplicitous enclaves of meaning.

The full implications of a constructionist approach are far from clear. We stand at a critical juncture: a radical departure from traditional assumptions about knowledge, persons, and the nature of illness and cure. Substantial deliberation and exploration are now required, and even then we shall have but additional fuel for a conversation that should ideally have no end. It is in this spirit that the remaining arguments are offered. In certain respects, current discussions of narrative meaning in therapy and counseling still retain significant vestiges of the modernist worldview. And, if the potentials of postmodernist constructionism are to be fully realized, we must ultimately press beyond narrative construction. The ultimate challenge for therapy, it may be ventured, is not so much to transform meaning, but transcend it, not to replace one client story with another, but to enable clients to participate in the continuous process of creating and transforming meaning. To appreciate this possibility, it is first necessary to explore the pragmatic dimension of narrative meaning.

THE PRAGMATICS OF NARRATION

Narrative accounts in modernist frame serve as potential representations of reality, true or false in their capacity to match events as they occur. If the accounts are accurate, they also serve as blueprints for adaptive action. Thus, in the therapeutic case, if the narrative reflects a recurring pattern of maladaptive action (Mader, this volume), one begins to explore alternative ways of behaving. Or, if it captures the formative processes for a given pathology, palliatives can be prescribed. Within the modernist view, the therapist's narrative has a privileged status in prescribing an optimal way of life. In contrast, for most therapists informed by the perspectivalism of the postmodern era, the modernist concern with narrative accuracy ceases to compel. Narrative truth cannot be distinguished from historical truth, and when closely examined, even the latter concept is found to be an imposter. What, then, is the function of narrative reconstruction? Most existing accounts now point to the potential of such reconstructions to reorient the individual, to open new courses of action that are more fulfilling and more adequately suited to the individual's capacities and proclivities. Thus, the client may alter or dispose of earlier narratives, not because they are inaccurate, but because they are dysfunctional in his or her particular circumstances.

Yet, the question must be raised, in precisely what way(s) is a narrative "useful." How does a language of self-understanding guide, direct, or inform lines of action? What does the story do for (or to) the client? Two answers to this question pervade post empiricist camps at present, and both are importantly flawed. On the one side is the metaphor of language as a lens. On this account, a narrative construction is a vehicle through which the world is *seen*. It is through the lens of narrative that the individual identifies objects, persons, actions, and so on. As many argue, it is on the basis of the world as seen, and not on the world as it is, that the individual determines a course of action. Thus, one who sees their life as a tragic fall (Ruth & Öberg, this volume), would perceive life's unfolding events in these terms. Yet, to take this position is to view the individual as isolated and solipsistic, simply stewing in the juices of his/her own constructions. The possibilities for survival are minimal, for there is no means of escaping encapsulation in the internal system of construals. Further, such an account buys a range of notorious epistemological problems. How, for example, does the individual develop the lens? From whence the first construction? For is there is no world outside that which is internally constructed, there would be no means for understanding, and thus of developing or fashioning the lens. How can we defend the view that the sounds and markings employed in human interchange are somehow transported into the mind to impose order on the perceptual world? This was indeed Benjamin Lee Whorf's proposal, but it is a view that never succeeded in being more than controversial. The argument for language as lens seems poorly taken.

The major alternative to this view holds that narrative constructions are internal models, forms of story that can be interrogated by the individual as guides to action. Again, there is no brief made for the truth of the model; the narrative operates simply as an enduring structure that informs and directs action. Thus, for example, a person who features himself as a hero whose feats of bravery and intelligence has prevailed against all odds, now finds the challenges too daunting. Through therapy he realizes that such a view not only places him in impossible circumstances, but works against close feelings of intimacy and interdependence with his wife and grandchildren. A new story is worked out in which the individual comes to see himself as a champion not for himself, but for his family. His heroism will be achieved through their feelings of happiness, and will thus depend importantly on their assessments of his actions.

It is this transformed image that is to guide subsequent actions. While there is a certain wisdom to this position, it is again problematic. Stories of this variety are in themselves both idealized and abstract. As such, they can seldom dictate behavior in complex, ongoing interaction. What does the new story of self say, for example, about the best reaction to his wife's desires for him to spend more time on ("feminine") domestic chores, or how should he respond to a new business offer, challenging and profitable, but replete with risk? Stories as internal models are not only bare of specific directives or implications, but they remain static. The individual moves through numerous situations and relationships, his son has a problem with drugs, medical insurance runs out, one loses night vision, and so on. At the same time, the narrative model remains inflexible, unbending and of obscure relevance. The "model in the head" is largely useless.

Yet, there is a third way of understanding narrative utility, one that grows out of the constructionist emphasis on the pragmatics of language. As proposed, narratives gain their utility primarily within social interchange. They are constitutive components of ongoing relationships, essential for maintaining the intelligibility and coherence of social life, useful in drawing people together, creating distance, and so on. Stories of the self enable public identities to be established, the past to be rendered acceptable, and the rituals of relationship to unfold with ease. The utility of these stories derives from their success as moves within these relational arenas, in terms of their adequacy as reactions to previous moves, or as instigators to what follows.

Consider, for example, a story of failure, how one tried one's best to succeed at a career but was only mediocre. As we have seen, the story is neither true nor false in itself; it is simply one construction of events among many. However, as this story is inserted into various forms of relationship, into the games or dances of the culture, its effects are strikingly varied. If a friend has just related a story of great personal achievement, one's story of failure is likely to act as a repressive force, and alienate the friend who otherwise anticipated a congratulatory reaction. If, in contrast, the friend had just revealed a personal failure, to share one's own failings is likely to be reassuring and to solidify the friendship. Similarly, to relate one's story of failure to one's mother may elicit a warm and sympathetic reaction, in effect, enabling her to be a "mother"; but to share it with a wife who worries each month over making ends meet may produce both frustration and anger.

To put it otherwise, a story is not simply a story. It is itself a situated action, a performance with illocutionary effects. It acts so as to create, sustain, or alter worlds of social relationship. In these terms, it is insufficient that the client and therapist negotiate a new form of self-understanding that seems realistic, aesthetic, and uplifting within the dyad. It is not the dance of meaning within the therapeutic context that is primarily at stake. Rather, the significant question is whether the new shape of meaning is serviceable within the social arena outside these confines. How, for example, does the story of oneself as "hero of the family group" play for a wife who dislikes her dependent status, a boss who is a "self-made woman," or a rebellious son? What forms of action does the story invite in each of these situations; what kinds of dances are engendered, facilitated, or sustained as a result? It is evaluation at this level that seems most crucial for the joint consideration of therapist and client.

TRANSCENDING NARRATIVE

The focus on narrative pragmatics sets the stage for perhaps the most critical argument of this chapter. For many therapists and counselors making the postmodern turn in therapy, the narrative continues to be viewed as either a form of internal lens, determining the way life is seen, or an internal model for the guidance of action. In light of the preceding discussion of pragmatics, these conceptions are found lacking in three important respects. First, each retains the *individualist* cast of modernism, in that the final resting place of the narrative construction is within the mind of the single individual. As we have reconsidered the utility of the narrative, we have moved outward, from the individual's mind to the relationships constituted by the narrative in action. Narratives exist in the telling, and tellings are constituents of relational forms, for good or ill. Second, the metaphors of the lens and the internal model both favor *singularity* in narrative. That is, both tend to presume the functionality of a single formulation of self-understanding. The individual possesses "a lens" for comprehending the world, it is said, not a repository of lenses; and through therapy one comes to possess "a new narrative truth," it is often put, not a *multiplicity* of truths. From the pragmatic standpoint, the presumption of singularity operates against functional adequacy. Each narrative of the self may function well in certain circumstances, but lead to miserable outcomes in others. To have only a single means of making self intelligible, then, is to limit the range of relationships of situations in which one can function satisfactorily. Thus, for example, it may be very useful to be able to "do anger" scenarios effectively, and to formulate accounts to justify such activity. There are certain times and places in which anger is the most effective move in the dance. At the same time, to be overskilled or overprepared in this regard, such that anger is virtually the only means of performing in trying circumstances, will vastly reduce one's relationships altogether. From the present perspective, narrative multiplicity is vastly to be preferred (for a discussion of whether we are *one* story or many, see Kenyon, this volume; Ruth & Kenyon, this volume).

Finally, both the lens and the internal model conceptions favor belief in our commitment to narrative. That is, both suggest that the individual lives within the narrative as a system of understanding. One "sees the world in this way," as it is said, and the narrative is thus "true for the individual." Or the transformed story of self is "the new reality"; it constitutes a "new belief about self" to support and sustain the individual. Again, however, as we consider the social utility of narrative, belief and commitment become suspect. To be committed to a given story of self, to adopt it as "true to me," is to vastly limit one's possibilities of relating. To believe that one is successful is thus as debilitating in its own way as believing that one is a failure. Both are only stories, after all, and each may bear fruit within a particular range of contexts and relationships. To crawl inside one and take root is to forego the other, and thus to reduce the range of contexts and relationships in which adequacy is achieved.

To frame the issue another way, postmodern consciousness favours a thoroughgoing relativism in expressions of identity. On the metatheoretical level it invites a multiplicity of accounts of reality, while recognizing the historically and culturally situated contingency of each. There are only accounts of truth within differing conversations, and no conversation is transcendentally privileged. Thus, for the postmodern practitioner a multiplicity of self-accounts is invited, but a commitment to none. From this standpoint the client should be encouraged, on the one hand, to explore a variety of narrative formulations, but discouraged from commitment to any particular "truth of self." The narrative constructions thus remain fluid, open to the shifting tides of circumstance, to the forms of dance that provide fullest sustenance.

Can such a conclusion be tolerated? Is the individual thus reduced to a social con artist, adopting whatever posture of identity that garners the highest payoff? Certainly the constructionist emphasis is on flexibility in self-identification, but this does not simultaneously imply that the individual is either duplicitous or scheming. To speak of duplicity is to presume that there is a "true telling" that is otherwise available. Such a view is deeply problematic and thus abandoned. One may interpret one's actions as duplicitous or sincere, but these ascriptions are, after all, simply components of different stories. Similarly, to presume that the individual possesses private motives, including a rational calculus of self-presentation (the psychological basis of a "con") is again to sustain the modernist view of the self-contained individual. From the constructionist standpoint the relationship takes priority over the individual self. That is, selves are only realized as a byproduct of relatedness. Thus, to shift in the form and content of self-narration from one relationship to another is neither deceitful nor self-serving in the traditional sense. Rather, it is to honor the various modes of relationship in which one is enmeshed. It is to take seriously the multiple and varied forms of human connectedness that make up a life. Adequate and fulfilling actions are only so in the terms of criteria generated within the various forms of relationship themselves.

THERAPEUTIC MOVES

From the present perspective, therapy or counseling as a means toward narrative reconstruction or replacement fails both in realizing the full implications of constructionist theory and in facilitating the full possibilities for human functioning. From a thoroughgoing constructionist view, the emphasis is placed on narrative within the broader social process of generating meaning. This involves an appreciation of the contextual relativity of meaning, an acceptance of indeterminacy, the generative exploration of multiplicity of meanings, and the understanding that there is no necessity for adhering to an invariant story or searching for a definitive identity. "Reauthoring" or "re-storying" (Randall, this volume) seems then, but a first order therapeutic approach, one which implies the replacement of a dysfunctional master narrative with a more functional one. At the same time this result carries the seeds of a prescriptive rigidity, one which might also serve to confirm an illusion that it is possible to develop a set of principles or codes which can be invariantly applied, irrespective of relational context.

From a certain standpoint, one may also venture that this very rigidity is constitutive of the difficulties which people often bring to the therapeutic situation. This possibility is worthy of attention. Just as psychotherapists may be restrained by a limiting code, so people who describe their lives as problematic often seem trapped within a limiting vocabulary, behavioral codes, and constitutive conventions from which the contours of their lives are molded. Acting in terms of a singular narrative and its associated actions, one is not only restrained from exploring alternative possibilities, but can become imprisoned in painful transactional patterns with those about them.

Heinz von Foerster once made the acute observation that we are blind until we see that we cannot see. If language provides the matrix for all human understanding, then psychotherapy may be aptly construed as "linguistic activity in which conversation about a problem generates the development of new meanings" (Goolishian & Winderman, 1988, p. 139). Put differently, psychotherapy may be thought of as a process of *semiosis:* the forging of meaning in the context of collaborative discourse. It is a process through which the meaning of events is transformed via a fusion of the horizons of the participants, alternative ways of narrating events are developed, and the new stances toward self and others evolve. A crucial component of this process may inhere not only in the alternative ways of accounting generated by the discourse, but also in the different orders of meaning that concurrently emerge.

To help another achieve the perspective that comes from seeing that we cannot see implies first a release from the tyranny of the implied authority of governing beliefs. Given the linguistic constitution of our world models, required is a transformation dialogue in which new understandings are negotiated together with a new set of premises *about* meaning. Further, we must nourish an expectant attitude toward the as yet unseen, the as yet unstoried, the "meaning ahead of the text" (Ricoeur, 1971). In terms of Bateson's (1972) distinctions between levels of learning, it is a move beyond learning to replace one punctuation of a situation with another (Level 1), to learning new modes of punctuation (Level 2), to evolving what Keeney (1983) calls "a change of the premises underlying an entire system of punctuation of habits (p. 159)" (Level 3). It is a progression from learning new meanings, to developing new categories of meaning, to transforming one's premises about the nature of meaning itself.

For any of these transformations to occur, a context needs to be established which facilitates their emergence. At the outset there is much to be said for Goolishian & Anderson's (1991) emphasis on creating a climate where clients have the experience of being heard, of having both their point of view and feelings understood, of feeling themselves confirmed and accepted. Invited are endeavors to understand the client's point of view, to convey an understanding of how it makes sense to the person, given the premises from which the viewpoint arises. At the same time this does not imply a necessary commitment to the client's premises. Rather, it serves as a contextual validation for a particular account, a validation that enables client and therapist to reconstitute this reality as a conversational object, now vulnerable to a new infusion of meaning.

How is this process to proceed? There is no single answer to this question, just as there can be no principled constraint over the number of possible conversations. However, therapists sensitive to the postmodern dialogues have been highly creative in developing conceptually congenial practices. Hoffman (1990) sets the contours for an *art of lenses*. Goolishian and Anderson (1992) employ a form of *interested inquiry*, asking questions that simultaneously credit the client's reality while pressing it toward evolution. Andersen and his colleagues (1991) have developed the practice of the *reflecting team*, individuals who observe the therapeutic encounter and then share their opinions with both therapist and client. In this way, the aura of single authority (the therapist) is reduced, appreciation for multiple realities is generated, and the client is furnished with a variety of resources for proceeding. White and Epston (1990) employ letters (and other written documents) to help clients to reauthor their lives. Letters may be written by both clients and the therapist. Penn (in press) also relies on client letter-writing, but with the major emphasis on generating a dialogic process within the clients' stories, so that new openings are subsequently forged for conversations with others.

O'Hanlon and Wilk (1987) lay out an array of conversational means by which client-therapist *negotiation* may proceed toward a dissolution of the putative problem. DeShazer (1991) encourages conversation *on solutions* (as opposed to problems), and Friedman and Fanger (1991) on *positive possibilities*. Lipchik (1993) emphasizes client talk about *balancing* the various goods and bads in exciting alternatives, to replace an either/or orientation with a both/and perspective. Many therapists place a strong emphasis on *positive construction* of self and life circumstances (see, for example, Durrant & Kowalski, 1993). Fruggeri (1992) encourages different descriptions of given events, new ways of connecting behaviors and events, and a process of continuous reflexivity.

Yet simply because these therapeutic forms grow from the soil of postmodern constructionism, does not mean that all other therapies are outmoded or abandoned. On the contrary, a constructionist standpoint, unlike empiricism, does not attempt to eradicate alternative languages of understanding and their associated practices. Such prefixes as "is true," "is objective," "is more successful in producing cures," may be removed from discussions of the alternatives. However, all theories of therapy, all forms of therapeutic practice, must be considered in terms of what they add (or subtract) from the conversational matrix we call therapy. Couches, dream analysis, positive regard, strategic interventions, circular questioning, are all entries into the broader vocabulary of the profession. They invite certain lines of interchange and action, and suppress others.

By the same token, we must view the modernist attempt to replace lay languages (of "ignorance") with scientific languages, and typically a univocal language of the true, as unnecessarily and detrimentally constraining. The common languages by which people live their daily lives have enormous pragmatic potential. Living room languages, street languages, spiritual languages, New Age languages, these and others are prime movers in the culture. To restrict their entry into the therapeutic setting is to reduce the possibilities for conversation. Belief is not in question here, for the concept of belief (as indexing a mental state) is itself deeply suspect. Rather, the major challenge concerns the potential of the therapeutic conversation to alter the course of events.

More generally, we may ask whether our languages and practices can liberate participants from static and delimiting conventions of understanding and enable a full flexibility of relationship. Can those turning to the therapist in times of trouble come to transcend the restraints imposed by their erstwhile reliance on a determinate set of meanings and be freed from the struggle that ensues from imposing their beliefs on self and others? Hopefully for some, new solutions to problems can become apparent, while for others a richer set of narrative meanings will emerge. For still others a stance toward meaning itself can perhaps evolve; one which betokens that tolerance of uncertainty, that freeing of self which comes from acceptance of the unbounded relativity of meaning. For those who adopt it, this stance offers the prospect of a creative participation in the unending and unfolding meaning of life.

13

Restorying a Life: Adult Education and Transformative Learning

William L.Randall, Ed.D.

TRANSFORMATIVE LEARNING

In the field of adult education, the academic agenda is seldom divorced from the activist one. With a heritage of programs whose goals range from job training to personal growth and from organizational development to social change, adult educators have traditionally been concerned not merely to fathom learning but to foster it as well–not just to study it, but to stimulate it too. From one context to another the kind of learning sought will naturally vary, whether it be in terms of knowledge, attitudes, or skills. Though learning in any of these domains may be said to *transform* the learner to some degree, one kind of learning has come to be identified as explicitly "transformative" in nature.

Transformative learning goes to the roots of our being. It is not a matter of merely adding to our store of information. It involves critical self-reflection. It is "a process of questioning the assumptions and values that form the basis for the way we see the world" (Cranton, 1992, p. 146). For Jack Mezirow (1978), the scholar often credited with originating the concept, tranformative learning goes beyond "learning how to do something" or "the way something works." And it is more than "learning what others expect of me" or forming "an evolving concept of myself as a person with certain values." Transformative learning is metalearning. A sort of secular conversion, it involves "learning how we are caught in our own history and are reliving it" (Mezirow, p. 102). The essence of such learning is that:

> We learn to become critically aware of the cultural and psychological assumptions that have influenced the way we see ourselves and our relationships and the way we pattern our lives. (Mezirow, p. 101)

It is my thesis in this chapter that the "transformation" in transformative learning can be conceived as *restorying.* This concept is a logical extension of a metaphor that is implicit in much of this volume; indeed, it is the *method* in that metaphor. I refer to "the story of my life"–a story of which I am arguably, at once, author, narrator, protagonist, and reader–a lived story that can be discussed in the same terms we use to analyze a literary one; a story that is "slowly unfolding according to [my] own inner theme and plot" (Bridges, 1980, p. 71).

I begin, then, by examining the complexity of the idea itself: the *story* of a life. Next, I consider the dynamics of stor*ying* a life, in particular the element of plotting and genre-ating that is involved. This leads to a look at "storying styles," then at the influence of the larger stories within which our personal ones are lived. I next sketch the process of *re*storing a life, especially the roles we educators can play in its facilitation. In doing so, I consider how transformative learning has what is in effect a *therapeutic* component, though one in which the personal is enmeshed with the political. Finally, I outline certain implications and questions raised by a story model for research, theory, and practice in adult education, an exercise which I conclude with some speculation on the convergences between that field and the field of gerontology with respect to biography and aging.

I should stress at the start that this is an exercise in the realm more of the humanities than of the social sciences, and this because essentially I am playing with a metaphor. In adult education, as in gerontology (Kenyon, Birren, & Schroots, 1991), metaphor may be our last resort in the face of the mystery of learning, our studies and statistics notwithstanding. In the house of metaphor, however, are many rooms, such as life-as-puzzle, life-as-battle, and life-as-journey (Daloz, 1986; Kenyon, 1991). Life-as-story can claim no special status. Yet allusions to it and variations on it sprinkle our everyday speech: "tale of woe," "sob story," "end a chapter," "turn over a new leaf," and so on. Furthermore, as educators, we know that the people we work with are never just disembodied brains. Bundled into the "baggage" they bring to each event (Even, 1987) is a unique set of memories and hopes, of experiences and expectations–a set of tales they carry around inside them (long and short, happy and sad, general and precise) about their past, present, and future. Without them, they can scarcely tell us who they are or relate to what they are learning (Schank, 1990). In the end, their stories may be their most precious, perhaps their sole, possession. By interfacing life and story, then, two otherwise separate realms, we set off a shower of alluring possibilities for understanding the meaning-making mechanisms that are central to being human.

THE STORY OF A LIFE

As the second in their list of thirty-six "adult learning principles," researchers Brundage and MacKeracher (1980) observe that:

> Adults enter learning activities *with an organized set of descriptions and feelings about themselves* which influence their learning processes. The descriptions are the *self-concept;* the feelings are the *self-esteem.* Both are based on *past experience* and on how that experience was *interpreted and valued* by the learner. (p. 97; emphasis mine)

The reason such a principle is ranked so high is that the items italicized in it are considered to have a profound influence on how, what, and why adults actually learn–not just positively, but negatively as well. As regards past experience, for instance, "the past experience an adult learner brings to any learning activity is both a helpful resource for further learning and an unavoidable potential hindrance" (Brundage & MacKeracher, p. 98). Indeed, even though it "becomes increasingly important as an adult grows older, its potential for helping or hindering also increases" (Brundage & MacKeracher, p. 99).

It is my assessment that the same italicized items can all be subsumed under "the story of my life." My story, for example, includes the organized set of descriptions and feelings I have about myself. It is thus the basis for my self-concept, that is, as it extends forward and backward in time to encompass my account of both where I have come from and where I am going. It is, moreover, the source of my self-esteem, though my version of it may change from one day to the next. That is, a bad story–"my family was no good," "my education was no good," "I'll never amount to no good," usually coincides with a bad day. As one critic reminds us, "stories are not innocent" (Rosen, 1986, p. 236). As a linking of my life from its dimly recalled beginning to its projected end through its ever-changing middle (of both good days and bad), my story is the source of my sanity too (Sacks, 1985; Winquist, 1974). This means that though it contains what I have interpreted and valued from my *past* experience, it includes what I anticipate in my *future* experience as well–just as in making sense of a story I am in the middle of reading, I look ahead to its end no less than I look back to its beginning.

On closer inspection, however, the concept of "lifestory" is as complex as it is commonplace. Its very presence in our vocabulary (and of other terms derived from it) signals a curious gap between the life we actually live and the account we fashion of it for others and ourselves; a gap that is aesthetic in nature; a gap between biology and biography (Weintraub, 1975), between life and lifestory. We get a sense of this gap by looking at lifestory in terms of at least four overlapping levels: existence, experience, expression, and impression.

Existence: The Outside Story

This level takes in all of the uninterpreted, unevaluated events of my existence, one after the other, from morning to night, conception to now, bottom to top: from the domain of the atomic and biochemical to that of my conscious thoughts and actions. None of these "events" are intrinsically more important than any others, though they are on different scales, size-wise. This level is "my life", then, in the sense that it is the total of the raw "facts" of my life. As such, it is my *whole* story. It is merely the *outside* story, though, for, if knowable at all, it is only by some colossal computer (or deity) at the edge of space-time in which everything is recorded in excruciating detail. In this respect, it may be my "true" story too, objectively speaking, but it remains outside my ken since "I" am inside of it, like an infant within a womb.

Experience: The Inside Story

The second level, then, is comprised of what I *make* of these facts–or make up from them,–within me, subjectively. It is the storehouse, as it were, of the countless smaller, shorter stories I weave around them. Impelled by a kind of "autobiographical imperative," however, these many stories are held together within me as one more or less integrated whole. This one story can be thought of as the story-*behind*-the story: the *inside* story. It is my experience: that swirling mass of "quasi-narrative" inner material (Casey, 1987, p. 43) that "used to be called the Soul" (Laing, 1967, p. 18).

My experience is a rather different story from my existence, since it is but a digest of it and so only ambiguously related to it. Indeed, it is often contradictorily related to it. What I remember does not always jibe with what happened and what I anticipate is frequently far from what will be. When I am sufficiently out of synch with the facts of my existence, I am deemed to be deluded. In synch or not, my experience is a vast realm in its own right, for it is the host not only of my memories of the past, but also of my anticipations for the future, as well as of all the meanderings of my mind and heart in the present.

My inside story is "my life," then, in one of the senses suggested by the platitude: "Life is what you *make* it." It is my life not in the sense of "how it is" or "how it was" but of "how it is interpreted and reinterpreted, told and retold" (Bruner, 1987, p. 31). It is "that story of our own lives which we narrate to ourselves in an episodic, sometimes semiconscious, virtually uninterrupted monologue" (Polkinghorne, 1988, p. 160).

Expression I: The Inside-Out Story

On this next level, I take my inside story, abridge it, edit it, and package it for others. In other words, I transform the facts of my life (leastwise those I have internalized) into the "artifacts" I recount to the world (Renza, 1980, p. 269). I do this, whether wittingly or not and formally or not, according to the storytelling conventions of everyday social interaction (Schank, 1990). Indeed, much of my "socialization" is a schooling in the culturally accepted ways of sequencing and weighting the events I wish to relate, of characterizing myself amid them, and of providing my audience both sufficient setting to take them in context and enough suspense to make them worth hearing. This is my "inside-out" story. However, depending on my audience, my motive, or my mood at any given time, plus my skills with the (intrinsically distorting) tool of language itself, the countless possible versions of it I convey can vary widely both from each other and from the original inside me from which they arise (Ruth & Kenyon, this volume). That is, I seldom say *exactly* what I mean or reveal precisely how I feel, a fact that can lead to my being confusing not only to others but also to myself.

This story is "my life" in the sense of the face and voice I project to the world, the set of accounts of me, verbal and nonverbal, with which I go public. It is the level of expression . It is also the level of my autobiography, or at least of my autobiographical *activity* , since so few of us have the time, talent, or temerity to put it in a publishable form (Eakin, 1985). It is my "life-story" as that term is used by Sharon Kaufman (1987).

Expression II: The Outside-In Story

This is the level of those various interpretations read into part or all of my life, and often imposed upon me, by the people and powers around me. It is "my life" in the sense of what is made of me by others, of how I am constructed in their imagination. It is my "outside-in" story, any one version of which will generally be inaccurate and incomplete: a crude "storyotype", a shadow of who I really am. In other words, in the lifestory of another, whether parent, partner, or peer, I am never more than a character (as s/he is in mine), no matter how major I might fancy myself or how fairly I might be composed. All I need do is listen to how I am portrayed in the anecdotes s/he tells about me to others. Yet as I internalize what I perceive is that person's version of me and accept it as "official" (as I "experience" it and make it part of my inside story), it can be frighteningly influential in the shaping of my sense of self: past, present, and future. It can make a great impression upon me, so much so that I may spend much time and energy in "impression management" (Goffman, 1959), adjusting my story inside-out either to reflect or to reject it. This level of impression , then, is the level of my biography, the story not that I tell the world but that the world tells of me. It is my "life history" (Kaufman, 1987). (For a further discussion of the outside story in relation to aging, see Kenyon, this volume).

The Links Between the Levels

In rough terms, if the outside story is what happens to me, then the inside story is what I make of what happens to me and tell to myself. On this view, the inside-out story is what I *tell* and show to others (Schafer, 1983, p. 222)–of what I make of what happens to me, while the outside-in story is what others make of me on their own, with or (usually) without my consent.

Two crude analogies illustrate the links and lags between these levels. In manufacturing terms, my outside story is the raw material from which I fashion my inside story. In turn, the inside story is the raw material from which I fashion the stories I tell inside-out. Accordingly, not everything that *could* be used from the outside story is used. Much is jettisoned as slag. By the same token, not everything that *could* be used from the inside story is used when I move inside-out. Much remains buried, or is left aside as scrap to be used on a later occasion. Still more of me will usually be scrapped by others in composing the commonly cardboard storyotype through which alone they can deal with me.

In publishing terms, my outside story corresponds to the physical object of a particular novel. It is the paper, ink, and binding that comprise the thing itself, as well as the history of its manufacture. My inside story, however, is the novel as I *experience* it, as I reconstruct it in the reading: its atmosphere, its unfolding in time, its reality within me as an entire story-world. My inside-out story is my summary of part or all of that world for the purpose of communicating about it with others. My outside-in story, then, is the set of versions that these others entertain of the same world, or read into it, on the basis of a review, the notes on the jacket, or the design on the cover.

From this, it should be clear that the "organized set of feelings and descriptions" about ourselves that influences what and how we learn lies on the level of the inside story: "that most human of "regions" between an event and a reaction to it - the place where the event is privately composed, made sense of, the place where it actually *becomes* an event for that person" (Kegan, 1982, p. 2). This is the realm of my "personal, practical knowledge" (Connelly & Cladinin, 1988). By practical is meant all the things I "know" about the world and about living in general, frequently without knowing that I know them: for example, "how to do something" or "the way something works" (Mezirow, 1978, p. 100). By personal is meant all that I "know" concerning myself. The way I know myself, however, is conceivably akin to the way I know a story I am in the process of reading. Poised constantly in its middle, somewhere between its beginning and its end, I hold it together, more or less successfully, in my memory and imagination. As Polkinghorne (1988) puts it, "We live immersed in narrative, recounting and reassessing the meanings of our past actions, anticipating the outcomes of our future projects, situating ourselves at the intersection of several stories not yet completed" (p. 160).

Personal knowing, then, the foundation of all abstract knowing (Brady, 1990, p. 50), is "narrative knowing" (Polkinghorne, 1988, this volume); it is an accomplishment in the domain of "narrative thought" (Bruner, 1986). Personal knowing, and personal learning, occurs in the domain of the inside story. It is on the formation and transformation of this inside story that I shall therefore be focussing in the next two sections.

THE STORYING OF A LIFE

To say that an event is "privately composed" (Kegan, 1982, p. 2) is to say that we do not receive it ready-made, with its "meaning" inherently assigned. Rather, we make its meaning for it; we construct the event ourselves. We story it, as we do our entire past. "We tell ourselves stories of our past, make fictions or stories of it," writes Carolyn Heilbrun (1988), "and these narrations *become* the past, the only part of our lives that is not submerged" (p. 51). To appreciate, though, how we compose our past, as well as our future and indeed our life overall (Bateson, 1989), many elements need to be considered. They are story elements actually, the same ones we employ in analyzing any short story, play, or novel. Alongside of character, point of view, and theme (Csikszentmihalyi & Beattie, 1979; Kaufman, 1987), each of which is worthy of its own analysis in this context, perhaps the most basic element is plot.

Plot in Literature and Life

The plot of a story, says Aristotle in the *Poetics*, is "the arrangement of the incidents" (1961, p. 62). It is what connects them in a continuous story-line with a beginning, middle and end. Tight or slack, this line is the skeleton of the story (Scholes & Kellogg, 1966, p. 238), its backbone. Naturally, plot-as-connection is different things from different perspectives. From that of the protagonist, it is just the way things are, one damned thing after another: the flow of "fate" with which one has little choice but to go. For the narrator, however, it is the way things *were*, since most narration is past tense. For the reader, it is what one follows expectantly into the future and figures out after the fact (Brooks, 1985, pp. 22f). To paraphrase Kierkegaard, one reads the story forward but understands it backward. For the author, finally, the plot is the "plan" of where things *ought* to go, more or less controllable depending on how formulaic or emergent is the design. Each of these perspectives mediates not just a different dimension of plot, however, but also a different story.

With respect to a novel, there is the story (or stories) the author conceives it to be not just before, but also during and after its composition. As well, there is the story as perceived by the narrator through whom it is told, though this may not at all be the same story as envisioned by the author. In addition, there is the story each of its characters would perceive it to be from one scene to another, if ever they were in a position to talk about it. Finally, there is the story that is read into and out of the novel by each of the readers into whose hands it falls. They in turn, as and when they read it and talk about it with other readers, will entertain one theory after another as to what sort of story it is and what it "means." Thus, a story is never simply one story but always many within the one.

Rebelled against by many modern authors for its association with conventions and rules, and by many critics for inviting the lowest form of reading (Brooks, 1985, p. 4), plot does more than merely connect events like beads on a string or lines on a blueprint. It constructs them. It "is what *makes* events *into* a story" (Ricoeur, 1980, p. 167). It rescues them from randomness by conferring on them a relevance, a purposefulness, because of the role they play in relation both to each other and to the story overall. Accordingly, the story goes somewhere (Gardner, 1985, pp. 48f), for plot connects events not just chronologically but causally as well. Because A happened, we discover (always in retrospect), it was possible for B and C to happen too. Each event "means something" in terms not of itself, that is, but of its place within an unfolding narrative context: past, present *and* future. Indeed, "the interpretation of current events is as much future-shaped as it is past-determined" (White & Epston, 1990, p. 10). As the story "unfolds" into the future, then, fresh events possess increased meaning potential over those preceding them. In a word, the plot "thickens."

Furthermore, the plot controls which of all of the events that *might* make it into the story actually do, as well as the relative weighting which each is assigned, that is, which is major and which minor, which is an important "turning point" and which is not. Also, the plot coordinates several strands of action and relationship by means of a system of intertwining *sub*plots. If it did not, the stuff of the story would not be integrated, would not constitute one story. Thus, plot gives the story its coherence.

It also gives the story its drive. Except in the fashionably slim plot of the average best-seller, which keeps a tight rein over its cast of stock heroes and villains, plot is tightly entwined with character. "What is character," asks Henry James, "but the determination of incident," and "What is incident but the illustration of character?" (Lynch & Rampton, 1992, p. 8). Plot is the crucible of character. It is the cradle of the conflict, the "agon," without which no "character" could ever be built and no story unfold. Count on a calm beginning and hope for a happy end, but have a quiet middle–with no problem to be overcome, no mystery to be solved, no battle to be won–and you have no tale. This central conflict, whether within characters, among characters, or between characters and their environment, is the engine that impels the story on. How this conflict is conceived and resolved determines, in turn, what sort of story we have, what "genre." There may be an infinite number of stories, says Northrop Frye, but only so many kinds (1988, p. 54). Criticizable for its crudeness, his typology is famous: tragedy, comedy, romance and irony (Keen, 1986, p. 175).

Given its conflict, every story is thus implicitly moral. There is a right to be upheld and a wrong to be put down, a good to be sought and an evil to be eschewed, however little resemblance each bears to the code of a conventional ethic or religion. In this way, the plot of a story mediates its "meaning" in both an aesthetic sense and an ethical one. A story has to have some point, that is: some bias or bottom line, some message, however innocuous. Again, stories are not innocent.

So, as the medium of coherence and conflict, morality and meaning, the plot of a story is not just its skeleton but also, as Aristotle saw, its soul. In these various respects, plot has its counterpart in the story of a life.

On a broad level, a life is plotted insofar as it has its own blunt brand of beginning, middle, and end; of calm, conflict, and conclusion. "We're born, we suffer, we die" (Gardner, 1985, p. 43). In this general way, "each person's life is a story that is telling itself in the living" (Bridges, 1980, p. 71). On a more specific level, however, plotting is involved in the process of composing a life insofar as not all of the events of my life in fact *become* events for me (Kegan, 1982, p. 2). Indeed, of the vast majority I seem to make nothing at all. Not all of my existence is experienceable, impressionable, at the time, nor is all of it, by any means, remeḿberable and accessible after the fact. Not every "real event," that is, is transformed into an "experienced event" (Neisser, 1986, p. 71). This does not mean it makes no impression whatever, simply that my consciousness as such is choosy.

Witness the last long trip we took and the precious few specifics we can later recall of all we surely saw and said, heard and felt. With much of our everyday life lived on "automatic pilot" (according to habits, scripts, routines), something somehow determines what we notice and what we ignore, what we retain in our story and what we release, what is important and what is not, what sinks in and what floats by on time's ever-rolling stream. This phenomenon pertains not just during a particular drive, of course, but on the journey of life in general. No doubt many factors are at work in it, from our learning style to our personality type, from our interests at a given time to our overall "frame of mind" (Gardner, 1990)–not to mention our "current developmental tasks, social roles, life crises and transition points" (Brundage & MacKeracher, 1980, p. 41). (See also McAdams, this volume; de Vries & Lehman, this volume; and Ruth & Öberg, this volume.) But through all of these run subtler, more aesthetic factors, ones which concern not only *what* we notice but *how*.

Storying Styles

Two people endure what seems the same event, yet their respective accounts of it are commonly different in both content and kind. This is the mystery of perception: one sees a rabbit; the other, a duck. Each extracts from the event, and focusses on, a certain set of features. Each fits the event as a whole into a particular narrative context, past, present *and* future. Each uniquely emplots it into, and explains it in terms of, a likely story. Each files it away into that rich repository of all the other stories that make him, biographically if not biologically, the unique individual he is (Sacks, 1985). Each thus "makes meaning" of it in an idiosyncratic manner (Kenyon, this volume), that is, according to a distinctive "storying style."

To entertain the notion of storying style, which I have elaborated elsewhere (Randall, 1955), means to consider not just the *content* of our self-storying (which will obviously be "novel" for each of us) but also the *form*. It means considering the varieties of self-plotting (and sub-plotting) and of self-characterization. It means considering the special set of themes (McAdams, this volume) that our self-story reveals and the unique atmosphere which, to others, it exudes. It means being alert to the features which the young Robert Coles (1989) was admonished by his mentor to listen for in the tales of his patients during his residency as a psychiatrist:

> He urged me to be a good listener in the special way a story requires: note the manner of presentation; the development of plot, character; the addition of new dramatic sequences; the emphasis accorded to one figure or another in the recital; and the degree of enthusiasm, of coherence, the narrator gives to his or her account. (p. 23)

To entertain the notion of styles means to ask whether, when people think of "their life," some do so primarily in terms of the outside level (outer events); some, of the inside (inner experiences); some, of the inside-out level (their expression to others); and some, of the outside-in (less what they think of themselves than what others think of them). It also means to consider the different points of view from which people may operate in relating to the stuff of their lifestory. The question of point of view can be discussed in terms not just of the tense toward which a story is tilted (past-, present-, or future-oriented) and of the person in which it is told (first, second, or third), but also of the angle from which it is perceived.

Scholes and Kellogg (1966) note that there are three points of view at work "in any example of narrative art, those of the characters, the narrator, and the audience" (p. 240). Might some of us relate to the story of our life primarily as *readers*, for example, forever wondering where it is going next or what are its principal themes, or what is the "meaning" of this event in the present relative to others preceding it in the past or following it in the future? Might some of us read primarily for the plot; others, for the point, the characters, the atmosphere, the themes (Beach, 1990)? On the other hand, might some of us be essentially *protagonists*; so immersed in the central action of our story, in the conflict or "agon", that any analysis, any reading, seems a waste of energy and time? Similarly, might some of us be basically *narrators*, endowed with "the chronicling gift" (Edel, 1973, p. ix), never more involved in our lifestories than when we are telling them, relaying play-by-play to whomever will listen the sometimes scarcely digested events of our existence, able to make so much of so frequently little. ("Stories happen," says Henry James, "to those who can tell them" (Bruner, 1987, pp. 11f)). And, as we are all narrators at some point, how "reliable" might we be with respect to the life we are narrating: how omniscient, how detached, how ironic, how identified with one character within us as opposed to another (Booth, 1961)?

Finally, what of ourselves as *authors* of our stories? What is the relationship between narrating our lives and authoring them? This is a metaphysical, even theological, question–the degree to which we *create* our lives. Though an answer is beyond the scope of this chapter, we can still ask how much of our self-authorship we normally "squander" and why (Polster, 1987), and what would be entailed in our taking on more? In the words of philosopher David Carr

(1988), "the self does not author itself, does not create itself *ex nihilo* out of the chaotic night of temporal incoherence." Nonetheless, "the narrative coherence of a life-story is a struggle, and a responsibility which no one else can finally lift entirely from the shoulders of the one who lives that life." (1986, p. 96)

Genre

The idea of storying styles also leads us to consider differences between people in terms of genre. "The manner in which we tell ourselves what is going on," says one psychoanalyst, Hillman (1975), "is the *genre* through which events become experiences (p. 146). Accordingly, "the way we imagine our lives is the way we are going to go on living our lives" (Hillman, 1975, p. 146). We see this all the time, however clumsy our categories (Keen, 1986). Some people experience and express their life events–that is, those they do experience and can express, according to what seems basically the tragic genre (Ruth & Öberg, this volume). No matter how normal or serene their life seems outside-in, the tales they tell of it are routinely fraught with conflict, and they are chronically the victim. We hear it in their voices, watch it in their posture, see it in their eyes: woe is perpetually them. The world is against them (Keen, 1986). For others, no matter how painful their life by other accounts, both what we hear and apparently what they feel is either a comedy (in the case of a "real character"), an adventure, or a parable of something else (Ruth & Öberg, this volume).

Writers investigating "personal mythology" argue the need to bring these genres to consciousness, to name the story-patterns by which we construct our lives and navigate our world (Feinstein Krippner, & Granger, 1988). Carol Pearson (1989), who identifies six such patterns or "hero" archetypes (innocent, orphan, martyr, wanderer, warrior, and magician), stresses the necessity of making explicit the myths that govern our lives. Otherwise, she says, "we are hostages to them and can do nothing else but live out their plots to the end" (Pearson, 1989, p. xx). In going through deep change, perhaps what transpires is describable then not just as "perspective transformation" (Mezirow, 1978) but as a re-*genre*—ation of the story of our life. That is, perhaps we can regenerate our lives overall, in the same way as, over time, we frequently reframe individual events within them: today's horror on the highway becomes tomorrow's tragedy, next week's exciting adventure, next month's amusing anecdote, and old age's illustration of the irony of life.

Though such differences in self-storying are put down by some simply to "temperament" or "disposition," even genetics, appreciating the subtler features of them is crucial to understanding the vast variety of ways in which we frame the world (Ruth & Kenyon, this volume). As the lenses through which we filter it, they influence what we make of it, what is in it to which we are open or closed, what we value and how we act in its midst. As Bruner (1987) observes, "A life as lived is inseparable from a life as told (p. 31)." With this link between living and telling (indeed, between ethics and aesthetics) as a reference point, we are led then to a fresh appreciation of Dewey's (1966) view of education as "the continuous reconstruction of experience (p. 66)". Before I focus on restorying, however, there is one other point to stress.

Larger Stories

We never story our lives in a vacuum. How we compose them, how we plot our experience, what we value and how, is necessarily influenced by the stories we consume from the world around us: through reading newspapers and novels, watching movies and television, or listening to the stories of others (Brookfield, 1990b; Coles, 1989; Greene, 1990). The "forms of self-telling" (Bruner, 1987, p. 16) are influenced even more profoundly, however, by the several *larger* stories within which we live and breathe because of being rooted in certain relationships, in a particular family, or in a specific sequence of lifestyles, communities, cultures, classes, and creeds–above all, in a given race and gender.

Like us as individuals, each of these systems has its saga. Each structure has its story, in the sense of both its distinctive history within the world and, though variously versioned by its members, its own "organized set of descriptions and feelings" about itself, that is, its own themes, conflicts, morality, message (Brundage & MacKeracher, 1980, p. 97).With some larger stories, the packaging and propagation of this message is the explicit agenda, as in most religions, which prescribe for us *master narratives* (Cupitt, 1991) or *sacred masterplots* (Brooks, 1985) to understand who we are as human beings in general, where we have come from and where we are going.

Inside each of these stories, each of us is a character in turn. For example, I am never simply who I am; I am always a character in the story of my family or clan, a story which was well underway before I arrived on the scene–with themes unfolding, conflicts brewing, and a cast of characters playing roles already established. In the same way, I am a character in the college story, company story, community story, country story, and so on.. I may, of course, not be a terribly compliant character in these stories, but rather a self-willed sort with which good authors must often contend. Such mutinous souls, says novelist E.M. Forster, (1962) "run away":

> they "get out of hand"; they are creations inside a creation, and often inharmonious towards it; if they are given complete freedom they kick the book to pieces,

and if they are kept too sternly in check they revenge themselves by dying, and destroy it by intestinal decay. (p. 72)

Ultimately, my self-story is also a world-story. My participation in each of these larger stories, that is, represents an extension of the boundary of my individual story. Simply put, somewhere in the story that I tell myself about who I am (past, present, and future) must be an account of what my family is as well, my community, culture, and planet. More than this, how I play the part I see myself to have within the world-story helps determine how *its* plot goes as well: what twists it takes, what themes it traces, whether it unrolls with business as usual or is kicked to pieces. In this basic way, the personal is always the political; individual change is necessarily social change.

THE RESTORING OF A LIFE

Unquestionably, we change. We change on the outside and we change on the inside. Inside change is change in our inside story. It is re-storying, "*the re-storying of experience* " (White & Epston, 1990, p. 14). If storying a life is a complex process, restorying a life is no less so.

Restorying *per se* is of course a fact of life, as natural as aging itself. Our story world is continually expanding, like the world of a novel the further we read. We get married, have children, pursue a career, and more events must be accomodated, more characters added in, more subplots worked into the main one, more themes raised and explored, and more layers of possible meaning piled up. Like a river the nearer it reaches the sea, our story-world widens and deepens, more complicated by cross-currents and more teeming with life. Its plot grows thicker with each new page, and it becomes for that reason more difficult to put down, and more resistant to radical change. That is, "Each of us resists change because a story is a self-coherent world with its own kind of immune system" (Bridges, 1980, p. 71). (See also Mader, this volume.) And all of this thickening happens so gradually we scarcely notice it. But happens it must, for the river must flow; the story cannot stand still.

Some restorying can occur quite suddenly, however, without our permission: a car crash, a test result, a betrayal, and we are launched out of one way of storying our lives and landed, quite rudely, amidst another. Indeed, we are *de-storied* and must story ourselves afresh. In such a situation, as one source has put it, our life is like a diary in which we mean to write one story but are forced to write another. Some re-storying, however, occurs of our own volition.

By a variety or combination of means, we sometimes seek to be restoried, down the route of religion perhaps, the path of therapy, or the trail of learning.

What stimulates this search is our realization that our old story, both of ourselves and our world, is no longer working, that it has itself become a hindrance to further learning (Kenyon, this volume). We seek restorying, that is, "when the narratives in which [we] are "storying" our experience, and/or in which [we] are having [our] experience "storied" by others, do not sufficiently represent [our] lived experience, and ... significant aspects of [our] lived experience contradict these dominant narratives" (White & Epston, 1990, p. 14). Put another way, we seek restorying when our current lifestory (inside at least) no longer coheres within itself, when it becomes incoherent, when the many are at war with the one. We seek it when our central self-story has either too little conflict and so fails to go anywhere, or too much and so threatens to fly apart, or when it is too small–meaning that it cannot make sufficient sense of our actual existence, of "the facts" of our life.

We might seek restorying, for example, when a particular episode fails to fit with the dominant story we tell ourselves about who we are, where we have come from, and where we are going. If that story is the story of a *down-home-boy-who-is-hard-working-and-honest*, then certain engagements may need editing out, such as the one about the creditor breathing down my neck about an overdue account, or the shady deal I made to cut a few corners, or the torrid affair with an employee behind my spouse's back. We may seek restorying, that is, because we are unsettled by our awareness of the gaps between our outside and inside stories, or between our inside story and the various versions of it that we express to others inside-out. This means the awareness that we are either hypocritical, self-deceived, or insane.

Deliberate restorying can also be prompted by the awareness that many of the several larger stories in which our personal one is embedded are too restrictive. That is, their plotlines are too tight, the characterizations (roles) they prescribe for us too stock, the themes they value not our themes, their conflicts (and morality) not ours. It can begin in the realization that we are "miscast in the family plot" (Kopp, 1987, p. 4) or that "we are caught in our history and are reliving it" (Mezirow, 1978, p. 101). The result, if not despair, will be to awaken in us a thirst for more author-ity, for greater novel-ty, for telling and living what is, so to speak, *our* story, our *whole* story, and *nothing* but our story.

Education as Therapy

As educators–whether as mentors, consciousness-raisers, or facilitators (Cranton, 1992)– we are accustomed to encountering people who are "in transition." This may be due to the loss of a job, the end of a life-style, the demise of a relationship, or the death of a dream. Helping them cope with and comprehend these transitions lends a therapeutic component to our work. Therapy, says James Hillman (1975), "is a restorying of life" (p. 168). It is concerned with enabling us to "construct a more contradiction-free and generative narrative" of our life (Bruner, 1986, p. 9). It changes "the meanings [we] attach to things and events" and so "reconstrues [our] world" (Jourard, 1971, p. 99). Such a perspective implies that the person in transition is "a victim not of her history but of the story in which she [has] put that history" (Hillman, 1989, p. 79);– a victim not of her existence but of her experience. It is not the person that needs doctoring, that is, but the story. "Successful therapy," insists Hillman (1989), is "a re-visioning of the story into a more intelligent, more imaginative plot (p. 80)." Its operative principle is captured by the quip that "if you want to change history, then become a historian."

In therapy proper, we seek to understand the story of our life with an unusual profundity and focus. We do so by learning to ask of it certain key questions. "Personal analysis," says psychoanalyst Roy Schafer, "changes the leading questions that one addresses to the tale of one's life and the lives of important others" (1983, p. 219). This self-questioning in fact "alter[s] the context of memory" so that we "then re-collect our individual stories under an enlarged horizon" (Winquist, 1980, p. 50).

The Stages of Re-Storying

The therapeutic process can be seen to proceed in three overlapping stages, each with its accompanying key question and its role for the therapist. Admittedly, these stages represent a simplification of the lengthy and intricate work that will be done by any given counsellor and client. Yet they are a valid if broad brush picture of the dynamics involved in "care of the soul" (Moore, 1992); not just in therapy, of course, but in any context where such care occurs, including a classroom, a support group, friendship, or even self-care, as in keeping a journal; which Anais Nin calls a "safe word-shop for self-creation" (cited in Friedman, 1988, p. 44).

The first stage of restorying is that of narrating my story, which means simply telling it, venting it, getting it out, with an intensity and honesty I may never have experienced before. Of course, it may not come out as a seamless whole, rather as a series of anecdotes of specific events, still lifes of particular moments, outpourings of pain, and bits of impressions from all across the years. But behind the many lurks the one: "The many stories clients use are attempts to convey the story of their lives" (Kennedy, 1977, p. 105). "First *stories*," says Frederick Wyatt (1986), "later *the* more or less coherent *story* urging to be told (p. 205)."

At this stage the guiding question is simply "What is my story? " However, such narrating does not mean that I am telling "simply" the same old story. Narrating this intensively and extensively means that something new is being brought about in my life, a distinct degree of self-*creation* occurs. "We are simply more than we were before" (Winquist, 1980, p. 60). At this stage the therapist is primarily a *listener* of an open, supportive, yet neutral kind I may seldom have had in the past (Schafer, 1983), and further, one who is alert not only to the content of the stories I recount (and of the stories behind the stories) but also, as I mentioned, to the form, to *how* they are told (Coles, 1989).

The second stage is that of *reading* the story of my life, which means, having told it, then studying it, evaluating it, critiquing it, with an honesty I may never before have experienced. My key question here is "What *kind* of story is my story? " "What *genre* of story has it been? " At this stage I might look closely at my central or signature stories, assessing what themes they reveal, how I have plotted them and characterized myself in their midst (as what sort of "hero"), and what they would be like if I told them from another point of view. This is a strategy used by literature teachers to stimulate fresh insights in students' minds: How would story X be different, for instance, if told not from the narrator's perspective but from that of the main character, a minor character, or the reader?

This stage is a distancing, a steppingback, from my lifestory. It is a stage of deliberate *de*—storying, which means entering a state of relative storylessness where everything about my life as *composed* is, in principle, up for review. Often it involves a close review of my family story–its themes, characters, author-ity, plot-line, genre–but it can also mean inquiring into the themes, characters, and so forth of the many larger stories that envelope my life. There is much vulnerability in this state, of course, as I allow myself to question my entire way of being in the world and to peer into parts of my experience perhaps long ago submerged. The therapist's role is correspondingly delicate. It may still not be, though, "to *change* the story, for this is to deny it; it is, rather, to *expand and deepen* the story, thus releasing the energy bound within it "(Houston, 1987, p. 99). (See also Gergen, this volume).

Through both the narrating and reading, then, another question comes to motivate me. It is this: "How can I *change* my story –re-genre-ate, re-author it – now that I have told it and am clearer on what kind of story it is and how it has affected my life? "Specifically, it is the question as to how I can compose a story *big* enough, with a horizon *broad* enough, to account for as much as possible of my actual life and render it available to me as a coherent, re-membered whole. As I ask this question, I enter the third stage of the therapeutic process, the stage of "re-writing the inner story so far" (Glover, 1988, p. 153)– the stage at which restorying my soul becomes particularly possible. It is the stage of "*retelling* a life" (Schafer, 1992).

The Role of the Educator in Restorying

Weaving from one to the other and back, I do not advance through these stages in lockstep fashion, for they are tightly entwined. In the words of one source, "we tell a story in order to find a story" (Winquist, 1980, p. 43). But throughout this subtle process, what again is the therapist? Robert Kegan (1982) sees the therapist as a "holding environment": a culture for the client to grow in, a "culture of embeddedness. (p. 276)" Such a culture performs three functions. The first is Confirmation. As the restorier discloses and vents, the therapist-as-holding-environment "holds on," refusing to be driven away by the content or force of the telling. The second function is Contradiction. As the restorier begins to distance from her story, the therapist too "must let go," must stand back and ask, with the patient, what kind of story it is. The third function is Continuity. As the restorier experiments with a new way of telling and living, the therapist "sticks around so that it can be reintegrated" into the fabric of her everyday life (Kegan, 1982, p. 121).

Relating these functions to our work as educators in transformative learning (Daloz, 1986), there are certain overlapping roles we may play in the process of people's restorying. First, besides whatever we are to ourselves and whatever other roles we play for them, we are *characters* in their life-story: storyotypes in a chapter marked "back to school."

Second and more seriously, we can be *keepers* of their story. We can provide them a safe, hospitable space in which they can tell their story, can get it out and get it straight. We can be an open and impartial audience who receives it, listens to it, and thus confirms it in a relatively unbiased, nonstoryotypeing manner. We can help them, that is, shift from being a character who is unquestioning within it, going along with its flow, to being its narrator, one step closer to being its author.

Third, as their story begins to come out, we can help them step back from it and, with them, become its *critics*. We become a "helpful editor" (Bruner, 1990, p. 113 who contradicts their story and so assists them in moving from mere narration to self-reading. This means analyzing, with a view to reworking, how they have emplotted their life so far, or specific incidents or chapters therein. It means considering, for example, what kind and degree of conflict has been integral to it; what they have seen and how they have valued as its turning points; how they have characterized themselves and others in the midst of it (as what sorts of heroes or villains); in terms of what point of view they tend to see it; which level of it they identify with most; what themes it reveals (Birren & Birren, this volume; Birren & Deutchman, 1991; McAdams, this volume) and genres it reflects. It means inquiring how it has been restricted and misshaped by the larger stories in which they have lived–stories which are always that, stories, never givens: structures that are not cast in stone but can themselves be restructured, recomposed.

Fourth, with them we can then *co-author* (Schafer, 1992) a more comprehensive, more plausible story, perhaps a re-generated story: say, from tragedy to adventure. And, as we have opportunity over time, we can continue to be around for them while they integrate their life into their new lifestory. At the very least, we can be a *catalyst* for them as they fashion an inside story that is more reflective of the breadth and complexity of their actual existence and more in harmony with their expression to the outside world: A story over whose unfolding they have greater author-ity, greater control. As coauthors, however, we may be coauthored by them in turn, insofar as in the process of providing them care (Daloz, 1986), of edu-care, we are commonly restoried ourselves.

LIFE-AS-STORY: QUESTIONS AND IMPLICATIONS

Any metaphor must be used in moderation, and life-as-story is no exception. Clearly, it cannot tell us the whole story about about transformative learning. Nonetheless, it can tell us more than we might think. It raises key questions and has important implications for theory and practice in adult education, as well as for the thinking done about "biographical aging" (Kenyon, this volume) in both that field and gerontology.

Theory

A story approach invites us to examine the aesthetic aspects of the continual reconstruction of personal experience (past, present, and future) that is integral to making meaning, both within us and between us and others. It raises the question of the limits of restorying and the reasons for our resistance to it: the question of why some seem to restory more profoundly or frequently than others, of whether it is possible to restory too often or too much. Philosophically, it raises the issue of whether radical restorying is realistic in the first place (whether the leopard can change its spots), or if, despite my testimony to the contrary, I end up telling and living "the same old story." That is, it raises the issue of existentialism vs. essentialism, of freedom vs. determinism–that is, whether I can compose the story of my life however I like (within the limits, at least, of the larger stories in which it is set) or "unfolds" as it must, with me as its hostage (Pearson, 1989); from what Henry James calls a central story "seed" (Allen, 1949, pp. 155f) to a destiny I can neither envision nor escape.

A story approach pushes us to consider the links between literacy, literature, learning, and life; to wrestle with the rhetoric of self-telling and how we acquire and cultivate it; to examine the degree of blending of lifestory genres and the possibility that, ultimately, each person's lifestory represents a genre of its own–is therefore "novel" (Polster, 1987). Furthermore, it forces us to research what Bruner (1987) calls "the development of autobiography, how our way of telling about ourselves changes, and how these accounts come to take control of our ways of life (p. 15)." It begs us to ask not just about "learning styles" but about "storying styles" too, and if such styles are genetic, if they are gendered, if and how they are rooted in and arise out of certain families, religions, classes, and cultures. It leads us to reconsider the formation of values; the dynamics of friendship and intimacy; and the narrative dimensions, and educational implications, of such common phenomena as secrecy and self-deception (Polonoff, 1987) gossip and prejudice, irony and humour, nostalgia and regret.

A story approach also entices us to reconceive the invisible line that adult educators are wont to draw between adulthood and childhood. Relevant in this regard are the words of the controversial French writer, Samuel Beckett, in particular these of the narrator on the final pages of his novel *The Unnameable* (cited in Estess, 1974):

> you must go on, I can't go on, you must go on, I'll go on, you must say words, as long as there are any, until they say me. . . perhaps it's done already, perhaps they have said me already, perhaps they have carried me to *the threshold of my story*, before the door that opens on my story, that would surprise me, if it opens, it will be I, it will be the silence. (p. 424, emphasis mine)

Borrowing from Beckett, we can see "adulthood" as that unspecifiable phase when the autobiographical imperative peaks within us and we stand on the *threshold* of our story: when we come alive to our story (or to our "roots"), or at least to our need for a *sense* of our story. This would be the stage in our development when "dawning in earnest" upon us is "the startling and novel idea that [we] have a story" (Johnston, 1993, p. 3). Though it would surely vary with each individual, our approach to this threshold could well coincide with the emergence of a sense of our own ending (Kermode, 1966) –a sense which can hit us as early as adolescence or as late as never at all. Our approach to it could also be said to begin when we feel the weight of our past piling up behind us, as well as the need to digest it, make sense of it, find a framework to fit it all together. It could begin with the awareness that our success in managing our life depends on coming to grips with not only the content of our lifestory but also the form: its plot and subplots, its principal themes, its genre, the characterization of our self it assumes. It could also be the point when we acquire a feel for the *several* stories of our life (outside, inside, etc.), of the gaps between them, and of the relationship between the many and the one.

Finally, as regards research, a story approach honors the textual complexity of the interview process often employed to extract "data" to generate new theories or substantiate those already devised. Surely such data are inseparable from the "story" of the subject's life, a story of considerable complexity (de Vries & Lehman, this volume) which is composed afresh through the interview process itself, and which afterward the researcher artfully "smooths" (Mishler, 1986, pp. 67ff).

Practice

Implicit in the metaphor of life-as-story is a method of adult education, another conceptual and practical tool to add to our kit. In general, a story approach points to the need for an explicitly autobiographical component in any curriculum whose duration and subject suits it. Impelled by the autobiographical imperative, students can thus begin (or continue) to get their stories out and straight so they can then be more open to the intensive restorying that is central to transformative learning. Provided a learning environment and teaching style that are appropriately confidential, this initial self-storying stage can be invited informally, in the course of normal class discussions. Indeed, rare is the class discussion in which such storytelling is not, sooner or later, the central activity, and the most significant as far as learning is concerned. Or it can be facilitated formally, by assigning the writing of a learning journal or life review or by asking learners to plot a lifeline to trace and interpret what they see as the turning points, the key conflicts, the "critical incidents" (Brookfield, 1990a, p. 31f), the pivotal experiences in the course of their lives.

In my own teaching, I use a variety of exercises to help learners see not only that they *have* a story (or stories) but that they themselves have composed it and can therefore *re*compose it, both inside and inside-out. In one, I ask them to make a quick list of all the specific (not general) things they can recall doing, saying, thinking, feeling, and seeing from the day before yesterday, then to reflect on the factors behind why so little of their existence seems to make it inside–for example, triggering question, learning style, degree of "importance" or unusualness. In another, I have them list the questions with which they would have to wrestle in preparing their formal autobiography, such as what audience to aim at, what to include and exclude, what themes to explore, what tone to strike, how to arrange and relate the incidents, what guiding metaphor to use, and what moral or message to push. I then invite them to consider how this formal autobiographical process relates to the informal autobiographical activity in which they are engaged each day (Eakin, 1985); moreover, how both are essentially *literary* enterprises (Polonoff, 1987, p. 46). In a third exercise, playful but insightful, I assign different small groups the same list of arbitrary "events" or narrative units. I then ask them to compose, and later recount to the whole group, a story that links these units together, sequentially and consequentially, according to a particular genre. The resultant range of stories serves to illustrate the polyplottable, regenreable nature of the "facts" of their own lives.

Because the life-as-story metaphor sensitizes us to the fine line between story and life, it increases our respect, and concern, for the power of stories generally (heard, read, or viewed, fiction or nonfiction) to colour our world; to "instruct and delight;" to either emancipate us (Greene, 1990) or entrench us more stubbornly in our preferred modes of interpreting our world. While acknowledging, though, that stories are never innocent (thus raising the question of censorship), the reading of assigned novels, biographies, and autobiographies can nonetheless put flesh on the bones of the theories to which learners are being exposed.

Finally, a story approach underlines the therapeutic and thus ethical side of our work as educators, helping people to restory their lives and relationships, to critique the larger stories in which they have been rooted or cast, and to author for themselves a more complete self-story and thus world-story–or simply to find such a story in the first place (Daloz, 1986; Mezirow, 1978). As such, it also raises the issue of the relationship to our own lifestory that is required by the roles we play as auditor, editor, and (co)-author in the reworking of theirs (Ruth & Kenyon, this volume).

Biographical Aging

A story approach raises questions concerning the increased importance of "past experience" as both a resource and potential hindrance to our learning the older we grow, where past experience is understood in terms of the broader concept of lifestory. It also raises questions about the nature both of meaning-making on an everyday basis and of the *search* for meaning overall,– of our own life and of "life in general." Insofar as this search intensifies with the passing of years, perhaps it can be seen as connected to the surfacing of our more self-reading side. The heightening of our hunger to understand the "reasons" things have happened to us as they have, that is, would then be seen in terms of that increase in the meaning potential of each event in our life*story* that inevitably accompanies the "thickening" of its plot. As there is more material for us to mull over, we thus spend more time in "ruminescence," a process which Edward Casey says is stimulated by "*thickening of memory* " (Casey, 1987 pp. 265, 275).

A story approach pushes us to inquire about not just the psychological but also the aesthetic and ethical ramifications when life outlasts lifestory (Schiebe, 1986, p. 143). It forces us to consider the effect on some people's self-storying of their belief that their lifestories do not end with death but are "to be continued," to have a sequel. It invites us to count the cost, both personal and cultural, of the stories that are left untold. As novelist Alex Haley puts it, "when an old person dies it's like a library had burned down" (Polster, 1987, p. 96). It also raises the question of what is entailed and implied in "de-storying."

As I have suggested, in order to restory, a certain destorying must first be done: deconstructing the old, no longer workable story of our life to make way for a newer, more comprehensive, more serviceable one. This happens as a natural part of the self's movement through its successive evolutionary stages, like the proverbial chambered nautilus that builds itself ever "more stately mansions", (Tennyson, "The Chambered Nautilus") But there is a more unnatural form of destorying that can go hand in hand with growing old, over and above the obvious kind entailed when, with "senility" itself, a person's memory is impaired. It is one we initiate, that is, when we are obliged to place someone in an institution for months or years on end, confining them to one room, with a few photos and a stranger for a roommate, a familiar chair from the house in which they no longer can live, and fewer friends visiting them who *know* their story (outside-in, at least) or loved ones outliving them in whose stories they have been characters in turn.

Yet, destorying may not be the indignity we can be quick to assume. Nearly all novels, Forster (1962) reminds us, "are feeble at the end. This is because the plot requires to be wound up" (pp. 93ff.). As a story unfolds, its plot progressively thickens, but it also, of necessity, narrows. It tapers down to a smaller and smaller ranger of possible endings until finally, as it were, it is the butler who did it and no one else. As with story, so with life. We begin it in the cradle, with no story of our own. Then, as the crucible of conflict completes its work, the story we have managed to spin for ourselves (Dennett, 1991) fades feebly away, narrowing down to its one, inevitable end–inevitable yet aesthetically necessary. We compose a life, that is, living and telling and weaving a story that is uniquely ours, that is novel; however, toward its end a certain de-composing, a denouement, must eventually occur. But this denoument need not be seen as a diminishment, in our eyes or those of others. For with it, is there not, as in story *per se*, the potential for a kind of aesthetic integrity to the course of our life as a whole, an integrity for which one word is "wisdom"? "When at last age gas assembled you together," asks Florida Scott-Maxwell, "will it not be easy to let it all go, lived, balanced, over?" (1968, p. 42).

TOWARD A POETICS OF ADULT LEARNING

The metaphor and method explored in this chapter promise to offer a more soulful sense of adult learning than do many of the arid categories on which we must otherwise rely. To play with it, however, is to embark on a journey without maps, for it lures us into a conceptual netherland on the frontier between several fields at once. As philosopher Herbert Fingarette has observed, "the idea that we are constitutive of our own experience crosses philosophy, theology, literary criticism, and psychology" (Kegan, 1982, p. 11). Such an exploration leads us into the land of poetics really, of *poiesus*, broadly defined as "the act of making with the imagination into words" (Hillman, 1975, p. 124). In this land, "we are what we imagine;" "our very existence consists in our imagination of ourselves" (Winquist, 1974, p. 1). We do not receive our life, that is; we compose it (Bateson, 1989).

To take a poetic approach to learning, as to aging, is to be lured into the company of novelists and raconteurs. With their counsel concerning the intricacies of the storymaking art, we have to factor different things into our equations: for instance, the role played by stories themselves in forming and transforming our "meaning perspectives" (Mezirow, 1978, 1990) and thus changing our lives (Greene, 1990), or the role of conflict, since conflict *per se* is not to be avoided, but affirmed. Without it, there is little to recall and less to recount. Indeed, no trouble, no tale; no pain, no gain–and no learning. To pursue the poetics of learning pulls us into a territory, that is, where learning itself is a lifelong adventure: where no incident is "unusable" in illustrating, indeed building, our character (Sarton, 1980); no event inherently meaningless; and no situation devoid of some clue to our particular destiny, to our unique message, to the "meaning" of our life.

In the end, we have hardly begun to frame, let alone answer, the beguiling questions that concern "the fictional side of human nature" (Hillman, 1975, p. 128). As the thinking represented in this volume attests, however, we have at least raised the lid of the box in which, till lately, they lay. We have little choice but to open it all the way.

14

Life Review and Reminiscence in Nursing Practice

Irene Burnside, R.N., Ph.D., F.A.A.N.

INTRODUCTION

Over the past two decades nurses have implemented life review and reminiscence as therapeutic interventions for older adults. Nurses continue to incorporate them into clinical practice, especially reminiscence (Burnside, 1990; Daly, McCloskey, & Bulechek, 1994; Hamilton, 1985, 1992; Ryden, 1981; Snyder, 1985). However, one educator believes that reminiscence may be an underused nursing resource (MacRae, 1982). Another well-known gerontological nurse states:

> I do not believe that many nurses in any field of practice use reminiscence by design. They have not been educated to do so and probably do not view it as an intervention for therapeutic caring. However, nurses do employ reminiscence in many day-to-day care settings; for example, doctors' offices, community health nursing, and home care nursing. (B. Steffl, personal communication, August 10, 1994)

In a recent survey of nurses by Daly, McCloskey and Bulechek (1994) regarding interventions for diagnostic purposes, it was found that one of the common interventions in long-term care is reminiscence therapy.

Ruth and Kenyon (this volume) point out that, "The way individuals have lived their lives and the way they have perceived their lives is of vital importance, not only as a means of exploring the aging process, but also as a guideline for the delivery of care." Reminiscence may be used in nursing assessments (Jessup, 1984; Mezey, Rauckhorst, & Stokes, 1980) to gather pertinent data for a care plan, or it may be implemented as an independent nursing intervention (Burnside, 1988; Snyder, 1985), for a treatment following a nursing diagnosis (Hamilton, 1985, 1992) or to improve the quality of life, especially in a nursing home (Fuller, 1988; Hala, 1975; Hogan, 1982; Matteson, 1986). The nursing literature indicates that life review is used with cancer patients (O'Connor, Wicher, & Germino, 1990), homebound elderly (Haight, 1988, 1990) and dying patients (Chubon,1980; de Ramon, 1983).

A lack of descriptive studies of these modalities has hampered the nurse's understanding of where, when, and how nurses conduct these treatments. However, one reason for the proliferation of intervention studies over other types of research may be nurses' eagerness and/or commitment to help persons with health problems, as well as to enhance quality of life. The latter is a viable rationale for the use of biographical materials (Ruth & Kenyon, this volume) in the care of older adults.

Lest one think the modalities are only for the alert, it is important to realize that the modalities are used with persons who are cognitively impaired (Norris & Eileh, 1982). Kenyon (1993) states that an individual with dementia, "remains a person with moral worth and that they still have a story to tell (p. 417)". That sage advice is sometimes forgotten in the day-to-day nursing care of persons with dementia Ruth and Kenyon (this volume), state that a person with dementia is a legitimate candidate for biographical forms of interventions, both in the context of assessment and diagnosis, for example, in a geriatrics unit or in a nursing home. There continues to be a need for therapeutic milieus for older patients with dementia and within those milieus, Taft, Delancy, Seman, & Stansell, (1993) state, "Reminiscence helps the client to experience being cared for and understood as a unique individual and allows them to maintain continuity of self despite the impact of disease (p. 34)".

Romaniuk (1983) proposes that

> reminiscing, with the aid of a photo album, can be employed as an assessment methodology to promote the establishment of rapport and client cooperation, to more accurately determine the extent of memory dysfunction, and to elicit the disclosure of key historical information and current problems. (p. 37)

Props have also been recommended by other professionals (Burnside, 1994; Lewis & Butler, 1974; Burnside, 1994b; Rodriguez, 1990). Nurses who implement life review or reminiscence would concur with Birren and Deutchman (1991) that "Memories provide material that can be used in structuring cognitive activities and stimulating mental ability (p. 19)."

TERMS

When one conducts a literature search, it is extremely difficult to ferret out nursing research and/or articles about the biographical modalities because of the current confusion we have in differentiating life review therapy from reminiscence therapy. Terms are used interchangeably and as though they were the same modality (Burnside & Haight, 1992). Added to this problem is the coining of terms; for example, (a) "reminiscing psychotherapy" (King, 1992), (b) "reminiscing: the life review therapy" (Dietche, 1979; Lappe, 1987) and "reminiscing counseling" (Youssef, 1990). However, other disciplines also coin terms for reminiscence; for example, "milestoning" (Lowenthal & Mazzarro, 1990).

DEFINITIONS

Another problem one quickly discovers when conducting a search of the nursing literature about the two modalities is the lack of definitions. The most common definition of life review used by nurses is that of Butler (1963), who states that it is

> a naturally occurring, universal mental process characterized by the progressive return to the consciousness of past experience, and, particularly the resurgence of unresolved conflicts, simultaneously and normally, these revived experiences and conflicts can be surveyed and reintegrated. Presumably this process is prompted by the realization of approaching dissolution and death, and the inability to maintain one's sense of personal invulnerability. (p. 66)

Haight's definition is, "a retrospective survey of existence, a critical study of a life, or a second look at one's life" (Burnside & Haight, 1992, p. 856). Haight believes that a life review implemented as a nursing intervention is not a natural occurring process, because it has been elicited (see also Ruth & Kenyon; Kenyon, this volume). According to Haight, a life review has unique characteristics which are outlined in Table 14.1.

Haight's criteria contain some of the same elements found in the work of

TABLE 14.1 Unique Characteristics of a Life Review

- One-to-one interaction between interviewer and reminiscer.
- Use recall.
- Evaluation.
- Integration.
- Cover the entire life span.
- Address both sad and happy times.
- Focus on self.
- Take 4–6 weeks to complete.

Note: From "Reminiscence and life review: Analyzing each concept" by I. Burnside & B.K. Haight, 1992, *Journal of Advanced Nursing*, 17, p. 857.

Webster and Young (1988), who state a life review must contain (a) recall, (b) integration, and (c) evaluation. The goal of a life review, according to Haight, always is to obtain integrity. Birren (1993) stated it well, "Life review is not merely a perfunctory reliving of the past. It has to have a purpose and that purpose must be the discovery of meaning and the achievement of integrity. We might also call it cohesiveness" (p. 20).

Cora (1989) defined reminiscence as "a process of recalling past life experiences. (p. 1)" It may be silent or spoken, solitary or with someone, spontaneous or structured. King (1982) stated that, "the individual's selective processes influence what is remembered and how the memories are evoked (pp. 21–25)" . Another nurse definition for reminiscence as implemented in long-term care is "Using the recall of past events, feelings, and thoughts to facilitate adaptation to present circumstances" (Daly, McCloskey, & Bulechek, 1994, p. 43).

DIFFERENTIATION

One of the basic differences in life review and reminiscence is that life review is a psychoanalytically based intervention (Lewis & Butler, 1974), and reminiscence is a psychosocial intervention (Burnside, 1988). It is clear that one of the current and urgent tasks of gerontological and geropsychiatric nurses is to differentiate between life review therapy and reminiscence therapy in nursing practice. Haight (1988, 1990) has done a masterful job of refining life review therapy as conducted by a nurse. She developed a "Life Review Experiencing Form" for a structured life review in the dyad (Haight, 1990).

To better elucidate the differences, a concept analysis was done of each modality by Burnside & Haight (1992). They offered the following suggestions to help identify the appropriate planned intervention: (a) Read current literature to better understand the two concepts, (b) state specific goals for the intervention planned, (c) select literature findings to support and validate the chosen intervention, (d) identify model cases of each modality, (e) identify one's own bias regarding the modality, and (f) carefully followup the intervention for the purpose of recording outcomes.

The lack of protocols for life both review and reminiscence interventions has also hampered nurses in adequately explaining or describing the two processes. Burnside and Haight (in press) have begun preliminary work in this area by designing protocols for both life review and one-to-one reminiscence. Another recent endeavor to provide a protocol for nurses implementing reminiscence therapy is designed specifically for residents in long-term care (Daly, McCloskey, & Bulechek, 1994). Guidelines for reminiscence groups have been provided by one author, Osborn (1989), and Wysocki (1983) wrote guidelines for life review therapy as conducted by a nurse.

Nurses have relied heavily on the frameworks of Erikson (1963) and Butler (1963). Erik Erikson (1963) provided the eight stages of man model and nurses use the last stage, that of integrity versus despair as a framework for their research (Cook, 1988). Robert Butler (1963) is a geropsychiatrist whose seminal article about life review and older people has been the basis for both reminiscence and life review research by a variety of professionals. These are the two most common frameworks nurses incorporate into their research. That is expected to change as student nurses are encouraged to embrace the work of nurse therorists in practice and research.

The purpose of this chapter is to trace the history of both life review and reminiscence in the nursing literature. Part I traces the history of the modalities in the nursing literature. Part II describes implementation in nursing practice. Part III presents some perspectives about women and life review and reminiscence.

PART I: HISTORICAL VIEW

In the decade of the 60s, no nurse-written articles were located about dyad life review. No empirical studies about life review therapy as a specific therapeutic intervention in the one-to-one interaction appear until the 1980's (Haight, 1988, 1990; Haight & Bahr, 1984).

According to the anecdotal literature in the decade of the 80s, the most common rationale for nurses implementing one-to-one life review is to assist a dying person to come to terms with his or her life (Chubon, 1980; de Ramon, 1983). It is interesting to note that Merriam (1993) challenges the fact that the life review is precipitated by approaching death. Nonetheless, nurses deem it a viable pre-death intervention. For example, life review was implemented and recorded with a group of cancer patients (O'Connor et al., 1990).

Further, de Ramon (1983), a Mexican nurse, describes the life review for the dying patient as "the final task." She suggests writing specific objectives. She recommends further counseling when patients have unresolved memories of stressful experiences. The patient should be made aware that even though he/she may be dying, he/she can still make decisions. Her suggestions are: (a) make yourself genuinely available, (b) respect confidentiality, (c) help the patient see the value of his life experiences, (d) time your visits so patient is feeling up to the process, (e) involve family members to share the patient's experiences, (f) use touch, (g) accept retreat or other adaptive behaviors, and (h) suggest that the patient see other professional help if you cannot help or work with the individual. In contrast to Haight's use of a structured format, de Ramon states that a life review need not have any special, structured format.

Black and Haight (1992) view the life review as one of the development tasks of the last stage of life, and call it "past-scanning". These authors differentiate reminiscence and life review: "Life review is not random sharing of pleasurable events, but rather a structured process containing a component of self-evaluation" (p. 9).

Wysocki (1993), an Australian nurse, offers suggestions to help an elderly patient achieve an improved state of mind through a life review. She suggests that one begin by explaining to the patient what a life review is, then plan for short, frequent visits to prevent fatigue. Also, she suggests, make sure the patient is physically comfortable before you begin, and open each visit with "some friendly, appropriate but small talk" (p. 47). Do try to bring up some major events of the patient's younger years; for example, ask about "firsts." Use pictures as props. About five minutes before completing the interview, bring the patient back to the present time and place. Finally, before leaving, remind the patient of the day and hour of the next visit. An important element of Wysocki's list of guidelines is her sensitive attention to the patient's physical comfort.

Life review group therapy has received little attention by nurses. The classic article on group life review therapy by Lewis and Butler (1974) has no counterpart in the nursing literature. As noted earlier, confusion exists about the definition of life review group therapy. In articles about group life review, the process described gave this reader the impression that the modality being described was not life review group therapy (Dietsche, 1979; Ellison, 1981; Giltinan, 1990; Lappe, 1987) but reminiscence group therapy. In an article entitled group reminiscing (Matteson & Munsat, 1982) the themes were selected "to provide for an orderly life review (p. 180)" and "the small number of sessions allowed for too limited a time for an adequate life review for all group members" p. 186). An analysis of the content of the articles in the review by Haight (1991) indicates that reminiscence is used more frequently than life review as an intervention by nurses. Furthermore, the literature reveals that nurses implement life review as a one-to-one modality and reminiscence as a group modality (Burnside & Haight, in press; Haight & Burnside, 1993).

The first account of a nurse using reminiscence on a one-to-one basis was by Jessie Breeze (1909). She described the importance of listening with sensitivity to memories of her private duty patients. Nurses first wrote about reminiscence as a nursing intervention in the early 70s (Burnside, 1973, p. 12), a decade after Butler's (1963) seminal article appeared (see Table 14.2 for empirical studies on reminiscence by nurses).

The first empirical study of reminiscence implementing a one-to-one interaction (Dibel, 1971) was an intervention study to reduce depression in older patients in a Veterans' Hospital in Boston. A sample of 30 males reminisced for 1 hour weekly for 8 weeks. There was no significant relationship identified between reminiscence and depression.

One of the newer forms of one-to-one reminiscence is noted in recent nursing literature. Nurses have encouraged reminiscence from a spiritual stance (Murphy, 1992; Turner, 1992) or implemented it from a Biblical perspective (Lashley, 1992). Sr. Pat Murphy (1992) writes that reminiscence is a way to relieve pressures long contained. Turner (1992) described her one-to-one interactions with a man terminally ill with an inoperable brain tumor. He advised her to "always listen to your patients" (p. 13). Lashley (1992) wrote that the major purpose of storytelling is "to help others find meaning in their individual experiences and to show God's divine guidance and faithfulness as a pattern throughout their lives." (p. 6). However, none of these writers termed their intervention life review therapy.

Nurses also implement the lifehistory (Ruth & Kenyon, this volume; Ruth & Öberg, this volume) in qualitative research. Bramwell (1984) wrote about the life history for pattern identification and for health promotion. Hagemaster (1992) used the lifehistory method

> to identify and document health patterns of individuals and groups as it challenges the nurse to understand an individual's current attitudes and behaviors and how they may have been influenced by initial decisions made at another time and in another place. (p. 1122)

Jones (1994) wrote a sensitive account of failed reality orientation sessions with an elderly veteran. This nurse manager knew the patient's background; he was a cobbler. The nurses entered Sam's world and let his room be a shoe shop because

> in guided reminiscence exercises, we teach our patients how to recall their past experiences and draw on points they already have. Yet with a confused patient, we

Table 14.2 Empirical Studies on Reminiscence by Nurses by Decade

1970's	Variable	1980's	Variable	1990's	Variable
1971 Hibel	depression	1981 Michelson	depression		
1974 Wichita	nonverbal response	1984 Moore	self-esteem morale	1990 Bramlett	creativity
1978 King	life satisfaction	1986 Hogan	information to train volunteers	1990 Burnside	depression life satisfaction fatigue
1978 Matteson	depression	1986 Parsons	depression		
				1990 Rodriguez	props
1978 Wilinoson	social interaction	1987 Lappe	self-esteem	1990 Youssef	depression
				1992 Levy	characteristics of reminiscence
1979 Mace	self-esteem	1987 Lovelady	self-esteem		
		1988 Cook	ego integrity		
		1988 Tourangeau	depression self-esteem		
		1989 Baumann	personal control		

Source: Author

don't want him to use these reference points. We don't want him to take refuge in his memories. (p. 51)

As a summary of one-to-one interactions, Hamilton (1992) states that, "Reminiscence therapy is a nursing intervention in which the normal process of reminiscence combines with nursing knowledge and communication skills to support the patient's life situation (p. 203)."

Butler, Lewis, and Sunderland (1991) state that, "Group therapy has been more widely used in work with the elderly in and out of institutions than is generally realized or reflected in professional or scientific literature. Nurses probably conduct more group work with older persons than do other professionals." (p. 421) As stated earlier, these are not life review groups, but reminiscence groups. The first empirical study about reminiscence as a group intervention was a master's thesis by Wichita (1974). She endeavored to reduce apathy and withdrawal in residents of a long-term care facility by leading a reminiscence group early in the morning. She observed and recorded nonverbal behaviors in the subjects and noted changes and improvement in demeanor.

In the 1970s most articles (Hala, 1975) and chapters in books (Blackman, 1980; Ebersole, 1976; Stange, 1973) about reminiscence group therapy were anecedotal. The first empirical studies were master's theses or projects (King, 1979; Matteson, 1978; Michelson, 1981; Wichita, 1974; Wilkinson, 1978). Wilkinson (1978) described the implementation of sociograms to better understand the interaction of group members. Wilkinson's (1978) study and King's (1979) were the first to mention the use of themes and/or props, common accoutrements of nurse-led reminiscence groups today. King (1979) offered a list of themes in her study as a protocol. It is now more common to include lists of themes for reminiscence groups (Burnside, 1993; Cook,1988; Giltinan, 1990; Lovelady, 1987; Matteson & Munsat, 1982). A descriptive study about props used with older persons (Rodriguez, 1990) helps provide a foundation for reminiscence group leaders.

Nurse researchers have studied the effectiveness of reminiscence group intervention on depression (Parsons, 1986; Tourangeau, 1988; Youssef, 1990). Tourangeau (1988) studied depression in nursing home residents in Canada using three groups: (a) reminiscence, (b) current events, and (c) no intervention group. She found a significant decrease in depression scores in the reminiscence group subjects. Parsons (1986) conducted reminiscence group therapy with six depressed women in a nursing clinic in a housing facility. There was a statistically significant decrease in Geriatric Depression Scale scores after completing the group reminiscence therapy. Youssef (1990) found that the differences before and after the reminiscence counseling sessions were statistically significant in the group of younger subjects (65 to 74 years) and insignificant in the group of older subjects (over 74 years). The sample consisted of nursing home residents.

Nurses have also used reminiscence therapy to study self-esteem (Lappe, 1987; Lovelady, 1987). Lovelady (1987) studied 20 residents in a nursing home. They met for 1 hour weekly for 10 consecutive weeks. The Rosenberg Scale of self-esteem was used and analysis of data revealed the experimental group had an overall increase in self-esteem. Lappe (1987) also studied nursing home residents. She also used the Rosenberg Scale. The interventions included reminiscence and current event groups. Results of the study suggest that reminiscence group therapy increases self-esteem scores of older persons in nursing homes to a greater degree than do current events group sessions. Tourangeau (1988) studied self-esteem as well as depression in nursing home residents. There was a significant increase in self-esteem. The subjects in the current events and control group did not demonstrate significant changes over the same treatement period.

In summary, the literature reveals nurses have generally implemented reminiscence therapy groups as an intervention for depressed older persons. Furthermore, most of the reports are about institutionalized elders and therefore not generalizable.

PART II: IMPLEMENTATION OF LIFE REVIEW AND REMINISCENCE

Research indicates that life review is successfully used with community-based older adults on a one-to-one basis (Haight, 1984, 1988, 1991; Haight & Bahr, 1994; Haight & Olson, 1989). However, it is unclear from the literature just how life review groups are implemented by nurses. The dearth of definitions, goals, and outcomes contribute to this lack of clarity. For example, as stated earlier, what is called a life review appears to be, in fact, a reminiscence group.

It is not clear from the literature who is deemed qualified to conduct life reviews. Some believe (Haight & Olson, 1989) that nurses aides can implement life review; others believe that only professional nurses with adequate background should conduct a life review. Ruth and Kenyon (this volume) state that properly trained interventionists are required and that techniques and training are necessary. This stance is also the one taken by Birren and Deutchman (1991).

There has been a steady increase in published articles by nurses concerning reminiscence. However, reviewers indicate there are some important obstacles to overcome (Haight, 1991; Kovach, 1990). The obstacles include problems with operational definitions, sampling procedures, and methodological shortcomings. Webster (1993) points out that, "One of the most common stumbling blocks to integration of existing evidence is the paucity of psychometrically sound instruments for assessing reminiscence dimensions." (p. 256)

Settings and Reminiscence

Nurses implement reminiscence in a dyad situation at the bedside, in acute care (Beadleson-Baird & Lura, 1988; Kibbee & Lackey, 1982), in the community while doing home nursing (I. Eide, April 20, 1994, personal communication); while taking a health history (Bramwell, 1984; Jessup, 1984; Mezey, Rauckhorst, & Stokes, 1980); and in the nursing home (Fuller, 1988).

Acute Care Settings

Nurses find it necessary to gain instant rapport with hospitalized older adults for the purpose of establishing trust and cooperation and in order to reduce anxiety. Nowhere is this more true than in acute care hospitals where confusion and fear may be rampant. Newly admitted persons are fearful and often cannot "read" or understand the new milieu. Rapid changes, relocation trauma, drugs, anesthetics and sensory overload can all cause confusional states in older persons (Wolanin & Phillips, 1981). Reminiscence interventions help to achieve rapport because the intervention focuses intently and intensely on the patient, not the tubes, monitors, and technical paraphernalia.

The future-oriented older person may refuse to engage in reminiscence not only with the nurse in acute care, but a nurse anywhere. Such individuals have a pejorative attitude about the reminiscence process and feel it is a sign of regression or approaching dementia. It has been my experience in group work that affluent older persons often have this deeply embedded view, and it can be most difficult to elicit "comfortable" reminiscence from them.

In acute care settings, nurses deliberately elicit reminiscence. Beadleson-Baird and Lura (1988, pp. 84-85) offer guidelines:

1. Listen (for statements about the past).
2. Initiate (ask memory-evoking questions).
3. Reinforce (encourage and support by verbal comments).
4. Accept (acknowledge both the positive and negative feelings).

Ryden (1981) offers similar guidelines for the nurse planning to introduce reminiscence: (a) initiate reminiscing, (b) reinforce reminiscing, (c) help the person deal with feelings associated with reminiscing, and (d) help the family role model reminiscence interventions. It will be noted that the first two guidelines of Ryden's are identical to 3 and 4 of Beadleson-Baird & Lura.

Beadleson-Baird & Lura (1988) state that the recall of past events is intensified when the person is acutely ill or dealing with a life-threatening situation. The importance of reminiscence with the acutely ill is noted by Enloe (1993), who reported that older persons discharged from hospitals in New York who had reminisced during hospitalization tended to survive longer and had fewer admissions than "those who focused on a bleak present. . ." (p. 256).

The work of psychologists Rybarczyk and Auerbach (1990) has important implications for nursing practice. These researchers found that a standard reminiscence interview "that focused on successfully met challenges reduced state anxiety and enhanced coping self-efficacy when measured against both attention-placebo and no-intervention control groups in a sample of 104 elderly male patients facing surgery" (p. 522). They suggest that techniques to manage presurgical stress should be designed to better match needs of older patients. It is hoped a similar study will be done on a female sample, and that nurses will incorporate the above research findings into daily practice.

The nursing literature does not clearly spell out how nurses effectively use reminiscence in taking a history, but it is alluded to frequently. Gerontological nurses (Mezey, Rauckhorst, & Stokes, 1980) remind the reader that it may be difficult to keep the client on the topic, and it is helpful to state precisely the amount of time the interviewer will spend with the client. Wolanin and Phillips (1981) state "The life history of the older person is important because of its extensive and cumulative nature" (p. 72) and go on to state that, "Recording the information about the life history and culture of the client is a matter of synthesis and winnowing. Life history is shared with individuals who are trusted" (p. 73). The matter of synthesis and winnowing can be difficult for beginning nurses because of the overload of information obtained.

This is particularly true with respect to octogenarians, nonagenarians, and centenarians who have much to tell because of their longevity and/or loquacity. It does require skillful interviewing to refocus, redirect and isolate the needed information germane to designing a nursing care plan. Some nurses find it difficult to interrupt because of fear of hurting the feelings of these older persons, being rude, or simply because they are mesmerized by the older person's memories, or even the wonderful way they relate memories. The nurse does the older person a disservice by allowing them to ramble too much, as it may increase the patient's anxiety. Still another difficulty in the interview may lie in the ageism of the nurse, who is negative about the entire process because she or he has bought into these ideas: (a) old people are garrulous, (b) old people constantly repeat themselves, and (c) reminiscence is a sign of dementia. Often, one successful reminiscence experience with an old person is sufficient to turn the nurse around.

As mentioned earlier, one difficulty may lie in the belief of the older person him or herself. Some believe adamantly that one should live for the future and cannot see any value in reminiscing; these persons will indeed be challenges for the nurse who tries to implement reminiscence. One important responsibility of the nurse not often mentioned in the literature is support. Continued support in the eliciting of memories is suggested by Jessup (1984, p. 157), a nurse practitioner: "Long after the formal history-taking process is over, the nurse can continue to support the aged person as he feels his way through these memories" (p. 167). The lack of follow-up support and continuity in health care is well-known to nurses.

While taking a history, the response of the older person often evokes a reminiscing exchange which enhances communication as well as provides information for the nursing care plan (B. Steffl, August 10, 1994, personal letter). For example:

> *Nurse:* Have you had any surgical operations?
> *Patient:* Yes, my first was for appendicitis when I was 9 years old. My father drove me to the hospital in a Model T Ford in a terrible snow storm. It took us two hours to go 10 miles.

Nurse: Go on.
Patient: I had ether for the operation and had to stay in the hospital for 20 days because it was ruptured. I got to be the nurse's pet patient. They spoiled me.
Nurse: Where did this happen?

Clinics

Clinics may be another setting in which reminiscence therapy is a viable treatment modality (McWhorter, 1980; Parsons, 1986). Geropsychiatric nurses use reminiscence in psychotherapy with older adults. Cutillo-Schmitter (1993) incorporates genograms into her therapy sessions with clinic clients. A great deal of information can be acquired in a short period of time from a genogram, but as she pointed out some clients may need help with the process, either because of problems with writing, comprehension, or vision.

Home Care

Nurses also implement reminiscence in home care nursing, but their ability and understanding may vary widely (I. Eide, April 20, 1994, personal communication). Home care and community health nurses elicit reminiscing by such simple remarks as, "I look forward to seeing that picture or book (or whatever) next time I come." For home care nurses implementing reminiscence, a review of the history and ethnicity of the client can enhance the nursing care plan or help with a problem such as nutrition. Example:

- An older Greek woman who is not eating well and getting weaker in hospital. Reminiscing and learning about food habits and favorites from childhood could be helpful.
- Insufficient intake of fluids—explore beliefs about types of fluids preferred in a family and as a child—hot? cold? sweet? sour? bitter? What must be avoided. (B. Steffl, August 10, 1994, personal letter.)

In two of the most comprehensive chapters about the use of reminiscence in nursing practice, Hamilton (1985, 1992) listed nursing diagnoses for which reminiscence is an appropriate intervention. In 1985, Hamilton identified 11; in 1992, the list had grown to 19. The increase indicates the momentum reminiscence has gained among nurses as a viable therapeutic intervention. However, there is little research to validate the effectiveness of reminiscence with each of the above interventions. Table 14.3 lists the diagnosis for which reminiscence may be used as an independent nursing intervention.

TABLE 14.3 Nursing Diagnoses for Which Reminiscence is Implemented

Altered growth
Anticipatory grieving
Anxiety
Decisional conflict
Diversional activity deficit
Family coping: potential for growth
Fear
Health-seeking behaviors
Hopelessness
Impaired judgment
Ineffective denial
Ineffective family coping
Ineffective individual coping
Powerlessness
Self-esteem disturbance
Social interaction impaired
Social isolation
Spiritual distress

Note: From "Reminiscence therapy" by D.B. Hamilton, 1992, in G.M. Bilechek & J.C. McColskey (Eds.), *Essential nursing treatment* (2d ed.), pp. 295–296.

It is important to note that there are persons for whom reminiscence may not be an appropriate or therapeutic nursing intervention: (a) agitated persons, (b) persons in pain, (c) persons with low energy level (especially those with chronic diseases), (d) persons who manifest paranoid behavior, and (e) persons with very traumatic, sad lives; for example, those who were in the Holocaust (Burnside, 1990). There are exceptions to any of these situations and it becomes a nurse's judgement call to decide who will benefit from reminiscence.

The nursing literature is much richer regarding group reminiscence. In a literature review (Haight, 1991) of a sample of 98 articles, 11 were identified as reminiscence group therapy by nurses. As stated earlier, nurses began implementing reminiscence groups with older adults two decades ago. In spite of sometimes disappointing research findings, nurses recognize the potential and cost-effectiveness of reminiscence group therapy (RGT).

One might ask how nurse leadership of RGT differs from that of another discipline. Quickly one thinks of the holistic approach imbued in nurses' training and how that would permeate both their leadership style and strategies. For example, a nurse would be sensitive to a member's pain and might check out pain medication immediatedly prior to the group meeting. Energy levels are monitored. Or a nurse might notice a member has an edematous foot and find a chair and pillow to support the extremity. A nurse might also be sensitive to slight behavioral changes in the group (for example, falling asleep) and pursue the cause. Nurses might also assess hearing and visual problems and take necessary steps; for example, checking batteries for hearing aid or cleaning extremely dirty glasses (Burnside, 1994b). Matteson and Munsat (1982) have spelled out the leader's tasks and emphasize the need to help members with hearing losses. Matteson (1986, p. 293) states that, "physical disabilities greatly interfere with group participation" (p. 293). She further states that "a physical disability may be an underlying reason for depression" (p. 293) and could rule such a situation out for a patient the group experience because of transportation difficulties to and from the group.

Nurses continue to seriously consider the importance of reminiscing for older adults. To the casual observer reminiscence may be viewed as "fun and games" type of intervention. That is not to deny that it cannot have its merry moments, but gerontological nurses realize the complexity of reminiscence interventions. Such interventions should not be underestimated because, "reminscence is a much more dynamic process than just talking. The nursing interventions involved in the process are more complex and exacting than simply providing a free ear" (Clements, 1986, p. 116, see also Ruth & Kenyon, this volume). However, it is most important that the nurses who implement reminiscence share the information with other team members so that a coordinated care plan can be provided (B. Steffl, personal letter, August 10, 1994).

PART III: GENDER, LIFE REVIEW AND REMINISCENCE

A literature search reveals that the research and implementation of life review and reminiscence in nursing has been carried out predominantly by women. One article in nursing literature was authored by men, a psychologist and a nurse (Norris & Eileh, 1982). This is not surprising, since nursing is comprised mostly of women, and a male gerontological nurse is quite rare, in spite of the rapid rate of increase in number of men who are registered nurses, which rose by 343 % during the past two decades (Glick & Bolyard, 1993).

The literature indicates that many of the studies were conducted in nursing homes which are predominantly women's residences; 71% of institutuionalized residents are women (George, 1984). Toseland (1990) states that gender influences how older people participate in a group. There is research indicating gender differences may be particularly important in later life development (Bengtson, Reedy and Gordon, 1985; Hagestad & Neugaraten, 1985). Little attention has been paid in the literature to gender differences in reminiscence and life review. Birren and Deutchman (1991) found that men and women were about equally interested in autobiography.

It is not easy to find accounts about single-sex groups (Burnside, 1989; Middleton, 1987), and yet they are common in current practice. There are reasons for selecting all women, all men or a heterosexual group. A leader may select a group of all women simply because men refuse to participate, as can happen in a nursing home. Or a leader may choose all women to better understand older women in the group setting (Burnside, 1989). Women may show up for treatment at a clinic more frequently than men, and therefore are placed in groups (McWhorter, 1980; Parsons, 1986). In contrast, veterans' hospitals contain predominantly men, so heterosexual groups are almost impossible to coordinate (McMahon & Rhudick, 1964; Reed & Cobble, 1986). One of the differences in all-men's groups pointed out by Reed and Cobble (1986) is that the themes and props introduced should appeal to men. For all-women's groups, dolls, cooking utensils, and preparing meals are favorite topics, the Model-T Ford, however, is a popular item to discuss for both genders (Rodriguez, 1990).

It has been my experience that older women in groups tend to open up more quickly and seem to reveal more intimate information about their lives than older men. In that respect, all-women groups tend to make the group leading easier. However, the interaction of men and women in the group can be advantageous to the members. One rather obvious observation, especially in nursing homes, is the increased interest in personal hygiene and appearance. In one such group a member would not come to group until she had put on her makeup. It will add to a leader's skill and expertise to conduct all three types of groups: (a) all men, (b) all women, (c) combined, and record the differences observed within each group and between groups.

Summary

The focus of this chapter was on life review and reminiscence in nursing practice. The history of life review empirical research was traced back to the 80s for one-to-one interactions; anecdotal articles indicate that nurses implement life review with dying individuals. The literature reveals confusion about differentiating life review group therapy and reminiscence group therapy.

Reminiscence in the one-to-one and group modality was traced back through the 70s. The literature is rich with materials about reminiscence group therapy conducted by nurses; however, there is less available information about the one-to-one reminiscence interactions. Nurses elicit reminiscence in all of the settings where they care for older adults; acute care, community settings, nursing homes, and day care centers. The nurse group leader ideally should have specific goals and a list of nursing diagnoses for which reminiscence is a treatment.

As research is refined, nurses will have a firmer foundation for their interventions. More qualitative studies would help us better understand the phenomena of life review and reminiscence. Qualitative studies by nurses about reminiscence have begun to appear in the literature (Bramwell, 1984; Hagemaster, 1992; Kovach, 1991a). Research will demand: (a) refined tools, (b) improved methodology, (c) replication studies, and (d) a variety of populations studied.

The importance of the two modalities, reminiscence and life review, to be included in the gerontological or geropsychiatric nurse's repertoire could improve psychosocial nursing care and the quality of life for the older adult. As Beadleson-Baird and Lura (1988) stated, "A sensitive, respectful nurse who sees reminiscence as having potentially therapeutic value is an asset to any treatment area. (p. 87)." To that could be added life review as well. O'Malley (1981) said that, "Memory is a crazy woman that hoards colored rags and thrown away food" (p. 134). As nurses we need to better understand the need to hoard memories as well as the need to throw away some memories.

15

Biographical Assessment in Community Care

Brian Gearing, Ph.D. and Peter Coleman, Ph.D.

This chapter describes the development of a biographical approach to the assessment of the health and social care needs of older people living in the community, an approach first developed in the Care for Elderly People at Home (CEPH) research project in Gloucester (1985-89).

COMMUNITY CARE FOR OLDER PEOPLE IN THE U.K.

Although older people comprise a highly heterogeneous group crossing more than three decades of the lifespan, community services for older people in the U.K. have fallen within a very limited range; typically, those comprising a home carer assisting with household tasks, a delivered meal, home aids and adaptations, possibly nursing care, sometimes day care to relieve loneliness, and where these services seem insufficient, assessment of eligibility for a place in a residential home. A limited view of old age and what it is like to be old seems to underlie such provision: a picture of an older person whose needs are predominantly physical, who is dependent, isolated and lonely; and undifferentiated in such characteristics from other people of his or her age. However, such services do not begin to match the diversity of capacities, attitudes, interests, and other attributes found among individuals in their seventh, eighth, and ninth decades.

Moreover, the *way* such services are provided often involves a rigidity which is insensitive to the changing nature of the circumstances of older individuals, and their capacity to contribute their views to an assessment of their own needs and the kinds of help they would like. This contrasts with the standard expected of work with children and young people. Here a value is placed in both training and practice on careful assessment, needs are defined holistically as being both material and socioemotional, and casework or counseling are considered an essential component of the work.

This is a longstanding problem. In 1967, in an article called *Towards a Developmental View of Aging for Social Work*, Pincus attributed the problem to the influence of Freudian psychoanalysis on social work theory, which had produced a view of aging as constituting a gradual descent from the peak of maturity attained in the early years of adulthood. In Pincus's view, this pessimistic orientation, combined with an understandable professional focus on those older people with social and economic problems, had led social workers "to regard aging primarily as a disease process rather than a natural process" (Pincus, 1967, p. 34). Nearly 30 years after Pincus's article, the Freudian influence in social work has receded. However, a pessimistic and unimaginative view of human aging has ensured that social work with older people is still accorded a low priority in the allocation of trained, skilled staff who are concerned to address older people's practical and emotional needs (Phillips, 1992; Stevenson & Parsloe, 1978).

Recently, social work practice with older people in the U.K. has received fresh consideration as a result of the reorganization of community care services brought about by the 1990 National Health Service and Community Care Act. Essentially, the 1990 Act addressed the longstanding organizational problem in the U.K. of the lack of coordination of health (nonmedical) care and social services for all ages of people in the community. Historically, these have been provided by different agencies (for example, health authorities and social services departments) and different professional workers (nurses, health visitors, social workers, home care workers, occupational therapists, and physiotherapists). The Act resulted in local authority social services departments being given the responsibility for allocating public funds for the assessment of need and coordination of care. Local authorities were expected to appoint care managers (roughly synonomous with case managers) who, on the basis of assessment, should decide what "package of care" matched the needs of the individual client concerned, and should also monitor and review the provision of that care.

The Act also gave prominence to assessment. Without good quality assessments, care packages cannot be devised and services cannot be coordinated to meet client needs appropriately. In the past, local authority staff have assessed needs and also had the responsibility for providing services. However, the Act separates out the assessment function from the service response by requiring that, following an assessment of need by one agency, care and services be "purchased" from the provider agency, which may be located in the private or volunteer sector. In making an independent needs-led assessment central to the new community care approach, the Act has implicitly raised fundamental questions about the role and meaning of assessment for community care.

ASSESSMENT AND BIOGRAPHY

Assessment has long been regarded as a core social work skill. Early attempts to establish a professional status and role for social work comparable to that secured by the medical profession were paralleled by social work texts which borrowed some of the medical terminology. For example, early social work texts referred to assessment as "social diagnosis" (Hollis, 1939). The importance of assessment was affirmed in subsequent gerontology texts for social workers by Paul Brearley (1975), Cherry Rowlings (1981), and Mary Marshall (1983), the latter also suggesting, significantly, that "biographical listening" is a prerequisite for understanding the needs for older people.

Under the community care legislation, assessments must be multidisciplinary, covering needs and problems which once were considered the sole or main responsiblity of health care professionals, as well as social workers. Anxiety has been expressed, however, about the kind of assessment which will be practiced in the brave new world of care management ushered in by the Act. Preliminary findings from an ESRC research project monitoring the implementation of the Act indicate that resource-constrained social service departments are having considerable difficulty in ensuring that assessment is needs-led (Lewis, 1994). Earlier, fear had been expressed that holistic assessment and counseling skills are likely to be disregarded when so much importance is placed in the Act on the organizational and technical skills or coordination, care packaging, budget holding, and resource allocation (Phillips, 1992). Is the traditional social work principle of valuing the whole person and his or her individual needs in danger of being forgotten? It is here, we argue, that a biographical approach can make a significant contribution. Within lifespan psychology an understanding of an individual's biography is fundamental to assessment at any stage of life. Many now acknowledge the influence of Henry Murray (1938) and other psychologists, who continued to pursue a holistic and lifespan approach to studying human lives in opposition to the fashion of the postwar years, which was to analyze particular behaviors and usually only in their immediate context (see, for example, McAdams, 1990). Of particular significance for the study of aging have been the writings of Erik Erikson and their emphasis on development over the whole life course (Erikson, 1965; Ruth & Kenyon, this volume). Erikson refers to capacities such as "trust," "intimacy," and "generativity," which are shaped over a lifespan and continue to seek a positive resolution before death.

Erikson's writings have been a source of inspiration also in long-term care settings. Archer, for example, provides a telling account of how she came to find added meaning in work with mentally infirm older people on British psychogeriatric wards, through a consideration of each of Erikson's stages of development. It allowed her to recognize each person's individuality, their own particular achievements, and their struggles. More recently, Helen Kivnick (1991) has developed a method for assessing what she describes as "life strengths" in elderly clients in long-term care. These strengths are based on updated versions of Erikson's eight concepts: hope and faith; willfulness, independence, and control; purposefulness, pleasure, and imagination; competence, and hard work; values and sense of self; love and friendship; care and productivity; and, wisdom and perspective. When care staff consider a resident's or client's functional needs in isolation from these strengths and values, they depersonalize them and exaggerate the relative importance of their disabilities (Ruth & Kenyon, this volume). The proposed approach to biographical assessment reflects the emphasis in Erikson's later thinking (Erikson, Erikson, & Kivnick, 1986) on the continuing relevance of previous life tasks. Although each task does have its focal period, the issues continue to return in various forms throughout life. The need to work at early "themes" in late life is a function of current life demands, not only of previous success or failure with similar issues. Aging is viewed as ongoing reinvolvement in life, building on past strengths, interests and achievements, as well as correcting past faults (see also Svensson, this volume). This view provides a helpful context for defining rehabilitation and long-term care goals.

The task of the last stage of life for Erikson is to attain "ego integrity", an assured sense of meaning and order in one's life and in the universe, as against despair and disgust. As a result, too, of Robert Butler's discovery of the significance of "life review" in clinical practice with older people (Butler, 1963) this perspective created a more positive attitude to older people's reminiscing among professional workers (see also Burnside, this volume). Subsequent research and theory have drawn attention to other qualities in reminiscence, especially the satisfaction achieved from passing on one's lifestory and experience to others. This reflects the traditional role of the older person as a moral storyteller, while at the same time helping to maintain his or her sense of identity (Coleman, 1994).

The lifestory that is created not only has to make sense to the person but also has to be communicated to a wider audience if it is to have continued meaning. This is a major task, and one which we may at times need to help people to achieve, or even stand in their place to create for them if frailty has taken away their mental powers. Studies on elderly care wards in Southampton, England, indicate that a substantial minority, perhaps as many as one-third, of very old people feel they would like to tell their lifestory but do not have available listeners. Even with people in advanced states of dementia, recall of significant parts of the person's story may be possible given patience, care, and empathy (Mills & Coleman, 1994). Although the formulation of an ever more coherent story that demands to be told can be considered as an ultimate goal for many (Kenyon, this volume), the obstacles along the way to its fulfillment will vary. Some may have literally forgotten what they have done, perhaps because they have never learned to value their achievements and experience. Others may not be able to see that a connection can be made between what they have achieved in the past and the challenges that face them now. There may be particular episodes in some people's lives which they have deliberately and successfully shut out of consciousness because they were unable to come to terms with them. Yet now they may feel the need to tell the whole story. Some indeed, may feel overwhelmed by a sense of dissatisfaction and apply a theme of failure to their whole lifestory. A common approach to people's reminiscences does not appear feasible or appropriate.

Nevertheless, this does not mean that normative theories of psychosocial change with age do not also promote understanding of reminiscence. In his book *Reclaimed Powers*, David Gutmann (1987) sets out the evidence for his ambitious theory that older people have a biological role within human society, contributing to its welfare and survival. This view is supported by certain interpretations of the results of studies on autobiographical memory, which indicate enhanced recall of older people's memories of their youth (Rubin, Wetzler, & Nebes, 1986). It is possible to suggest that this ability gives older people a significant function, especially in pre-literate societies, in preserving the memory of infrequent but important occurrences such as natural disasters. Other sociobiographical evidence suggests that older people are more effective communicators about past events, speaking about them in a more digestible mode, and in a voice that will draw the attention of their listeners (Mergler & Goldstein, 1983). These notions remain speculative at present, but at the very least they indicate a greater readiness to appreciate the social functions of older people's reminiscences.

Interest in reminiscence in Britain gained momentum during the 1970s as a result of developments in oral history, which treated memories of the past as valid evidence, and community publishing, which drew on people's writing and the unearthing of ordinary people's autobiographies and memories (Bornat, 1989). But the interest in historical accuracy does not rule out an appreciation of lifestories in their own regard as products of ordinary people's search for order, intelligibility, and meaning in their lives (Cohler, 1982). Because perceptions of pasts, presents, and futures are closely interwoven, exploration of the former leads naturally to the latter; including perception of appropriate help.

THEORETICAL BACKGROUND TO THE GLOUCESTER PROJECT

Interest in the U.K. in using life history and reminiscence to meet older people's health and social care needs can be attributed to Malcolm Johnson's 1976 paper, *That Was Your Life: A Biographical Approach to Later Life*, which influenced gerontological thought about the value of the past in understanding old age. Underlying Johnson's critique was a view that theory and research into old age are flawed by social gerontology's functionalism and empiricism. In embodying these characteristics, much of gerontological research had ignored the meaning of older people's lived experiences and denied them a part of defining their own needs. His alternative biographical approach drew on the strengths of two related social science traditions in the United States: symbolic interactionism and the life history approach in sociology (see also Ruth & Kenyon, this volume).

A distinctive feature of Johnson's (1976) critique was that it encompassed both gerontological theory and research, and health and social care provision for older people. Johnson argued that the dominance of "objective" measures of older people's needs in research and practice (survey questions and assessment scales to measure capacity and incapacity) had resulted in a narrow view of old age as a time of dependency:

> Just as social workers who disburse these benefits are constrained by the nature of existing provision, so are many researchers, who cast their studies in terms of what is, or might easily be, available. Thus there is a reinforcing process which lends a spurious legitimacy to giving older people the nearest thing you have from a minute range of provisions. One of the major flaws in this allocation process is the failure to properly diagnose the elderly person's true 'needs'. . . . (p. 154)

Johnson argued that this position could be turned around by valuing the older person's subjective view of his or her situation and that a "biographical approach" could reveal how life histories have shaped present concerns. This would in turn uncover a greater diversity of need, which could be matched only by a broader range of services and flexible helping strategies.

Since Johnson's paper a number of gerontological studies in Britain have used a biographical or life history method. These have focused on diverse topics, which include: older people's nutritional preferences (Johnson, de Gregorio, & Harrison, 1980); their strategies for "managing" old age (di Gregorio, 1986,

1987); "confusion" in later life (Sidell, 1986); and the beliefs of older people about health and old age (Cornwell & Gearing, 1989). However, the Gloucester CEPH Project represents the only known systematic attempt to develop the biographical approach as a form of health and social care practice aimed at assessing health and social service needs.

THE DEVELOPMENT OF THE BIOGRAPHICAL APPROACH TO ASSESSMENT

This brings us to the key question for this chapter. What relevance does a biographically based interview method have to the assessment of the health and social care needs of older people living in the community? We will answer it through a description and analysis of the Gloucester Care for Elderly People at Home Project, of which the development of a biographical approach was one part.

The CEPH Project ran from 1985 to 1989 and was based on three "Care Coordinators" who took on the role of keyworkers with older people (see Dant, Carley, Gearing, & Johnson, 1989). The project was set up in collaboration with the Gloucester Health Authority which employed the Care Coordinators in its Community Unit. The Care Coordinators were located in three primary health care teams (that is, community-based teams of GPs with a nurse) professionally oriented to social work. The three people were not professionally trained, but were chosen for their personal skills, abilities, and formal qualifications not necessarily related to the position (for example, degrees, teaching, and nursing qualifications).

The Care Coordinators worked as key workers for older people in the community. Key-working is essentially an attempt to solve the problems of noncoordination referred to earlier: of the neglect, fragmentation and overlap which arise through different agencies and professions providing the range of services which are potentially available to older people living in their own homes in the community (Dant & Gearing, 1990).

The Care Coordinators undertook a role which included assessment, planning a care package, operating the package, monitoring, and reviewing its effects. Each Care Coordinator carried a caseload of older people referred to them by members of the primary health care teams as being "at risk", according to certain explicitly defined criteria. They were distinctly more dependent than the group of clients served by the local authority's Home Care Service, while not being so dependent as the residents of Gloucestershire County Council's Elderly Persons Homes (Dant et al., 1989).

On the basis of needs following a biographical assessment, the Care Coordinator set up a "package of care" linking statutory, voluntary, and informal services to enable the older person to remain at home. Such a package included, for example, nursing services, day care, and other provision, as well as the "buying in" of informal care. An important part of coordination was to link such services with care provided by relatives, friends, and neighbors.

The approach to biographical assessment used by the Care Coordinators was developed jointly with the Project's research team during the three years of the Project. A main assumption of the research team in the CEPH Project was that the health problems of older people are inter-related with their social situation–that "needs" are not simply "social" or "medical" but are particular to the life history and current life circumstances of the individual. Members of the research team had previously carried out biographical studies of older people's needs and beliefs relating to health and social care (Cornwell & Gearing, 1989; Johnson et al., 1980). Drawing on this experience, they drew the following three conclusions which seemed relevant to assessment:

First, those who listen to the life stories of older people whom they wish to help gain markedly different pictures of the person and their needs, from those who administer traditional assessment techniques (This concurs with the view of Ruth and Kenyon, stated in the introductory chapter of this volume, that lifestories can form a basis for action). The second conclusion was that self-esteem can be greatly enhanced by skillful encouragement of reminiscence. The third was that the way people cope with the multiple losses associated with later life is directly dependent on earlier life experience and present relationships, roles, and activities.

The aim of research was to develop an approach to assessment which reflected these principles and, moreover, was demonstrably effective and efficient in the context of the everyday practice of community-based professionals. Crucially, it had to work within that particular context in order to meet the objective of eliciting a view of the individual's needs which would also lead to more appropriate and acceptable forms of assistance. This professional context and purpose led the research team to devise a different interview method from that of the oral historian or the life history researcher. Whereas historians of both these kinds are interested in the past for its own sake, the CEPH Project research team adopted a more instrumental biographical approach, their primary interest being what the past revealed about the older person's current life situation and the formation of his or her current needs and preferences. This involved innovation as there was no known experience elsewhere which could be applied in a community care context. The research team and the Care Coordinators therefore developed the approach gradually in the light of experience gained through working with clients during the Project. Their structural location within primary health care teams greatly facilitated this objective. Early ideas and methods devised by the research team were considerably modified in the light of the Care Coordinators' actual experience of working with their older clients.

Initially, the Care Coordinators were prepared for this task through an education and training process (see Johnson, Gearing, Carley, & Dant, 1988). This included three main stages: working systematically through an Open University study pack *Caring for Older People*, designed for those involved in practical work with older people; reading, discussing, and viewing material on biographical research; and analysis including interview styles and methods, and carrying out pilot biographical interviews which were tape recorded, transcribed, and discussed with the research team. The following were provided for this purpose:

- a *Checklist for Interviewers* which reminded them of basic rules for biographical interviewing.
- a *Biographical Interview Schedule* which constituted a "route map" of the biographical territory to be explored, rather than a questionnaire. No form of words in a question format were supplied, but a chronological and thematic schema was provided, which started with childhood and family of origin, and progressed through numerous common life stages and life events, leading up to present circumstances, including health and dependency in retirement, and self-assessment of health and health-related needs.
- a *Lifetime Chart* which was essentially a schematic summary of the areas covered in the schedule which the Coordinators could refer to easily during the interviews.
- an *Analysis Sheet* to be completed at the end of an interview which also proposed a set of consequent actions.

The resulting pilot interviews ranged from 1¼ hours to over 4 hours. The Care Coordinators ended this induction phase with enthusiasm for the biographical approach but had several reservations. These concerned: the length of time the interviews took; the stage of the helping relationship when biographical interviews were useful; conducting interviews when people had acute needs to be attended to; asking people to tell their lifestories when the need for help was manifestly clear; and conducting interviews with deaf or confused people, though this was possible.

As the Care Coordinators worked on developing and refining the biographical approach to assessment, they learned that it had to be used flexibly. For example, rather than pursuing a systematic and strictly chronological progression through the stages of someone's life from childhood onwards, using the Biographical Interview Schedule, the Coordinators found it was often more realistic and productive to attend to immediate presenting needs and then work back as opportunities allowed in the course of an interview, to discuss earlier experiences, attitudes, and relationships (using the Lifetime Chart as a schema and prompt sheet.) Eventually, an acceptable way of meeting people's needs emerged, in most cases, but this could vary in the time it took, from one or two lengthy sessions lasting around an hour, to a less concentrated interaction in which different parts of the life history were disclosed and pieced together, over several visits, while other more immediate or practical problems were also discussed. This gradual, flexible approach could, we believe, also be used by professionals such as social workers, health visitors, GPs, or district nurses (Boulton, Gully, Mathews & Gearing, 1989).

THE VALUE OF THE BIOGRAPHICAL APPROACH

The way the biographical approach developed in practice is best demonstrated through case studies. We present three of them in this section.

Case Study 1: Mr. Fred Allen

Mr. Allen first came to the attention of the Care Coordinator through referral by a neighbor who said that Mr. Allen wasn't looking well and his general appearance had deteriorated. Mr. Allen had earlier refused a potential offer of help when visited by a member of the primary health care team, making it clear that he was managing very well, thank you. Subsequently, he requested several home visits in quick succession, not appearing to remember the previous visit. Mr. Allen was formally referred on to the Care Coordinator whose informal, noninterrogative, listening approach and encouragement to talk about his life quickly seemed to gain his confidence. The interviews revealed that Mr. Allen had worked first as an insurance agent, which he had disliked, moving from there to the Ministry of Labour, where he held a clerical post until he retired in 1979.

On being asked when specific events happened Mr. Allen showed considerable uncertainty of recall, but he talked about losing his wife many years before and how he had brought up his only son single-handed. Mr. Allen was explicit about revealing his loneliness. He had suffered considerably after his wife's death and said he dreaded putting the key in the lock; "there was nothing to come home for". However, he claimed to do things he had always enjoyed, like walking, betting on the dogs, and calling into the Soldiers and Sailors Club most lunch times. But his home showed signs of being neglected for some time; not only was it untidy but littered with the remains of food. According to Mr. Allen, he was managing, but the Care Coordinator had her doubts about how well and regularly he ate. If asked what he had eaten that day, he would look to the table for clues and clearly there were occasions when he could not remember whether he had eaten at all. He was of the habit of writing notes to himself as if to prop up his failing memory. Mostly he sat watching the television and smoking cigarettes. A lifetime of heavy smoking had taken its toll in the form of chronic bronchitis and constant shortness of breath.

It transpired that one of the practice receptionists had known Mr. Allen and his family for many years and the Coordinator was able to check out some aspects of his life story. Mr. Allen's wife had in fact died more recently than he remembered. His son, John, had left home some time before this. His visits to different places were now the exception rather than the rule: the barman at the Soldiers and Sailors confirmed that Mr. Allen had not been there for some time. On the occasions he had been seen there, he would forget he had paid for a drink, returning to the bar more than once to offer money.

The Care Coordinator's use of the biographical approach helped her to share Mr. Allen's life experiences and to better understand his mental health needs. It became clear that he had suffered a marked loss of short-term memory and, when questioned, relied on his more accurate long-term memory. Consequently, the description he gave of his current circumstances only gave an accurate picture of how he had *once* managed, not of his present lifestyle. Without a biographical assessment it seems unlikely that Mr. Allen would have received the kind of help he needed and found acceptable. It helped the Care Coordinator to get to know Mr. Allen over time and in a way which enabled him to relax and give his trust. It helped in the assessment of his mental health needs and, this, in turn, helped other workers who were later involved in his care. Through her knowledge of his past life, the Care Coordinator learned about Mr. Allen's relationship with his neighbor, and she was able to revive a family friendship which had faded over the years. This also led to the help provided by his neighbour's daughter-in-law, something which was acceptable to Mr. Allen and maintained him happily in his own home for several months. When his physical health deteriorated, private nursing care provided the only alternative for the last weeks of his life.

In summary, the main way in which the biographical approach proved valuable in Mr. Allen's case was in constructing a full and credible account of his past life, including the part played by his family and other significant relationships. This greater understanding contributed to an assessment of Mr. Allen's mental health. The biographical approach was also instrumental in getting Mr. Allen to accept help and in establishing a network of friendship and practical support which he found acceptable.

Case Study 2: Mrs. Jackson

Mrs. Jackson was referred by her GP, as she was finding it difficult to cope with life after the sudden death of her husband a few weeks earlier.

The biographical approach helped the Care Coordinator see Mrs. Jackson as someone who had always been resourceful and determined and much influenced by a childhood in the Depression of the 1930s, when her father couldn't afford shoes to send her to the local technical college. She had been careful with money for most of her life, supporting her husband in business and making sacrifices to give her daughter and granddaughter the education of which she felt deprived and considered all-important. Mrs. Jackson would not spend any of her savings on herself and was quite adamant that she would leave her estate to help secure her grandchildren's future. Her continuing desire to help her family financially, in particular her adult disabled twin grandsons, led her to economize as much as possible. For this reason, she refused the Council's Home Care Service, which she regarded as too expensive. Because the Care Coordinator understood this she was able to facilitate an acceptable substitute, the less expensive private cleaning service.

Biographical knowledge contributed in other ways to the help that was given to Mrs. Jackson. After the recent and sudden death of her husband, Mrs. Jackson became particularly concerned to remain in the home which he had chosen and which had been the focus of their activities and friendships. However, Mrs. Jackson recognised that she would have a problem in maintaining the house and, following several falls, was also worried about being alone. An important part of the Care Coordinator's role was to help Mrs. Jackson explore housing alternatives such as warden-controlled flats, conversion, and letting.

The Care Coordinator drew up a package of care which included referrals to the Gloucester Community Programme for help with the garden and household repairs, and for the installation of secure locks after an attempted break-in. Following a fire in her kitchen, Age Concern, a local voluntary organization, was contacted and provided a smoke alarm, which gave her some peace of mind.

The Care Coordinator also counselled Mrs. Jackson in her bereavement. Mrs. Jackson did not want to worry her daughter, whose own husband had just recently died, suffered from migraines, and had four children to look after, including adult disabled twin sons.

Mrs. Jackson's restricted mobility had prevented her from pursuing some interests, such as playing bowls, but she was able to find a new source of interest in a nearby Family Centre to which the Care Coordinator introduced her. Biographical assessment had revealed that she had a lifelong interest in the roles of women and in children. At the Centre she was able to talk to the mothers and their children, and contribute to the Centre's activities.

In summary, we can say that in Mrs. Jackson's case the biographical approach was found to be particularly useful in establishing meaningful connections between significant past events (disappointment at not going to the technical school) and present attitudes towards finances, the role of women and women's education, and family responsiblities. This led to an understanding of Mrs. Jackson's refusal of certain services, which was important in preventing her from being labelled a "difficult" client. The biographical approach adopted by the Care Coordinator also incorporated therapeutic counseling following Mrs. Jackson's bereavement and it led directly to meaningful activites and to a package of care which she found acceptable and which enabled her to stay home.

Case Study 3: Mrs. Peters

Mrs. Peters was referred to the Care Coordinator by her family doctor, as she felt that Mrs. Peters was lonely and isolated. The immediate community did not offer any social amenities, and Mrs. Peters' mobility was restricted.

Mrs. Peters' family was very important to her. In her 87 years, she had suffered many tragedies and upheavals, including the death of her father and two husbands who had both died of cancer. A recent move from another part of England to live in a mobile home in Gloucestershire nearer to her daughter had left her feeling isolated. Her limited mobility prevented her from getting the bus into town. Nonetheless, she had an extroverted and lively outlook on life, responding to the situation in which she found herself as positively as she could. Her daughter lived near enough to visit every morning and evening to help her with housework and shopping, though her own work prevented her from taking Mrs. Peters outdoors.

Following the biographical assessment, the Care Coordinator perceived her main task as trying to find some kind of stimulating outlet for Mrs. Peters. The local authority Social Services department could only offer her a local privately run day home which she rejected as a place where older, disabled people sat in their chairs all day with nothing to do. Social Services were critical of her refusal of this service, feeling she was "difficult" and did not know what she wanted. Knowing Mrs. Peters and her history, the Care Coordinator felt that, on the contrary, she was a person who very much knew what she wanted. She certainly knew what she didn't want! The Care Coordinator felt it was her job to persevere until she found the right place for Mrs. Peters.

During the next few months the Care Coordinator arranged for Mrs. Peters to attend the Saturday club at the local hospital's Elderly Care Unit, where she enjoyed the company of the younger volunteers, as well as the activities and organized talks. She became physically more active, going on short walks around the corridors surrounding the Unit and attending keep-fit sessions, which the

Care Coordinator had instigated knowing how important it was to Mrs. Peters, a former dance teacher, that she kept as physically active as her mobility would allow.

The Care Coordinator also arranged a voluntary visitor through the local Age Concern group, which partly mitigated the isolation she felt at not being able to walk outside her home. However, because Mrs. Peters needed to get out of the house more often and transport was available, the Coordinator switched Mrs. Peters' chiropidy from domiciliary home visits to outpatient attendance at the local clinic. The Coordinator's knowledge of Mrs. Peters' past interests also led her to suggest and then arrange membership of a recently formed University of the Third Age branch in the city.

Overall, we can say that Mrs. Peters had strong feelings about "being old and inactive" which the biographical approach uncovered. It also revealed past interests and preferences which formed the basis for developing a package of care which gave her more activity and stimulation and relieved some of the pressure on her daughter. It may also have averted depression and made decreased mobility and a permanent residential placement less likely.

THE CASE STUDIES: SOME OBSERVATIONS

From these cases and others in the Project (Boulton, Gully, Mathews, & Gearing, 1989) we can say that the biographical approach has been particularly useful in the following circumstances:

1. Eliciting older people's attitudes to a broad range of things and experiences (old age, life-style, interests, relationships, personal standards, and residential care) (Mr. Allen, Mrs. Jackson, and Mrs. Peters).
2. Understanding family relationships (Mr. Allen and Mrs. Jackson).
3. Finding out about relationships between carers and the older person (Mrs. Peters).
4. Discovering various kinds of help and services, which would be acceptable and unacceptable, in order to provide a package of care (Mrs. Jackson and Mrs. Peters).
5. Relating to and understanding people labeled as "difficult" (Mrs. Jackson and Mrs. Peters).
6. Hearing how people coped with past difficulties and hardships, with a view to how they might cope in the future (Mrs. Jackson and Mrs. Peters).
7. Eliciting a different picture of someone's needs (Mrs. Peters).
8. Understanding and relating to people who suffer dementia (Mr. Allen).

9. Helping individuals to put traumatic events into perspective (Mrs. Jackson).
10. Uncovering particular talents and aspirations which may suggest future activities (Mrs. Peters).

The case studies demonstrate three main ways in which a biographical approach is of value in the assessment of older people's needs in this context.

First, it leads to the practitioner gaining a greater understanding of and respect for the individual older person. The case studies would suggest that this occurs in part through the way the diversity of experiences and personal characteristics among older people are revealed through the telling of their life stories.

Second, this feeling of being understood and appreciated as an individual can undoubtedly be beneficial in itself, giving or restoring to the older person concerned a feeling of self-worth (Birren & Birren, this volume; Kenyon, this volume; Randall, this volume), but it also facilitates a good relationship between worker and client, one characterized by trust, acceptance, and a feeling of security. This is important if personal and sometimes sensitive issues, needs, and problems are to be frankly discussed (see also Ruth & Kenyon, this volume).

Third, biographical knowledge can directly influence decisions made about the service or package of care most appropriate to the client's needs. This study suggests that service providers need to ask themselves whether older people are able to relate their present circumstances to the life they have lived (Coleman, 1994).

More speculatively, perhaps, we would suggest that a further value associated with biographical assessment is that it gives the older person the opportunity to tell their story as the end of life comes nearer. As one of us has suggested elsewhere (Coleman, 1994), one of the essential tasks for the aging individual is not only to make sense of their own lifestory but, if that life is to have continued meaning, to communicate it to others; something which older people, living alone or without close friends or confidants are unable to do. Furthermore, we would suggest that the life story is something which is as much constructed through the act of telling as it is reconstructed or recalled (Wallace, 1992): an appropriate context and a sympathetic, sensitive listener are essential ingredients if older people are to have this opportunity.

ISSUES ARISING FOR WIDER USE

In describing and commenting upon the development of a biographical approach to assessment through the Gloucester CEPH Project, our aim is to bring to wider attention a way of working with older people which we believe has value for the work of care managers, social workers, community nurses, and other professionals involved with older people. However, we need to acknowledge that there are also difficulties attached to this approach to assessment and meeting needs which have to be confronted. Two which we discuss here are the time required for the operation of the biographical approach and the circumstances in which it is most likely to be useful. The biographical interviews carried out by the Care Coordinators varied in length, but could take up to an hour. As suggested above, it was essential that time and attention were given to the older person in the context of a supportive and sympathetic relationship; listening, and allowing people to express themselves in their own way and at their own pace, were things which both the exploration of the life history and the building of the relationship demanded. The Care Coordinators' caseloads were smaller than that usually carried by other health and social work professionals working with older people in the community, although the intensity of the cases, which involved many very dependent people of an average age of just under 80 years, ensured that the Coordinators were kept very busy. Nonetheless, the question remains: how practical is the biographical approach to assessment? Can it work other than in a research "experiment": in the context of everyday practice with all its demands and constraints? Two further questions are relevant here. (1) Can an assessment based on this approach save time, in the long run? (2) Are there particular cases where the biographical approach is likely to be particularly effective, and others where it would not be needed or may simply be a luxury?

It is clear that time and resources are wasted in community care through hasty, superficial assessments and the inappropriate use of resources. In practice, this can mean that the right service is not given at the time it is needed, or it may be continued when no longer needed; or conversely, an inappropriate service may be given in the first place (Carpenter & Paley, 1984). This is something which the newly operationalized NHS and Community Care Act with its emphasis on assessment and the effective use of resources is intended to change. The crux of the problem, however, is the timely matching of appropriate resources to sensitive and accurate assessments of need. It is far from certain that the Act will achieve this. As our case studies demonstrate, a thorough and careful process of assessment, based on knowledge of the client and carers, can lead to the uncovering of multiple needs within a single case. Moreover, in such complex cases, needs frequently change over time, so assessments have to be reviewed and changes made accordingly in the package of care to ensure that resources continue to match needs. This is unlikely to save time in individual cases, particularly in the short run. However, the Care Coordinators' sensitive use of the biographical approach did eventually lead to an effective use of a wider range of resources which met client needs appropriately through individualized packages of care.

This leads us to the second question asked earlier: Where is the biographical approach to assessment likely to prove most effective? The Care Coordinators were referred only certain kinds of cases: those involving older people thought to be "at risk", according to certain measures, of not being able to continue to live in their own homes. From a comparison made with other caseloads outside the CEPH Project (using measures of dependency) the Care Coordinators were judged to be working at the "heavy end" of the spectrum of need (Dant et al., 1989). We would suggest that it is in cases of this kind, where there are "at risk" factors and the likelihood of multiple problems, that such an approach is particularly well justified. These are not cases that are ever likely to be solved by superficial assessments and the hasty or inflexible use of resources. They contrast with many other cases where older people's community care needs are relatively straightforward: where they know what they want, and where there is no problem about providing it, or of them accepting it. There is, after all, no point in taking a life history from someone who simply wants help in cleaning their house, or who requires a bath-aid. It would be an imposition (Ruth & Kenyon, this volume).

CONCLUSION

What can we learn from this research project which is relevant to the assessment of older people's community care needs? A main conclusion is that, if a biographical assessment is to be incorporated into the everyday practice of professionals, it has to be promoted in such a way that these professionals understand and feel comfortable with the principles of the approach and can incorporate it into their own way of working. Success in the Gloucester Project resulted from a sensitive and flexible application of the principles of an approach to biographical assessment by the Care Coordinators to the differing personalities and circumstances of their clients. Strict adherence to a preformulated set of methods and processes devised initially by the research team had to be abandoned in the light of the Coordinator's experience with their clients. In other words, the biographical approach to assessment should be regarded as precisely that–an approach which can be learned, adapted, and applied in the light of different circumstances and in different professional contexts, rather than a "tool" or method which practitioners should be expected to use in a fixed or uniform way. The best way of achieving this may be through education and training programs for professional community care workers in the principles and processes involved in the biographical assessment of older people: Drawing on what is known about the value, principles, and approaches to life history and reminiscence work with older people; incorporating interviewing and counseling skills training; and identifying those kinds of cases where a biographical approach is likely to be most appropriate and effective. What is not required is the codification of yet another set of assessment methods or schedules which could be used indiscriminately on older people.

Earlier in this chapter we argued that the low status of social work with older people and the recognition of a narrow range of community care needs did not match the diversity of older people's lives and took little account of their own perception of their needs. As long ago as 1967 Pincus (1967) argued that the focus of a pathological view of aging had led social workers to take a generally negative and pessimistic view of working with older people. He advocated a developmental view of aging:

> His viewpoint frees the worker from the narrow perspective of measuring successful aging against a single model of a previous life stage and forces the recognition that old age hold its own potentials for psychological well-being. It takes the emphasis off general prescriptions for all aging clients and helps the worker to guide the client down his unique path of successful ageing (p. 41).

Today, this view still seems relevant, both as a comment on the negative orientation of much work with older people and the need for an approach which recognizes diversity and developmental potential. Increasingly, Pincus also argued that a developmental view of aging would make us aware of the necessity of examining the appropriateness of diagnostic and treatment techniques. The biographical approach to assessment can be seen as one outcome of such an examination. If used more widely in community care it can contribute to a re-evaluation of later life as a time of continuity and personal growth and development, as well as loss and decline.

ACKNOWLEDGMENT

The authors wish to acknowledge the contribution of members of the Gloucester CEPH Project (1985–89) research team, Michael Carley, Tim Dant, and Malcolm Johnson, to the development of ideas in this paper.

16

Autobiography: Exploring the Self and Encouraging Development

James E. Birren, Ph.D. and Betty A. Birren

There are many uses of autobiography: a) as a source of psychological and social science research material, b) as a source of historical material for family and community, c) as a means of promoting personal insight, and d) as preparation for changes in life. The authors have been working with guided autobiography for over 15 years and have at times been involved with all of the uses listed above.

An autobiography may be defined as the history or story of a life written by the person who has experienced it. Since autobiographies contain descriptions of events as they have impacted on individuals, they provide readers with information about how lives have been experienced and how events have been interpreted at different stages of life and in different historical eras.

Guided autobiography is a method of obtaining histories of lives organized according to major themes that are commonly experienced. In addition to writing accounts of their lives, the writers read aloud their narratives in small groups. Group participation helps sensitize the participants to early experiences and enlarges the scope of their recall. By developing trust among the participants, the small groups also encourage an open and intimate sharing of the many experiences of growing up and growing old.

An important use of autobiography in psychology was offered in the volumes of *A History of Psychology in Autobiography* which began publication in 1930. These volumes recreate some of the academic climate in which psychology developed (Murcheson, 1930). The early history of psychology is a combination of administrative and social decisions, the economics of the period, and of particular institutions, as well as the individuals involved. Careers of scholars cannot be reconstructed solely from published scientific papers and books. Their motivations, their disputes with colleagues, their fortuitous interactions with foundations or individual benefactors, and their personal experiences of social unrest, wars, and economic depression all influence their development, their science, and their institutions. Knowledge of the intellectual climate of a period can only come from accounts of the individuals who experienced it. Not unimportant in understanding the development of a science are the goals and strategies that individuals used in the pursuit of their careers. Their fascination with particular ideas, unanticipated events, and other aspects of personal background are part of the picture of why and how sciences and institutions have developed. The reasons for having chosen psychology, sociology, biology, or business for a life career must be answered through *personal statements about the decision and its context.*

A paradox about the abundance of autobiographies by early eminent psychologists is why they bothered to write about their lives at all. By the professional standards of psychology of their day, autobiography was "soft" subjective material. Those early eminent psychologists must have believed that something of value is transferred through written autobiography that is not transmitted through published scientific articles. What did they expect to achieve by publishing their autobiographies? Late in his life, the prototypic behaviorist, B. F. Skinner, published his autobiography, which seems inconsistent with the principles of human behavior he espoused. That is, if one believes that rewards and punishment are the only basis for shaping behavior, what value is there in reading or writing an autobiography? Clearly, more is involved in shaping behavior than is apparent from the behavior itself.

It is important to examine the paradox presented by the early leaders of psychology who wrote autobiographies. These writers were distinguished psychologists who focused their careers on the emergence of experimental science in the late 19th century. They believed in the "objective" study of behavior, but even so, they wrote autobiographies, perhaps the epitome of the subjective interpretation of life (Ruth and Kenyon, this volume). They must have believed that there was value to be gained in writing an autobiography as well as in reading one. What did they think their autobiographies' value was to their contemporaries and to their successors? Were their statements contributions to science, or to literature and society, or were they merely personal statements?

This paradox, and the lack of its discussion in psychology, suggests to the authors that there is a considerable amount of exploration to be done about the significance of the objective and subjective, the external and the internal, and the externally perceived and the internally perceived ways of viewing life (These issues are explored in detail in various chapters of this volume).

The opportunity of examining published autobiographies has enabled us to gain insights into the elements of the course of life (de Vries & Lehman, this volume). A major drawback of this approach is that published autobiographies usually represent society's elite who are verbally facile. These works are products of people who have established public reputations or who have the financial resources to publish their autobiographies.

One of the authors was asked to interview a distinguished elderly international figure in psychology. The intent was to obtain an autobiography that could be part of an archive. The autobiographical interviews produced many hours of material that was taped and transcribed. This material was given to the individual to check for accuracy. However, in editing the transcript, the individual deleted personal information about key turning points in life, presumably to protect the person's public image that had been developed during a long and productive career. The resulting archive document is truthful or faithful to the interview, but it does not contain all of the material known by the person to have been the basis for some important life decisions. The user of autobiographical material should also keep in mind that selective recall can be both a conscious as well as a subconscious influence.

CLUES FROM GUIDED AUTOBIOGRAPHY FOR FUTURE RESEARCH

Many of the theories about development that still shape scientific thought were in part derived from analyzing personal statements. G.S. Hall, one of the founders of child psychology early in the twentieth century, used diaries and autobiographies as sources in constructing his theories on adolescence (Ruth & Kenyon, this volume). Freud developed many of his ideas about development by listening to the accounts and experiences of his patients (de Vries, Birren, & Deutchman, 1990). Murray (1938) used diaries and autobiographies, in addition to other techniques, in constructing his theories of personality.

Bertaux and Kohli (1984) pointed to the importance of autobiographical statements and oral life stories to the substantive, or theoretical, questions of sociology. They noted that many contemporary sociologists use such sources to investigate sets of social relationships. The same may be said for many anthropological studies. They reasoned that this interest is due to the efforts needed to understand sociohistorical processes in which both action and subjectivity play a part. Of particular relevance is the importance of autobiographical data in research aimed at understanding the impact of social history on personal development (Kohli, Rosenow, & Wolf, 1983), as well as the "socio-cultural changes that take place in the development of individuality" (Roos, 1988, p. 3).

The effects of social events on lives are reflected in the narratives or life stories that people tell. Sociologists Elder (1974, 1977, 1987), Elder and Baily (1981), and Elder and Caspi (1990) have looked at the effects of war mobilization and other social changes as they are reflected in personal narratives. Looking at the content of lives over the lifespan involves the examination of an individual's interaction with events, which combines the perspectives of both the fields of personality and of developmental psychology (Runyan, 1984). A recent book examines this blending of viewpoints, entitled *Studying Lives Through Time* (Funder, Parke, Tomlinson-Keasey, & Widaman, 1993). Although this study concentrates on early development, it has implications for the development of the person across the entire lifespan.

Ethnomethodology is a third area of sociological research in which the use of autobiographical data plays a vital role. According to Benson and Hughes (1983), ethnomethodology is research aimed at "the ordinary, common-sense, mundane world in which members live and do so in a way that remains faithful to the methods, procedures, practices, etc., that members themselves use in constructing and making sense of this social world" (p. 30). For the most part, anthropological research that draws on autobiography as a data source is rooted in the life history method. One example of relevance to gerontological research is Myerhoff's (1978) book about an older-adult Jewish community in California, *Number Our Days*, which is the result of research utilizing the life history method (see also Cohler & Cole, this volume).

Recently, there has been a return to the use of autobiographical data from earlier periods to understand more fully political history and the role of the individual in the formation of public policy. Wachter's (1988) bibliography of works about life-writings contains many examples of how autobiographical statements can shed light on the political climate of past eras as well as on previously neglected or overlooked individuals. It is particularly important because of past neglect to have autobiographical data of women (Blanco, 1986; Geiger, 1986) and minority groups (Kim, 1987). In the past these groups have held little political power and were usually disregarded in the political writings of earlier eras. Through the analysis of autobiographical statements, a new perspective on both the often unacknowledged roles these groups played in the formation of policy and on social changes, as well as the impact of policies on individual people, can be gained.

The humanities traditionally have been the most accepting of autobiography as a data source, because they are focused on the totality of human beings. The humanities span the study of history, literature, philosophy, theology, and the arts. Autobiography also has been used in the search for understanding the motivations and influences that form the perspective of the artist. Rich (1988) demonstrated how the creative processes of writing and revising a novel can reveal key aspects of an author's life history. Stout (1987) traced one author's use of biography as a part of a search for self-presence.

RETROSPECTIVE ACCOUNTS OF DECISION-MAKING

Individuals make choices under the influence of many variables. These variables include contrasting values, reasoning, information sources and other support resources, and emotions and moods. That is, an individual may have made an important choice while angry or enraged that later statements may be able to place in the proper context. Individuals may quit a job in a dispute with the boss, a marriage may break up following an emotional outburst, or other major psychological investments may shift in an emotional context. Research on the determinants of decisionmaking can be expanded to include autobiographical material on major life decisions. Present perceptions of the determinants of decision choices may be contrasted with later retrospective perceptions and accounts of the outcomes of choice.

Older and younger individuals may differ in their decisionmaking processes because of differing values. That is, an older adult may choose to conserve energy and use a principle of least effort in making choices and may also avoid social confrontations that have emotional overtones. An older person's decision may give the appearance of lack of reasoning and suggest a reduced cognitive capacity, whereas the underlying factor is actually just a value judgement. In an autobiographical account, an older consumer may state that he or she did not wish to protest a product failure or service inadequacy because of not wanting to "make a scene" or to "bother with the matter," whereas a younger person may do more comparison shopping before making a major purchase.

THE GUIDED AUTOBIOGRAPHY METHOD

It was not mentioned above that participation in guided autobiography (Birren & Deutchman, 1991) by researchers can lead to new clues about latent elements of people's lives, as well as the identification of interactions that seem to be important in shaping the structure of individual lives. Participation in a guided autobiography group by a researcher may lead to new hypotheses and insights into important and heretofore overlooked aspects of life. The explanation of the outcomes of particular events depends not only on the characteristic of the event, but on the context in which the event occurs, and the characteristics of the individual experiencing the event. The interactions of the person, event, and context is seen in guided autobiography and may reveal clues about previously unexpected issues.

The literature supports the view that autobiography provides unique insight into the internal world of the individual. Guided autobiography is a resource for understanding that world. It has been further posited that autobiography provides unique insights into issues of spiritual development and the role of religion in adaptation and maturation. For example, Hedlund (as cited in Birren & Hedlund, 1987) analyzed 145 autobiographical essays on the meaning of life and found that the item "religious or individual belief system" was among the four major categories of life meaning, which included altruism or service, personal growth, personal relationships, and beliefs. In general, psychology has avoided study of the importance of religion or spirituality in individual's lives, possibly because of past conflicts between church authority and intellectual freedom. However, currently there is a movement toward looking into the subject. While scholars in theology and letters have looked at confessional literature, it is only recently that psychology and the social sciences have recognized that many older persons interpret their lives in religious or spiritual terms. Soon to be published is a handbook of religion and aging that attempts to bridge views of religion and aging from the viewpoints of the empirical sciences as well as religion and pastoral care (Kimble, McFadden, Ellor & Seeber, 1995).

One way of describing the experience of doing one's autobiography and sharing it with a small group is that one's life becomes more integrated and more acceptable. Birren and Deutchman summarized the positive outcomes of studies on autobiography as follows (1991):

- Sense of increased personal power and importance;
- Recognition of past adaptive strategies and application to current needs and problems;
- Reconciliation with the past and resolution of past resentments and negative feelings;
- Resurgence of interest in past activities or hobbies;
- Development of friendships with other group members;
- Greater sense of meaning in life;
- Ability to face the nearing end of life with a feeling that one has contributed to the world (p. 4).

The authors prefer guided autobiographies, rather than chronological autobiographies, as sources of information about life for several reasons (Birren & Deutchman, 1991). Many people need the incentive of group support and a system or general road map before they are able to do an autobiographical review, unlike the person who publishes his or her autobiography, and who often is motivated to present a self-defined public image, earn a profit, or defend a previously taken stand on an important public issue. To some extent, an element of justification of the way a life has been lived is always a component of autobiography. A published account, however, may present an undue amount of public justification which, in a privately prepared autobiography, is not necessarily required. The latter, particularly in its early stages, can be used as an inquiry, an untangling of the threads of life, and the achieving of insight, in addition to telling the tale of a life as it has been lived. A full account of the guided autobiography process has been described by Birren and Deutchman (1991) (see also Mader, 1993).

Guided autobiography stimulates people to write about the principal themes that characterize most lives: 1) account of major branching points, 2) family, 3) life-work, 4) health, 5) sexual identity and behavior, 6) the role of money, 7) loves and hates, 8) experiences with death and dying, 9) and life's aspirations and goals. Omitted from the above list is spirituality. The role of religion and spirituality in the individual's life is often very significant. It does not, however, occur in every life. Therefore, it is a theme to be used with those for whom the spiritual component is one of life's main supports.

Writing and sharing the details of one's life is often a high point of an individual's experience. Providing social support and mental stimulation for adults to review and share their life stories is the context for guided autobiography. Participation appears to lead to a heightened sense of self-awareness, social acceptance, and self-esteem. For many older adults, events of daily life often damage feelings of identity and self-worth. Writing one's autobiography can enhance the conviction that one's life is meaningful.

After being involved with over 300 people who have written their autobiographies, the authors are impressed with the insight of Hemingway's observation that the world breaks everyone but many are stronger at the broken places. In reviewing the details of their lives with the support of the small group, people become impressed, if not amazed, by how much they have experienced. The coming alive of old memories and emotions, and the revitalization of power and meaning in life, can be extremely satisfying for all participants in the guided autobiography group process. It is our belief that through guided autobiography adults can be helped to come to terms with their lives and to meet future changes with increased confidence and competence. From the viewpoint of development, it is important to gain a perspective on life and to find clarity and understand more deeply the meaning of the experiences of a lifetime. Particularly in the later years, an individual needs to believe that his or her life has mattered. An understanding of the fabric of one's life can make a significant contribution to one's well-being. Guided autobiography:

> combines individual and group experiences and autobiography, incorporating (1) group interaction and leadership to sensitize people to the overlooked and unappreciated past and to generate new perspectives on issues of their lives; (2) private reflection and the writing of two-page life stories on selected life themes; and (3) reading these life stories and sharing thoughts in a mutually encouraging group, moderated by a group leader. (Birren & Deutchman, 1991, p. 1)

In contrast to guided autobiography, other life-review techniques have evolved different principles (Burnside, this volume). Butler (1963) emphasized proximity to death as a stimulus to the resurgence of old memories. Other reminiscence methods (Ingersoll & Silverman, 1978; Kaminsky, 1978) utilize spontaneous and free-flowing memories. Guided autobiography is an efficient way to review a life by following a proven series of evocative themes and responding to questions of other group members. Themes are presented and discussed sequentially so that recollections can be fit into a picture of the individual life.

A key feature of guided autobiography is the developmental change that arises from a mutual sharing among members of who they are and from where they have come. As each group member reads his or her story in the small group, a context is developed for new friendships and for greater self-esteem. In addition, we believe that the confidence and trust built through a small group experience enhances both recall and the ease of translating life's experiences to the written page.

> In guided autobiography, participants are asked to write and share with the group a series of brief autobiographical life stories based on assigned themes. A guided autobiography group meets a minimum of ten times for at least two hours each time. Sessions consist of a discussion of the next meeting's theme, to be written in advance of that meeting, and members' reading and discussing the life stories written at home on the theme assigned for the current day. (Birren & Deutchman, 1991, p. 2)

Guided autobiography is not designed to be formal therapy. It is not directed toward the cure or amelioration of disease. It does, however, have a therapeutic effect. Similarly, various things such as friendships, relaxation time, confidant relationships, gardening, and playing a musical instrument are therapeutic without being therapy. Like these other activities that have therapeutic qualities, guided autobiography has "healing powers" which result from a reconciliation of longstanding issues. Substantial research was reviewed by Birren and Deutchman (1991) that supports guided autobiography groups for older adults due to the apparent emotional and pragmatic gains.

These positive outcomes are encouraging to professionals who seek to increase competence and confidence in adults. Most older adults need to reconcile past values and goals with present realities, as they needed to do in previous periods of transition, such as leaving school, making a job change, entering retirement, or when the youngest child leaves home. These issues, however, are most salient when future opportunities for altering the life course are perceived as limited. Renewed confidence in one's capacity to adapt, along with increased understanding of one's personal agenda, can form the basis for successful future choices. The writing and sharing of one's lifestory leads to a stronger sense of identity, about who and what one is.

A study by Birren, Hoppe, and Birren (unpublished) of 363 participants in guided autobiography identified 17 words most frequently used by persons in describing themselves. The five most commonly used descriptive words were friendly, intelligent, loving, sensitive, and caring. The most common first word was friendly, although only 18 of 363 people chose it. We may conclude that identity is a very individual matter. It was also noted that the commonly chosen descriptive words were largely behavioral rather than physical attributes.

The above study was carried out on the first day of ten autobiography sessions. The approach, however, lends itself to a before-and-after-design in which individuals list their self-descriptors on the first and last day, and possibly after 6 months or more. If the guided autobiography has an effect on self-evaluation, more positive words will be used after the experience. If the effect lasts, months later there should be measurable effects of a more integrated and satisfactory view of the self.

Individuals construct an identity based on differences in three versions of the self: (1) the "real self" as defined by personal interpretation, (2) the "ideal self," a model of the "perfect" self as one would like to be, and (3) the "social-image self," a person's perception of how other people view him or her. A large discrepancy between these images of the self leads to tension and discomfort. A high level on congruence of the images is presumed to lead to contentment and security in relation to others (Birren & Deutchman, 1991).

Another issue raised by research is whether or not an individual's view of other people is more labile than one's self-view. Specifically, if one shares one's autobiography in a small group, and trust develops between group members, then one's behavior may change and there is more acceptances of other persons as they are and also one discovers that "they are more like me than I thought." Here the research issue is being raised of the interaction between one's self-concept and one's concept of the other person. In one unpublished study, views of other people proved more subject to change than views of self (Reedy & Birren, 1980). If such findings are substantiated, a working hypothesis becomes apparent in which one's self-concept is stable but one's self-esteem improves in guided autobiography because others become viewed as more like oneself.

Perhaps as one grows older and participates in autobiography, an acceptable or comfortable view emerges that, "after all, we are human beings with a lot in common," or "we are all sinners." This runs counter to the contemporary point of view which emphasizes diversity of the population. Perhaps one of the issues to be resolved by mature persons is the melding of concepts about the uniqueness of the individual, the diversity of the population, and the impact of unique events or major historical events that marks people from a particular era, such as economic depressions, wars, and natural disasters. In her comments on the study of the life course, Hagestad (1990) said that, "After nearly two decades of writing and research in this area, investigators are still struggling to find integration between macro- and microlevel views of lives; between insiders' and outsiders' perspectives; between prospective and retrospective accounts; between patterns of diversity and themes of uniformity" (p. 152). The stamp that social events place on individuals has been well studied by Elder (1974, 1985, 1989). Perhaps the study of autobiography will help provide insight into human similarity and individuality, between the effects of personal choice and those of external events, in the course of life (Tyler, 1978).

In guided autobiography, a person not only recalls the facts of his or her past, but his or her memories enter awareness together with their past and present emotions which helps provide a basis for integration of the cognitive and emotional content of the past into the present. Increased confidence from group support and from integration appears to lead to motivation. Older adults comment that after participating in guided autobiography, they become energized to meet new challenges with greater optimism and vitality.

Grotjahn (1989) pointed out that the "assignment for the elderly is the integration of past-life experiences into final identity formation" (p. 110) (see also Sherman, 1991). Guided autobiography fills a specific need for an individual to strengthen the management of life's negative elements by emphasizing strengths manifested in the past, and by the growing realization that there may be alternatives for the future. If a life can be described as a spider web, it might be said that it has main threads that give supporting structure to life and circular threads that form its pattern. An alternative metaphor is that of the fabric of life in which the warp and the woof cross cut, and on to which are woven patterns.

GUIDED AUTOBIOGRAPHY AS A THERAPEUTIC PROCESS

An area that uses autobiographical data for much of its research is counseling psychology. Birren and Hedlund (1987) pointed out that during recent decades this area has shown the largest increase of studies utilizing autobiographical data. Research directed at clinical treatment has proposed autobiographical data as a means of increasing insights on the part of counselors (Baird, 1957; Toblert, 1959) and of providing meaningful services to older adults (Bratter & Tuvman, 1980; Burnside & Schmidt, 1994; Butler & Lewis, 1982; Gergen, this volume). An example of these services was presented by Green (1982) in her analysis of life review as a technique for clarifying family roles in adulthood.

Guided autobiography is an absorbing life therapy process in which "getting one's life together" improves one's self-esteem and self confidence. Most therapy, on the other hand, is problem-centered, during the course of which the individual focuses primarily on a bothersome problem or problems. This problem may have broad roots which can be seen as part of a system of thinking about the self and the way decisions are made. The process of therapy, however, begins with an individual's presenting a specific problem. This is different from examining one's life in guided autobiography in which both the past and present with successes and failures are reviewed. In their autobiographies, people reveal a remarkable capacity of adaptability to the many challenging conditions of life, and emerge with a considerable sense of strength and integrity. Thus, in the integration of lives from a guided autobiographical point of view, people put together pluses and minuses, pitfalls, successes, and loves and hates into a complete and coherent picture that can be described in terms of evolving developmental principles of life.

The healing that comes from being part of an autobiography group often has special value at selected phases of the lifespan. Retirement is an advantageous time to review one's life, as new plans or alternative pathways for the future evolve. Returning to school is another time when a life review is a good preparation for going forward. Following certain life events such as the loss of a job, financial reversal, or health changes are also appropriate times to look to the past in order to see more clearly one's strengths that can influence future actions.

It has been noted that guided autobiography can be of value in senior centers, continuing education facilities, and institutional groups for the disabled. All of these applications have therapeutic and research implications. Many institutions offering therapy frequently have waiting lists. Wait-listed individuals who write autobiographies can gain valuable insight into themselves and have a better focus on the issue of their lives when they ultimately begin desired therapy or are admitted to appropriate institutions.

Church groups are often fertile ground for undertaking guided autobiography. Here, the theme of life as a spiritual journey is a particularly provocative topic. Another helpful use of guided autobiography is to create a common experience for individuals who are to be introduced into a new environment, such as a life-care facility, or a newly formed group of veterans, members who have recently joined a church, or individuals participating in activities of a community senior center. Other special populations exist for whom guided autobiography would be beneficial. For instance, women serving long-term prison sentences can write and share their autobiographies so that when they are released, they will have a more coherent view of themselves and their life circumstances.

There are, of course, other contexts for using guided autobiography. For example, English composition can be taught through the medium of autobiography. Students can write selected essays about their lives using the themes of guided autobiography. They can also read examples of their writing in their classrooms, thereby gaining skills in English composition and rhetoric as well as insight into themselves.

DIDACTIC USE OF GUIDED AUTOBIOGRAPHY

Trainees in helping professions such as nursing, psychiatry, medicine, psychology, social work, and religious ministry all benefit from participating in the guided autobiography experience. This not only gives them an opportunity to review, integrate and express the important elements of their own development, but it enables them to examine the similarities and contrasts of the development of other individuals. More systematically stated, the individuals can review their lives while learning about the differences associated with gender, culture, age, and individual differences in personality and temperament.

Contemporary seminars in social and behavioral sciences teach that the important elements of life are attributed to cohort differences, time of measurement, and ontogenetic change. These remain abstract principles unless they are seen in the context of an individual life. Although the elements of sequential longitudinal design of research and statistical methods for identifying change can be found, it is through the experience of an individual life that these contributors to human experience are seen in their relative strengths (Ruth & Kenyon, this volume).

Among the social and behavioral sciences in which research training can be enhanced by participating in a didactic, guided autobiography group are: anthropology, sociology, psychology, and in some instances, economics, and political science. In addition to the research aspects relevant to these groups, teaching skills are enhanced by participation in a guided autobiography group. This use of guided autobiography provides a context within which a teacher can give differential emphasis to different components of the life span, but at the same time can be aware of the process of simplification that goes on in most disciplinary training. Partitioning dependent variables and the independent variables that is part of the process of scientific analysis, benefits from the perspective provided by participating in guided autobiography. That is, the individual teacher or researcher becomes increasingly sensitive to new unsuspected variables in people's lives, as well as becoming sensitive to the positive and negative outcomes of the same event. What makes a difference in the outcomes of traumatic experiences is still puzzling. In some instances individuals are stronger after adversity. For others, the same adversity may temporarily or permanently reduce them to a marginal life.

From participating in a guided autobiography group, scholars can learn in concrete detail that major historical phenomena such as wars, business recessions, and natural disasters such as floods, hurricanes, and fires occur to many people and that these events may have varying positive and/or negative effects on the development of a particular individual. During a war, an infant may be left in the care of its mother while its father goes into military service, perhaps never to return. Other fathers who were exempt from military service because of physical disabilities prospered greatly in the civilian economy because they performed needed functions. Thus, while there are general trends in the effects of war on families and individuals, there are individual differences as well.

The Great Depression of the 1930s was a traumatic event for many families who lived in urban areas, but some farm families were not very affected by the poor economy. Thus, there are clusters of different outcomes of major historic events. In a similar way, growing up as a boy or as a girl in different historic periods has had different outcomes. In the beginning of World War II, women were welcomed into the American labor force but then were excluded as the returning veterans needed employment. It is important to the helping professions to understand different patterns of development for males and females and also to understand generational differences.

RESEARCH PROSPECTS FOR GUIDED AUTOBIOGRAPHY

Individuals may write their autobiographies privately with little or no interaction with others. They may be surprised to discover that as they write, they gain increasing recall of past events. They may also use family archival materials that provoke historical and personal references. However, preparing an autobiography may best be done in the guided form, in which there is both a general format for reviewing life and also a group discussion of life themes. Participation in guided autobiography requires reading one's autobiographical statement in a small group. Not only does the recitation of this material help to enlarge the reader's perspective, but this perspective is also enhanced by hearing other people's statements, which then leads to the recall of other dormant and overlooked memories. In brief, the group enhances, elicits, or cues the recall of earlier memories. At the same time, there is a refinement of one's own perspective as contrasts and similarities are offered by other group members of the accounts of their lives. Research should be directed at the kind of change induced in the participants by the process. Presumably, future research will also be focused on the measurement of before and after effects of the perceptions of doing guided autobiography and on the dynamics of the process.

As described earlier, attempts by the authors to measure changes in self-concept before and after autobiography resulted in the finding that the primary change was in the view of other people, not of the self (Reedy & Birren, 1980). Therefore, in addition to the prospect of changing one's view of oneself, there is perhaps even more important possibility of changing one's view about other people. If other people come to be seen as more like you, then you are more likely to respect and interact with them and to consider them as social resources. If research on autobiography continues to expand, then more efforts should be directed at identifying its effects on the concepts of self and others and the processes by which changes occur.

To determine how these processes are brought about by participation in guided autobiography, interviews and measurements can be conducted with individuals before and after participation. In addition, follow-up interviews 6 months later can also be conducted. The primary question would be what, from the individual's points of view, changed during the course of writing their autobiographies, and whether or not they view their lives differently after the guided autobiography experience.

Another opportunity for evaluating the changes that occur in individuals as a result of participating in guided autobiography is to study reunion groups. Autobiography participants often wish to stay in contact with each other to exchange comments on the progress of their lives. Focusing such groups on the question of how they changed may lead to new perspectives about what changed and how change was brought about. Post-autobiography group meetings could be scheduled to systematize their explorations and avoid seeing only the positive examples of individuals who believe there were important personal changes introduced by their participation.

What changes and how change is brought about in guided autobiography needs fuller exploration. Why did a group listen so carefully to the moving description by an elderly black woman of walking to school down a dusty

Mississippi road as a girl while the white children were driven by in their bus? How did she go from rural poverty to receiving an honorary degree from a major university? Equally startling was the parallel story of the industrialist who rebuilt his family fortune after WWII. Why do these people listen to one another? There was the elderly nun who dedicated her life to God in elementary school and the woman who became aware that her sons were sexually molested by a supposedly good man in their school. All of these people told their stories in similar groups. What is the nature of the binding power of individuals and groups? Perhaps it lies in our capacity to have different life experiences and yet, at the same time, to identify with the feelings and emotions of other persons. The commonality of people may lie in the emotional domain while their differences lie in cognition, the interpretation of events. These are "hunches" drawn from experiences in autobiography groups that have to be replaced by information from research.

Increasingly, it is expected that research on guided autobiography will be used to study the course and principles of human development, as well as to study groups of particular interest. Autobiographies can be obtained from individuals who are young and old, male and female, poor and wealthy, educated and uneducated, heterosexual and homosexual, criminals and victims, and members of ethnic groups selected for contrast. Retrospective examination of gang behavior can be obtained by correcting autobiographies from, for example, groups of older gang members now in prison, those leading marginal lives in the community, and those who are no longer gang members but have accepted more conventional patterns of life. What would be their perspectives on their earlier lives? What inferences could we make about the determining elements in the ways their lives flowed, so that we could use the knowledge to help others? Similarly, we could examine the lives of older people who have been perceived as being wise in the management of their lives and those who have been judged to have been unwise. An examination of autobiographies from these various groups might shed some light on the choices and strategies that produced different outcomes in life.

There are other research areas that are amenable to an autobiographical approach. A common experience in contemporary life is that of divorce. A research project might be built around this issue by obtaining sequential autobiographies at different intervals after separation and divorce. Autobiographies could also be obtained from support group members. From retrospective accounts of the way lives have flowed, it may be possible to identify principles about satisfying lives that were developed after divorce, as well as about long-lasting marriages, and about noncontractual living arrangements.

Another topic that can be studied through autobiography is that of the frequent traumatic experience that comes as a result of a "whistleblower's" action.

Confronted with unethical or illegal practices of colleagues or superiors in a business or other organization, the whistleblower often volunteers information that brings public attention to the situation. Rather surprisingly, the consequences are often severely damaging for the whistleblower. He or she may lose employment, be shunned by peers, and his or her family may disintegrate under the pressure of social ostracism and financial reversal. What are the principles by which one may live a moral life according to long–standing ethical principles, and yet achieve an acceptable balance among conflicting values? Selected guided autobiographies can be obtained from whistleblowers, or other victims of traumatic experiences, which may provide useful research information.

The foregoing suggests the value of selecting groups according to contrasting behavior patterns or outcomes in securing autobiographical material. Since prospective studies require years to yield results, it is expected that there will be increasing *post hoc* studies of individuals selectively sampled. Early longitudinal studies of human aging were often based on *ad hoc* or opportunist samples of people. Samples for current longitudinal studies are now being defined more rigorously. In a similar manner, it is expected that autobiographical research will be conducted on defined or specially selected samples.

Autobiographies may be gathered as part of other psychological, social, and biological studies of the lifespan and from participants in ongoing longitudinal studies. It should be possible to identify not only developmental changes in individuals, but also the individuals' perceptions of these changes and their contrasting outcomes. There is also, of course, the possibility of comparing different cohorts of individuals and their autobiographies in relation to different events that they have experienced. This also suggests the opportunity to contrast retrospective accounts of life choices with those derived from contemporaneous perceptions.

SUMMARY AND DISCUSSION

Autobiographical material is increasingly being regarded as a valuable source of information on the course of human lives. It has not, however, replaced early quantitative measurements and their longitudinal follow-up. What it does is provide information about the way people interpret their lives and the reasons they give for outcomes. Perhaps in the future we will see autobiographical statements included in longitudinal studies. These statements can help to capture cohort effects or transient ways of interpreting life experiences that reflect contemporary metaphors or views. But they can also give us insight into the way life is experienced in ways that measurements cannot. The chapters of this book describe many approaches to gathering, analyzing, and interpreting narrative accounts of the ways people experience their lives that do not replace data from observation and measurements. They offer a rich supplement to our sources of information about the commonality and uniqueness of human life.

The guided autobiography process is favored for older adults because the small groups act as a peer support method and as a way of stimulating and enhancing the recall of earlier life experiences. The guided autobiography process is an important experience for participating individuals, but it also is a method that has great application as an adjunct to research on other topics. That is, selected samples of people may be drawn to study the importance of such things as education, gender, or occupation in the flow of life. While the primary focus of guided autobiography lies in the benefits for participating individuals, there are important research byproducts.

Increasingly, research will need to be focused on the measurement of "before and after" effects of the change brought about by guided autobiography and the processes by which those effects are brought about. It is expected that future research on autobiography will greatly expand. This expansion may also take the form of autobiography serving as an adjunct to designed studies, such as sequential longitudinal studies of aging in population groups. Exploring the inside of life (Ruth & Kenyon, this volume) through guided autobiography is an enriching human experience. It can enhance our sense of self and prepare us for a change of direction. "You don't know where you are going unless you know where you have been."

References

Achenbaum, A. (1991). Time is the messenger of the gods: A gerontologic metaphor. In G. Kenyon, J. Birren, & J. J. Schroots (Eds.), *Metaphors of aging in science and the humanities* (pp. 83–101). New York: Springer.

Agren, M. (1992). *Life at 85: A study of life experiences and adjustment of the oldest old.* Gothenberg, Sweden: University of Gothenberg.

Ainsworth, M. D. S., & Bowlby, J. (1991). An ethological approach to personality development. *American Psychologist, 46,* 333–341.

Alasuutari, P. (1990). Desire and Craving. *Acta Universitatis Tamperensis*, ser A, Vol. 288. Academic dissertation. Tampere, Finland: University of Tampere.

Alheit, P. (1992). The biographical approach to adult education. In W. Mader (Ed.), *Adult education in the Federal Republic of Germany: Scholarly approaches and professional practice.* Vancouver: Centre For Continuing Education, University of British Columbia.

Alheit, P. (1993). Transitorische bildungsprozesse: Das "biographische paradigma" in der weiterbiildung. In W. Mader (Ed.), *Weiterbildung und gesellschaft* (pp. 343–417). Bremen: Universität.

Alheit, P. (forthcoming). *The biographical question as a challenge.* Genf: University.

Allen, W. (1949). *Writers on writing.* London: E.P. Dutton.

Allport, G. W. (1942). *The use of personal documents in psychological science.* New York: Little, Brown.

Allport, G.W. (1962). The general and the unique in psychological science. *Journal of Personality, 30,* 405–422.

Allport, G. W. (1968). *The person in psychology*. Boston: Beacon Press.

Amoss, P. T., & Harrell, S. (1981). *Other ways of growing old: Anthropological perspectives.* Stanford: Stanford University Press.

Anderson, J. E. (1980). Developmental principles in childhood and maturity. In J. E. Birren (Ed.), *Relations of development and aging* (pp. 11–28). New York: Arno Press.

Anderson, T. (1991). *The reflecting team: Dialogues and dialogues about the dialogues.* New York: Norton.

Angyal, A. (1972). *Foundations for a science of personality*. New York: Viking Press.

Annis, A. P. (1967). The autobiography: Its uses and value in professional psychology. *Journal of Counseling Psychology*, *14*(1), 9–17.

Antonovsky, A. (1987). *Unraveling the mystery of health: How people manage stress and stay well.* San Francisco: Jossey-Bass.

Archer, J. L. (1982). Discovery and philosophy for working with the elderly mentally infirm. *Social Work Service,* (43–49, Summer.

Aristotle, (1981). *Poetics.* Translated by S. H. Butcher. New York : Hill and Wang

Atkinson, J. W., Heyns, R. W., & Veroff, J. (1954). The effect of experimental arousal of the affiliation motive on thematic apperception. *Journal of Abnormal and Social Psychology*, *49*, 405–410.

Averill, J. R. (1984). The acquisition of emotions during adulthood. In C. Z. Malatesta & C. E. Izard (Eds.), *Emotion in adult development* (pp. 23–43). London: Sage.

Averill, J. R. (1988). A Ptolemaic theory of emotion. *Cognition & Emotion, 2,* 81–87.

Back, K. W. (1987). Continuing theory. In G. L. Maddox (Ed.), *The encyclopedia of aging* (pp. 144–145). New York: Springer.

Baird, C. R. (1957). The autobiography. *Education Digest*, 19: 39–43.

Bakan, D. (1966). *The duality of human existence: Isolation and communion in Western man.* Boston: Beacon Press.

Baker-Brown, G., Ballard, E. J., Bluck, S., de Vries, B., Suedfeld, P., & Tetlock, P. E. (1992). The conceptual/integrative complexity scoring manual. In C. P. Smith (Ed.), *Motivation and personality: Handbook of thematic content analysis* (pp. 401–418). New York: Cambridge University Press.

Bakhtin, M. (1986). *Speech genres and other late essays* (Trans. V.W. Mcgee & Ed.. C. Emerson and M. Hoquist). Austin, TX: The University of Texas Press.

Ballard, E. J. (1983). Canadian prime ministers: Complexity in political crises. *Canadian Psychology, 24,* 125–129.

Baltes, P. B. (1987). Theoretical propositions of life-span developmental psychology: On the dynamics between growth and decline. *Developmental Psychology, 23,* 611–626.

Bandura, A. (1982). The psychology of chance encounters and life paths. *American Psychologist, 37*, 747–755.

Bateson, G. (1972). *Steps to an ecology of mind.* New York: Ballantine.

Barthes, R. (1984). *Image Music Text,* New York: Hill and Wang.

Bateson, G. (1979). *Mind and nature.* New York: Dutton.

Bateson, M. C. (1989). Composing a life. New York: *Atlantic Monthly.*

Baumann, M. (1989). *The effect of reminiscence group therapy on personal control of institutionalized elders.* Unpublished master's thesis, Medical College of Georgia, Augusta, GA.

Baumeister, R. F. (1986). *Identity: Cultural change and the struggle for self.* New York: Oxford University Press.

Beach, R. (1990). The creative development of meaning: Using autobiographical experiences to interpret literature. In D. Bogdan & S. B. Straw (Eds.), *Beyond communication: Reading comprehension and criticism* (pp. 211–235). Portsmouth, NH: Boyton/ Cook Heinemann.

Beadleson-Baird, M., & Lura, L. L. (1988). Reminiscing: Nursing actions for the elderly ill geriatric patient. *Issues in Mental Health Nursing, 9*(1), 83–94.

Bearon, L. B. (1988). Conceptualizing quality of life: Finding the common ground. *Journal of Applied Gerontology, 7,* 275–278.

Beck, U. (1986). *Risikogesellschaft - Auf dem weg in eine andere moderne.* Frankfurt: Suhrkamp.

Becker, E. (1973). *The denial of death.* New York: The Free Press.

Bellah, R. N., Madsen, K., Sullivan, W. M., Sandler, A., & Tipton, S. M. (1985). *Habits of the heart.* Berkeley, CA: University of California Press.

Bengtson, V. L. (1989). The problem of generations: Age group contrast, continuities, and social change. In V. L. Bengtson & K. W. Schaie (Eds.), *The course of later life:Research and reflections* (pp. 25–54). New York: Springer.

Bengtson, V. L., Reedy, M. N., & Gordon, C. (1985). Aging and self-conception: Personality processes and social contexts. In J. E. Birren and K. W. Schaie (Eds.), *Handbook of psychology of aging* (2nd ed.) (pp. 544–593). New York: Van Nostrand-Reinhold.

Benner, P. (1984) *From Novice to Expert.* Addison-Wesley Publishing. Menlo Park, Ca.

Benson, D., & Hughes, J. A. (1983). *The perspective of ethnomethodology.* New York: Longman.

Bergen, R. C. (1992) Expanding options in the long-term care of our elderly. *Caring 11*(3), 66–68

Berger, L. (1974). *From instinct to identity: The development of personality.* Englewood Cliffs, NJ: Prentice-Hall.

Berman, H. (1988). Admissible evidence: Geropsychology and the personal journal. In S. Reinhartz & G. Rowles (Eds.), *Qualitative gerontology,* (pp. 47–63). New York: Springer Publishing Company.

Berman, H. (1994). Analyzing personal journals of later life. In J. Gubrium & A. Sankar (Eds.), *Qualitative methods in aging research* (pp.211–226). Thousand Oaks, CA: Sage Publications.

Berman, M. (1982). *All that's solid melts into air: The experience of modernity.* New York: Simon & Schuster.

Berne, E. (1964). *Games people play.* New York: Grove.

Bertaux, D. (1977). Ecrire la sociologie. *Soc, Sci, Inf., 19,* 7–25.

Bertaux, D. (Ed.) (1981). *Biography and society: The life-history approach in the social sciences.* Beverly Hills, CA: Sage Publications.

Bertaux, D,. & Bertaux-Wiame, I. (1981a). Lifestories in the baker's trade. In D. Bertaux (Ed.), *Biography and society: The life history approach in the social sciences* . Beverly Hills, CA: Sage.

Bertaux, D., & Bertaux-Wiame, I. (1981b). Artisanal bakery in France: How it lives and how it survives. In F. B. Bechofer & B. Elliot (Eds.), *The petite bourgeoisie: Comparative studies of a easy stratum.* London: Macmillan

Bertaux, D., & Kohli, M. (1984). The lifestory approach: A continental view. *Annual Review of Sociology, 10,* 215–237.

Birren, J. E. (1987, May). The best of all stories. *Psychology Today,* 74–75.

Birren, J. E. (1988). A contribution to the theory of the psychology of aging: As a counterpart of development. In J. Birren and V. Bengtson (Eds.), *Emergent theories of aging* (pp.153–177). New York: Springer.

Birren, J. E., & Deutchman, D. E. (1991). *Guiding autobiography groups for older adults.* Baltimore: Maryland: The Johns Hopkins University Press.

Birren, J. E. (1993). Understanding life backward: Reminiscing for a better old age. In R. N. Butler & K. Kiikuni (Eds.), *Who is responsible for my old age?* (pp.18–29). New York: Springer.

Birren, J. E., & Hedlund, B. (1987). Contribution of autobiography to developmental psychology. In N. Eisenberg (Ed.), *Contemporary topics in developmental psychology* (pp. 394–415). New York: John Wiley and Sons.

Birren, J. E., Hoppe, C., & Birren, B. *Identity and autobiography.* Unpublished manuscript, University of Southern California.

Birren, J. E. & Schroots, J. J. F. (1984). Steps to an ontogenetic psychology. *Academic Psychology Bulletin, 6,* 177–190.

Black, G., & Haight, B. K. (1992). Integrality as a holistic framework for the life review process. *Holistic Nursing, 7*(1), 7–15.

Blackman, J. (1980). Group work in the community: Experiences with reminiscence. In I. Burnside (Ed.), *Psychosocial nursing care of the aged* (2nd ed.) (pp. 126–144). New York: McGraw-Hill.

Blanco, A. (1986). In their chosen place: On the autobiographies of two Spanish women of the left. *Genre, 19*: 431–45.

Blasi, A. (1988). Identity and the development of the self. In D. K. Lapsley & F. C. Power (Eds.), *Self, ego and identity: Integrative approaches* (pp. 226–242). New York: Springer-Verlag.

Blumer, H. (1969). *Symbolic interactionism, perspective and method.* Berkeley: University of California Press.

Blytheway, B. (1993). Aging and biography: The letters of Bernard and Mary Berenson. *Sociology, 27,* 153–165.

Boetzkes, E. (1993). Autonomy and advance directives. *Canadian Journal on Aging, 12,*(4), 441–452

Bolles, E. B. (1991). *A second way of knowing.* New York: Prentice-Hall.

Booth, W. C. (1961). *The rhetoric of fiction.* Chicago: University of Chicago Press.

Bornat, J. (1989). Oral history as a social movement: Reminiscence and older people. *Oral History,*16–23.

Boulton, J., Gully, V., Mathews, L., & Gearing, B. (1989). *Developing the biographical approach in practice with older people (Project Paper No. 7 of the Gloucester Care of Elderly People at Home Project).* Obtainable from School of Health, Welfare and Community Education, The Open University, Milton Keynes, MK7 6AA, England.

Bourdieu, P. (1992). *Réponses. Pour un anthropologie reflexive.* Paris: Seine.

Brady, E. M. (1990). Redeemed through time: Learning through autobiography. *Adult Education Quarterly, 41,* 43–52.

Bramlett, M. H. (1990). *Power, creativity and reminiscence in the elderly.* Unpublished doctoral dissertation, Medical College of Georgia, Augusta, GA.

Bramwell, L. (1984). Use of life history in pattern identification and health promotion. *Advances in Nursing Science: Research Tools, 7*(11), 37–44.

Bratter, T. E., & Tuvman, E. (1980). A peer counseling program in action. In S. Stanfeld Sargent (Ed.), *Nontraditional therapy and counseling with the aged.* New York: Springer.

Brearley, P. (1975). *Social work, ageing and society.* London: Routledge and Kegan Paul.

Breeuwsma, G. (1990). Individuele Variatie in de Levensloop. In R. L. Loth, H. Bosma, G. Breeuwsma, & P. van Geert (red.), *De Menselijke Levensloop. In Perspectief Van Een Persoonlijk Wereldbeeld. Deel 1. De Structuur Van De Levensloop* (pp. 75–107). Heerlen: Open Universiteit.

Breeze, J. (1909). The care of the aged. *American Journal of Nursing, 9*, 826–831.

Breisach, E. (1983). *Historiography: Ancient, medieval, and modern.* Chicago: University of Chicago Press.

Brider, P. (1991) Who killed the nursing care plan? *American Journal of Nursing*, (May), 35

Bridges, W. (1980). *Transitions: Making sense of life's changes.* Toronto: Addison-Wesley.

Briggs, J. C. (1970). *Never in anger: Portrait of an Eskimo family.* Cambridge, MA: Harvard University Press.

Bringuier, J. C. (1980). *Conversations with Piaget.* (Trans. B. M. Gulati, trans.). Chicago: The University of Chicago Press.

Brookfield, S. D.(1990a). *The skillful teacher.* San Francisco: Jossey-Bass.

Brookfield, S. D. (1990b). Analyzing the influence of media on learners' perspectives. In J. Mezirow (Ed.), *Fostering critical reflection in adulthood* (pp. 235–250). San Francisco: Jossey-Bass.

Brooks, P. (1985). *Reading for the plot: Design and intention in narrative.* New York: Vintage.

Brundage, D. H., & MacKeracher, D. (1980). *Adult learning principles and their application to program planning* Toronto: Ontario Ministry of Education.

Bruner, J. S. (1986). *Actual minds, possible worlds.* Cambridge, MA: Harvard University Press.

Bruner, J. S. (1987). Life as narrative. *Social Research, 54*, 11–32.

Bruner, J. S. (1990). *Acts of meaning.* Cambridge, MA: Harvard University Press.

Bruner, J. S. (1993). The autobiographical process. In R. Rolkenflik (Ed.), *The culture of autobiography: Constructions of self-representation* (pp. 38–56). Stanford, CA: Stanford University Press.

Buhler, C. , (1933). *The human life course as a psychological problem.* Leipzig: Hirzel Verlag.

Buhler, C., & Massarik, F. (1968). *The course of human life.* New York: Springer.

Burgos, M. (1988). *Life stories: Narrativity and the search for the self.* (Research Unit for Contemporary Culture Publications no. 9). Jyvaskyla: University of Jyvaskyla.

Burke, N., & Cohler, B. (1992). Countertransference and psychotherapy with the anorectic adolescent. In J. Brandell (Ed.), *Countertransference in child and adolescent psychotherapy* (pp. 163–189). New York: Aronson.

Burnside, I. (1973). *Psychosocial nursing care of the aged.* New York: McGraw-Hill.

Burnside, I. (1988). Reminiscence and other therapeutic modalities. In I. Burnside (Ed.), *Nursing and the aged: A self-care approach* (3rd ed.) (pp. 645–686). New York: C.V. Mosby.

Burnside, I. (1989). Group work with older women: A modality to improve the quality of life. *Journal of Women & Aging*, (1) Vol. 1, Nos. 1–3 , 265–290.

Burnside, I. (1990). Reminiscence: An independent nursing intervention for the elderly. *Issues in Mental Health Nursing, 11*, 38–48.

Burnside, I. (1993). Themes in reminiscence groups with older women. *International Journal of Aging and Human Development, 37*(3), 177–189.

Burnside, I. (1994a). Group work with the physically impaired. In I. Burnside, M. G. Schmidt, (Eds.), *Group work with older persons: Group process & techniques* (3rd ed.). Boston: Jones & Bartlett.

Burnside, I. (1994b). Themes and props: Adjuncts for reminiscence therapy groups. In B. Haight & J. Webster (Eds.), *The art and science of reminiscing: Theory research, methods and application.* Washington, DC: Taylor & Francis.

Burnside, I., & Haight, B. K. (1992). Reminiscence and life review: Analyzing each concept. *Journal of Advanced Nursing, 17*, 855–862.

Burnside, I., & Haight, B. K. (In press). Protocols for reminiscence and life review therapy.

Burnside, I., & Schmidt, M. G. (Eds.) (1994). *Working with older adults.* Boston: Jones & Bartlett.

Butler, R. N. (1963). The life-review: An interpretation of reminiscence in the aged. *Psychiatry, 26*, 63–76.

Butler, R. N., & Lewis, M. I. (1982). *Aging and mental health*, (3rd ed.), St. Louis: Mosby.

Butler, R. N., Lewis, M., & Sutherland, G. (1991). *Aging and mental health: Positive psychosocial and biomedical approaches*. New York: Macmillan.

Campbell, J. (1949). *The hero with a thousand faces.* New York: Bollingen Foundation

Carlson, R. (1988). Exemplary lives: The use of psychobiography for theory development. In D. P. McAdams & R. L. Ochberg (Eds.), *Psychobiography and life narratives* (pp. 105–138). Durham, NC: Duke University Press.

Carp, F. M. (1976). Housing and living environments of older people. In R. H. Binstock & E. Shanas (Eds.), *Handbook of aging and the social sciences*. New York: Van Nostrand Reinhold

Carpenter, M., & Paley, J. (1984). A culture of passivity. *Community Care, 13*, 24–25.

Carr, D. (1986). *Time, narrative, and history*. Bloomington: University of Indiana Press.

Carr, D., Taylor, C., & Ricoeur, P. (1991). Discussion: Ricoeur on narrative. In D. Wood (Ed.), *On Paul Ricoeur: Narrative and interpretation* (pp. 160–187). London: Routledge.

Casey, E. S. (1987). *Remembering: A phenomenological study*. Bloomington, IN: Indiana University Press.

Charme, S. T. (1984). *Meaning and myth in the study of lives: A Sartrean perspective.* Philadelphia: University of Pennsylvania Press.

Chatman, S. (1978). *Story and discourse: Narrative structure in fiction and film.* Ithaca, NY: Cornell University Press.

Checkland, D., & Silberfeld, M. (1993). Competence and the three a's: Autonomy, authenticity, and aging. *Canadian Journal on Aging, 12*, (4), 453–468.

Chomsky, N. (1975). *Reflections on language.* New York: Pantheon.

Chubon, S. (1980). A novel approach to the process of life review, *Journal of Gerontological Nursing, 6*, 543–546.

Chused, J. (1991). The evocative power of enactments. *Journal of the American Psychoanalytic Association, 39*, 615–639.

Clark, P. G. (1988). Autonomy, personal empowerment, and quality of life in long-term care. *Journal of Applied Gerontology, 7*, 279–297.

Clements, D. B. (1986). Reminiscence: A tool for aiding families under stress. *Maternal Child Nursing, 11*, 114–117.

Clifford, J. (1986). Introduction: Partial truths. In J. Clifford & G. Marcus (Eds.), *Writing culture: The poetics and politics of ethnography* (pp. 1–26). Berkeley, CA: University of California Press.

Clifford, J., & Marcus, G. (Eds.)(1986). *Writing culture: The poetics and politics of ethnography*. Berkeley, CA: University of California Press.

Coachman, W. (1987). Getting to know. *Nursing Times, 83*(28), 57–58.

Cohler, B. J. (1982). Personal narrative and life-course. In P. Baltes & O. G. Brim, Jr. (Eds.) *Life span development and behavior, 4* (pp. 205–241). New York: Academic Press.

Cohler, B. J. (1988). The human studies and the life history. *Social Service Review, 37*, 552–575.

Cohler, B. J. (1993). Aging, morale, and meaning. In T. Cole, A. Achenbaum, P. Jakobi, & T. Kastenbaum (Eds.), *Voices and visions of aging* (pp. 107–133). New York: Springer.

Cohler, B. J. (1994). The lifestory perspective within the human sciences. *Journal of Contemporary Psychology, 39*, 137–139.

Cohn, J., & Tronick, E. (1987). Specificity of infants' response to mothers' affective behavior. *Journal of the American Academy of Child and Adolescent Psychiatry, 28*, 242–248.

Colby, A., & Damon, W. (1991). *Some do care*. New York: The Free Press.

Cole, M. (1985). The zone of proximal development; Where culture and cognition create each other. In J. Wertsch (Ed.), *Culture, communication, and cognition: Vygotskian perspective*. Cambridge, England: Cambridge University Press.

Cole, T.R. (1992). *The journey of life: A cultural history of aging in America*. Cambridge, England: Cambridge University Press.

Cole, T. R. (1995). *No color is my kind: The life of Eldrewey Stearns, Texas integration leader*. Austin, TX: The University of Texas Press.

Cole, T. R., Achenbaum, A., Jakobi, P., & Kastenbaum, R. (Eds.). (1993). *Voices and visions of aging*. New York: Springer.

Cole, T. R., & Premo, T. (1986). The pilgrim of Joel Andrews: Aging in the autobiography of a Yankee farmer. *International Journal of Aging and Human Development, 24*, 79–85.

Coleman, P. (1986). *Ageing and reminiscence processes: Social and clinical implications*. New York: Wiley.

Coleman, P. (1990). Ageing and the life history: The meaning of reminiscence in later life. In L. Dex (Ed.), *Life and work history analysis: Qualitative and quantitative development (pp. 120–143). Sociological Review Monographs Vol. 37.*

Coleman, P. (1994). Reminiscence within the study of ageing: The social significance of story. In J. Bornat (Ed.) *Reminiscence reviewed: Evaluations, achievements, perspectives.* Buckingham, United Kingdom: and Philadelphia: Open University Press.

Coles, R. (1989). *The call of stories: Teaching and the moral imagination.* Boston: Houghton Mifflin.

Connelly, E. M., & Clandinin, D. J. (1988). *Teachers as curriculum planners: Narratives of experience.* New York: Teachers College Press.

Connor, S. (1984). *Postmodernist culture, an introduction to theories of the contemporary.* Oxford, Great Britain: Blackwell.

Cook, E. A. (1988). *The effect on reminiscence on psychological measures of ego integrity in elderly nursing home residents.* Unpublished doctoral dissertation, The University of Texas, Austin, TX.

Cora, V. L. (1989). *Recollection of our past: A program for families with elders.* Unpublished manuscript.

Cornwell, J., & Gearing, B. (1989). Doing biographical interviews with older people. *Oral History, 17*(1), 36–43.

Cortazzi, M. (1993). *Narrative analysis.* London: Falmer.

Coupland, N., & Nussbaum, J. F. (1993). *Discourse and life span identity.* Newsbury Park: Sage.

Cranton, P. (1992). *Working with adult learners.* Toronto: Wall & Emerson.

Crapanzano, V. (1977). On the writing of ethnography. *Dialectical Anthropology, 2,* 69–73.

Crapanzano, V. (1980). *Tuhami: Portrait of a Moroccan.* Chicago: The University of Chicago Press.

Csikszentmihalyi, M., & Beattie, O. V. (1979). Life themes: A theoretical and empirical exploration of their origins and effects. *Journal of Humanistic Psychology, 19*(1), 45–63.

Cupitt, D. (1991). *What is a story?* London: SCM.

Cutillo-Schmitter, T. (1993, May). *Psychotherapy in the elderly: Key issues and techniques.* Paper presented at the Conference on Gerontological Nursing, Philadelphia, PA.

Daloz, L. A. (1986). *Effective teaching and mentoring: Realizing the transformational power of adult learning experiences.* San Francisco: Jossey-Bass.

Daly, J. M., McCloskey, J. C., & Bulechek, G. M. (1994). Nursing interventions classification use in long-term care. *Geriatric Nursing, 15*(1), 41–46.

Danielsen, K. (1992) Boys like us. Old men retelling their lives. Olson: Pax. Forlage.

Dannhauer, H. (1977). *Heredity and personality.* Berlin: VEB Deutscher Verlag der Wissenschaften.

Dant, T., Carley, M., Gearing, B. & Johnson, M. (1989). *Coordinating care: The final report of the care for elderly people at home project, Gloucester.* United Kingdom: Milton Keynes, The Open University.

Dant, T., & Gearing, B. (1990). Keyworkers for elderly people in the community: Case managers and care co-ordinators. *Journal of Social Policy, 19*(3), 331–360.

De Beauvoir, S. (1973). *The coming of age.* New York: Warner.

Del Togno-Armanasco V., Olivas G., & Harter S. (1989). Developing an integrated nursing case management model, *Nursing Management 20*(5), 26–29.

Dennett, D. (1991). *Consciousness explained.* Boston: Little, Brown.

Denzin, N. K. (1970). *The research act.* Chicago: Aldine.

Denzin, N. K. (1984). Interpreting the lives of ordinary people: Sartre, Heidegger, and Faulkner. *Life Stories, 7.*

Denzin, N. K. (1989a). *Interpretive biography.* Newbury Park, CA: Sage.

Denzin, N. K. (1989b). Interpretive interactionism. *Applied Social Research Method Series,* Vol. 16. Newbury Park, CA: Sage.

Denzin, N. K. (1993). *Studies in symbolic interaction* (Vol. 14). London: Jai Press.

Denzin, N. K., & Lincoln, Y.S. (1994). (Eds.). *Handbook of qualitative research.* Thousand Oaks, CA: Sage.

deRamon, B. (1983). The final task: Life review for the dying patient. *American Journal of Nursing, 13*(2), 44–49.

DeShazer, S. (1991). *Putting differences to work.* New York: Norton.

Devereux, G. (1980). *Basic problems in ethnopsychiatry.* Chicago: University of Chicago Press.

de Vries, B., Birren, J. E., & Deutchman, D. E. (1990). Adult development through guided autobiography: The family context. *Family Relations, 39,* 3–7.

de Vries, B., Birren, J. E., & Deutchman, D. E. (in press-a). The method and uses of the guided autobiography. In B. K. Haight & J. D. Webster (Eds.), *The art and science of reminiscing: Theory, research, methods, and applications.* Washington, DC: Taylor and Francis.

de Vries, B., Blando, J. A., & Walker, L. J. (in press-b). The review of life's events: An exploratory analysis of content and structure. In B. K. Haight & J. D.Webster (Eds.), *The art of science and reminiscing: Theory, research, methods, and applications.* Washington, DC: Taylor and Francis.

de Vries, B., Bluck, S., & Birren, J. E. (1993). The understanding of death and dying in a life-span perspective. *The Gerontologist, 33,* 366–372.

de Vries, B., & Shannon, D. (1992, July). *Thinking about the self in relationships.* Paper presented at the International Conference on Personal Relationships, Orono, Maine.

deVries, B., & Walker, L. J. (1986). Moral reasoning and attitudes towards capital punishment. *Developmental Psychology, 22,* 509–513.

de Vries, B., & Walker, L. J. (1988). Conceptual/integrative complexity and attitudes toward capital punishment. *Personality and Social Psychology Bulletin, 13,* 448–457.

de Vries, B., & Watt, D. (in press). A lifetime of events: Age and gender variations in the life story. *International Journal of Aging and Human Development.*

deWaele, J. -P. (1983). History of individual psychology: In R. Harré & T. Lamb (Eds.), *The encyclopedic dictionary of psychology,* 300–302. Cambridge, MA: MIT Press.

DeWaele, J.W. (Ed.). [In press]. *Handbook of the case study.* London: Wiley.

Dewey, J. (1966). *Democracy and education.* New York: The Free Press.

Dibel, D. (1971). *The relationship between reminiscence and depression among thirty selected institutionalized aged males.* Unpublished doctoral dissertation, School of Nursing, Boston University, Boston, MA.

Dietche, L. M. (1979). Facilitating the life review through group reminiscences. *Journal of Gerontological Nursing, 5*(4), 43–46.

di Gregorio, S. (1986). Understanding the management of everyday living. In C. Phillipson, M. Bernard, & P. Strang (Eds.) *Dependency and interdependency in later life: Theoretical perspectives*. London: Croom Helm.

di Gregorio, S. (1987). Managing - A concept for contextualising how people live their later lives. In S. di Gregorio (Ed.), *Social gerontology: New directions*. London: Croom Helm.

Dilthey, W. (1976). *W. Dilthey: Selected writings* (H.P. Rickman, Trans. and Ed.). Cambridge, England: Cambridge University Press.

Dilthey, W. (1988). *Introduction to the human sciences* (R. J. Betanzos, Trans.). Detroit: Wayne State University Press. (Original published 1883)

Dinneen, F. P. (1967). *An introduction to general linguistics*. New York: Holt, Rinehart and Winston.

Dittmann-Kohli, F. (1990). The construction of meaning in old age: Possibilities and constraints. *Ageing and Society, 10,* 279–294.

Dollard, J. (1935). *Criteria for the life history: With analysis of six notable documents*. New Haven: Yale University Press.

Durrant, M., & Kowalski, K. (1993). Enhancing views of competence. In S. Friedman (Ed.), *The new language of change*. New York: Norton.

Dwyer, K. (1977). On the dialogic of field work. *Dialectical Anthropology, 2,* 143–151.

Dwyer, K. (1979). The dialogic of ethnology. *Dialectical Anthropology, 4,* 205–224.

Eakin, P. J. (1985). *Fictions in autobiography: Studies in the art of self-invention*. Princeton, NJ: Princeton University Press.

Ebersole, P. P. (1976). In I. Burnside (Ed.), *Nursing and the aged* (pp. 214–230). New York: McGraw-Hill.

Ebersole, P. P. (1978). Establishing reminiscence groups. In I. M. Burnside (Ed.), *Working with the elderly: Group process & techniques* (pp. 236–254).

Eckert, J. K. (1988). Ethnographic research on aging. In S. Reinhartz & G. D. Rowles (Eds.), *Qualitative gerontology* (pp. 241–255) New York: Springer.

Edel, L. (1973). Introduction. In J. Glassco (Ed.), *Memoirs of Montparnasse*. Toronto: Oxford University Press.

Efran, J., Lukens, M., & Lukens, R. (1990). *Language structure and change*. New York: Norton.

Elder, G. H. Jr. 1974. *Children of the great depression*. Chicago: University of Chicago Press.

Elder, G., Jr. (1984). *The course of life: Developmental, social, and historical perspectives*. Ithaca, New York: Cornell University Press.

Elder, G. H. Jr. (Ed.) 1985. *Life course dynamics, trajectories, and transitions, 1968–1980*. Ithaca, N. Y.: Cornell University Press

Elder, G. H., Jr., & Bailey, S. L. (1988). The timing of military service in men's lives. In, J. Aldous & D. Klein, *Social stress and family development*, pp. 157–174. New York: Guilford.

Elder, G. H., Jr., & Caspi, A. (1988). Studying lives in a changing society: sociological and personological explorations. In, A. I. Rabin (Ed.) *Studying persons and lives: the Henry A. Murray Lectures in personality*. New York: Springer.

Elder, G. H., & Caspi, A. (1990). Studying lives in a changing society: Sociological and personalogical explorations. In A. I. Rabin, R. Zucker, R. Emmons, & S. Frank (Eds.), *Studying persons and lives* (pp. 201–247). New York: Springer Publishing Company.

Elias, N. (1991). On human beings and their emotions: A process sociological essay. In M. Featherstone & M. Hepworth (Eds.), *The body* (pp. 103–125). London: Sage.

Elkind, D. (1981). *Children and adolescents* (3rd ed.). New York: Oxford University Press.

Ellison, K. B. (1981). Working with the elderly in a life review group. *Journal of Gerontological Nursing, 7*(9), 537–541.

Enloe, C. (1993). Managing daily living with resources and losses. In D. L. Carnavali & M. Patrick (Eds.), *Nursing management for the elderly* (3rd ed.) (pp. 250–258). Philadelphia, PA.

Epstein, S. (1973). The self-concept revisited, or a theory of a theory. *American Psychologist, 28*, 404–416.

Erikson, E. H. (1958). *Young man Luther: A study in psychoanalysis and history*. New York: W. Norton.

Erikson, E. H. (1959). *Identity and the life cycle*. New York: Norton.

Erikson, E. H. (1963). *Childhood and society* (2nd ed.). New York: Norton.

Erikson, E. H. (1965). *Childhood and society*. London: Penguin.

Erikson, E. H. (1968). *Identity: Youth and crisis*. New York: Norton.

Erikson, E. H. (1969). *Gandhi's truth: On the origins of militant nonviolence*. New York: Norton.

Erikson, E. H. (1976). Psychological reality and historical actuality. In E. Erikson (Ed.), *Insight and responsibility* (pp. 161–215). New York: Norton. (Original work published 1968).

Erickson, E. H. (1979). Reflections on Dr. Borg's life cycle. In D. Van Tassel (Ed.), *Aging, death, and the completion of being*. (pp. 29–67). Philadelphia: University of Pennsylvania Press.

Erikson, E. H. (1982). *The life cycle completed: A review*. New York: Norton.

Erikson, E.H. (1984). Reflection on the last stage - and the first. *Psychoanalytic Study of the Child, 39*, 155–165.

Erikson, E. H., Erikson, J. M., & Kivnick, H. Q. (1986). *Vital involvement in old age: The experience of old age in our time*. New York: Norton.

Eskola, (1993). On the methodological paradigms of psychological peace research. In K. S. Larson (Ed.), *Conflict and social psychology*. London: Prio, Oslo & Sage.

Estess, T. L. (1974). The inenarrable contraption: Reflections on the metaphor of story. *Journal of the American Academy of Religion, 42*(3), 415–434.

Even, M. (1987). Why adults learn in different ways. *Lifelong learning: An omnibus of practice and research, 10*(8), 22–27.

Fagot, B., Leinbach, M. & O'Boyle, C. (1992). Gender labeling, gender stereotyping and parenting behavior. *Developmental Psychology, 28*(2), 225–230.

Fairbairn, W. R. D. (1952). *Psychoanalytic studies of the personality: The object relations theory of personality*. London: Routledge and Kegan Paul.

Fay, B. (1987). *Critical social science*. Ithaca, NY: Cornell University Press.

Featherstone, M. (1992). The heroic and everyday life. *Theory, culture & society, 9*, 159–182.

Featherstone, M., & Hepworth, M. (1991). The mask of ageing and the postmodern life course. In Featherstone, M., et al. (Eds.), *The body*. London: Sage.

Feinstein, D., Krippner, S., & Granger, D. (1988). Mythmaking and human development. *Journal of Humanistic Psychology, 28*(3), 23–50.

Feldman, C. F., Bruner, J., Renderer, R., & Spitzer, S. (1990). Narrative comprehension. In B. K. Britton & A. D. Pellegrini (Eds.), *Narrative thought and narrative language*. Hillsdale, NJ: Lawrence Erlbaum.

Fell, A. T. (1992). Epistemological and ontological queries concerning David Carr's *Time, Narrative, and History*. *Philosophy of the Social Sciences, 22* (3), 370–380.

Fiehler, R. (1990). *Kommunikation und emotion*. Berlin: de Gruyter.

Fischer, L. (1994). Qualitative research as art and science. In J. Gubrium & A. Sankar (Eds.), *Qualitative methods in aging research* (pp. 3–14). Thousand Oaks, CA: Sage Publications.

Fliess, R. (1944). The metapsychology of the analyst. *Psychoanalytic Quarterly, 11*, 211–227.

Fliess, R. (1953). Countertransference and counteridentification. *Journal of The American Psychoanalytic Association, 1*, 268–284.

Foster, H. (Ed.) *The anti-aesthetic: essays on postmodern culture*. Port Townsend, WA: Bay Press.

Forster, E. M. (1954). *Aspects of the novel*. San Diego, CA: Harcourt Brace.

Foucault, M. (1970). *The order of things: An archaeology of the human sciences*. New York: Vintage Books.

Fowler, J. (1981). *Stages of faith: The psychology of human development and the quest for meaning*. New York: Harper & Row.

Frank, G. (1979). Finding the common denominator: A phenomenological critique of the life history method. *Ethos, 7*, 68–94.

Frankl, V. (1962). *Man's search for meaning*. New York: Simon & Schuster.

Franscina, F.. & Harrison, C. (1982). *Modern art and modernism*. London: Open University Press.

Franz, C. E., & Stewart, A. J. (1994). (Eds.). *Women creating lives: Identities, resilience, resistance*. Boulder, CO: Westview.

Freeman, M. (1993). *Rewriting the self: History, memory, narrative*. New York: Routledge.

Frenkel, E. (1936). Studies in biographical psychology. *Character and Personality, 5*, 1–35.

Freud, S. (1897/1985). Letter of September 21, 1987. In J. M. Masson (Ed.), *The letters of Sigmund Freud to Wilhelm Fliess, 1887–1904* (pp. 263–267). Cambridge, MA: Harvard University Press.

Freud, S. (1900/1958). The interpretation of dreams. In J. Strachey (Ed.and trans.), *The standard edition of the complete psychological works of Sigmund Freud* (Vols. 4–5). London: Hogarth Press.

Freud, S. (1905a/1953). Fragment of an analysis of a case of hysteria. In J. Strachey (Ed. & trans.) *The standard edition of the complete psychological works of Sigmund Freud* (Vol. 8) (pp. 7–124). London: Hogarth Press.

Freud, S. (1905b/1960). Jokes and their relation to the unconscious. In J. Strachey (Ed. and trans.), *The standard edition of the complete psychological works of Sigmund Freud* (Vol. 8). London: Hogarth Press.

Freud, S. (1906/1953). My views on the part played by sexuality in the aetiology of the neuroses. In J. Strachey (Ed. and trans.), *The standard edition of the complete psychological works of Sigmund Freud* (Vol. 7) (pp. 271–282). London: Hogarth Press.

Freud, S. (1910a/1957). Five lectures on psychoanalysis (The Clark Lectures). In J. Strachey (Ed. and trans.), *The standard edition of the complete psychological works of Sigmund Freud* (Vol. 11) (pp. 9–58). London: Hogarth Press.

Freud, S. (1910b/ 1957). A special type of choice of object made by men (Contributions to the psychology of love, 1). In J. Strachey (Ed. and trans.), *The standard edition of the complete psychological works of Sigmund Freud* (Vol. 11) (pp.165–175). London: Hogarth Press.

Freud, S. (1911/1958). *Formulations regarding the two principles in mental functioning.* In J. Strachey (Ed. & trans.) *The standard edition of the complete works of Sigmund Freud* (Vol. 12). London: Hogarth Press, (213–226).

Freud, S. (1912/1958). Recommendations to physicians practicing psychoanalysis, *The standard edition of the complete psychological works of Sigmund Freud,* (Vol. 12) (pp. 109–120). London: Hogarth Press.

Freud, S. (1923). *The ego and the id.* London: Hogarth.

Freud, S. (1930/1961). Civilization and its discontents. In J. Strachey (Ed. and trans.), *The standard edition of the complete psychological works of Sigmund Freud* (Vol. 21) (pp. 59–145). London: Hogarth Press.

Freund, E. (1987). *The return of the reader: Reader-response criticism.* New York: Methuen.

Friedman, S. S. (1988). Women's autobiographical selves: Theory and practice. In S. Benstock (Ed.), *The private self: Theory and practice of women's autobiographical writings* (pp. 34–62). Chapel Hill, NC: University of North Carolina Press.

Friedman, S., & Fanger, M. (1991). *Expanding therapeutic possibilities: Putting grief psychotherapy to work.* New York: Livingston.

Frijda, N. H., & Swagerman, J. (1987). Can computers feel? Theory and design of an emotional system. *Cognition & Emotion, 3,* 235–257.

Frisby, D. (1985). *Fragments of modernity.* Cambridge: Polity Press.

Fruggeri, L. (1992). Therapeutic process as the social construction of change. In S. McNamee & K. Gergen (Eds.), *Therapy as social construction.* London: Sage.

Frye, N. (1957). *Anatomy of criticism.* Princeton, NJ: Princeton University Press.

Frye, N. (1988). *On education.* Toronto: Fitzhenry & Whiteside.

Fuller, L. (1988). Reminiscence: Using memories to improve the quality of care for elderly patients. *Journal of Practical Nursing, 38*(3), 30–35.

Gadamer, H-G. (1981). *Reason in the age of science* (F. G. Lawrence, trans.). Cambridge, MA: MIT Press.

Gadow, S. (1986). Frailty and strength: The Dialectic of aging. In T. Cole & S. Gadow (Eds.), *What does it mean to grow old: Reflections from the humanities.* Durham, NC: Duke University Press.

Galatzer-Levy, R., & Cohler, B. (1993). *The essential other: A developmental psychology of the self.* New York: Basic Books.

Gallie, W. B. (1968). *Philosophy and historical understanding.* New York: Schocken Books.

Gardner, H. (1983). *Frames of mind: The theory of multiple intelligences.* New York: Basic Books.

Gardner, H. (1990). *Frames of mind: The theory of multiple intelligences.* San Francisco: Basic Books.

Gardner, J. (1985). *The art of fiction: Notes on craft for young writers.* New York: Vintage.

Gardner, R. (1987). *Self-inquiry.* Hillsdale, NJ: The Analytic Press. (Originally published 1983).

Gardner, R. (1993). On talking to ourselves: Some self analytical reflections on self-analysis. In J. Barron (Ed.), *Self-analysis: Critical inquiries, personal visions* (pp. 147–170). Hillsdale, NJ: The Analytic Press.

Garfinkel, H. (1967). *Studies in ethnomethodology.* Englewood Cliffs, NJ: Prentice-Hall.

Gearing, B., & Dant, T. (1990). Doing biographical research. In S. M. Peace (Ed.), *Researching social gerontology: Concepts, methods and issues.* London: Sage Publications.

Geiger, S. N. (1986). Women's life histories: Method and content. *Signs,* 334–51.

Gendlin, E. T. (1992). Thinking beyond patterns: Body, language, and situations. In B. D. Ouden & M. Moen (Eds.), *The presence of feeling in thought* (pp. 21–151). New York: Peter Lang.

George, L. (1984). The institutionalized in famous aged. In E. Palmore (Ed.), *Handbook on the aged in the United States* (pp. 339–354). Westport, CT: Greenwood Press.

George, L. K., & Bearon, L. B. (1980). *Quality of life in older persons: Meaning and measurement.* New York: Human Sciences Press.

George, L. K. & Siegler, I. C. (1982). Stress and coping in later life. *Educational Horizons, 60,* 147–154.

Gergen, K. J. (1990). Social understanding and the inscription of self. In J. W. Stiegler, R. A. Sneider, & G. Herdt: *Cultural psychology: Essays on comparative human development.* Cambridge, England: Cambridge University Press.

Gergen, K. J. (1991). *The saturated self: Dilemmas of identity in contemporary life.* New York: Basic.

Gergen, K. J., & Gergen, M. (1983a). Autobiographies and the shaping of gendered lives. In N. Coupland & J. F. Nussbaum (Eds.), *Discourse and the lifespan identity* (pp. 28–54). Newbury Park, CA: Sage.

Gergen, K. J., & Gergen, M. (1983b). Narratives of the self. In T. R. Sarbin & K. E. Scheibe (Eds.), *Studies in social identity (pp.* 245–273). New York: Praeger.

Gergen, K. J., & Gergen, M. (1986). Narrative form and the construction of psychological science. In T. Sarbin (Ed.), *Narrative psychology: The storied nature of human conduct* (pp. 22–44). New York: Praeger.

Gergen, K. J. (1993). *Toward transformation of social knowledge* London: Sage.

Gergen, K. J. (1994). *Toward the transformation in social knowledge* (2nd ed.) London: Sage.

Gergen, M. & Gergen, K. (1984). The Social Construction of narrative accounts. In K. Gergen & M. Gergen (Eds.), *Historical social psychology,* (pp. 173–189). Hillsdale, Nj: Erlbaum.

Gergen, M. (1988). Narrative structures in social explanation. In C. Antaki (Ed.), *Analysing everyday explanation: A casebook of methods* (pp. 94–112). London: Sage.

Gilligan, C. (1982). In a *different voice: Psychological theory and women's development.* Cambridge, MA: Harvard University Press.

Giltinan, J. M. (1990). Using life review to facilitate self-actualization in elderly women. *Gerontology & Geriatrics Education, 10(4),* 75–83.

Giorgi, A. (1970). *Psychology as a human science: A phenomenological based approach.* New York: Harper & Row.

Giorgi, A. (1975). An application of phenomenological method in psychology. In A. Giorgi, C. T. Fisher, & E. L. Murray (Eds.), *Duquesne studies in phenomenological psychology (No. 2)* Pittsburgh, PA: Duquesne University Press.

Giorgi, A. (1986). Status of qualitative research in the human sciences: A limited interdisciplinary and international perspective. *Methods,* 1, 29–62.

Glaser, B., & Strauss, A. L. (1965). *Awareness of dying.* Chicago:

Glaser, B., & Strauss, A. L. (1967). *The discovery of grounded theory.* Chicago: Aldine.

Glaser, B., & Strauss, A. L. (1968). *Time for dying.* Chicago:

Glass, A. L., Holyoak, K. J., & Santa, J. L. (1979). *Cognition.* Reading, MA: Addison-Wesley.

Glick, P. C., & Bolyard, M. (1993). Women and men in non-traditional occupations: Their growing numbers and their marital stability. *International Journal of Family and Marriage, 1*(3), 1.

Glover, J. (1988). *I: The philosophy and psychology of personal identity.* London: Penguin.

Goffman, E. (1959). *The presentation of self in everyday life.* New York: Doubleday.

Goffman, E. (1972). *Interaction ritual: Essays on face to face behavior.* London: Penguin Press.

Good, B. (1994). *Medicine, rationality, and experience: An anthropological perspective.* New York: Cambridge University Press.

Goolishian, H., & Anderson, H. (1991). Language systems and therapy: An evolving idea. *Journal of Psychotherapy, 24,* 529–38.

Goolishian, H. & Anderson, H. (1992). The client is the expert: A not-knowing approach to therapy. In S. McNamee & K. Gergen (Eds.), *Therapy as social construction.* London: Sage.

Goolishian, H., & Winderman, L. (1988). "Narrative and the self as relationship" In L. Berkowitz (Ed.), *Advances in experimental social psychology (Vol. 21).* (pp. 17–56). New York: Academic Press.

Gould, R. (1978). *Transformations, growth and change in adult life.* New York: Simon and Schuster.

Green, M. (1989). *Theories of human development: A comparative approach.* Englewood Cliffs, NJ: Prentice Hall.

Green, R. R. (1982). Life review: A technique for clarifying family roles in adulthood. *Clinical Gerontologist*, 1(2), 59–67.

Greene, M. (1990). *The emancipatory power of literature*. In J. Mezirow (Ed.), *Fostering critical reflection in adulthood* (pp. 251–268). San Francisco: Jossey-Bass.

Greenwald, A. (1980). The totalitarian ego: Fabrication and revision of personal history. *American Psychologist, 35*, 603–618.

Grotjahn, M. L. (1989). Group analysis in old age. *Group Analysis, 22*, 109–11.

Gubrium, J., & Sankar, A. (Eds.) (1994). *Qualitative methods in aging research*. Thousand Oaks, CA: Sage.

Gubrium, J. F. (1993). *Speaking of life: Horizons of meaning for nursing home residents*. Hawthorne, New York: Aldine de Gruyter.

Gullestad, M. (1989). *Kulthr og hverdagsliv (Culture and everyday life)*. Oslo: Universitetsforlaget.

Gutmann, D. L. (1977). The cross-cultural perspective: Notes toward a comparative psychology of aging. In J. E. Birren & K. W. Schaie (Eds.), *Handbook of the psychology of aging*. New York: Van Nostrand Reinholt Co.

Gutmann, D. L. (1987). *Reclaimed powers: Towards a new psychology of men and women in later life*. New York: Basic Books.

Haan, N. (1977). *Coping and defending: Processes of self-environment organization*. New York: Academic Press.

Hagemaster, J. (1992). Life history: A qualitative method of research. *Journal of Advanced Nursing, 17*(9), 1122–1128.

Hagberg, B. (In press). The individual's life history as a formative experience to ageing. In B. K. Haight & J. Webster (Eds.), *The art and science of reminiscing: Theory and practice*. Washington, DC: Francis & Taylor.

Hagestad, G. O. (1990). Social perspectives on the life course. In, R. H. Binstock & L. K. George (Eds.), *Handbook of aging and the social sciences*, pp. 151–168. New York: Academic Press.

Hagestad, G. O., & B. L. Neugarten (1985). Age and the life course. In R. H. Binstock & E. Shanas (Eds.), *Handbook of aging and the social sciences* (2nd ed.), (pp. 35–61). New York: Van Nostrand Reinhold.

Haight, B. K. (1988). The therapeutic role of a structured life review process in homebound elderly subjects. *Journal of Gerontology*, 43(2), 40–44.

Haight, B. K. (1991). Reminiscing: The state of the art as a basis for practice. *International Journal of Aging and Human Development*, 33(1), 1–32.

Haight, B. K., & Bahr, R. (1984). The therapeutic role of the life review in the elderly. *Academic Psychology Bulletin, 6*, 287–289.

Haight, B. K., & Burnside, I. (1993). Reminiscence and life review: Explaining the differences. *Archives of Psychiatric Nursing, 7*(2), 91–98.

Haight, B. K., & Olson, M. (1989). Teaching home health aids the use of life review. *Journal of Nursing Staff Development*, 5(1), 11–16.

Hala, M. (1975). Reminiscence group therapy project. *Journal of Gerontological Nursing, 1*, 34–41.

Haldemann, V. (1993). "Les methodes qualitatives - Pourquoi?" [Qualitative methods: Why?] *Canadian Journal on Aging, 12*, (2), 117–128.

Hall, G. S. (1922). Senescence: The last half of life. New York: Appleton, Century, Crafts.

Hall, G., George, A., & Rutherford, W. (1987) *Measuring stages of Concern About the Innovation: A Manual for use of the SoC Questionnaire* Austin: Research and Development Center for Teacher Education, The University of Texas.

Hamilton, D. B. (1992). Reminiscence therapy. In G. M. Bulechek & J. C. McCloskey (Eds.), *Essential nursing treatments* (2d ed.), (pp. 292–303). Philadelphia: W. B. Saunders.

Hamilton, D. B. (1985). Reminiscence therapy. In G. M. Bulechek & J. C. McCloskey (Eds.), *Nursing interventions: Treatments for nursing diagnoses* (pp. 139–151). Philadelphia: W. B. Saunders.

Handel, A. (1987). Personal theories about the life-span development of one's self in autobiographical self-presentation of adults. *Human Development, 30,* 83–97.

Hankiss, A. (1981). On the mythological rearranging of one's life history. In D. Bertaux (Ed.), *Biography and society* (pp. 203–209). Beverly Hills, CA: Sage.

Hare-Mustin, R. & Marecek, J. (1988). The meaning of difference: gender theory, postmodernism and psychology. *American Psychologist, 43,* 455–64.

Harre, R. (1989). Language games and the texts of identity. In J. Shotter & K. J. Gergen (Eds.), *Texts of identity* (pp. 20–35). London: Sage.

Harris, R., & Gillett, G. (1994). The discursive mind. Thousand Oaks, CA: Sage.

Harrison, C. (1993). Personhood, dementia and the integrity of a life. *Canadian Journal on Aging, 12,* (4), 428–440.

Hart, D. (1988). The adolescent self-concept in social context. In D. K. Lapsley & F. C. Power (Eds.), *Self, ego, and identity: Integrative approaches* (pp. 71–90). New York: Springer-Verlag.

Harter, S. (1983). Developmental perspectives on the self-system. In P. H. Mussen (Ed.), *Handbook of child psychology (4th ed.): Vol. 4: Socialization, personality, and social development* (pp. 275–386). New York: Wiley.

Harvey, O., Hunt, D., & Schroder, H. (1961). *Conceptual systems and personality organization.* New York: Wiley.

Hedlund, B.L. (1987). *The development of meaning-in-life in adulthood.* Unpublished doctoral dissertation, University of Southern California, Los Angeles.

Heidegger, M. (1962). *Being and time* (J. Macquarrie & E. Robinson, trans.). New York: Harper & Brothers.

Heikkinen, R-L. (1988). Laadullisen Neuvonta-aineiston Valottama Terveyskasvatusanalyysi [Analysis of Health Education Based on a Qualitative Counselling Material.] (Doctoral thesis. Laitos, Julkaisusarja A., Tutkimusraportti N:o 42, Tampere.

Heikkinen, R-L. (1993). Patterns of Experienced aging with a Finnish cohort. *Journal of Aging and Human Development,* 36, 269–277.

Heilbrun, C. (1988). *Writing a woman's life.* New York: Ballantine.

Heinriz, C. (1991). Les Archives Biographiques en Allemagne. (The biographical archives in Germany.) *Cahiers de Semiotique Textuelles,* 20, 87–102.

Hempel, C., & Oppenheim, P. (1948). Studies in the logic of explanation. *Philosophy of Science, 15,* 135–178.

Hermans, H. J. M., & Kempen, H. J. G. (1993). *The dialogical self: Meaning as movement.* San Diego, CA: Academic Press.

Hesse, H. (1990). *Mit der reife wird man jünger - Betrachtungen und gedichte über das alter.* (With maturation one becomes younger–reflections and poems on aging.) Frankfurt: Insel.

Hibel, D. E. (1971). *The relationship between reminiscence and depression among 30 selected institutionalized males.* Unpublished doctoral dissertation, Boston University School of Nursing, Boston, MA.

Higgins, E. T. (1987). Self-discrepancy: A theory relating self and affect. *Psychological Review, 94,* 319–340.

Hillman, J. (1975). The fiction of case history: A round. In J.B. Wiggins (Ed.), *Religion as story* (pp. 123–173). New York: Harper & Row.

Hillman, J. (1989). *A blue fire.* New York: Harper & Row.

Hoffman, L. (1990). Constructing realities: An art of lenses. *Family Process, 29,* 1–12.

Hogan, J. (1982). *The use of non-professional leaders in reminiscing groups for the institutionalized elderly.* Unpublished master's thesis, Department of Nursing, San Jose State University, San Jose, CA.

Höjrup, R. (1984). Begrepet Livsform. En Formspecificerande Analysmade Anvent Pa Nutidige Vesteuropeiske Samfund. (The way of life concept. A form specifying analysis applied on contemporary West-European societies.) Fortig Og Nytid 2.

Holliday, S., & Chandler, M. (1986). *Wisdom: Explorations in adult competence.* Basel: Karger.

Hollis, F. (1939). *Social casework in practice: Six case studies.* Family Service Association of America.

Horner, J. (1982). *That time of year: A chronicle of life in a nursing home.* University of Massachusetts Press.

Houston, J. (1987). *The search for the beloved: Journeys in sacred psychology.* Los Angeles: Jeremy P. Tarcher.

Howard, G. S. (1991). Cultural tales: A narrative approach to thinking, cross-cultural psychology, and psychotherapy. *American Psychologist, 46,* 187–197.

Humphrey, R. (1993). Life stories and social careers: Ageing and social life in an ex-mining town. *Sociology, 27,* 166–178.

Hunsberger, B. (1991, August). Integrative complexity and religion. In P. Suedfeld (Chair), *New directions in research on integrative complexity.* Symposium conducted at the meeting of the American Psychological Association, San Francisco.

Hunt, D. E., & Dopyesa, J. (1966). Personality variation in lower-class children. *Journal of Psychology, 62,* 47–54.

Husserl, E. (1931). *Ideas: General introduction to pure phenomenology.* (W. R. Gibson, Trans.). New York: Macmillan. (Original work published 1913)

Husserl, E. (1960). Cartesian Meditations: An introduction to phenomenology (Trans. D. Cairns). The Hague: Martinus Nijoff

Hyland, D. T., & Ackerman, A. M. (1988). Reminiscence and autobiographical memory in the study of personal past. *Journal of Gerontology, 43*(2), 35–39.

Hyland, D. T., & Ackerman, A. M. (1992). International yearbook of oral history and life stories. Oxford, UK: Oxford University Press.

Ingersoll, B., & Silverman, A. (1978). Comparative group psychotherapy for the aged. *Gerontologist, 18*, 201–206.

Iser, W. (1978). *The act of reading: A theory of aesthetic response.* Baltimore, MD: Johns Hopkins University Press.

Jackson, S. (1992). The listening healer in the history of psychological healing. *American Journal of Psychiatry, 149*, 1623–1632.

Jacobs, T. (1986). On countertransference enactments. *Journal of the American Psychoanalytic Association, 34*, 289–307.

Jacobs, T. (1991). *The use of the self: Countertransference and communication in the analytic situation.* Madison, CT: International Universities Press.

Jaffe, D. (1986). Empathy, counteridentification, countertransference: A review with some personal perspectives on the "analytic instrument." *Psychoanalytic Quarterly*, 215–243.

Jefferson, A., & Salovey, P. (1993). *The remembered self: Emotions and memory in personality.* New York: The Free Press.

James, W. (1892). *Psychology: A briefer course.* Greenwich, CT: Fawcett.

Jessup, L. (1984). The health history. In B. Steffl (Ed.), *Handbook of gerontological nursing* (pp. 150–160). New York: Van Nostrand.

Johan, M. (1992). (Panel Reporter). Enactments in psychoanalysis, *Journal of the American Psychoanalytic Assocation*, *40*, 827–841

Johnston, J. (1993, April 25). Fictions of the self in the making. *New York Times Book Review*,_pp. 3, 29, 31, 33.

Johnson, M. (1987). *The body in the mind: The bodily basis of meaning, imagination, and reason.* Chicago: University of Chicago Press.

Johnson, M. L. (1976). That was your life: A biographical approach to later life. In J. M. A. Munnichs & W. J. A. Van Den Heuval (Eds.), *Dependency and interdependency in old age.* The Hague: Martinus Nijhoff.

Johnson, M.L. (1988). Biographical influences on mental health in old age. In *Mental health problems in old age: A reader.* UK: Milton Keynes: The Open University.

Johnson, M. L., di Gregorio, S., & Harrison, B. (1980). *Ageing, needs and nutrition.* Leeds: Centre for Health Service Studies University of Leeds.

Johnson, M. L., Gearing, B., Carley, M., & Dant, T. (1988). *A biographically based health and social diagnostic technique: A research report, Project Paper No. 4 of the Gloucester Care of Elderly People at Home Project.* Milton Keynes, England: The Open University. Obtainable from School of Health, Welfare and Community Education, The Open University, Walton Hall, Milton Keynes, MK7 6AA, England.

Joint Commission on Accrediation of Healthcare Organization. Oakbrook Terrace, Illinois

Jones, C. P. (1994). In Sam's shop. *American Journal of Nursing, 94*(3), 50–52.

Josselson, R. (1993). A narrative introduction. In R. Josselson & A. Lieblich (Eds.), *The narrative study of lives* (pp. ix-xv). Newbury Park, CA: Sage.

Josselson, R., & Lieblich, A. (Eds). (1993). *The narrative study of lives.* Newbury Park, CA: Sage.

Jourard, S. (1971). *The transparent self.* New York: Litton.

Jung, C. G. (1953). *Collected works.* New York: Pantheon.

Jung, C. G. (1961). *Memories, dreams, reflections.* New York: Vintage.

Jylhä, M. (1994). Perceived health in old age: Two methodological approaches. In P. Öberg, P. Pohjolainen, & I. Ruoppila (Eds.), *Experiencing ageing.* Helsinki: SHSK Skrifter No. 4.

Kaminsky, M. (1978). Pictures from the past. The use of reminiscence in casework with the elderly. *Journal of Gerontological Social Work. 1*, 187–194.

Kaminsky, M. (1992). Introduction. In B. Myerhoff, (Ed.) *Remembered lives: The work of ritual, storytelling and growing older* (pp. 1–99). Ann Arbor: The University of Michigan Press.

Kant, I. (1965). *Critique of pure reason* (unabridged ed.). (N. K. Smith, Trans.). New York: St. Martin's. (Original work published 1781)

Kappeli, S. (1984). *Towards a practice theory of relationships of self-care needs, nursing needs and nursing care in the hospitalized elderly.* Unpublished doctoral dissertation. Manchester, England: The University of Manchester.

Karl, F. D. (1991). *Die älteren - Zur lebenssituation der 55 - Bis 70 jährigen.* Bonn: Dietz.

Kastenbaum, R. (1980). Habituation as a partial model of human aging. *International Journal of Human Development, 13,* 159–170.

Kastenbaum, R. (1983). Time course and time perspective in later life. In C. Eisdorfer (Ed.), *Annual Review of Gerontology and Geriatrics.* (Vol. 3) (pp. 80–101)New York: Springer.

Katz, J. (1976). Development of the mind. In J. Katz & R. T. Harnett (Eds.), *Scholars in the making: The development of graduate and professional students* (pp.107–126). Cambridge, MA: Ballinger Publishing Company.

Kaufman, S. (1986). *The ageless self.* New York: New American Library.

Keen, E. (1986). Paranoia and cataclysmic narratives. In T. Sarbin (Ed.), *Narrative psychology: The storied nature of human conflict* (pp. 174–190). New York: Praeger.

Keeney, B. (1983). *Aesthetics of change.* New York: Guilford Press.

Kegan, R. (1982). *The evolving self; Problem and process in human development.* Cambridge, MA: Harvard University Press.

Kelly, G. A. (1955). *The psychology of personal constructs: A theory of personality* (Vol. 1). New York: Norton.

Kemper, S. (1984). The development of narrative skills: Explanations and entertainments. In S. A. Kuczaj II (Ed.), *Progress in cognitive development research* (pp. 99–124). New York: Springer-Verlag.

Kennedy, E. (1977). *On becoming a counselor: A basic guide for non-professional counselors.* New York: Continuum.

Kenyon, G.M. (1980). The meaning of death in Gabriel Marcel's philosophy. *Gnosis, 2,* 27–40.

Kenyon, G.M. (1985). The meaning of aging: Vital existence vs personal existence. *Human Values and Aging Newsletter, 8,* 2.

Kenyon, G. M. (1988). Basic assumptions in theories of human aging. In J. Birren & V. Bengtson (Eds.), *Emergent theories of aging.* New York: Springer.

Kenyon, G. M. (1989a). *Enhancing personal meanings of aging: The importance of biography.* Paper presented at the 14th International Congress for Gerontology, Acapulco.

Kenyon, G. M. (1989b). Health care intervention with the elderly: A philosophical perspective. In J. J. F. Schroots, A. Bouma, G. Braam, A. Groeneveld, D. Ringoir, & C. Tempelman (Eds.), *Health and Aging.* Assen: Van Gorcum.

Kenyon, G. M. (1991). Homo viator: Metaphors of aging, authenticity and meaning. In G. Kenyon, J. Birren, & J. J. F. Schroots (Eds.), *Metaphors of aging in science and the humanities* (pp. 17–35). New York: Springer.

Kenyon, G.M. (1992). Aging and possibilities for being. *Aging and the Human Spirit, 2,* 1.

Kenyon, G. M. (1993). Editorial: Aging and the humanities. *Canadian Journal on Aging, 12*(4), 416–418.

Kenyon, G., Birren, J., & Schroots, J. J. F. (Eds.), (1991). *Metaphors of aging in science and the humanities.* New York: Springer.

Kerby, A. T. (1991). *Narrative and the self.* Bloomington: Indiana University Press.

Kermode, F. (1966). *The sense of an ending: Studies in the theory of fiction.* New York: Oxford University Press.

Kibbee, P. E., & Lackey, D. S. (1982). The past as therapy: An experience in an acute setting. *Journal of Practical Nursing, 32*(9), 29–31.

Kim, S. G. (1987). Black Americans' commitment to communism: A case study based on fiction and autobiographies by black Americans (Doctoral dissertation, University of Kansas, 1987). *Dissertation Abstracts International*, *48*, 34215–6B. University of Kansas.

Kimble, M.A., McFadden,. S. H., Ellor, J.W., & Seeber, J.J. (Eds.), (1995). *Aging, religion, and spirituality: A handbook.* Minneapolis: Fortress Press.

King, K. (1979). *Reminiscing group experiences with aging people.* Unpublished master's thesis, College of Nursing, University of Utah, Salt Lake City.

King, K. (1982). Reminiscing psychotherapy with aging people. *Journal of Psychosocial Nursing and Mental Health Services, 20*(2), 21–25.

King, K. (1984). *Reminiscing as a means of counseling.* Unpublished paper.

Kirk, S. (1986). *The phenomenological concept of the body as a grounding for the new epistemology in family therapy.* The Pennsylvania State University UMI Dissertation Information Service.

Kivnick, H. Q. (1991). *Living with care, caring for life: The inventory of life strengths.* Minneapolis; School of Social Work, University of Minnesota.

Kleemeier, R. W. (1962). Intellectual changes in the senium. *Proceedings of the American Statistical Association, 1,* 290–295.

Klemola, T. (1991). *Liikunta tiena kohti varsinaista ItseauU.* Filosofian Tutkimuksia Tampereen Yliopistosta . (Vol 12). Tampere: Tampereen Yliopisto.

Kluckhohn, C., & Murray, H. A. (1953). Personality formation: The determinants. In C. Kluckhohn, H. A. Murray, & D. Schneider (Eds.), *Personality in nature, society and culture* (pp). New York: Knopf.

Knowles, E. S., & Sibicky, M. E. (1990). Continuity and diversity in the stream of selves: Metaphorical resolutions of William James's one-in-many-selves paradox. *Personality and Social Psychology Bulletin, 16*, 676–687.

Kohlberg, L. (1984). *Essays on moral development: The psychology of moral development (Vol. 2)* San Francisco: Harper & Row.

Kohli, M. (1981). Biography: Account, text, method. In D. Bertaux (Ed.), *The life history approach in the social sciences.* (pp. 61–75). Beverly Hills, CA: Sage Publications.

Kohli, M., Rosenow, J. & Wolf, J. (1983). The social construction of aging through work: Economic structure and life-world. *Aging and Society, 3,* 23–42.

Kohut, H. (1971). The analysis of the self: A systematic approach to the psychoanalytic treatment of narcissistic personality disorders (Monography 1) of *The Psychoanalytic Study of the Child Series*. New York: International Universities Press.

Kohut, H. (1977). *The restoration of the self*. New York: International Universities Press.

Kohut, H. (1978). Introspection, empathy and psychoanalysis: An examination of the relationship between mode of observation and theory. In P. Ornstein (Ed.), *The search for the self: Selected writings of Heinz Kohut, 1950–1978*. (Vol. 1) (pp. 205–232). New York: International Universities Press. (Originally published 1959).

Kohut, H. (1984). *How does analysis cure?* Chicago: The University Press.

Kolakowski, L. (1972). *Positivist philosophy: From Hume to the Vienna circle* (N. Guterman, trans). London: Penguin Books.

Kolberg, L. (1984). *Essays on moral development: The psychology of moral development* (Vol. 2). San Francisco: Harper & Row.

Kopp, S. (1987). *Who am I ... really?: An autobiographical exploration on becoming who you are*. Los Angeles: Jeremy P. Tarcher.

Kotre, J. (1984). *Outliving the self: Generativity and the interpretation of lives*. Baltimore, MD: Johns Hopkins University Press.

Kovach, C. (1990). Promise and problems in reminiscence research. *Journal of Gerontological Nursing, 16*, 10–14.

Kovach, C. R. (1991a). Content analysis of reminiscence of elderly women. *Research in Nursing & Health, 14*, 287–295.

Kovach, C. R. (1991b). Reminiscence behavior: An empirical exploration. *Journal of Gerontological Nursing, 17*(12), 23–27.

Kovach, C. R. (1991c). Reminiscence: A closer look at content. *Issues in Mental Health Nursing, 12*, 193–204.

Kovel, J. (1989). The American mental health industry. In D. Ingleby (Ed.), *Critical psychiatry: The politics of mental health*. New York: Pantheon.

Kozulin, A. (1990). *Vygotsky's psychology: A biography of ideas*. Cambridge, MA: Harvard University Press.

Kraut, R. (1986). Feelings in context. *The Journal of Philosophy, 11*, 642–652.

Krohn, L. (1993). Tribar. Porvoo: Werner Söderström Osake Yhtiö.

Krohn, S. (1990). Muuttumaton muutoksessa, kehityksessä ja edistyksessä. (The unchangeable in transition, in development and progression.) In I. Halonen & H. Häyry (Eds.), *Muutos* (pp. 137–145). Helsinki: Suomen Filosofinen Yhdistys.

Kuhn, T. S. (1970). *The structure of scientific revolutions*. Chicago: University of Chicago Press.

Kusch, M. (1988). Kertova minä. (Narrative self.) In I. Niiniluoto & P. Stenman (Eds.), *Minä (Self)* (pp. 152–164). Helsinki: Suomen Filosofinen Yhdistys.

Kvale, S. (1977). Dialectics and research on remembering. In N. Datan & H. W. Reese (Eds.), *Life-span developmental psychology : Dialectical perspectives on experimental research* (pp. 165–189). New York: Academic Press.

Kvale, S. (1989). The primacy of the interview. *Methods: A Journal for Human Science*. Annual edition. 3–37.

Kvale, S. (Ed.) (1992). *Psychology and postmodernism*. Newbury Park, CA: Sage.

Labov, W., & Waletzsky, J. (1966). Narrative Analysis: Oral versions of persona experience. In J. Halor (Ed.), *Essays on the verbal and visual arts* (pp. 12–44). Seattle, WA: American Ethnological Society, Annual Spring Meeting.

Laine. T. (1993). Aistisuus, kehollisuus ja dialogisuus (Sensuousness, bodiliness and dialogue. Basic Principles in Ludwig Feuerbach's philosophy and their development in the anthropologically oriented phenomenology of the 1900's). Jyväskylä Studies in Education, Psychology and Social Research (No. 96). Jyväskylä, Finland: University of Jyväskylä.

Laing, R. D. (1967). *The politics of experience.* New York: Ballantine.

Lakoff, G. (1987). *Women, fire, and dangerous things: What categories reveal about the mind.* Chicago: University of Chicago Press.

Lamb, R. (1987). Objectless emotions. *Philosophy and Phenomenological Research, 1,* 107–117.

Langbaum, R. (1982). *The mysteries of identity: A theme in modern literature.* Chicago: University of Chicago Press.

Lappe, J. M. (1987). Reminiscing: The life review therapy. *Journal of Gerontological Nursing, 13*(4), 12–16.

Larson, R. (1978). Thirty years of research on the subjective well-being of older Americans. *Journal of Gerontology, 33,* 109–125.

Lasch, C. (1979). *The culture of narcissism*. New York: Norton.

Lashley, M. (1992). Reminiscences: A Biblical basis for telling our stories. *Journal of Christian Nursing*, Summer, 4–8.

Latour, B., & Woolgar, S. (1986). *Laboratory life: The construction of scientific facts* (2nd ed.). Princeton, NJ: Princeton University Press.

Lawton, M. P. (1972). Assessing the competence of older people. In D. Kent, R. Kastenbaum, & S. Sherwood (Eds.), *Research, planning, and action for the elderly.* New York: Behavioral Publications.

Lawton, M. P. (1975). Competence, environmental press and the adaptation of older people. In P. G. Windley, T. O. Byerts & F. G. Ernst (Eds.), *Theory development in environment and aging.* Washington, DC: Gerontological Society.

Lawton, M. P. (1980). *Environment and aging.* Monterey, CA: Brooks/Cole.

Lawton, M. P. (1983). Environment and other determinants of well-being in older people. *The Gerontologist, 23,* 349–357.

Lawton, M. P. (1991). A multidimensional view of quality of life in frail elders. In J. E. Birren, D. Deutchman, J. E. Lubben, & J. Rowe (Eds.), *The concept and measurement of quality of life in the frail elderly.* (pp. 3–27) San Diego: Academic Press.

Lawton, M. P. & Simon, B. (1968). The ecology of social relationships in housing for the elderly. *The Gerontologist, 8,* 108–115.

Lax, W. (1992) Postmodern thinking in a clinical practice. In S. McNamee & K. Gergen (Eds.), *Therapy as social construction.* London: Sage.

Levenson, M. (1984). A genealogy of modernism. Cambridge, MA: Cambridge University Press.

Levinson, D. J. (1978). *The seasons of a man's life*. New York: Knopf.

Levy, K. A. (1992, April). *Characteristics of reminiscence in nursing home residents.* Paper presented at research conference, University of Virginia, School of Nursing, Charlottesville, VA.

Lewin, K. (1936). *Principles of topological psychology*. New York: McGraw-Hill.

Lewin, K. (1951a). Field theory in social science. In *Selected theoretical papers*, D. Cartwright (Ed.) New York: Harper & Brothers.

Lewin, K. (1951b) Group decision and social change. In *Readings in Social Psychology*. T. Newcomb and E. Hartley, (Eds). New York: Holt, Rinehart and Winston.

Lewis, J. (1994). Care management and the social services: Reconciling the irreconcilable. *Generations Review, 4*(1), 2–4.

Lewis, M., & Brooks-Gunn, J. (1979). *Social cognition and the acquisition of self*. New York: Plenum.

Lewis, M. I., & Butler, R. N. (1974). Life-review therapy: Putting memories to work. *Geriatricas, 29*(11), 165–173.

Lewis, O. (1961). *Children of Sanchez: Autobiography of a Mexican family*. New York: Random House.

Lifton, R. J. (1979). *The broken connection: On death and the continuity of life*. New York: Simon and Schuster.

Linde, C. (1990). *Life stories: The creation of coherence*. (Monograph No. IRL90–0001). Palo Alto, CA: Institute for Research on Learning.

Lipchik, E. (1993). "Both/And" solutions. In S. Friedman (Ed.), *The new language of change*. New York; Guilford Press.

Loevinger, J. (1966). *Ego development: Conceptions and theories*. San Francisco: Jossey-Bass.

Loftus, E. (1993). The reality of repressed memories, *American Psychologist, 48*, 518–537.

Loftus, E., & Kaufman, L. (1992). Why do traumatic experiences sometimes produce good memory (flashbulbs) and sometimes no memory (repression)? In E. Winograd & U. Neisser (Eds.), *Affect and accuracy in recall: Studies of "flashbulb" memories* (pp. 212–223). New York: Cambridge University Press.

Lovelady, M. S. (1987). The effect of reminiscence therapy on self-esteem in the institutionalized elderly. Unpublished master's thesis, Troy State University, New York.

Lowenthal, M., Thurner, M., & Chiriboga, D. (1975). *Four stages of life. A comparative study of women and men facing transitions*. San Francisco: Jossey-Bass.

Lowenthal, R. I., & Mazzarro, R. A. (1990). Milestoning: Evoking memories for resocialization through group reminiscence. *The Gerontologist, 30*(2), 269–272.

Luborsky, M. (1993). The romance with personal meaning in gerontology: Cultural aspects of life themes. *The Gerontologist, 33*(4), 445–452.

Lundh, L. (1983). Mind and meaning. Unpublished doctoral dissertation. Uppsala University, Sweden.

Lynch, G., & Rampton, D. (Eds.) (1992). *Short fiction: An introductory anthology*. Toronto: Harcourt Brace Jovanovich.

Lynch, M. (1993). *Scientific practice and ordinary action: Ethnomethodology and social studies of science*. New York: Cambridge University Press.

Lynch-Sauer, J. (1985). Using a phenomenological research method to study nursing phenomena. In M. M. Leininger (Ed.), *Qualitative research methods in nursing*. Orlando: Grune & Stratton.

Lyons, N. (1983). Two perspectives: On self, relationships, and morality. *Harvard Educational Review, 53*, 125–145.

MacIntyre, A. (1984). *After virtue*. Notre Dame, IN: University of Notre Dame Press.

MacRae, I. (1982). An underused nursing resource. *Nursing Papers Perspective in Nursing, 14*(1), 52–54.

Maddi, S. (1988). On the problem of accepting facticity and pursuing possibility. In S. Messer, L. Sass & R. Woolfolk (Eds.), *Hermeneutics and psychological theory* (pp. 182–209). New Brunswick, NJ: Rutgers University Press.

Mader, W. (1991). Aging and the metaphor of narcissism. In G. Kenyon, J. Birren, & J. J. F. Schroots (Eds.), *Metaphors of aging in science and the humanities.* (pp. 131–153). New York: Springer.

Mader, W. (1993). Thematically guided autobiographical reconstruction. Paper presented at seminar on life-history and biographical research, Geneva.

Maeland, J. G. (1989). Helse og livskvalitet. Begrepper og definisjoner. (Health and quality of life. Concepts and definitions.) *Tidsskrift for den norske laegeforening, 109,* 1311–1315.

Mahoney, M. (1991). Human change processes. New York: Basic Books.

Malatesta, C. Z., & Izard, C. E. (Eds.) (1984). *Emotion in adult development.* London: Sage.

Malinowski, B. (1989). *A diary in the strict sense of the term.* Stanford, CA: Stanford University Press. (Original work published 1967).

Mancuso, J. C. (1986). The acquisition and use of narrative grammar structure. In T. R. Sarbin (Ed.), *Narrative psychology: The storied nature of human conduct* (pp. 91–110). New York: Praeger.

Mandl, H., & Huber, G. L. (1983). *Emotion und kognition.* (Emotion and cognition). München: Urban & Schwarzenberg.

Mandelbrot, B. B. (1983). *The fractal geometry of nature.* New York: W.H. Freeman.

Mandler, J. M. (1984). *Stories, scripts, and scenes; Aspects of a schema theory.* Hillsdale, NJ: Lawrence Erlbaum.

Mannheim, K. (1952). *Essays in the sociology of knowledge.* (P. Kecskemetti, trans.). New York: Oxford University Press. (Original work published 1928.)

Marcel, G. (1962). *Homo viator.* New York: Harper & Row.

Marcia, J. E. (1966). Development and validation of ego-identity status. *Journal of Personality and Social Psychology, 3,* 551–558.

Marcia, J. E. (1976). Identity six years later: A follow-up study. *Journal of Youth and Adolescence, 5,* 145–160.

Marcus, J., & Tar, Z. (Eds.) (1984). *Foundations of the Frankfurt school of social research.* New Brunswick, NJ: Transaction Books.

Markus, H. R., & Herzog, A. R. (1992). The role of the self-concept in aging. In K. W. Schaie & M. P. Lawton (Eds.), *Annual Review of Gerontology and Geriatrics.* (Volume 11) (pp. 110–143.) New York: Springer.

Markus, H., & Nurius, P. (1986). Possible selves. *American Psychologist, 41,* 954–969.

Marshall, M. (1983). *Social work with old people.* London: MacMillan.

Maslow, A. (1968). *Toward a psychology of being.* New York: Van Nostrand.

Maslow, A. (1976). *The farther reaches of human nature.* New York: Penguin.

Mathews, S. H. (1983). Definitions of friendship and their consequences in old age. *Ageing and Society, 3,* 141–155.

Matte, M. A., & Munsat, E. M. (1982). Group reminiscing therapy with elderly clients. *Issues in Mental Health Nursing, 4*(3), 177–187.

Matteson, M. A. (1978). Group reminiscence: Treatment for the depressed institutionalized elderly client. Unpublished research paper, Duke University, Durham, NC.

Matteson, M. A. (1986). Group reminiscing for the depressed institutionalized elderly. In I. Burnside (Ed.), *Working with the elderly: Group process and techniques* (2nd ed.),(pp. 287–298). Boston: Jones & Bartlett.

Mattingly, C. (1989). Thinking with stories: Story and experience in a clinical practice. Unpublished doctoral dissertation, The Massachusetts Institute of Technology, Cambridge, MA.

McAdams, D. P. (1982). Experiences of intimacy and power: Relationships between social motives and autobiographical memory. *Journal of Personality and Social Psychology, 42*, 292–302.

McAdams, D. P. (1984). Love, power, and images of the self. In C. Z. Malatesta & C. E. Izard (Eds.), *Emotion in adult development* (pp. 159–174). Beverly Hills, CA: Sage.

McAdams, D. P. (1985a). A life-story model of identity. In E. Hogan & W. Jones (Eds.), *Perspectives in personality.* New York: Plenum.

McAdams, D. P. (1985b). *Power, intimacy, and the life story: Personological inquiries into identity.* New York: Guilford.

McAdams, D. P. (1987). A life-story model of identity. In R. Hogan & W. H. Jones (Eds.), *Perspectives in personality* (Vol. 2, pp. 15–50). Grenwich, CT: JAI Press.

McAdams, D. P. (1989). *Intimacy: The need to be close.* New York: Doubleday.

McAdams, D. P. (1990). Unity and purpose in human lives: The emergence of identity as a life story. In A. I. Rabin, R. A. Zucker, R. E. Emmons, & S. Frank (Eds.), *Studying persons and lives* (pp. 148–200). New York: Springer.

McAdams, D. P. (1993). *The stories we live by: Personal myths and the making of the self.* New York: Morrow.

McAdams, D.P., Booth, L., & Selvik, R. (1981). Religious identity among students at a private college: Social motives, ego stage, and development. *Merrill-Palmer Quarterly, 27*, 219–239.

McAdams, D.P., & de St. Aubin, E. (1992). A theory of generativity and its assessment through self-report, behavioral acts, and narrative themes in autobiography. *Journal of Personality and Social Psychology, 62*, 1003–1015.

McAdams, D.P., de St. Aubin, E., & Logan, R. L. (1993). Generativity among young, midlife, and older adults. *Psychology and Aging, 8*, 221–230.

McAdams, D.P., Ruetzel, K., & Foley, J. M. (1986). Complexity and generativity at midlife: Relations among social motives, ego development, and adults' plans for the future. *Journal of Personality and Social Psychology, 50*, 800–807.

McAdams, D. P., & Ochberg, R. L. (Eds.) (1988). Psychobiography and life narratives [Special Issue]. *Journal of Personality, 56*(1).

McGuire, M. (1990). The rhetoric of narrative: A hermeneutic, critical theory. In B. K. Britton & A. D. Pellegrini (Eds.), *Narrative thought and narrative language* (pp. 219–236). Hillsdale, NJ: Lawrence Erbaum.

McLane, A. (1987) *Classification of nursing diagnoses: Proceedings of the seventh conference.* St. Louis: The CV Mosby Co.

McLaughlin, J. (1991). Clinical and theoretical aspects of enactment. *Journal of the American Psychoanalytic Association, 39*, 595–614.

McLaughlin, J. (1993). Work with patients and the experience of self-analysis. In J. Birren (Ed.), *Self-analysis: Critical inquiries, personal visions* (pp. 63–82). Hillsdale, NJ: The Analytic Press.

McClelland, D. C. (1961). *The achieving society*. New York: D. Van Nostrand.

McMahon, A. W., & Rhudick, P. J. (1964). Reminiscing: Adaptational significance in the aged. *Archives of General Psychiatry, 10*, 292–298.

McNamee, S. (1992). Reconstructing identity: The communal construction of crisis. In S. McNamee & K. J. Gergen (Eds.) *Therapy as social construction*. London: Sage.

McWhorter, I. M. (1980). Group work for high utilizers of clinic facilities. In I. Burnside (Ed.), *Psychosocial nursing care of the aged*, (pp. 114–125). New York: McGraw-Hill.

Mead, G. H. (1934). *Mind, self, and society*. Chicago: University of Chicago Press.

Mead, M. (1975a). *Coming of age in Samoa: A psychological study of primitive youth for Western civilization*. New York: Morrow-Quill. (Original work published 1928).

Mead, M. (1975b). *Growing up in New Guinea: A comparative study of primitive education*. New York: Morrow-Quill. (Original work published 1930).

Meeks, S., Carstensen, L., Tamsky, B. F., Wright, T., & Pellegrini, D. (1989). Age differences in coping: Does less mean worse? *International Journal of Aging and Human Development, 28*, 127–140.

Mergler, N. L., & Golstein, M. D. (1983). Why are there old people? Senescence as biological and cultural preparedness for the transformation of information. *Human Development, 26*, 72–90.

Merleau-Ponty, M. (1962). *Phenomenology of perception* (C. Smith, trans.) London: Routledge & Kegan Paul. (Original work published 1945).

Merriam, S. B. (1993). Butler's life review: How universal is it? *International Journal of Aging and Human Development*, 37(3), 163–175.

Merriam, S. B., & Cross, L. (1982). Adulthood and reminiscence: A descriptive study. *Educational Gerontology, 8*, 275–290.

Mezey, M. D., Rauckhorst, L. H., & Stokes, S. A. (1980). *Health assessment of the older individual*. New York: Springer.

Mezirow, J. (1978). Perspective transformation. *Adult Education, 28*(2), 100–110.

Mezirow, J. (1990). How critical reflection triggers transformative learning. In J. Mezirow (Ed.), *Fostering critical reflection in adulthood* (pp. 1–20). San Francisco: Jossey-Bass.

Michelson, S. A. (1981). Reminiscence as a means of decreasing depression in the aged. Unpublished manuscript. Boston College, Boston

Michotte, A. E. (1963). *The perception of causality* (T. Ricoeur, & E. Miles, Trans.). London: Methuen. (Original work published 1946)

Middleton, R. (1987). Book review. *Social Work in Health Care, 12*(4), 119.

Miller, J. G. (1978). *Living systems*. New York: McGraw-Hill.

Millon, T. (1990). *Toward a new personology: An evolutionary model*. New York: John Wiley & Sons.

Mills, M., & Coleman, P. (1994). Nostalgic memories in dementia: A case study. *International Journal of Aging and Human Development, 38,* 203–219.

Mink, L. O. (1966). The autonomy of historical understanding. *History & Theory, 5,* 24–47.

Mishler, E. G. (1986). *Research interviewing: Context and narrative.* Cambridge, MA: Harvard University Press.

Mishler, E. (1990). Validation in inquiry-guided research: The role of exemplars in narrative studies. *Harvard Educational Review, 60,* 415–442.

Mishler, E. G. (in press). Validation: The social construction of knowledge: A brief for inquiry-guided research. *Harvard Educational Review.*

Mitchell, W. J. T. (1981). Foreword. In W. J. T. Mitchell (Ed.), *On narrative* (pp. vii-x). Chicago: University of Chicago Press.

Moody, H. (1988). Toward a critical gerontology: The contribution of the humanities to theories of aging. In J.E. Birren & V. Bengtson (Eds.), *Emergent theories of aging* (pp. 19–40). New York: Springer.

Moody, H. (1993). Overview: What is critical gerontology and why is it important? In T. Cole, A. Achenbaum, P. Jacobi, and R. Kastenbaum (Eds.), *Voices and visions of aging.* (pp. xv-xii). New York: Springer.

Moore, M. (1984). *Effects of reminiscing and touch in group therapy on the self-esteem and morale of institutionalized elderly.* Unpublished master's thesis, Department of Nursing, San Jose State University, San Jose, CA.

Moore, T. (1992). *Care of the soul: A guide for cultivating depth and sacredness in everyday life.* New York: Harper Perennial.

Munhall, P. L. (1988). Philosophical pondering on qualitative research methods in nursing. *Nursing Science Quarterly,* 20–28.

Munnichs, J. M. A. (1966). *Old age and finitude.* Basel: Karger.

Murcheson, C. (1930). *A history of psychology in autobiography.* (Vol. 1,) Worcester, MA.: Clark University Press.

Murphy, P., (1992). Reminiscence. *Aging and Spirituality,* 4(3), 2.

Murray, H. A. (1938). *Explorations in personality.* New York: Oxford University Press.

Myerhoff, B.G. (1978). *Number our days.* New York: Touchstone.

Myerhoff, B. G. (1982). Life history among the elderly: Performance, visibility and remembering. In Ruby, J. (Ed.), *A crack in the mirror: Reflexive perspectives in anthropology* (pp. 99–120). Philadelphia, PA: University of Pennsylvania Press.

Myerhoff, B. G. (1992). *Remembered lives: The work of ritual, storytelling and growing older.* Ann Arbor: The University of Michigan Press.

Myerhoff, B. G., & Ruby, J. (1982). Introduction. In J. Ruby, (Ed.), *A crack in the mirror: Reflexive perspectives in anthropology* (pp. 1–38). Philadelphia, PA: University of Pennsylvania Press.

Myerhoff, B. G., & Tufte, V. (1992). Life history as integration: Personal myth and aging. In B. Myerhoff (Ed.), *Remembered lives: The work of ritual, storytelling and growing older* (pp. 249–256). Ann Arbor: The University of Michigan Press.

Nagel, T. (1986). *The view from nowhere.* New York: Oxford University Press.

Neisser, U. (1986). Nested structure in autobiographical memory. In D. Rubin (Ed.), *Autobiographical memory* (pp. 71–81). New York: Cambridge University Press.

Nesselroade, J. R. (1988). Sampling and generalizability: Adult development and aging research issues examined within the general methodological framework of selection. In K. W. Schaie, R. T. Campbell, W. Meredith, & S. C. Rawlings (Eds.), *Methodological issues in aging research* (pp. 13–42). New York: Springer.

Neugarten, B. L. (1970). Dynamics of transition to old age. *Journal of Geriatric Psychiatry, 4*, 71–87.

Neugarten, B. L., Havighurst, R., & Tobin, S. (1968). Personality patterns of aging. In B. Neugarten (Ed.), *Middle Age and Aging*. Chicago: University of Chicago Press.

Neugarten, B. L. (1964). *Personality in middle and later life*. New York: Atherton.

Neugarten, B. L. (1977). Personality and aging. In J. E. Birren & K. W. Schaie (Eds.), *Handbook of psychology of aging* (pp. 626–649). New York: Van Nostrand Reinhold.

Neugarten, B., & Hagestad, G. (1976). Age and the life course. In R. Binstock & E. Shanas (Eds.), *Handbook of aging and the social sciences*, (pp. 35–55). New York: Van Nostrand Reinhold.

New York Psychoanalytic Institute (1963, October 14). Minutes of the faculty meeting (Unpublished).

New York Psychoanalytic Institute (1963, October 20). Minutes of the faculty meeting (Unpublished).

Nordbeck, B. (1989, June). *Quality of life, health and aging*. Paper presented at the 14th International Congress of Gerontology, Acapulco.

Norris, A. D., & Eileh, M. T. (1982). Reminiscence groups. *Nursing Times, 78*, 1368–1369.

Novey, S. (1968). *The second look: The reconstruction of personal history in psychiatry and psychoanalysis*. Baltimore, MD: Johns Hopkins University Press.

Öberg, P. & Ruth, J-E. (in press). Old age as reflected in the life stories of elderly Finns. In L. d'Epinay, C. Hummel, & J - C Rey (Eds.), *Images of aging*. (pp. xx) Geneva: Centre of Interdisciplinary Gerontology, University of Geneva.

O'Connor, A. P., Wicher, C. A., & Germino, B. B. (1990). Understanding the cancer patient's search for meaning. *Cancer Nursing, 13*(3), 165–175.

O'Hanlon, B., & Wilk, J. (1987). *Shifting contexts: The generation of effective psychotherapy*. New York: Guilford Press.

Olbrich, E. (1985). Coping and development in the later years: A process-oriented approach to personality and development. In J. Munnichs, P. Mussen, E. Olbrich, & P. Coleman (Eds.), *Life-span and change in a gerontological perspective*. New York: Academic Press.

Olivas G., Del Togno-Armanasco V., Erickson J., & Harter, S. (1989). Case management: A bottom-line management care delivery model, Part I: The concept, *Journal of Nursing Administration*: *19* (11), 16–20.

Olivas G., Togno-Armanasco V., Erickson J., & Harter, S. (1989). Case management: A bottom-line management care delivery model, Part II: Adaptation of the model, *Journal of Nursing Administration*: *19* (12), 12–17.

O'Malley, A. (1981). Quoted in E. R. Murphy 2.715. *One line quotations for speakers, writers, & raconteurs*. New York: Bonanza Books.

Orem, D. E. (1985) *Nursing Concepts of Practice* (3rd ed.) New York: McGraw-Hill.

Osborn, C. L. (1989). Reminiscence: When the past eases the present. *Journal of Gerontological Nursing, 15*(10), 6–12.

Palombo, J. (1992). Narratives, self-cohesion and the patients' search for meaning. *Clinical Social Work Journal, 20,* 249–270.

Panel (M.C. Winestine, Reporter). (1973). The experience of separation-individuation in infancy and its reverberations through the course of life: 1. Infancy and childhood. *Journal of the American Psychoanalytic Association, 21,* 135–154.

Parse, R. R. (1981). *Man–Living–Health: A theory of nursing.* New York: Wiley.

Parse, R. R. (1987). *Nursing science: Major paradigms, theories and critiques.* Philadelphia: Saunders.

Parse, R. R. (1990). Parse's research methodology with an illustration of the lived experience of hope. *Nursing Science Quarterly, 3,* 9–17.

Parse, R. R. (1992). Human becoming: Parse's theory of nursing. *Nursing Science Quarterly, 1,* 35–42.

Parsons, C. (1986). Group reminiscence therapy and levels of depression in the elderly. *Nurse Practitioner, 11*(3), 68–76.

Parsons, T. (1952). The superego and the theory of social systems. *Psychiatry, 15.*

Pearson, C.S. (1989). *The hero within: Six archetypes we live by.* San Francisco: Harper & Row.

Peitgen, H.O. & Saupe, D. (Eds.) (1988). *The science of fractal images.* New York: Springer-Verlag.

Penn, P. & Frankfurt, M. (In Press) Creating a participant text: Writing, multiple voices, narrative multiplicity. *Family process.*

Perakyla, A. (1988). An outline of the study of the social meanings of death in a modern hospital. Proceedings of the Finnish-Polish sociological conference. Sociological research on institutions and everyday life. Acta Universitas Lodzensir, Folia Socjologica.

Peterson, C., & McCabe, A. (1991). Linking children's connective use and narrative macrostructure. In A. McCabe & C. Peterson (Eds.), *Developing narrative structure* (pp. 29–53). Hillsdale, NJ: Lawrence Erlbaum.

Peterson, B., & Stewart, A. (1990). Using personal and fictional documents to assess psychosocial development: A case study of Vera Brittain's generativity. *Psychology and Aging, 3,* 400–411.

Phelan, J. (1989). *Reading people, reading plots: Character, progression and the interpretation of narrative.* Chicago: The University of Chicago Press.

Philibert, M. (1986). *L'Echelle des ages.* Paris: Editions du Seuil.

Phillips, J. (1992). The future of social work with elderly people. *Generations Review,* 2(4), pp. 12–14.

Piaget, J. (1952). *The origins of intelligence in children.* New York: International Universities Press.

Piaget, J. (1970). *Genetic epistemology.* New York: Columbia University Press.

Pincus, A., (1967). Towards a developmental view of aging for social work. *Social Work,* July, 33–41.

Pitts, R. C., & Lehman, A. J. (1994). [The relationship between integrative complexity and ego processes mechanisms]. Unpublished raw data.

Pitts, R. C., Walker, L. J., Chandler, M. J. & Lehman, A. J. (1992, November). *Faith or fiction? A construct validity study of Folwer's faith development theory*. Paper presented at the meeting of the Association for Moral Education, Toronto.

Plank, W. (1989). *Gulag 65: A Humanist Looks at Aging*. New York: Peter Lang.

Plath, D. (1980). Contours of consociation: Lessons fromn a Japanese narrative. In. P. B. Baltes and O.G. Brim, Jr. (Eds.) *Life-Span Development and Behavior* (Volume 3). (pp. 287–307). New York: Academic Press.

Poland, W. (1993). Self and other in self-analysis. In J. Barron (Ed.), *Self-analysis: Critical inquiries, personal visions* (pp. 219–240). Hillsdale, NJ: The Analytic Press.

Polkinghorne, D. (1983). *Methodology for the human sciences: Systems of inquiry*. Albany, NY: Press of the State University of New York.

Polkinghorne, D. E. (1991). Narrative and Self-concept, *Journal of Narrative and Life History*, 1(2–3), 135–153.

Polkinghorne, D.E. (in press). Narrative configuration in qualitative analysis. *International Journal of Qualitative Studies in Education.*

Polkinghorne, D. (1988). *Narrative knowing and the human sciences*. Albany, NY: State University of New York Press.

Polonoff, D. (1987). Self-deception. *Social Research, 54*(1), 45–53.

Polster, E. (1987). *Every person's life is worth a novel*. New York: W.W. Norton.

Pondy, L.R., Morgan, G., Frost, P.J.,, & Dandridge, T.C. (1983). (Eds.). *Organizational symbolism*. Greenwich, CT: JAI Press.

Popper, K. (1968). *The logic of scientific discovery* (Revised edition). New York: Harper and Row.

Porter, C. A.,, & Suedfeld, P. (1981). Integrative complexity in the correspondence of literature figures: Effects of personal and societal stress. *Journal of Personality and Social Psychology, 40*, 321–330.

Prado, C. (1986). *Rethinking how we age*. Westport, CT: Greenwood Press.

Pratt, M. W., Diessner, R., Hunsberger, B., Pancer, S. M., & Savoy, K. (1991). Four pathways in the analysis of adult development and aging: Comparing analyses of reasoning about personal-life dilemmas. *Psychology and Aging, 6*, 666–675.

Pratt, M. W., Hunsberger, B., Pancer, S. M., & Roth, D. (1992). Reflections on religion: Aging, belief orthodoxy, and interpersonal conflict in the complexity of adult thinking about religious issues. *Journal for the Scientific Study of Religion, 31*, 514–522.

Pratt, M. W., Hunsberger, B., Pancer, S. M., Roth, D., & Santolupo, S. (1993). Thinking about parenting: Reasoning about developmental issues across the life span. *Developmental Psychology, 29*, 585–595.

Pratt, M. W., Pancer, S. M., Hunsberger, B., & Manchester, J. (1990). Reasoning about the self and relationships in maturity: An integrative complexity analysis of individual differences. *Journal of Personality and Social Psychology*, *59*, 575–581.

Prigogine, I. (1979). *From being to becoming*. San Francisco: W. H. Freeman.

Prigogine, I. & Stengers, I. (1984). Order Out of Chaos: Man's New *Dialogue with Nature*. Toronto: Bantam.

Primm, P. (1986) Entry into practice: Competency statements for BSN and ADNs. *Nursing Outlook*, May-June, 135–137.

Randall, J. H. Jr. (1940). *The making of the modern mind.* Boston: Houghton Mifflin.

Reedy, M. N. & Birren, J. E. (1980). *Life review through autobiography.* Paper presented at the annual meeting of the American Psychological Association, Montreal.

Renza, L. (1980). The veto of the imagination: A theory of autobiography. In J.Olney (Ed.), *Autobiography: Essays theoretical and critical* (pp. 268–295). Princeton, NJ: Princeton University Press.

Rettig, R. P., Torres, M. J., & Garrett, G. R. (1977). *Manny: A criminal addict's story.* Boston: Houghton Mifflin.

Rich, S. L. (1988). Mirror, mirror: An autobiographical study in creative process. (Doctoral dissertation, New York University, 1988). *Dissertations Abstracts International, 48*: 1766A.

Ricoeur, P. (1971). The model of the text: Meaningful action considered as text. *Social Research, 38,* 529–562.

Ricoeur, P. (1977). The question of proof in Freud's psychoanalytic writings. *Journal of the American Psychoanalytic Association, 25,* 835–872.

Ricoeur, P. (1980). Narrative time. In W. J. T. Mitchell (Ed.), *On narrative* (pp. 165–186). . Chicago: The University of Chicago Press.

Ricoeur, P. (1984). *Time and narrative* (Vol. 1). (K. McLaughlin & D. Pellauer, Trans.). Chicago: University of Chicago Press.

Ricoeur, P. (1989). *Time and narrative* (Vol. 3). (K. Blamey & D. Pellauer, Trans.). Chicago: University of Chicago Press.

Ricoeur, P. (1992). *Oneself as another.* Chicago: University of Chicago Press.

Riegel, K. F. (1976). The dialectics of human development. *American Psychologist, 31,* 689–700.

Riegel, K. F., & Reigel, R. M. (1972). Development, drop, and death. *Developmental Psychology, 6,* 306–319.

Riesman, P. (1977). *Freedom in Fulani social life: An introspective biography.* Chicago: The University of Chicago Press.

Ritter, G., Fralic, M. F., Tonges, M. C. & McCormac, M. Rodriguez, A. W. (1992). Redesigned nursing practice: A case management model for critical care. *Nursing Clinics of North America,* 27 (1), 119–128.

Rodriguez, A. W. (1990). A descriptive study of selected props used to elicit memories in elders. Unpublished master's thesis, School of Nursing, The University of Texas, Austin, TX.

Romaniuk, M. (1983). The application of reminiscing to the clinical interview *Clinical Gerontologist, 1*(3), 39–43.

Roos, J. P. (1985a). Elämäntapaa etsimässä. (Searching for the way of life.) *Tutkijaliiton Julkaisusarja 34.* Jyväskylä: Gummerus.

Roos, J. P. (1985b). Life stories of social changes: Four generations in Finland. *International Journal of Oral History,* 6(3), 179–190.

Roos, J. P. (1988). Elämäntavasta elämäkertaan. (From way of life to history of life.) *Tutkijaliiton Julkaisusarja 52,* 139–154. Jyväskylä: Gummerus.

Roos, J. P. (1993). European lives, The question of cultural comparisons through life stories. *Autobiography 2,* 57–64.

Rorty, R. (1980). *Philosophy and the mirror of nature.* Princeton, NJ: Princeton University Press.

Rosaldo, R. (1993). *Culture and truth: The remaking of social analysis* (2nd ed.). New York: New York University Press.

Rosen, H. (1986). The importance of story. *Language Arts, 63*(3), 226–237.

Rosenau, P. M. (1992). *Post-modernism and the social sciences.* Princeton: Princeton University Press.

Rosenmayr, L. (1982). Biography and identity. In T. Hareven & K. Adams, (Eds.), *Aging and life course transitions: An interdisciplinary perspective* (pp. 21–53). New York: Guilford Press.

Rosenwald, G. C., & Ochberg, R. L. (1992). (Eds.). *Storied lives: The cultural politics of self understanding.* New Haven, CT: Yale University Press.

Ross, M., & Holmberg, D. (1992). Are wives' memories for events in relationships more vivid than their husbands' memories? *Journal of Social and Personal Relationships, 9,* 585–604.

Rotter, J. B. (1966). Generalized expectancies for Internal vs. external control of reinforcement. *Psychological Monographs, 80,* 1–28.

Rowlings, C. (1981). *Social work with elderly people.* London: George Allen and Unwin.

Rubin, D. C. (1986). *Autobiographical memory.* Cambridge: Cambridge University Press.

Rubin, D. C., Wetzler, S. E., & Nebes, R. D. (1986). Autobiographical memory across the life-span. In Rubin, D. C. (Ed.), *Autobiographical memory.* Cambridge: Cambridge University Press.

Rubinstein, R. L. (1988). Stories told: In-depth interviewing and the structure of its insights. In G. Rowes & S. Reinharz (Eds.), *Qualitative gerontology* (pp. 128–146). New York: Springer.

Rubinstein, R., Kilbride, J., & Nagy, S. (1992). *Elders living alone.* New York: de Gruyter.

Runyan, W. M. (1982). *Life histories and psychobiography: Explorations in theory and method.* New York: Oxford University Press. (paperback in 1984).

Runyan, W. M. (1990). Individual lives and the structure of personality psychology. In A. I. Rabin, R. Zucker, R. Emmons, & S. Frank (Eds.), *Studying persons and lives* (pp. 10–40). New York: Springer Publishing Company.

Ruth, J.-E. (1991). Reliabilitets och validitetsfragan i kvalitativ respektive kvantitativ forskningstradition. (The question of reliability and validity in the qualitative versus quantitative research tradition.) *Gerontologia, 5,* 277–290.

Ruth, J.-E. (1993). A dialectical model of resources, developmental tasks, organization of the self, adapting to life and well being in old age: Analytical scheme for the group for analyzing biography. UCLA. Published in Finnish in M. Isohanni et al. (Ed.) Vanhuusla Mielenterveys (pp. 49–69). Helsinki: WSOY.

Ruth, J.-E. (1989). The development of creativity during the life-span. *The Creative Child and Adult Quarterly, 14,* 3–4.

Ruth, J.-E. & Öberg, P. (1992). Expressions of aggression in the life stories of aged women. In K. Björkqvist & P. Niemelä (Eds)., *Of mice and women: Aspects of Female Aggression* (pp. 133–146). San Diego: Academic Press.

Ruth, J.-E., & Schultz-Jorgensen, P. (1984). Reviews of Scandinavian psychology: 3 Personality and developmental psychology. *Scandinavian Journal of Psychology, 25,* 97–116.

Rybarczyk, B. D., & Auerbach, S. M. (1990). Interviews as stress management interventions for older patients undergoing surgery. *The Gerontologist, 30*(4), 522–528.

Rychak, J. (1988). *The psychology of rigorous humanism* (2nd ed.). New York: New York University Press.

Ryden, M. B. (1981). Nursing intervention in support of reminiscence. *Journal of Gerontological Nursing, 7*(8), 461–463.

Ryff, C.D., & Heincke, S. G. (1983). Subjective organization of personality in adulthood and aging. *Journal of Personality and Social Psychology, 44,* 807–816.

Saarenheimo, M. (1989). Personallisuuden integraatio näkökulmana ikääntyneiden mielenterveyteen. elämäkertatutkimus 75–vuotiaista kotona asuvista helsinkiläisistä. Unpublished Licentiate thesis, University of Helsinki.

Sacks, O. (1985). *The man who mistook his wife for a hat, and other clinical tales.* New York: Summit.

Sampson, E. (1985). The decentralization of identity. *American Psychologist, 40,* (11), 1203–1211.

Sampson, E. E. (1989). The deconstruction of the self. In J. Shotter & K.H. Gergen (Eds.), *Texts of identity* (pp. 1–19). London: Sage.

Sarbin, T. R. (1986). *Narrative psychology: The storied nature of human conduct.* New York: Praeger.

Sarbin, T. R. (1993). *Constructing the social.* London: Sage.

Sarton, M. (1980). *Recovering: A journal.* New York:. W. Norton.

Sartre, J. P. (1955). *No exit.* New York: Vintage Books.

Sartre, J. P. (1956). *Being and nothingness.* New York: Simon & Schuster.

Sartre, J. P. (1957). *The transcendence of the ego; An existential theory of consciousness.* New York: Farrar, Straus and Giroux.

Sartre, J.P. (1965). *Essays in existentialism.* Secaucus, NJ: The Citadel Press.

Schafer, R. (1983). *The analytic attitude.* New York: Basic Books.

Schafer, R. (1959). Generative empathy in the treatment situation. *Psychoanalytic Quarterly, 28,* 342–373.

Schafer, R. (1980). Narration in the psychoanalytic dialogue. *Critical Inquiry, 7,* 29–53.

Schafer, R. (1981a). Narration in the psychoanalytic dialogue. In W. J. T. Mitchell (Ed.), *Recent theories of narrative.* Chicago:University of Chicago Press.

Schafer, R. (1981b). *Narrative actions in psychoanalysis.* Worcester, MA: Clark University Press.

Schafer, R. (1982). The relevance of the "here-and-now" transference interpretation to the reconstruction of early development. *International Journal of Psychoanalysis, 63,* 77–82.

Schafer, R. (1992). *Retelling a life: Narrative and dialogue in psychoanalysis.* New York: Basic Books.

Schaie, K. W., & Willis, S. (1991). *Adult development and aging* (3rd ed). New York: Harper Collins.

Schank, R. C. (1990). *Tell me a story: A new look at real and artificial memory*. New York: Scribner's.

Schiebe, K. E. (1986). Self-narratives and adventure. In T. R. Sarbin (Ed.), *Narrative psychology: The storied nature of human conduct* (pp. 129–151). New York: Praeger.

Scholes, R., & Kellogg, R. (1966). *The nature of narrative*. New York: Oxford University Press.

Shotter, J. (1993). *Conversational realities; Constructing life through language*. London: Sage.

Schroder, J. M., Driver, M. J., & Streufert, S. (1967). *Human information processing*. New York: Holt.

Schroots, J. J. F. (1988). On growing, formative change and aging. In J. E. Birren & V. L. Bengtson (Eds.), *Emergent theories of aging* (pp. 299–329). New York: Springer.

Schroots, J. J. F. (1990). Developments in the psychology of aging. In W. Koops, H. J-G. Soope, J. L. Vander-Linden, P. C. M. Molenaar & J. J. F. Schroots (Eds.), *Developmental psychology behind the dikes; An outline of developmental psychological research in the Netherlands* (pp. 43–60). Delft: Eburon.

Schroots, J. J. F. (1991). Metaphors of aging and complextiy. In G. M. Kenyon, J. E. Birren, & J. J. F. Schroots (Eds.), *Metaphors of aging in science and the humanities* (pp. 219–243). New York: Springer.

Schroots, J. J. F. (1994). Transformaties [Transformations]. In T. Bakker, A. Lit & J. J. F. Schroots (Eds.), *Naar een nieuwe psychogeriatrie: pluriform en complex [Toward a new psychogeriatrics: Pluriform and complex]* (pp. 79–106). Lisse: Swets & Zeitlinger.

Schroots, J. J. F. (1994, November). *Gerodynamics: Toward a branching theory of aging*. Paper presented at the 47th Annual Scientific Meeting of the Gerontological Society of America, Atlanta, GA.

Schroots, J. J. F. & Birren, J. E. (1988). The nature of time: Implications for research on aging. *Comprehensive Gerontology C, 2,* 1–29.

Schroots, J. J. F., Birren, J., & Kenyon, G. (1991). Metaphors and aging: An overview. In G. Kenyon, J. Birren, and J. J. F. Schroots (Eds.), *Metaphors of aging in science and the humanities* (pp. 116–243). New York: Springer.

Schroots, J. J. F. & Ten Kate, CA. (1989). Metaphors, aging and the life-line interview method. In D. Unruh & G. S. Livings (Eds.), *Current perspectives on aging and the life cycle: Vol. 3 Personal history through the life course* (pp. 281–298). London: JAI Press.

Schutz, A. (1957a/1966). The problem of transcendental intersubjectivity in Husserl. In. AA Schutz, *Collected Papers*. III: Studies in Phenomenological Philosophy (Ed. I. Schutz) (pp. 51–84) The Hague: Martinus Nijhoff.

Schutz, A. (1957b/1966). Answer to comments made in the discussion of "The problem of transcendental intersubjectivity in Husserl." In. A. Schutz, *Collected Papers*. III: Studies in Phenomenological Philosophy (Ed. I. Schutz) (pp. 87–91). The Hague: Martinus Nijhoff.

Schutz, A. (1967). *The phenomenology of the social world*. Evanston: Northwestern University Press.

Schutz (1970). *On phenomenology and social relations*. Chicago: The University of Chicago Press. (Original work published 1940).

Schutz, A. (1973). *Collected papers*. The Hague: Martinus Najhoff.

Schutze, F. (1980). Prozesstrukturen des lebenslaufs. (The process-structure of the life-span) In I. Matthes, A. Pfeifenberger, & M. Strosberg, M. (Eds.), *Biographie in handlungswissenschaftlicher perspektive*. (Biography in a behavioral perspective) Nürnberg: Nürnberger Forschungsvereinigung.

Schwaber, E. (1983). A particular perspective on analytic listening. *Psychoanalytic Study of the Child, 38*, 519–546.

Scott-Maxwell, F. (1986). *The measure of my days*. New York: Penguin.

Selman, R. (1976). Social cognitive understanding: A guide to educational and clinical practice. In T. Lickona (Ed.), *Moral development and behavior: Theory, research, and social issues*. New York: Holt, Rinehart & Winston.

Shaw, C. R. (1930). *The Jack Roller: A delinquent boy's own story*. Chicago: University of Chicago Press.

Shaw, C. R. (1931). *The natural history of a delinquent career*. Chicago: University of Chicago Press.

Shaw, C. R. (1936). *Brothers in crime*. Chicago: University of Chicago Press.

Sheehy, G. (1974). *Passages: Predictable crises of adult life*. New York: Bantam.

Shotter, J., & Gergen, K. J. (Eds.) (1989). *Texts of identity*. London: Sage.

Sidell, M. (1986). Coping with confusion: The experience of 60 elderly people and their informal and formal careers. Unpublished doctoral dissertation, University of East Anglia, Norwich.

Siedler, W. J. (1991). Liebe als erkenntnismittel - Das glück des sich-selbst-wiederfindens: Thomas Manns literarische essayistik. (Love as consciousness raising. - The happiness of recovering oneself: The literary essayistic of Thomas Mann) In *Süddeutsche zeitung No. 298*, p. 63.

Siegrist, J., & Junge, A. (1989). Conceptual and methodological problems in research on the quality of life in clinical medicine. *Social Science and Medicine, 29*, 463–468.

Siikala, A-L. (1984). Tarina ja tulkinta, tutkimus kanasankertojista. [Story and interpretation, a study of folk storytellers]. *Suomalaisen Kirjallisuuden Seuran Toimituksia 404*. Mänttä: Mäntän Kirjapaino.

Silverman, D. (1989). Telling convincing stories: A plea for cautious positivism in case studies. In B. Glaser & D. Moreno (Eds.), *The qualitative - quantitative distinction in social sciences* (pp. 57–77). Dordrecht: Kluwer Academic Publishers.

Silverman, D. (1993). *Interpreting qualitative data: Methods for analyzing talk, text, and interaction*. London: Sage.

Simmons, L. (1942). *Sun Chief: The autobiography of a Hopi Indian*. New Haven: Yale University Press.

Simonton, D. K. (1977). Creative productivity, age, and stress: A biographical time-series analysis of 10 classical composers. *Journal of Personality and Social Psychology, 35*, 791–804.

Singer, J. A., & Salovey, P. (1993). *The remembered self: Emotion and memory in personality*. New York: The Free Press.

Skinner, T. J. (1975). The processes of understanding in doctor-patient interaction. Unpublished doctoral dissertation, Rice University.

Slugoski, B., Marcia, J., & Koopman, R. (1984). Cognitive and social interactional characteristics of ego identity statuses in college males. *Journal of Personality and Social Psychology, 47*, 646–661.

Smith, H. (1993). Engagements in analysis and their use in self-analysis. In J. Barron (Ed.), *Self-analysis: Critical inquiries, personal visions* (pp. 83–116). Hillsdale, NJ: The Analytic Press.

Smith, L. (1994). The biographical method. In N. Denzin & Y. Lincoln (Eds.), *Handbook of qualitative research* (pp. 286–305). Thousand Oaks, CA: Sage Publications.

Snyder, M. (1985). Reminiscence. In M. Snyder (Ed.), *Independent nursing interventions*. New York: John C. Riley.

Solomon, P. (1992). The efficacy of case management services for severely mentally disabled clients. *Community Mental Health Journal, 28*(3), 163–180.

Sonnenberg, S. (1991). The analyst's self-analysis and its impact on clinical work: A comment on the sources and importance of personal insights. *Journal of the American Psychoanalytic Association, 39*, 687–704.

Spence, D. (1982). *Narrative truth and historical truth: Meaning and interpretation in psychoanalysis*. New York: Norton.

Sroufe, L.A. (1988). The role of infant-caregiver attachment in development. In J. Belsky & T. Nezworksi (Eds.), *Clinical implications of attachment* (pp. 18–38). Hillside, NJ: Erlbaum.

Stamps, P. L. & Piedmonte, E. B. (1986). *Nurse and Work Satisfaction: An Index for Measurement*. Health Administration Press Perspective, Ann Arbor, Michigan.

Stange, A. (1973). Around the kitchen table: Group work on a back ward. In I. Burnside (Ed.), *Psychosocial nursing care of the aged* (pp. 174–186). New York: McGraw-Hill.

Staudinger, U. M. (1989). The study of life review: An approach to the investigation of intellectual development across the life span. *Max-Planck-Institut für bildungsforschung. Studien und Berichte, 47*.

Steffl, B. (1994). Personal letter. Creating a therapeutic milieu in dementia care. *Journal of Gerontological Nursing*, 19(10), 30–39.

Stern, D. (1985). *The interpersonal world of the infant*. New York: Basic Books.

Stewart, A. J., Franz, C., & Layton, L. (1988). The changing self: Using personal documents to study lives. *Journal of Personality, 56*, 41–74.

Stigler, J. W., Shweder, R. A., & Herdt, G. (1990). *Cultural psychology: Essays on comparative development*. Cambridge: Cambridge University Press.

Stolorow, R., & Atwood, G.(1992). *Contexts of being: The intersubjective foundations of psychological life*. Hillsdale, NJ: The Analytic Press.

Stout, J. C. (1987). Antonin Artaud as a writer of biographies. (Doctoral dissertation, Princeton University 1987). *Dissertation Abstracts International* 48, 936A.

Strauss, A. (1987). *Qualitative analysis for social scientists*. Cambridge: Cambridge University Press.

Strauss, A., & Corbin, J. (1990). *Basics of qualitative research: Grounded theory procedures and techniques*. Newbury Park, CA: Sage.

Strauss, A., & Glaser, B., (1977). *Anguish: A case history of a dying trajectory*. Oxford: Robertson.

Streufert, S., & Streufert, S. (1978). *Behavior in a complex environment* . Washington, DC: Winston.

Suedfeld, P. (1980). Indices of world tension in the *Bulletin of the Atomic Scientists Political Psychology*, Fall/Winter.

Suedfeld, P., & Bluck, S. (1993). Changes in integrative complexity accompanying significant life events: Historical evidence. *Journal of Personality and Social Psychology, 64*, 124–130.

Suedfeld, P., & Coren, S. (1992). Cognitive correlates of conceptual complexity. *Personality and Individual Differences, 13,* 1193–1199.

Suedfeld, P., Corteen, R., & McCormick, C. (1986). The role of integrative complexity in military leadership: Robert E. Lee and his opponents. *Journal of Applied Social Psychology, 16,* 498–507.

Suedfeld, P., & Piedrahita, L. E. (1984). Intimations of mortality: Integrative simplification as a precursor of death. *Journal of Personality and Social Psychology, 47,* 848–852.

Suedfeld, P., & Rank, A. D. (1976) Revolutionary leaders: Long-term success as a function of changes in conceptual complexity. *Journal of Personality and Social Psychology, 34,* 169–178.

Suedfeld, P., & Tetlock, P. E. (1977). Integrative complexity of communications. *Journal of Conflict Resolution, 21,* 169–184.

Suedfeld, P., Tetlock, P. E., & Ramirez, C. (1977). War, peace, and intergrative complexity: UN speeches on the Middle East problem, 1947–1976. *Journal of Conflict Resolution, 21*, 427–442.

Suedfeld, P., Tetlock, P. E., & Streufert, S. (1992). Conceptual/integrative complexity. In C. P. Smith (Ed.), *Motivation and personality: Handbook of thematic content analysis* (pp. 393–400). New York: Cambridge University Press.

Sullivan, E., McCullough, G., & Stager, M. (1970). A developmental study of the relationship between conceptual ego, and moral development. *Child Development, 41,* 399–412.

Sullivan, H. S. (1953). *The interpersonal theory of psychiatry*. New York; Norton.

Sutton-Smith, B. (1986). Children's fiction making. In T. Sarbin (Ed.), *Narrative psychology: The storied nature of human conduct* (pp. 67–90). New York: Praeger.

Svensson, T. (1984). *Aging and environment: Institutional aspects.* Linköping, Sweden: Department of Education and Psychology.

Svensson, T. (1991). Intellectual exercise and quality of life of the frail elderly. In J. E. Birren, D. Deutchman, J. E. Lubben & J. Rowe (Eds.), *The concept and measurement of quality of life in the frail elderly*. (pp. 256–275.) San Diego: Academic Press.

Taft, L. B., Delancy, K., Seman, P., & Stansell, J. (1993). Creating a therapeutic mileau in dementia care. *Journal of Gerontological Nursing, 19*(10), 30–39.

Taylor, C. (1977). What is human agency? In T. Mischel (Ed.), *The self: Psychological and philosophical issues* (pp. 103–125). Oxford: Basil Blackwell.

Tetlock, P. E. (1981). Pre- to postelection shifts in presidential rhetoric: Impression manangement or cognitive adjustment? *Journal of Personality and Social Psychology, 41*, 207–212.

Tetlock, P. E. (1983). Cognitive style and political ideology. *Journal of Personality and Social Psychology, 45,* 118–126.

Tetlock, P. E. (1984). Cognitive style and political belief systems in the British House of commons. *Journal of Personality and Social Psychology, 46,* 365–375.

Tetlock, P. E. (1985). Integrative complexity of American and Soviet foreign policy rhetoric: A time-series analysis. *Journal of Personality and Social Psychology, 49,* 1565–1585.

Tetlock, P. E., Bernzweig, J., & Gallant, J. L. (1986). Supreme court decision making: Cognitive style as a predictor of ideological consistency of voting. *Journal of Personality and Social Psychology, 48,* 1227–1239.

Tetlock, P. E., Hannum, K. A., & Micheletti, P. M. (1984). Stability and change in the complexity of senatorial debate: Testing the cognitive versus rhetorical style hypothesis. *Journal of Personality and Social Psychology, 46,* 979–990.

Thomae, H. (1953). Über daseinstechniken social auffälliger jugendlicher. (The life techniques of socially deviant youngsters.) *Psychologische Forschung, 23,* 11–13.

Thomae, H. (1976). *Patterns of aging: Findings from the Bonn Longitudinal Study of Aging.* Basel: Karger.

Thomae, H. (1980). Personality and adjustment to old age. In J. E. Birren & R. B. Sloane (Eds.), *Handbook of mental health and aging.* (pp. 385–400). Englewood Cliffs, NJ: Prentice-Hall.

Thomae, H. (1987). Conceptualizations of responses to stress. *European Journal of Personality, 1,* 171–192.

Thomae, H. (1992). Contributions of longitudinal research to a cognitive theory of adjustment to aging. *European Journal of Personality, 6,* 157–175.

Thomas, L. E. (Ed.). (1989). *Research on adulthood and aging: A human science approach.* Albany: State University of New York Press.

Thomas, W. I. & Znaniecki, F. (1974). *The Polish peasant in Europe and America.* New York: Octagon Books - Farrar, Straus, and Giroux. (Earlier versions published 1918–1920, 1927)

Thompson, P. (1978). *The voice of the past: Oral history*. Oxford: Oxford University Press.

Thompson, P. (1992). I don't feel old: Subjective ageing and the search for meaning in later life. *Ageing and Society, 12,* 23–47.

Thompson, P., Itzin, C., & Abednstern, M. (1990). *I don't feel old: The experience of later life*. Oxford: Oxford University Press.

Thornton, S., & Brotchie, J. (1987). Reminiscence: A critical review of the empirical literature. *British Journal of Clinical Psychology, 26,* 93–111.

Tigerstedt, C., Roos, J. P., & Vilkko, A. (Eds.) (1992). *Självbiografi, kultur, liv. (Autobiography, culture, life)* Stockholm: Brutus Östlings Forlag Symposion.

Titon, J. T. (1980). The life story. *Journal of American Folklore, 93,* 276–292.

Todrov, T. (1984). *Mikhail Bakhtin: The dialogical principle* (W. Godzich, trans.). Minneapolis, MN: The University of Minnesota Press.

Tolbert, E. L. (1959). *Introduction to counseling*. New York: Appleton, Century, Crofts.

Tomkins, S. S. (1987). Script theory. In H. Aronoff, A.I. Rabin, & R.A. Zucker (Eds.), *The emergence of personality* (pp. 147–216). New York: Springer.

Tornstam, L. (1987). Ageing and self-perception: A systems theoretical model. In L. Levi (Ed.), *Society, Stress and Disease: Vol 5. Old Age* (pp. 38–43). New York: Oxford University Press.

Tornstam, L. (1989). Gero-transcendence: A meta-theoretical reformulation of the disengagement theory. *Aging: Clinical and Experimental Research, 1*, 55–63.

Toseland, R. W. (1990). *Group work with older adults.* New York: New York University Press.

Toulmin, S. E. (1972). *Human understanding: The collective use of concepts.* Princeton, NJ: Princeton University Press.

Tourangeau, A. (1988). Group reminiscence therapy as a nursing intervention: An experimental study. *ARRN Newsletter, 44*(8), 17–18; *44*(9), 29–30.

Townsend, P. (1957). *The family Life of old people.* London: Penguin.

Trevarthan, C. (1980). The foundations of intersubjectivity: Development of interpersonal and cognitive understanding of infants. In D. Olson (Ed.), *The social foundations of language and thought: Essays in honor of Jerome Bruner* (pp. 316–342). New York: Norton.

Trevarthan, C. (1989). Origins and directions for the concept of infant intersubjectivity, *Society for research in Child Development Newsletter*, Autumn, 1–4.

Trevarthan, C., Hubley, P. (1978). Secondary intersubjectivity: Confidence, confiders, and acts of meaning in the first year. In. A. Lock (Ed.) *Action, Gesture, and Symbol* (pp. 183–230). New York: Academic Press.

Tuchschmidt, A. (1988). Aging from a biographical persective. Unpublished doctoral dissertation, University of Fribourg.

Turner, T. L. (1992). The revealing of Mr. Stubbs: Stories from the heart. *Journal of Christian Nursing*, 9(3), 12–13.

Turski, G. (1991). Emotions and responsibility. *Philosophy Today*, 137–152.

Unruh, D. R. (1983). *Invisible lives. Social world of the aged.* Beverly Hills: Sage.

Vaillant, G. (1977). *Adaptation to life.* Boston: Little Brown.

Verwoerdt, A. (1981). Clinical geropsychiatry. Baltimore: William and Wilkens.

Vester, M. Oertzen, P., Geiling, H., Hermann, T., & Muller, D. (1992). *Neue soziale milieus and pluralisierte klassengesellschaft.*(New social environments and the pluralistic class society.) Hannover: Hannover Universität.

Vischer, A.L. (1961). *Seelische Wandlungen Beim Alternden Menschen.* (Psychological changes among aging human beings) Bazel/Stuttgart: Benno Schwabe.

Voepe-Lewis, T. & Poole, M. (1992). Case management for ambulatory surgery: An innovative approach to quality improvement. *Journal of Post Anesthesia Nursing*, 7(3), 221–222.

Voges, W., & Pongratz, H. (1988). Retirement and the lifestyles of older women. *Ageing and Society, 8*, 63–84.

von Wright, G. (1963). *The varieties of goodness.* London: Routledge & Kegan Paul.

Vygotsky, L. (1934). *Mind in society: The development of higher psychological process* (M. Cole, V. John-Steiner, S. Scribner & E. Souberman, Eds. and Trans.). Cambridge, MA: Harvard University Press.

Wachter, P. E. (1988). Current bibliography of life writing. *Biography: An Interdisciplinary Quarterly, 11*(4), 316–25.

Waerness, K., Ruth, J.-E., & Tornstam, L. (1993). *livslöp blant gamle i norden.* Olso: Norsk Gerontologisk Institutt, Rapport 2.

Wagner, J. D. & Menke, E. M. (1992). Case management of homeless families. *Clinical Nurse Specialist.* 6(2), 65–71

Wahlström, J. (1992). Merkitysten muodostuminen ja muuttuminen perheterapeuttisessa keskustelussa [Semantic change in family therapy] (Unpublished doctoral dissertation, University of Jyväskylä. Finland.

Wallace, E. R. (1985). *History and causation in psychoanalysis.* Hillsdale, NJ: Analytic Press.

Wallace, J. B. (1992). Reconsidering the life review: The social construction of talk about the past. *Gerontologist, 32*(1), 120–125.

Watzlawick, P., Beavin, J. & Jackson, D. (1967). *Pragmatics of human communication: A study of interactional patterns, pathologies and paradoxes.* New York: Norton.

Watkins, M. (1986). *Invisible guests: The development of imaginal dialogues.* Hillsdale, NJ: Analytic Press.

Watt, L. M., & Wong, P. T. (1991). A taxonomy of reminiscence and therapeutic implications. *Journal of Gerontological Social Work, 16,* 37–57.

Weber, M. (1947). *The theory of social and economic organizations.* New York: Oxford University Press.

Weber, M. (1949). *The methodology of the social sciences* (E. A. Shils & H. A. Finch, Trans.). New York: The Free Press.

Weber, M. (1958). *The Protestant ethic and the spirit of capitalism.* New York: Macmillan.

Webster, J. (1994). Predictors of reminiscence: A lifespan perspective. *Canadian Journal on Aging, 13*(1), 66–78.

Webster, J. D. (1993). Construction and validation of the reminiscence functions scale. *Journal of Gerontology: Psychosocial Sciences,* 48(5), 256–262.

Webster, J. D. (1989, October). *Individual differences in reminsiscence behavior: A lifespan perspective.* Paper presented at the meeting of the Canadian Association on Gerontology, Ottawa, Ontario.

Webster, J. D., & Cappeliez, P. (1993). Reminiscence and autobiographical memory: Complementary contexts for cognitive aging research. *Developmental Review, 13,* 54–91.

Webster, J. D., & Young, R. A. (1988). Process variables of the life review: Counseling implications. *International Journal of Aging and Human Development,* 26(4), 315–323.

Weenolsen, P. (1986). What's it all mean: We never stop asking? *APA Monitor, 17,* 20.

Weiland, S. (1989). Aging according to biography. *The Gerontologist, 29,* 191–194.

Weintraub, K.J. (1975). Autobiography and historical consciousness. *Critical Inquiry,* 821–848.

Wertsch, J. (1985). *Vygotsky and the social formation of mind.* Cambridge, MA: Harvard University Press.

Wertsch, J. (1991). *Voices of the mind: A sociocultural approach to mediated action.* Cambridge, MA: Harvard University Press.

West, B.J. (1987). Fractals, intermittency and morphogenesis. In H. Degn, A.V. Holden, & L.F. Olsen (Eds.), *Chaos in biological systems* (pp. 305–314). New York: Plenum.

Western Interstate Commission for Higher Education, *The Preparation and Utilization of New Nursing Graduates*. Boulder, Colorado: The Commission, 1985.

White, H. (1981). The value of narrativity in the representation of reality. In W. J. T. Mitchell (Ed.) *On narrative.* (pp. 1–23). Chicago: University of Chicago Press.

White, H. (1987). The question of narrative in contemporary historical theory. In H. White (Ed.), *The content of the form: Narrative discourse and historical representation* (p. 26–58). Baltimore, MD: Johns Hopkins University Press.

White, H. (1973). *Metahistory: The historical imagination in nineteenth-century Europe.* Baltimore: Johns Hopkins University Press.

White, M., & Epston, D. (1990). *Narrative means to therapeutic ends.* New York: W. Norton.

White, R. W. (1966). *The study of lives.* New York: Atherton.

White, R. W. (1972). *The enterprise of 1iving.* New York: Holt, Rinehart & Winston.

White, R.W. (1975). *Lives in Progress* (3rd ed.). New York: Holt, Rinehart and Winston (Original work published 1952).

Whorf, B. L. (1965). Language, thought and reality. Cambridge, MA: MIT Press.

Wichita, C. (1974). Reminiscing as therapy for apathetic and confused residents of nursing homes. Unpublished master's thesis, University of Arizona, Tucson.

Wilkinson, C. S. (1978). A descriptive study of increased social interaction through group reminiscing in institutionalized elderly. Unpublished master's thesis, School of Nursing, Tulane University, Tulane, LA.

Wilson, A., & Weinstein, L. (1992a). An investigation into some implications of a Vygotskian perspective on the origins of the mind: Psychoanalysis Vygotskian psychology: Part I, *Journal of the American Psychoanalytic Association, 40,* 349–379.

Wilson, A., & Weinstein, L (1992b). Language and the psychoanalytic process: Psychoanalysis and Vygotskian psychology, Part II. *Journal of the American Psychoanalytic Association, 40,* 725–760.

Windley, P. G., & Scheidt, R. J. (1980) Person-environment dialectics: Implications for competent functioning in old age. In L. W. Poon (Ed.), *Aging in the 1980's.* Washington, DC: American Psychological Association.

Winnicott, D. W. (1953). Transitional objects and transitional phenomena. In D.W. Winnicott, (Ed.) *Collected papers: Through pediatrics to psychoanalysis* (pp. 229–242). New York: Basic Books.

Winnicott, D. W. (1960). The theory of the parent-infant relationship. *International Journal of Psychoanalysis, 41,* 585–595.

Winquist, C. E. (1974). The act of storytelling and the self's homecoming. *Journal of the American Academy of Religion, 42*(1), 101–113.

Winquist, C. E. (1980). *Practical hermeneutics: A revised agenda for the ministry.* Chico, CA: Scholars Press.

Winter, D. G. (1973). *The power motive.* New York: The Free Press.

Winter, D. G., & Carlson, L. A. (1988). Using motive scores in the psychobiographical study of an individual: The case of Richard Nixon. *Journal of Personality, 56,* 75–104.

Winter, D. G., & Carlson, L. A. (1988). Using motive scores in the psychobiographical study of an individual: The case of Richard Nixon. *Journal of Personality, 56,* 75–104.

Wittgenstein, L. (1976). *Philosophical investigations.* Oxford: Basil Blackwell.

Wittgenstein, L. (1922). Tractatus Logico-Philosophicus. London: Routledge.

Wolanin, M. O., & Phillips, L. R. (1981). *Confusion: Prevention and Care.* St. Louis: Mosby.

Wolf, M.A. (1985). The meaning of education in late life: An exploration of life review. *Gerontology & Geriatrics Education, 5,* 51–59.

Wong, T. P., & Watt, L. M. (1991). What types of reminiscence are associated with successful aging? *Psychology and Aging, 6*(2), 272–279.

Wyatt, F. (1986). The narrative in psychoanalysis; Psychoanalytic notes on storytelling, listening, and interpreting. In T. Sarbin (Ed.), *Narrative psychology: The storied nature of human conduct* (pp. 193–210). New York: Praeger.

Wyatt, F. (1963). The reconstruction of the individual and the collective past. In R. W. White (Ed.), *The study of lives: Essays in honor of Henry A. Murray* (pp. 305–320). New York: Atherton Press/Aldine Publications.

Wyatt-Brown, A. M., & Rossen, J. (Eds.) (1993). *Aging and gender in literature: Studies in creativity.* Charlottesville: University Press of Virginia.

Wyatt-Brown, A. M. (1992). *Barbara Pym: A critical biography.* Columbia: University of Missouri Press.

Wysocki, M. R. (1983). Life review for the elderly patient. *American Journal of Nursing, 2,* 46–49.

Yates, F. E. (1987). *Self-organizing systems: The emergence of order.* New York: Plenum Press.

Yates, F. E. (1991). Aging as prolonged morphogenesis: A topobiologic sorcerer's apprentice. In G. M. Kenyon, J. E. Birren, & J. J. F. Schroots (Eds.), *Metaphors of aging in science and the humanities.* (pp. 199–218). New York: Springer Publishing Company. pp. 199–218.

Young, S. (1991). Differentiating nursing practice into the twenty-first century. Integrated care in the home health and hospice setting. *American Nurses Association Publication,* #G-182, 155–163.

Young, S. (1992) Team Work Product Management, Healthcare Micro systems, Inc. Torrence, CA.

Young, S. (1991) *The New Definition,* 6(3) the Center for Case Management, Inc., South Natick, MA.

Young, S. (1987) Surprise Discharge. UC San Diego, Continuing Care Network, San Diego, California.

Young, M., & Schuller, T. (1991). *Life after work: The arrival of the ageless society.* Hammersmith, London: Harper Collins.

Youssef, F. (1990). The impact of group reminiscence counseling on a depressed elderly population. *Nurse Practitioner, 15*(4), 32–38.

Index

D

M

N

O

P

Q

R

S

T

U

V

W

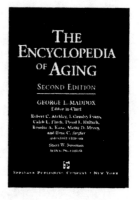